Professional's Guide to
PROCESS
IMPROVEMENT

Maximizing Profit, Efficiency, and Growth

Bennet P. Lientz

Kathryn P. Rea

Harcourt
Professional Publishing

SAN DIEGO   NEW YORK   CHICAGO   LONDON

Copyright © 2000 by Harcourt, Inc.

Portions of this work were published in previous editions.

Harcourt and the Harcourt logo are trademarks of Harcourt, Inc.

Printed in the United States of America.

ISBN: 0-15-607211-4

00 01 02 03 MG 4 3 2 1

PREFACE

For thousands of years, people and organizations have been working to establish and improve business processes. Records of process problems go back to ancient Egyptian tablets. In the 20th century, formal process measurement was established through detailed measurements (e.g., by efficiency experts). More recently, continuous small process, quality improvement, and radical reengineering were put forward as approaches. With all of the effort and methods, it is still the case that a large percentage of process improvement projects fail either partially or entirely.

This book reflects the following lessons learned from the failures:

- Information technology (IT) often was not considered as an integral part of the improvement method. There must be a strategic systems plan to support process improvement.

- Radical and conservative approaches appear to yield less than optimal results. A useful approach is a middle ground in which there is major, discrete improvement.

- Many process improvement efforts have not been organized as formal projects. There is benefit in using modern project management methods. Moreover, there is a need to manage multiple projects due to the complexity of the work.

- Process improvement and reengineering have often focused on single processes. In the real world, you must deal with a group of related processes. Critical processes do not stand alone.

- Many process improvement efforts have been started and ended without measurement. The lesson learned here is that measurement before, during, and after the process improvement work is important.

The approach of this book is step-by-step, from the initial understanding of the business through measurement after implementation of process change. The focus is on major, discrete change and improvement in groups of projects. Information technology is a major theme. Not only do you need a strategic systems plan for the enterprise and key departments, but a strategic plan is also an integral part of designing and implementing improved processes. Measurement is also a theme throughout the book.

CRITICAL SUCCESS FACTORS

There are a number of critical success factors to process improvement. The features of the book reflect these:

- Each of the steps has a logical start and finish and is supported by lessons learned and guidelines based on real-world process improvement projects.

- During the process improvement project, you identify quick-hit opportunities that can be implemented during the project. This builds confidence and morale. More important, it keeps the project going. Quick hits, of course, must be consistent with the analysis in the process improvement project. Quick hits can pave the way for longer-lasting, in-depth changes, thus creating a dual approach to process improvement.

- Much attention is given to implementation. Most books are not only narrow in scope, but also do not include implementation. It is often assumed that everything will turn out well after the new process is defined. However, the proof is whether the new process works.

- There is an emphasis on communications—project team, management, end user, and IT communications. Communications are a major factor in the success of a project.

- In addition to technology, the method includes procedures, policies, organization, and infrastructure—a multidimensional approach to address a multidimensional problem.

- People learn from examples. The book contains examples from different industries and organizations.

WHAT WILL YOU ACHIEVE?

With the material in this book, you will be better equipped to do the following:

- Understand the business and select the most appropriate processes for improvement
- Assess technology and develop a strategic systems plan for the enterprise and for key departments
- Create new business processes that work
- Define a project plan and team that can implement process improvement
- Market the new process to management and employees
- Develop an implementation strategy and plan
- Implement the new processes and measure the results
- Identify and solve problems and issues that arise during the entire project

WHO IS THIS BOOK FOR?

The book will be useful to the following audiences:

- Business managers interested in improving their business processes
- IT and systems managers and staff members who want to ensure that the investment in IT results in business improvement
- Employees and consultants involved in planning and implementing a process improvement project
- Consultants who want to pursue process improvement projects

Organizations generate earnings, provide services, and survive on the basis of their business processes. If you employ the right methods and techniques for process improvement, your organization can be a winner.

ABOUT THE AUTHORS

Bennet P. Lientz is Professor of Information Systems at the Anderson Graduate School of Management, University of California, Los Angeles (UCLA). Dr. Lientz was previously Associate Professor of Engineering at the University of Southern California and department manager at System Development Corporation, where he was one of the project leaders involved in the development of ARPANET, the precursor of the Internet. He managed administrative systems at UCLA and has managed projects and served as a consultant to companies and government agencies since the late 1970s.

Dr. Lientz has taught process improvement, information technology, project management, and strategic planning for the past 20 years. He has delivered seminars related to these topics to more than 4,000 people in Asia, Latin America, Europe, Australia, and North America. He is the author of more than 25 books and 70 articles on process improvement, information systems, planning, and project management. He has been involved in more than 70 process improvement projects in 15 industries.

Kathryn P. Rea is president and founder of The Consulting Edge, Inc., which was established in 1984. The firm specializes in process improvement, project management, and financial consulting.

Ms. Rea has managed more than 65 major technology-related projects internationally. She has advised on and carried out projects in government, energy, banking and finance, distribution, trading, retailing, transportation, mining, manufacturing, and utilities. She has successfully directed multinational projects in China, North and South America, Southeast Asia, Europe, and Australia. She has conducted more than 120 seminars around the world. She is the author of eight books and more than 20 articles in various areas of information systems and analysis. She has been an e-business project leader on ten projects and has been involved in several start-up e-business companies.

CONTENTS

ABOUT THE COMPUTER DISC

SYSTEM REQUIREMENTS

- IBM PC or compatible computer with CD-ROM drive
- Microsoft Word® 7.0 for Windows™ or compatible word processor, Microsoft® Excel 5.0 for Windows™ or compatible spreadsheet, Microsoft® PowerPoint 7.0, Microsoft® Project 98, and Microsoft Access
- 3 MB available on hard disk/drive

The CD-ROM provided with 2001 *Professional's Guide to Process Improvement* contains files to support use of the steps of process improvement presented in this book.

The word processing forms are intended to be used in conjunction with your word processing software. The word processing forms have been formatted in Word 7.0 for Windows. If you do not own this program, your word processing software may be able to convert the documents into a usable format. Check the user's manual that accompanies your word processing software for more information about the conversion of the documents.

Also included on the disc are Microsoft PowerPoint 7.0 presentations, Microsoft Project 98, Microsoft Access, and Microsoft Excel 5.0 for Windows™ or a compatible spreadsheet.

Subject to the conditions in the license agreement and the limited warranty, which is displayed on screen when the disc is installed and is reproduced at the end of the book, you may duplicate the files on this disc, modify them as necessary, and create your own customized versions. Installing the disc contents and/or using the disc in any way indicates that you accept the terms of the license agreement.

If you experience any difficulties installing or using the files included on this disc and cannot resolve the problem using the information presented in this section, call our toll-free software support hotline at (888) 551-7127.

INSTALLING THE TEMPLATES

To install the files on the disc using Windows 95 or above, select the Control Panel from the Start menu. Then choose Add/Remove Programs and select Install. You will be asked a series of questions. Read each question carefully and answer as indicated. If you are using Windows 3.1, choose File, Run from the Windows Program Manager and type D:/INSTALL in the command line or type D:/INSTALL at the DOS prompt.

First, the installation program will ask you to specify which drive you want to install to. You will then be instructed to specify the complete path where you would like the files installed. The installation program will suggest a directory for you, but you can name the directory anything you like. If the directory does not exist, the program will create it for you.

You can choose to install the Excel, PowerPoint, Project, and Microsoft Word. The program will automatically install the files in Excel, PowerPoint, Project, or Word subdirectories.

OPENING THE FILES

Open your word processing program. Choose Open from the File menu. Select the subdirectory that contains the loaded files to list the names of the files. Highlight the name of the file you want to open and click OK or press ENTER. You can also open a document in Windows Explorer (in Windows 95 or above), or in Windows 3.1 from the File Manager, by highlighting the name of the file you want to use and double-clicking your left mouse button.

Refer to the Disc Contents section of the book to find the file name of the document you want to use. The Disc Contents are also available on your disc in a file called "CONTENTS." You can open this file and view it on your screen or print a hard copy to use for reference.

Opening the Excel Spreadsheet

Open Excel 5.0 or higher or a compatible spreadsheet program. Choose Open from the file menu. Select the subdirectory that contains the loaded files to list the names of the files. Highlight the name of the file you want to open and click OK or press ENTER. You can also open a spreadsheet file from the File Manager (in Windows 3.1) or in the Explorer (in Windows 95) by highlighting the name of the file you want to use and double-clicking your left mouse button.

Spreadsheet Tips

Initially, only one spreadsheet file will exist in the spreadsheet installation directory. This is done to preserve an original copy of the Excel spreadsheet. After opening this file, simply select File and save to a new location and/or give the spreadsheet a different name. This will create a new file that will not be marked as read-only.

Opening the PowerPoint Tips

Open PowerPoint 7.0 or higher or a compatible program. Choose "Open an existing presentation" from the file menu. Click OK or press ENTER. Select the subdirectory that contains the loaded files to list the names of the files. Highlight the name of the file you want to open and click OK or press ENTER. You can also open a PowerPoint file from the File Manager (in Windows 3.1) or in the Explorer (in Windows 95) by highlighting the name of the file you want to use and double-clicking your left mouse button.

Opening the Project Tips

Open Project 98 or higher or a compatible program. Choose Open from the file menu. Select the subdirectory that contains the loaded files to list the names of the files. Highlight the name of the file you want to open and click OK or press ENTER. You can also open a Project file from the File Manager (in Windows 3.1) or in the Explorer (in Windows 95) by highlighting the name of the file you want to use and double-clicking your left mouse button.

Word Processing Tips

Wherever possible, the text of the documents has been formatted as tables so that you can modify the text without altering the format of the documents. To maneuver within a table, press TAB to move to the next cell, and SHIFT + TAB to move backward one cell. If you want to move to a tab stop within a cell, press CTRL + TAB. For additional tips on working within tables, consult your word processor's manual. It might be helpful to turn on the invisible table lines in Microsoft Word while modifying the document by selecting Gridlines from the Table menu.

Microsoft Word is equipped with search capabilities to help you locate specific words or phrases within a document. The Find option listed under the Edit menu performs a search in Microsoft Word.

Important: When you are finished using a file you will be asked to save it. If you have modified the file, you may want to save the modified file under a different name rather than the name of the original file. (Your word processing program will prompt you for a file name.) This will enable you to reuse the original file without your modifications. If you want to replace the original file with your modified file, save but do not change the name of the file.

PRINT TROUBLESHOOTING

If you are having difficulty printing your document, the following suggestions may correct the problem:

Microsoft Word

- Select Print from the Microsoft Word File menu. Then choose the Printer function.
- Ensure that the correct printer is selected.
- From this window, choose Options.
- In the media box, make sure that the paper size is correct and that the proper paper tray is selected.
- Check your network connections if applicable.
- If you still have trouble printing successfully, it may be because your printer does not recognize the font Times New Roman. At this point, you should change the font of the document to your default font by selecting the document (CTRL + A) and then choosing Font from the Format menu and highlighting the name

of the font you normally use. Changing the font of the document may require additional adjustments to the document format, such as margins, tab stops, and table cell height and width. Select Page Layout from the View menu to view the appearance of the pages before you try to print again.

DISC CONTENTS

The file names on the CD-ROM contain both the chapter reference and the titles. Files are in Microsoft Word, PowerPoint, Excel, Access and Project formats.

Description	File Name	File Type
Risk Assessment of Processes	01-01	Excel
Rating of Importance of Processes	01-02	Excel
Summary Rating of Processes	01-03	Excel
Process Questions and Checklist	01-04	Excel
Questionnaire on Potential Problems	01-05	Excel
Process Presentation	01-06	PowerPoint
GANTT Chart	02-01	Project
Business Process Improvement Method Presentation	02-02	PowerPoint
Issues Database	02-03	Excel
Managers and Staff	02-04	Excel
Development of the Plan	03-01	Word
Project Concept and Initial Planning	03-02	Word
Project Concept Presentation	03-03	PowerPoint
Issues	03-04	Access
Lessons Learned	03-05	Access
Issue Comments	03-06	Excel
Lessons Learned Database	03-07	Excel
Project Leader Evaluation	04-01	Word
Project Manager Evaluation	04-02	Word
Support for Project Managers	04-03	Word
Project Management Assessment	04-04	Word
Project Leader Skill	04-05	Excel
Project Leaders vs. Type of Project	04-06	Excel
Project Leaders vs. Phase	04-07	Excel
Team Member Project Evaluation	05-01	Word
Team Member vs. Skills	05-02	Excel

Description	File Name	File Type
Issues vs. Team Member	05-03	Excel
Team Member vs. Phase	05-04	Excel
The Project Budget	06-01	Word
Sample Common Resource Pool	06-02	Project
Budget Categories vs. Projects	06-03	Excel
Budget Categories vs. Risk	06-04	Excel
Budget Categories vs. Budget Categories	06-05	Excel
Methods vs. Tools	07-01	Excel
Methods vs. Staff	07-02	Excel
Methods vs. Projects	07-03	Excel
Business Objectives Assessment	08-01	Excel
Business Strategy Assessment	08-02	Excel
Business Issues vs. Processes	08-03	Excel
Organization vs. Processes	08-04	Excel
Infrastructure vs. Processes	08-05	Excel
Interdependence of Processes	08-06	Excel
Business Strategies vs. Processes	08-07	Excel
Example of Business Objectives vs. Processes	08-08	Excel
Process Step vs. Organization	09-01	Excel
Example of Transactions vs. Organization	09-02	Excel
Shadow Systems and Exceptions	09-03	Excel
Process Step vs. Technologies	09-04	Excel
Issues at the Step and Transaction Levels	09-05	Excel
Competition vs. Processes	10-01	Excel
Competitor vs. Financial Results	10-02	Excel
Issues vs. Current Technologies	11-01	Excel
Business Processes vs. Potential Technologies	11-02	Excel
Projects vs. Technologies	11-03	Excel

Description	File Name	File Type
Processes vs. Data Type	15-01	Excel
Processes vs. Issues	15-02	Excel
Processes vs. Processes	15-03	Excel
Key Process vs. Related Processes	16-01	Excel
Process Transaction Analysis	16-02	Excel
Group Process Analysis	16-03	Excel
Process Cost Analysis	16-04	Excel
Example of Process Groupings	16-05	Excel
Rework and Issues Checklist	16-06	Excel
Organization vs. Process Group	16-07	Excel
Infrastructure vs. Process Group	16-08	Excel
Test Your Knowledge Regarding Processes	16-09	Excel
Companies vs. Characteristics	17-01	Excel
Example of Process Alternative	17-02	Excel
Process Group vs. Firms	17-03	Excel
Sample Graph of Alternative Processes	17-04	Word
Alternative Process Solution Analysis	17-05	Excel
Alternative Process Solutions	17-06	Excel
Issues vs. Alternative Process Solutions	17-07	Excel
Process Scorecard	18-01	Excel
Vendor Scorecard	18-02	Excel
Organization Scorecard	18-03	Excel
Alternative Implementation Strategy Checklist	18-04	Excel
Potential Impact of Changes on Implementation Strategy	18-05	Excel
Management Contact Planner	19-01	Excel
Presentation of New Process	19-02	PowerPoint
Presentation of Issues	19-03	PowerPoint
GANTT Chart—II	20-01	Project
Milestone Table	20-02	Excel
Implementation Issues Checklist	20-03	Excel
Issues vs. Tasks	20-04	Excel

Description	File Name	File Type
Rylande Corporation	21-01	Word
Rylande Project Template for Process Improvement	21-02	Project
Rylande Project Plan	21-03	Project
Issues Presentation	22-01	PowerPoint
Multiple Projects Presentation	22-02	PowerPoint
Project Effectiveness Evaluation	23-01	Word
Project Review Checklist	23-02	Word
Project Review	23-03	Word
Collaboration in Projects	24-01	Word
Staff vs. Projects	24-02	Excel
Staff vs. Stages	24-03	Excel
Issues vs. Stages	25-01	Excel
Issues vs. Types of Issues	25-02	Excel
Questionnaire for Pilot Project Evaluation	27-01	Word
Analysis of Pilot Project Questionnaire Data	27-02	Excel
Current Technology vs. Process	28-01	Excel
New Technology vs. Process	28-02	Excel
Example of New Technology vs. Processes	28-03	Excel
Technology vs. Technology	28-04	Excel
Issues with Technology Checklist	28-05	Excel
Interfaces and Relationships	28-06	Excel
Benefits Achieved	29-01	Excel
Original Estimated Benefits Analysis	29-02	Excel
Original Issues Evaluation	29-03	Excel
New Issues	29-04	Excel
Organization vs. Processes	29-05	Excel
New Process Evaluation	29-06	Excel
Detailed Records	29-07	Excel
Business Measurement Checklist	30-01	Excel

Description	File Name	File Type
Systems and Technology Measurement Checklist	30-02	Excel
Issues vs. Results	30-03	Excel
Actions vs. Benefits	30-04	Excel
Potential Outsourcing Functions	32-01	Excel
Functions and Interfaces	32-02	Excel
Function Evaluation	32-03	Excel
Outsourcing Checklist	32-04	Excel
Vendor Table	32-05	Excel
Outsourcing Project Plan	32-06	Project
Glossary	34-01	Word
Web Sources	34-02	Word
Process Improvement Trends in Selected Vertical Markets	34-03	Word
Process Improvement Step-by-Step	34-04	Word

PART I ONE

GETTING STARTED

CHAPTER 1

INTRODUCTION

CONTENTS

1

INTRODUCTION

BUSINESS PROCESSES—OVERVIEW

Process improvement projects have been started at many companies. However, the success rate has been less than 50 percent. Why do these "reengineering" projects fail? How can you make sure your process improvement project succeeds? The answers to these questions are the focus of this book. Using proven guidelines and a step-by-step method, you will be able to improve your business processes successfully or turn around previous failures.

What is a business process? A *process* is a set of procedures and work-flow steps that carries out a specific business function. With this broad definition, company processes may encompass everything from issuing payroll to generating monthly company performance statistics. Processes exclude casual, ad hoc work. The most important processes are those that add to a company's competitive position and provide value to customers. It is these processes that process improvement addresses.

Standard terminology will be used throughout the book. Here are definitions of frequently-used terms:

- *Business process improvement*—A major change or improvement to a process or process group along with its technology, organization, and infrastructure support

- *Infrastructure*—Computers, communications, facilities, and any other physical support required by a business process, including equipment, information systems, general technology, and other resources that support implementing the process

- *Organization*—The business's structure and its employees

- *Process group*—A group of processes that are related through one facet of a business, such as organization, technology, suppliers, or customers

- *Technology*—All categories of technology involving computers and communications

These terms and others used in this book are defined in the glossary at the end of this chapter.

Looking at the organizations within a company, you discover that many processes cross over multiple internal organizations. This may be by design and division of control and is often for a sound business reason. It simply may have evolved this way. An organization may have changed, with no thought given to the processes.

Processes and Technology

What is the relationship between a business process and computer and communications technology and systems? The telephone system, computer network, electronic mail, voice mail, and facsimile machine are examples of infrastructure that supports process operation. If the business tailors a computer software system to the process, the computer system becomes a part of that process. The hardware, network, and other software necessary to run the systems are part of the infrastructure.

Formal vs. Informal Processes

Formal processes tend to be documented or at least acknowledged by the organization. Informal processes, which are more numerous, may be either manual or computer-based. For example, people invent forms or put data into a PC. These informal *shadow systems* can lead to trouble. The organization becomes dependent on these systems, which usually are set up by a computer-savvy employee, and builds processes around them. If the inventive employee leaves the organization, the informal process may not be usable.

Critical Processes

In this book, you will consider some processes that are critical. An organization may view some processes (such as payroll) as more important than others. The business process is *critical* if the performance of the process significantly impacts revenue or costs of the organization.

Changes to a Process over Time

How does a process evolve? A process frequently begins informally. The company grows and changes. No one pays much attention to the process, because it appears to function. Over time, the volume of work increases, the nature and range of transactions change, and the amount of work per transaction increases. The people who originally worked with the process disappear. People coming into the organization and process do not receive formal training. There is no on-the-job training.

Technology enters the picture. In some cases, people install a system, but it performs only part of the work of the process. Systems people concentrate on automating the easiest part of the process. People then institute workarounds for the system. The system itself begins to deteriorate into a maintenance mode. People discover that the process cannot handle all of the requirements. There are additional management reporting and functional requirements. People then generate shadow systems. This is a fairly typical picture of how processes change.

Here are some signs of deterioration to watch for:

- The process may work, but it is unresponsive.

- There are no up-to-date, formal procedures.

- Typically, one or two people have been with the process for a long time. They can provide history but are ignored by management.

- A number of add-on, replacement processes may come to surround the basic process. The result is a crazy quilt of patched processes.

- People may complain about the process, but they fear changing it.

Business Process Improvement Defined

Business process improvement, or more simply process improvement, consists of the efforts made to improve processes. These efforts can be incremental improvements, major rework, or even elimination. Some people attempt to differentiate improvements from "wholesale reengineering," but it is difficult to draw the line.

PROCESS IMPROVEMENT: WHY AND HOW

Process improvement can take place for both external and internal reasons. External reasons include changes in competition, supplier/customer relations, government regulation, and technology. Internal reasons may include management direction, lack of flexibility, and process obsolescence. Most process change is motivated by the simple fact that the existing process does not live up to expectations. Perhaps people have been focused on the "how" and not the "what," "who," or "where." Perhaps the people performing the steps in the process feel comfortable and secure with "the way it has always been" and haven't reevaluated the process for awhile. Whatever the reason, the process is failing or has already failed.

When change is called for, attention to the infrastructure or the organization doesn't necessarily improve the process. Treating a symptom may not cure the disease. Changing a process or a group of processes requires dedicated work that is political as well as technical. It requires time, because the culture surrounding the process in the organization must be altered.

Process Improvement Step by Step

First consider how to formulate the process improvement project., including the following aspects of the project:

- Developing the project plan
- Identifying the project leader
- Getting the project team together
- Obtaining funding and resources for the process improvement project
- Selecting the right project management methods and tools

Here is the sequence of steps of the method used in this book:

Understanding the business

> Step A: Grasp business goals and direction.
> Step B: Select the processes for improvement.
> Step C: Assess the competition and industry.

Technology and processes

Step D: Evaluate technology possibilities.

Step E: Develop an enterprise strategic systems plan.

Step F: Define departmental strategic systems plans.

Step G: Define the systems architecture.

Step H: Collect information for processes, infrastructure, and organizations.

Determining the new process

Step I: Analyze the information.

Step J: Define the new process.

Step K: Develop the implementation strategy.

Step L: Market the new process.

Step M: Develop the implementation plan.

Implementation and measuring results

Step N: Implement the new process.

Step O: Define and measure success.

Step P: Follow up after implementation.

Step Q: Measure plan results.

You will also address specific project management areas, including the following:

- Project communications
- Management communications and support
- Track and analyze project results and status
- Collaborative scheduling and work
- Managing project resources
- Overcoming project crises

New processes cost money and can generate controversy. Therefore, the process improvement project must be well organized and measurable. Since improvement projects often cross multiple departments and involve significant organization and infrastructure changes, an implementation strategy is needed.

Also, analysis does not translate into results. Therefore, there are steps to implementation planning, implementation, and post-implementation work. The detailed implementation plan supports the strategy. Post-implementation work supports measurement and often identifies where the effort should be directed next. Implementation includes both downsizing and outsourcing, each of which are addressed in later chapters.

Methods and Tools for Implementation

Implementation requires both methods and tools. Choosing the right ones is important. The wrong method or tool can be fatal to the process improvement effort.

A *method* is a technique for doing a specific piece of work on the project. Examples include collecting data, developing the new process, and testing the new process. A *tool* supports a method by making it easier and more effective to follow the method. Tools include process mapping, flowchart software, and simulation tools. Methods do not require tools but are enhanced by them. Tools, implemented without methods, often fail, because people do not know the proper use of the tool.

Downsizing/Rightsizing

Downsizing (or rightsizing, as it's sometimes called) is the process of reducing the organizational and infrastructure requirements for the process. After determination of how the new process should work, the organization and infrastructure are adjusted to fit. This can lead to tangible savings.

Examples of downsizing are doing the process with fewer people, using PCs instead of mainframe computers, and moving work out of the organization (outsourcing). Clearly, technology advances and increased labor costs tend to support downsizing.

Downsizing sometimes occurs before the process has been ana-lyzed. For example, layoffs occur, then the remaining employees are told they will have to carry on the work with less people to help out. This approach limits the number of solutions possible, lowers mo-rale, and tends to be counterproductive. Another problem with this approach is that managers often lay off the most junior employees, who may be the closest to the process. Thus, downsizing too soon may harm the process it was intended to aid.

Project Management

Process improvement projects differ from other projects. First, a process improvement project often crosses multiple organizations. Second, it often depends to some extent on technology. Third, the environment of the project is politically charged. A critical process touches many people who have a stake in the outcome.

A process improvement project also combines three project ar-eas—infrastructure, process, and organization—with three time spans for each—short-term, intermediate-term, and long-term. This adds up to nine related, integrated projects. This complexity must be addressed to prevent process improvement projects from running into trouble.

Becoming a Project Manager

Process improvement projects must compete with other projects for project managers and team members. Why would someone want to become a manager in a process improvement project? It looks like a lot of work. It entails career risk. If you are successful, you might just end up doing one project after another. All of this is true. Yet, people still seek to become project leaders. What is the positive side of being a project manager? For younger people it is an opportunity to gain the recognition and attention of management. A project is visible. A project manager is visible. A project manager may have more oppor-tunities for advancement than an employee stuck in a line organiza-tion. In process improvement, a leader gains experience and knowl-edge of processes that few have. This is extremely valuable for an organization.

Here are some additional reasons to become a project manager, beyond the potential of advancement:

- The project leaders gain valuable relationships with people across the organization through process improvement.

- A project is a chance to learn new skills and methods. In process improvement managers often get better at interpersonal skills and problem-solving abilities.

- Being a process improvement project leader may be your best shot at breaking into management.

- The role of project leader may be more challenging than your current position.

- Being a project leader will increase your range of contacts and personal network.

If you are a project manager with a known track record, you can wait to be called. Otherwise, how do you get started? Consider the old-fashioned approach of volunteering. Even if you are turned down for a particular project, people will see that you have an interest in the company. Second, you have shown initiative. How many people around you are doing that? Third, you are alerting people to your interest in projects and project management.

What should you do before volunteering? Scout the processes and project out. Gather information on business processes. Learn how the business works. Determine what you could add to the project. Don't stress the negative things in the project that you could fix. Focus instead on the opportunities in the project and the strengths you could bring to the table. Next, determine what you would do with the duties of your current job. You definitely don't want to say that these can be left undone. Instead, show that you can piggyback the project tasks on top of your normal work, even if this means extra work.

What if you want to volunteer to replace a current project manager? Do not undermine the current manager. How do you propose your services? The best technique for taking over a project is to volunteer to address the outstanding, unresolved issues in the project. Never emphasize administrative or communication skills unless there is a known problem here. You want to show that you care and want to help.

When you make your proposal to management, use the words "volunteer" and "assistance," and ask them to think about it. To avoid pressuring them for a decision, indicate that you will check with them in a week or so to see what they might suggest.

THE BENEFITS OF SUCCESS

Successful companies and managers cite a number of major benefits when process improvement projects are successful. Some of the more common ones are the following:

- **Improved staff productivity**

  This is an expected benefit.

- **Streamlined, simpler business processes**

  These processes are easier to staff, operate, manage, and measure.

- **Improved work quality**

  For this benefit to be achieved, it needs to be an original goal of process improvement.

- **Better decisions are made**

  This relates to the visibility of the process and its improvement as well as improved information.

- **Improved customer satisfaction**

  This occurs if it is an original focus of the process improvement effort.

- **Reduced expenses**

  Cost savings are sometimes achieved; however, the cost of the modified infrastructure and support consume savings realized from terminating the old system.

- **Improved employee morale**

  This can be credited to several factors, including attention given to the employees and their process, the investment in the process, and the changes made to the process.

- **Increased market share and sales**

  This is normally achieved on an individual basis and depends on factors other than the process improvement effort.

- **Flexibility to handle change**

  An efficient process can be scaled up or down to handle changes in volume or variations in transactions within limits.

WHY PROCESS IMPROVEMENTS PROJECTS FAIL

Here are some common reasons for process improvement failures:

- **High expectations**

  Management has lofty expectations created by attending seminars or excessive marketing.

- **Over-reliance on methods or tools that have too much jargon**

  The method cannot be used because it is too general or cannot be understood.

- **Too narrow a scope for the project**

  Changes are not supported because much is outside the scope.

- **Too wide a scope for the project**

  No major changes can occur because everything on the playing field is in play.

- **Settling for small changes**

  People become frustrated and want progress. They settle for small changes.

- **Overdependence on technology**

  People mistakenly believe that all problems can be overcome by moving to client-server, videotext, hypermedia, or any other technology.

- **Lack of technology planning**

  Process improvement often requires new technology and systems. There should be a strategic systems plan.

- **Lack of use of modern project management methods and tools**

  Often, an organization treats process improvement as just another project.

- **Over-control by vendor or consultant**

  The organization turns the project over to an outside firm. The new process never takes hold after the consultants leave.

- **Lack of consideration of the political environment**

  This often results when process improvement is treated as a technical project.

- **Underestimation of the changes in the infrastructure and technology required**
- **General resistance to change by the organization**
- **Lack of upper management support**

  While deep involvement is not necessary, management must provide a minimum level of support.

- **Excessive upper management involvement**

  This is the extreme in which managers attempt to micromanage the process improvement project.

DEBUNKING THE MYTHS

Here are some common myths concerning process improvement.

Myth 1: Change is continuous.

It is a myth that process improvement should be continuous, in which you constantly strive to improve processes in major ways. Unfortunately, this approach flies in the face of reality. People desire stable

KOUDRY

critical processes. Observe that after a major change, the process tends to be stable. It then begins to evolve on its own. Just like the old process, the new one undergoes maintenance. It can then begin to deteriorate.

Myth 2: Focus only on the critical processes.

The effort should focus on groups of processes containing some of the top 10 to 20 critical processes, but as long as you are working on process improvement, also take the time to fix less important, related aspects.

Myth 3: Process improvement is always the big project.

Substantial changes in procedures are possible with little expense. Making major infrastructure changes, on the other hand, requires more time and effort. Projects have been carried out in which simple changes in procedure resulted in significant improvements.

Myth 4: Top management has to participate actively in process improvement projects for the projects to succeed.

Participation by management may be desirable but it is not mandatory. What is essential is management support during the entire project.

Myth 5: The entire process is radically redesigned.

Radical change may not always be the best change. In radical redesign of a process, the organization or the infrastructure (or both) may foil you. Radical change has even driven firms into bankruptcy.

Myth 6: Information systems and technology play key roles in process improvement.

Whether this is true or not depends on scope. If you want fast results, focus on the procedures. If you want to have major, long-lasting change, move to the technology.

Myth 7: The process is started with a clean slate.

This might be good theoretically, but it ignores reality. Much of the organization and infrastructure must be accepted and taken as a constraint. Who has the time and money to keep a business going and, at the same time, totally reinvent its processes?

Myth 8: The golden method or tool will ensure success.

This is the vendors' dream: That their method or tool will solve all process improvement problems and result in new, widely acclaimed processes. If the method is so great, why isn't everyone using it? Methods and tools come and go. Don't pin all your hopes on a particular one.

Myth 9: If you do the process redesign right, the implementation will be successful.

What you learn in implementation may undo some of the original design. Also, politics appear in implementation to a greater extent than in redesign, so changes may be required.

TEN PRINCIPLES FOR PROCESS IMPROVEMENT

A series of principles for process improvement is defined here and expanded on and supported in later chapters.

Principle 1: A firm depends on its business processes for profitability.

To make money you must make something or provide a service. Doing this requires processes. Companies that are successful have integrated their organization and infrastructure with their processes.

Principle 2: Processes should be considered in groups.

There are few stand-alone, separate processes, and few of these are critical. A good example is the large-scale acquisition of stand-alone personal computers in the late 1980s. Much of their value was not realized until networks were established so that the technology and people could be linked to the processes.

Many times, the most successful companies have found a new and better grouping of processes. They then focused on having the organization and infrastructure support this group. One example is the retail company, Quick Response, which combined point of sale, scanning, electronic data interchange, bar coding, and shipping container marking.

Principle 3: Process performance and characteristics allow you to differentiate between companies in the same industry.

Look in newspapers or magazines. Successful companies are cited for their organizations (Hewlett-Packard) or their approach to infrastructure (Wal-Mart). Organizations and infrastructure are used to support processes. Why do other companies with similar organizations and infrastructures either fail or have less success? A key reason is failure to map the resources into the process. To see this in action, visit several chains who use point-of-sale systems. Look for differences in terms of how they have embedded the technology into the process.

Principle 4: The technologies and infrastructure that are important support or can potentially support critical processes.

Most technologies are irrelevant to processes. Even when they are relevant, their value is not automatically achieved. Adding a new technology creates gaps and problems in interfacing with the rest of the organization and infrastructure.

Consider the totality of all of the technologies supporting a business process. Watch for a technology's lack of applicability. Many new technologies don't work because they cannot easily interface with other parts of the infrastructure.

Principle 5: Processes must be maintained over time.

This is often ignored. People assume that either the process is self-maintaining or that the people involved will automatically keep the process up-to-date. If an organization fails to maintain its processes, it often withers and dies. Sears did not keep its processes current and so lost ground to mass merchandiser/discount chains.

Principle 6: Downsizing or rightsizing should follow process improvement analysis.

Downsizing can carry out the results of the business process improvement analysis. When combined, they provide a potent combination that can lead to a position of dominance in an industry.

Principle 7: Process improvement is best carried out in discrete steps as opposed to continuous improvement.

Process improvement requires considerable time, energy, and focus. If changes are made continuously, how can you be focused on anything else? Instead, improve the process and allow it to stabilize, be maintained, and evolve. It can then be revisited later as needed.

Principle 8: Employees should be valued based on their contribution to the critical processes.

The operative word here is *should*. Unfortunately, many companies reward people based on their value to the organization. Processes don't evaluate staff; managers do. Being valuable to the organization is different from being valuable to the process. One can be valued in an organization through politics and personal relationships. A process is not as emotional. When an organization rewards people for their contribution to process, the process often will improve. Other employees recognize such rewards because their contribution to a process was evident and the importance of the process was obvious.

Principle 9: Processes are easily and negatively impacted by organization and infrastructure policies.

An example is the behavior of clinging to mainframe computer systems for almost all computing, in spite of the rising tide of distributed systems in the late 1980s.

Principle 10: Changes in organization and infrastructure that are not made to improve processes tend to be transient and short-lived.

For example, some people think that changing managers will somehow transform processes. It usually does not happen, unless the new managers move quickly to improve the processes.

HOW TO USE THIS BOOK

Each of the process improvement steps is presented using the following:

- Introduction
- Purpose and scope
- End products of the activities
- Resources involved in that stage of work
- The approach to carry out the step in terms of actions
- Management presentation and cost-benefit analysis
- Status check (guidance on how to evaluate your work)
- Industry examples
- Detailed guidelines
- Action items (detailed steps you can take)

To support the overall sequence of steps, you will build a series of tables that show relationships between the business, the process, organization, infrastructure, competition and the industry, suppliers, and customers. The tables are based on the comparison factors defined in Table1-1. Constructing tables will help with understanding, analysis, decision-making, and action.

Table 1-1: Comparative Factors for Business Process Improvement

In other chapters you will be building comparison tables that show the results of analysis. These can be presented to management and will help with the implementation of the new process. The tables are based on the following factors:

Business

Business objectives—General goals of the business

Business issues—Regulatory, competitive, and industry pressures

Industry

Competitive and similar firms—Firms in the same industry or those with similar processes

Competitor's or other firm's process—Selected process for analysis

Industry averages/statistics—Ratios, trends, and statistics for the industry segment

Competition infrastructure—General components of the infrastructure of the competitor

Competition organization—Features of the organization (empowered, distributed, centralized, outsourced, etc.)

Organization

Organizations (old/new)—Features of the organization

Detailed organization (old/new)—Organizational units

Infrastructure

General

Internal infrastructure—Old/new

Candidate infrastructure

Technology

Architecture—Old/new

Internal technology—Old/new

Candidate technologies

Degree of automation—Old/new

General processes

Processes—All

Process groups

Process group

Process strategy

Processes

Process steps—Old/new

Process characteristics (age, etc.)—Old/new

Measurement

Benefits–Estimated/actual

Costs—Estimated/actual

Performance measure (response, time, effort, paper)—Estimated/actual

THE THREE INDUSTRY EXAMPLES

Three companies are used as examples and represent typical industries with processes that are common candidates for process improvement. Each faced a crisis and successfully resolved it. You will see how this was done step-by-step as you progress through the book.

Monarch Bank

At an international bank, Monarch Bank, the primary customers are consumers in the United States. The bank has the standard divisions, including consumer banking, commercial banking, international banking, trust. After growing rapidly for five years with its network expanding from 350 branches to more than 700 branches, Monarch's financial results were suffering. The increase in the number of employees outpaced the increase in sales. There was a profitability crisis. Losses were mounting. The auditors warned about risk and exposure of loans. The bank had to take drastic steps to turn around the situation, face a sharp downsizing, or suffer a hostile takeover. The process improvement project was headed up by a manager of project management. This person was ideal because he combined business knowledge with technical knowledge and structure through projects.

Monarch Bank is typical of the following industries and processes:

- Large international corporations
- Medical care and service
- Insurance, banking, and sales and servicing environments
- Accounting and finance processes, such as accounts receivable and payables

TRAN

The second example is TRAN, a government agency. TRAN supports the planning and operation of transportation operations (mainly buses) in an urban area. For years, the agency spent only a minimal amount on technology. While the agency fell behind, the number of employees increased. Efficiency dropped as traffic and customers increased. With technology improving and becoming more affordable, management thought that the systems and processes should be modernized. While the situation worsened gradually, an enormous financial crisis hit, causing an available funding loss in the millions of dollars. TRAN had to change its operations dramatically or cut public services by more than 50 percent.

Process improvement efforts were managed by several people. The most successful was a business manager who had experience in several departments and so could take a wider view of the business.

TRAN is representative of processes in defense, transportation, utilities, government agencies, and non-for-profit organizations.

Stirling Manufacturing

The third example involves a manufacturing firm that makes a specific range of engineering products in fairly small quantities. Stirling Manufacturing had been making these components for 20 years and was an industry leader. New competitors then entered the market and could make the same or similar products at much lower costs. Stirling faced the possibility of continuing eroding market share and leadership. The erosion caused the cost of making products to soar due to loss of economies of scale. The parent company was rumored to be considering a sale of the firm.

At Stirling, the project manager for process improvement came from both a business and technical background.

This example represents processes in manufacturing, distribution, project management, and construction.

ACTION ITEMS

Complete the following questions or use them as the basis of a short survey of managers to determine which processes managers and staff view as critical. These questions also raise interest in business process improvement by getting people involved.

1. Identify ten critical business processes. Rank these in order of importance to the business (1 is highest, 10 is lowest).

1. _____ 2. _____

3. _____ 4. _____

5. _____ 6. _____

7. _____ 8. _____

9. _____ 10. _____

2. Now take the same processes and rank them in terms of degree of problems and potential improvement on the same scale.

1. _____ 2. _____

3. _____ 4. _____

5. _____ 6. _____

7. _____ 8. _____

9. _____ 10. _____

3. Compute a total score for each process by multiplying the ratings for importance and potential for improvement. This approach helps you identify processes that rank highest overall.

	Process	*Score*
1.	_____	_____
2.	_____	_____
3.	_____	_____
4.	_____	_____
5.	_____	_____
6.	_____	_____
7.	_____	_____
8.	_____	_____
9.	_____	_____
10.	_____	_____

4. Based on your knowledge of business processes, indicate the degree to which you agree or disagree with the following statements on a scale of 1 to 5 (1–strongly agree, 2–agree, 3–indifferent, 4–disagree, 5–strongly disagree):

The most severe problems with processes lie in:

Organization	1	2	3	4	5
Information systems	1	2	3	4	5
Infrastructure (buildings, telephones, etc.)	1	2	3	4	5
Lack of management interest	1	2	3	4	5
Age of the processes	1	2	3	4	5
Bad information in the processes	1	2	3	4	5
Lack of formal processes	1	2	3	4	5
Staff turnover	1	2	3	4	5
Lack of process training	1	2	3	4	5
Interfaces between departments	1	2	3	4	5
Interfaces with suppliers	1	2	3	4	5
Interfaces with customers	1	2	3	4	5

5. For companies that have not been successful in previous business process improvement efforts, examine the following common reasons for problems in carrying out these efforts. Rate these on a scale of 1 to 5 (1 means it does not apply at all, 5 means it strongly applies). Your responses will help you determine what obstacles you will later overcome.

Lack of management involvement	1	2	3	4	5
Excessive management involvement	1	2	3	4	5
Method was oversold; raising excessive expectations	1	2	3	4	5
Lack of project management	1	2	3	4	5
Lack of measurement of current process and system	1	2	3	4	5
Project to implement was too large	1	2	3	4	5
Overdependence on consultants	1	2	3	4	5

CHAPTER 2

PROCESS IMPROVEMENT: CRITICAL SUCCESS FACTORS

CONTENTS

2

PROCESS IMPROVEMENT: CRITICAL SUCCESS FACTORS

CRITICAL SUCCESS FACTORS

Some of the most important factors that affect the success of the process improvement project are the following:

- Making the case to implement. This is the marketing and sales issue.
- Dealing with issues and potential crises that arise during the project.
- Addressing the cultural issues of the organization that affect the project.
- Establishing and keeping the right level of management attention.
- Ensuring that the infrastructure supports the process.

Keep these in mind as project management is discussed to ensure that you are armed with modern project management methods.

Definition of Major Deliverable Items

Over the years, a minimum list of deliverable items has been developed which sets apart serious efforts at process improvement from those that produce only stacks of reports. Here is a list of those items, along with the step in which you would generate the item:

- The recommended group of processes to be improved (Step B)
- The assessment of external information related to industry and competition (Step C)

- The evaluation of potential new technologies (Step D)
- The development of strategic systems plans for both the enterprise and critical departments (Steps E and F)
- The definition of the systems and technology architecture (Step G)
- The assessment of the current business processes in detail (Step H)
- The analysis of the information (Step I)
- Creation of the new process—how it will work, the benefits, and what changes are required to make it come true (Step J)
- Delineation of the implementation strategy for the processes (Step K)
- Development of the implementation plan (Step M)
- Measure the results obtained from the new process (Step R)

Create a Flexible Project Plan

The scope of an process improvement project can expand and contract with the progress of the work, requiring a flexible project plan. The project will begin with a low-level analysis of the business. Then a candidate group of processes will be defined. The project will expand to a more detailed external and internal data collection and analysis. This will lead to the development of the new processes. Implementation can bring more changes and redirection.

The scope can also change due to changes in management policy, organization, and other factors (both internal and external). Organization and infrastructure changes may set off a political battle. The project may be forced to go underground if a significant organizational battle surfaces.

Issues can arise that must be addressed and may change the scope. Outcomes of issue resolution often impact the plan.

Win Management Support

The ongoing support of upper management is so important that management presentations are addressed in each chapter. Resistance (both overt and covert), inertia, and the need to keep the business operating all combine against process improvement every step of the way. Without continuing management support, the project often falters.

On the other hand, managers have their normal jobs. Be aware that management's role may be limited to lending crucial support in specific crisis situations. They do not have the time or energy to be heavily involved in the day-to-day detail.

After the project has been initiated, you should broaden the base of support from management. This is a good time for a committee of managers and staff from the affected process group to become involved. This gives them an opportunity for ownership and a sense of participation. Keep the committee informal, as a formal committee may burden the project with overhead.

Some have suggested that a steering committee, consisting of a group of managers, should meet to review the progress of the project and resolve issues. This approach, however, has several pitfalls:

- **A steering committee makes the project visible.**

  In early stages, high-level visibility is useful, but during implementation, lower and mid-level involvement is better. Greater visibility means higher risk and exposure.

- **The review requirements of the project vary with the stage of the project.**

  The same steering committee should not work on every stage.

- **A steering committee assignment is political.**

  If higher level managers see that their peers are sending lower-level personnel to meetings in their place, they will also send substitutes. The result can be a lowest common denominator of employee.

- **A steering committee makes the review process too formal.**

  Most often, the project benefits from informality.

A process improvement project often requires only a few critical decisions. Get the support of the right manager. Give that manager the opportunity to sell the decision.

Review of the Process

As a reviewer, you should keep an eye on the scope of the project. What has changed? Look at the project factors before considering standard items such as budgeted vs. actual. Progress is not always traditional work but may be problem-solving work that involves policies, organization, or political conflict.

During the implementation of the process changes, use two review groups. One could be derived from the committee formed to deal with implementation. A higher-level group could deal with strategy and general process improvement approaches.

Polish Management Presentation and Cost-Benefit Analysis

At the start of the project (even when you are developing the plan), people expect you to have a great deal of detail. Be ready to respond to detailed questions at the front end of the project. Be purposely vague about the tasks and work that are further out in the future. After all, you do not know which processes are to be improved.

Be able to answer questions about project costs and benefits at the same time. However, make every effort to separate these from the schedule and the plan. The plan is the "how" you will do it. The costs and benefits are the effects of carrying out the project. For example, if someone says that some part of the project is too expensive, focus on the work itself and determine if there is any better way to do it. Always remember that costs and benefits are the impacts of the schedule.

Always track cumulative costs and benefits. Infrastructure change can absorb the largest part of the budget, so make sure that all infrastructure improvements and work map directly into benefits for the process. Infrastructure costs tend to occur at the front end. Benefits occur later. If you create a curve of benefits minus costs, the curve will be negative for some time. It is important to track when this curve goes positive. The negative value should give you a boost to obtain management support for organization change to take advantage of the process improvement.

Within the project itself you will be tracking actual vs. planned budget. This helps prevent diversions or delays in the project. During many of these projects, interesting opportunities surface as you look at a process in detail. Have the actual vs. planned budgets ready so that you can keep on track.

Termination of a Project

More than half of all process improvement projects fail or are cut down in scope prematurely. It would be better to end some of these early, in order to save time and money. How can you detect projects with major problems? What is the range of feasible actions? If you decide to end the project, how will you do that?

You usually know when something is not right on a project. People don't talk about issues. There may be little progress or effective work. Process improvement accelerates these and other symptoms because it places immediate stress on organization, infrastructure, and management. Process improvement often makes symptoms stand out earlier and in sharper contrast than standard work. Issues are often clearly in focus. Issues not addressed become even more obvious.

Confronting major issues is difficult. Here are some ways to deal with a crisis:

- **Continue the project as is.**

  In the midst of major upheaval, this alternative is infeasible. Much of the completed work will have to be redone.

- **Slow down the project but maintain momentum.**

  This alternative is not attractive, because resources are still being consumed and morale is plummeting.

- **Accelerate the project to force resolution and change.**

  Accelerating the project is a practical approach. In some cases, issues involving process and organization are vague. More attention, pressure, and effort may force the issue into the open. This saves money in the long run and prevents a process improvement project from dissolving into minor improvements.

- **Halt the project and examine the issues.**

  This forces people to address the issues because they will have to be reassigned if the issues are not resolved. This action takes management initiative and incurs risk. If there is no project change and work resumes, the project is more likely to fail.

- **Terminate the project.**

  Terminating a project is a major decision. It is not the ending of the project that is a consideration as much as what will follow. Some companies, such as Citibank, immediately started another process improvement project after failure. This shows management intent to get results. Many companies lack the will to do this. Management quietly drops the project and goes on about their business. Employees may think that management is not serious about improvement. Staff members who volunteered and participated in the project will be reluctant to get involved in another project and another failure.

When you terminate a project, it is important to move quickly to identify lessons learned. This does not refer to placing blame but rather means examining the entire range of the project to learn how to prevent future failure.

CHALLENGES TO ADDRESS UP FRONT

The project manager in a process improvement project faces challenges that are unique:

- **Technology infrastructure**

  The technology must integrate and support the process as well as the implementation.

- **Management**

  Coping with management obstruction and resistance to change is a challenge. This even occurs in cases in which there is strong top management support.

- **Staff**

  First, there is fear among the staff involved in the process. Second, there is fear among the team members in regards to their future after the project is completed.

- **The new process and organization**

  Specifying, designing, and developing the processes and the organization approach are a challenge.

- **A steady stream of results**

  Expectations are high. They continue to be so (and even rise) if some success is achieved.

- **Complexity of the project**

  Process improvement involves many groups within the organization as well as outside of the company, making the project a daunting political, technical, and organizational challenge.

Political Warfare

Misconceptions can give rise to political warfare. Some possibilities to be prepared for are the following:

- **Hostile takeover**

  A group feels threatened or wants credit so an offensive is mounted to take over the project.

- **Leaks from the project team**

  Be careful what you say in the presence of the team. Assume that everything you say will be available in print.

- **Flank attack**

  A group starts a "different" project. In fact, it is a competing project.

- **Hired guns**

  Some managers, feeling threatened, may seek to bring in outside consultants. Their charter may be to dismantle or change the project.

- **Forced failure and the left-handed compliment**

  A manager says the team is doing well and asks for an acceleration of the work. This increases pressure and may lead to project failure.

Given the extended duration of projects, consider battles won and lost as skirmishes. Final victory comes when you receive widespread support.

QUICK HITS AND LONG-TERM CHANGE—A DUAL APPROACH

Quick Hits Defined

Process improvement has as its core objective the long-term and in-depth positive change in business processes. The project is complex and can take a long elapsed time to get results. How do you cope with factors such as the following?:

- Management for business reasons needs fast results.
- Business and IT managers and staff do not have unlimited patience.
- The organization has not employed a process improvement method; uncertainty is magnified as time goes on in the project.
- Individual team members desire to return to their normal jobs more and more with the passage of time.

These factors put enormous pressure on the process improvement team to settle for less than adequate results.

To counteract these negatives, consider an approach in which, as you go through the steps, you identify *quick hit* opportunities. A quick hit opportunity is characterized by the following:

- A quick hit can be implemented without a major project plan or structure.
- Quick hits can be implemented within the existing organization.
- The results of quick hits can be measured easily and immediately.
- Quick hits most often will not result in major changes.

Benefits and Risks of Quick Hits

Besides addressing the pressure points listed above, quick hits also have the following benefits:

- The team gains confidence in its use of the process improvement methods. This definitely helps in the long haul.
- Management sees some results and gives ongoing support.
- Employees see the results of the quick hits and get on the bandwagon for longer term process improvement.

Quick hits are not without risk. There is a danger that management will declare the process improvement project over after the quick hits are implemented. To prevent this, the quick hits should be staged in implementation.

How do quick hits figure into the 17-step method in this book? For a quick hit, the technology change and assessment is eliminated; you have to accept the technology and systems as they are.

Identifying Quick Hits

Quick hits will surface as you collect data on the internal business processes. Encourage employees to make any type of suggestion— long-term or short-term. Separate out the short-term items and create a separate data base or list of these. As you identify a quick hit, have someone on the team or, better yet, an employee, write up one page or less on the following:

- Description of the quick hit
- Impact if the quick hit is not implemented
- Benefit if the quick hit is implemented
- Suggestions as to how to implement the quick hit

During the analysis of the quick hit opportunities, address whether the quick hit is consistent with the direction of the process improvement project. If the quick hit will later be undone or changed by the project, you still may to implement it if there are sufficient benefits.

You may next want to gather these write-ups and have them rated or scored on a scale of 1 to 5 in regard to benefits and, separately, on ease of implementation by a set of employees and the team. Both of these aspects of the quick hits should be rated because quick hits that require substantial effort but have benefits may need to be deferred due to the danger of diverting the team and project.

All of these activities proceed in parallel with the process improvement project. After you have a group of quick hits, you can seek management approval. After management approval, begin implementation. Implementation should proceed with the oversight of the improvement team , but the team should not be heavily involved in implementation.

EXAMPLES

Monarch Bank

The work at Monarch extended over seven years across six organizations and involved more than 20 processes. While no one could predict the duration at the start, there was a feeling that multiple processes would be modified and created over a number of years. One major decision was to create two general schedules. One, at a high level, was in a summary form for management. This schedule remained intact for almost eight years. The second schedule was a general implementation template. This schedule went through three major revisions.

Project reviews were undertaken in three ways. There were one-on-one meetings with the executive vice president. These meetings were sporadic, informal, and based on issues. The second type of project review addressed specific issues. The audience depended upon the issue. The third type of review was a periodic project team meeting. At all three reviews, very little time was expended on status. Records revealed that issues consumed over 80 percent of the time. Managers and staff became interested and involved in issue resolution. They saw the benefit of resolution at lower organization levels.

Initially, plans were maintained manually. This was a laborious effort, in which bars were created and moved by hand in GANTT charts. After a few months of this, off-the-shelf software was obtained. Using this, the project leader developed a one-page summary for project status and issues.

With a project of such duration, it was inevitable that the project would be buffeted by political, management, competitive, regulatory, and technology change. After dealing with two changes in an ad hoc manner, a pattern was established. A team member recorded all such issues and potential changes. Every year the project issued a list of changes and actions taken. Political factors never appeared in any document, but issues were clearly stated. The impact of change was clearly delineated.

TRAN

TRAN presented an interesting challenge when contrasted with Monarch. Management at the top wanted innovation and change. So did the workers at the bottom. Compounding the bureaucracy was an aging infrastructure and requirements to centralize to more convenient and useful facilities.

In response to the above conditions, the overall plan was informal. Surfacing it formally would have created more problems. Formal individual project plans were created for infrastructure and process change. This allowed people to focus on detail and not on the politics.

An effort was made in one project to employ process mapping software. Two people were sent to a one-week class. They returned and went to work with enthusiasm. Hopes were high that progress could be speeded up with this tool. Upon review, most time was spent collecting data. Time was wasted in data entry and debugging charts with the quirky software. Staff in the business department could not understand the drawings.

The most detailed project plans concerned infrastructure. Because infrastructure consumed the most money, people wanted detail. Infrastructure took the focus off politics and process.

Two types of project reviews were conducted: an informal review and a general project review. The informal review was unstructured and wide-ranging. The general review was highly structured and controlled by agenda. Over half of the issues (which were political) never saw the light of day in the general review meeting.

Stirling Manufacturing

Everyone at Stirling was supportive of process improvement—on the surface. Stirling had used project management for years. Over time, the nature of manufacturing and the types of products had evolved. Unfortunately, the organization had not. Each business area carried its own culture as baggage. Cultural differences meant that the process improvement approach had to be customized for each area.

Management at the top was inbred. People tended to stay on for years. They had preconceived ideas of what worked and what did not. It was important not to confront these beliefs, even though in some cases the new process contrasted with their styles.

There was an overall project plan, which was nonpolitical. A separate plan was employed for each business area. Politics and culture served as a guiding light to the project structure, and the review process was individually customized to each business area.

In reviews, the new process was demonstrated along with supporting systems over two months. This resulted in more support, which in turn helped overcome reluctance on the part of some managers.

GUIDELINES

- **Adequate and credible motivation are necessary to carry out change.**

  Change for the sake of change is not a reason for process improvement. Tearing everything up and starting over is too disruptive to take lightly. People must understand the importance of the process. They must be motivated to champion the process.

- **Emphasize that changes will occur in waves.**

  Continuous change and evolution is too destabilizing for most organizations to tolerate. As changes are implemented, revisit them for further improvement.

- **Base progress reports on results and recommendations, not on level of effort and activity.**

  Process improvement projects are never level-of-effort standard projects in which a specific set of resources is committed. They are based on substantial breakthroughs. A typical process improvement project offers many small victories for management to enjoy and savor. The review process should allow for this time to "smell the roses."

- **If people cannot understand a method or tool in simple English, avoid it.**

  There is a direct relation between the use of arcane jargon and symbols and time spent in explanation and training. This time should be spent in marketing or getting agreement. Training is overhead, and in a process improvement project, with tight time and resource schedules, it is very expensive overhead.

- **Have a strategy ready for the manager who runs to you with the latest buzz word from a seminar.**

  Get more details, analyze what the manager says, and return with an assessment of how this would or would not fit with the project. This strategy conveys that you value what the manager says.

ACTION ITEMS

1. Develop a general list of 50 tasks for a business process improvement project using the materials in this section. For each task enter the resources and predecessor task, if any. Enter these into a project management system through a copy and paste process.

2. For a sample process with which you are familiar develop a list of people who could serve as core members of the business process improvement project team. Identify their roles as well as what they are working on now. Think about how you could get them on your team.

	Person	Project	Role	Current Work
1.				
2.				
3.				
4.				
5.				

3. Now take a wider view and think about people you will need part-time for specific tasks based on their technical expertise or business knowledge.

Person	Expertise	Time Needed
1.		
2.		
3.		
4.		
5.		

4. Listed below are some common objections encountered in recruiting people to join a project. Think about which apply to the people you have listed. Also, begin to think of arguments that will overcome these objections.

- Work on other projects has priority.
- There appears to be nothing in it for me.
- I have never done a business process improvement project before.
- It is likely to fail so why should I get involved?

5. Given your knowledge of managers, identify who might serve as a project sponsor and who might serve on a steering committee. Also, indicate how much of their time would be needed.

6. What management style would you use for updating the committee and presenting issues for decisions?

7. What is the latest management fad or concept that your firm attempted to implement? What was the result? Were there tangible benefits? How were results measured?

8. What project management software tool do you have available? How proficient are you in the use of the tool? Is the tool endorsed by management? Are other tools in use? What political risk is involved in using the tool?

9. How are project issues resolved by management? What approach would you use for a process improvement issue?

CHAPTER 3

DEVELOPING THE PROJECT PLAN

CONTENTS

3

DEVELOPING THE PROJECT PLAN

PURPOSE AND SCOPE

The purpose of this chapter is to guide you in how to lay out the process improvement project. Studies and experience show that many failures can be traced back to this early period in the project. Had more analysis been performed, failure could have been averted.

Here are some examples where failure to plan caused failure of the project:

- A tank was designed by the military. It went into initial production. It was later discovered that the tank was too wide for most of the bridges in Europe.

- In California, the state transportation department attempted to create a high occupancy lane from the west side of Los Angeles over steep hills to the San Fernando Valley. Only the week before it was to open a test was performed. A bus was sent up the hill. By the time it reached the crest of the hill, its top speed was just 25 miles per hour. The project was halted.

- The Aswan Dam in Egypt was built to provide power and water control for the Nile. It was constructed in the tropical and desert areas of Africa. After construction it was discovered that evaporation and leakage to underground, inaccessible reservoirs drained much of the water. For years it was too expensive to route the power north.

The scope in this chapter begins with the initial concept of a project and ends with the completed detailed project plan.

END PRODUCTS

The primary end products for the process improvement project are the following:

- The project concept—the basis for the entire process improvement project
- The process improvement project plan

The secondary end product is consensus and support for the process improvement project.

RESOURCES

Obviously, you will be the one who will do much of the work and preparation, but you will need the participation of others in formulating and reviewing the project concept.

APPROACH

You are now ready to begin to develop the process improvement plan. Answer some basic questions first:

- What is the purpose of the project? Answer this from different perspectives, including the perspectives of management, the business process, technology, and customers or suppliers.
- What is the scope of the project? What is not included within the project? What are the boundaries?
- What are the tangible benefits from completing the project? Again, answer this from different points of view. Ask the reverse question. If the project were not done or if it failed, what would be the impact?
- What will be the roles of various organizations in process improvement?
- What are some of the likely issues that you will face when the project is underway?

These questions will be addressed through the ***project concept***. The project concept paves the way for a common understanding of the process improvement project. Only with the project concept agreed to should you proceed to the project plan.

Action 1: Determine the Project Concept

Why do all of this now? Because you want everyone involved to have the same common vision of what the project is to accomplish. If you don't define the vision early, there will be more problems later. Your project, for example, will be more prone to scope creep, which refers to a gradual expansion of the project with no additional time or resources.

Objectives and Scope

If you define a narrow set of objectives and scope, you risk having a completed project with little impact. If you define it too broadly, you risk failure and noncompletion. Scope generally relates to complexity—the wider the scope, the greater the complexity.

For example, construction projects may seem to have obvious objectives and scope, but they typically have political objectives as well as construction objectives. When a city builds a park, it is for the use of its citizens. However, it is also an opportunity to name the park and give someone recognition. How many parks do you know of that are not identified by name?

Consider developing the project concept prior to developing a detailed plan. The ingredients of the project concept are as follows:

- Purpose of the project

- Scope of the project—you will want to define scope in terms of both business and technology.

- Benefits of the project—you will want to define benefits for process improvement from different perspectives: business employees, the business process, business managers, IT managers and staff, and general, upper management.

- General roles of the project—which organizations are going to do what

- Basic issues that the process improvement project may face. Examples are resource-oriented issues (getting people or equipment), political issues, and issues of participation if organizations are very busy.

How do you evaluate specific objectives and scope? Here are some tests you can use:

- Do the objectives and scope fit with the organization? Are the purpose and scope aligned with each other?
- Are the objectives too broad or too focused?
- Are potential resources available for the objectives and scope you have defined? Have you already defined a project that is not feasible?
- Where are the areas of risk—both technical and managerial? This ties in with the issues.
- Are the benefits reasonable given the purpose and scope? In information technology, if the purpose is to install a system and the benefits are to increase productivity, you are not likely to achieve benefits because the purpose is too narrow. It does not include the business process improvement after the system has been installed. Is it any wonder that many IT projects are completed successfully without tangible benefits? The process was not changed.

Subprojects

Based on the scope of the project, you can decide how to divide the process improvement project into subprojects. The more subprojects you create, the simpler the project, but the more complex are the interfaces between the subprojects. It's a trade-off. Several ways to divide the project are defined below. Each of these has pluses and minuses.

- **By organization** This ensures greater accountability for each subproject but may make coordination between the subprojects a nightmare. This is typical when installing large financial software systems. This was also typical in Roman times when the military had strong leadership.
- **By project leader** This approach starts with the people and divides up the work according to their skills and experience. This is a good approach with the right people. However, if you have gaps with no leader or if a leader moves on, you could be in trouble.

- **By function**   Here you would partition the project into parts that apply to specific functional activities. An example is a construction project, which has electrical, plumbing, and carpentry subprojects.
- **By geography**   This is the historic approach to managing large projects where authority was delegated to specific regions. Today, with the Internet and rapid communications, this approach may not be necessary.
- **By time**   This is also a traditional approach. You divide a project into phases. Each phase follows another. Each phase is a subproject. The problem here is that it forces the project to be sequential. It is difficult to establish a parallel effort if only one or two phases are active at one time.
- **By interface**   Here you begin by assuming that risk lies in interfaces between parts of the project. Therefore, you organize the project to concentrate on interfaces at the start.

A typical set up for failure is to divide the project by line organization. The line organizations will not get along. The issues and problems will not be resolved at the interfaces between organizations. The project will likely fail even if the parts in each organization succeed, which is doubly frustrating.

Having divided the project into subprojects, you are now ready to evaluate these. Here are some suggested questions to ask. Ask the same questions if you want to attach the new project to an existing project.

- How will you gather data across the subprojects to get a sense of what is going on overall?
- How will you identify issues that cross multiple subprojects and get them resolved?
- Is the risk spread among the various subprojects, or does it fall in one subproject?
- Are some subprojects too small to be viable and likely to fall within another subproject?
- Have you ensured accountability? Or, have you set up a situation in which project leaders from different subprojects may blame each other?
- Can resources be moved and shared between subprojects?

Action 2: Assess the Improvement Project in the Business, Technology, Industry, and Organization Environment

Here is a list of factors that might impact a project:

- Technology
  - —New tools are available to make products
  - —Technology can be used to test quality
  - —Improved technology is available for sales and distribution of products
- Competition
  - —Ideas or concepts can be gathered from firms in other industries.
  - —Services or products are improved by competition.
  - —Your target market is invaded by the competition.
- Government regulation
  - —Increased government reporting is required.
  - —Regulations impact your subcontractors.
  - —Methods or tolls are regulated or prohibited in the project
- Politics
  - —A change of the party in power results in priority changes
  - —The project is canceled or redirected.
  - —The project is accelerated.
- Cross-impact examples
  - —Technology makes different products more competitive with yours.
  - —Government regulation restrains your competition, thereby reducing the need for your project.

How should you employ this list? First, determine which items can be employed in the project. Second, try to determine where risks lie up front, before the project is started. Third, use the list to validate your objectives and scope. Consider how the items in the figure could disrupt the project if changes occurred.

Action 3: Develop a Strategy for the Process Improvement Project

A project strategy will be your approach for attaining the objectives within the scope and the environment. The strategy provides focus for the "how" of the process improvement project, just as the project concept provides the vision and focus for management.

A strategy must address all parts of the scope. Thus, if the scope includes political factors, you must have a political strategy—even if you don't advertise it. A political strategy is an approach for dealing with potential problems, for advertising and marketing the project, and for getting support. You may have a stated strategy and several unstated strategies. For example, in a reengineering project the stated strategy might be to improve process and design and implement a new computer system at the same time. The unstated strategies might be to rightsize and restructure the organization.

What should your strategy address?

- How you will organize the project
- How you will select the project leader and team
- What will be the role of the team in project management
- How you will manage risk and address issues

In order to develop a strategy, define your approach for each of the above items. Consider political, organizational, and technological factors to refine the strategy. Define several alternatives for each, then evaluate the alternatives with the following questions:

- What is the least expensive strategy? The most expensive strategy?
- What is the strategy that will produce results most quickly?
- What is the strategy that is "politically correct"?
- What is the strategy that can minimize risk?

The more thinking and analysis that you do here, the clearer the strategy will be.

Action 4: Identify the Major Milestones and Initial Schedule

A good engineer and project manager in the 1800s could visualize the project plan based on experience. Without computers and extensive paper files, he had to keep a lot of information in memory. He had to be able to visualize the following initial milestones: route determined, survey completed, land and right-of-way obtained; materials and people procured; and work started.

Milestones

A milestone in the plan is a task that has no length or duration. It must be capable of being evaluated or tested to see if it has been achieved. Draw up at least 10 to 20 milestones for each subproject.

- Logically relate the milestones between the subprojects in terms of dependencies. If you have a dangling milestone that you know should relate to another subproject, you are probably missing a milestone. You will likely need to add some milestones.
- Take a piece of paper and lay it out sideways (landscape). The long side of the paper is the timeline and the short side is for the subprojects. Draw a horizontal line for each subproject. Put the milestones on each line for the corresponding subproject. Draw lines between the milestones to show dependencies. A general example is shown in Figure 2.1.

Figure 2.1: General Example of Subprojects and Timeline

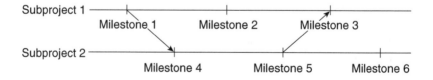

Initial Schedule

Make several copies of this chart. On one, start backward from the target date for completing the overall work. This will tell you when things will have to start so as not to delay the end date. On another chart, start at the beginning and estimate as you go. On a third, take a colored marking pen and highlight the milestones for which you perceive risk in their underlying tasks. Which milestones are these? They are the ones in which you have the least experience, the ones in which you really don't know how the work will be done, or the ones in which problems have occurred in the past with similar projects. Define the schedule based on these risky tasks.

Put all the charts side by side and create a fourth chart that reconciles these three. You can use the computer to do this. However, using manual methods gives you more flexibility.

Action 5: Define the Initial Budget, Using the Milestones

Think about what resources will be necessary to achieve each milestone. List 4 or 5 key resources for each milestone. Now develop an initial budget by milestone for each subproject. Always develop your initial budget bottom up. If you do it top down, you will miss part of the plan and resources. After you have completed this, you can estimate overhead and other resources as a group. Include facilities, supplies, and equipment as well as personnel.

Here are some common mistakes that people make:

- Failure to adequately consider downtime waiting or rework.
- Failure to allow for some change of scope in the project.
- Failure to consider potential additional tasks and work, resulting in underestimation.

In doing your budgeting, plan on holding onto resources only as long as needed. In modern projects you seek to release resources as soon as possible to reduce costs. For personnel costs, use a high average cost for an employee. Add the overhead cost in as well. For facilities and equipment include the set up time and tear down time, if applicable. If you are involved in new technology or methods, include training costs along with potential travel costs.

Many projects have two budgets. Since the project plan cannot detail all of the costs, use a spreadsheet to develop the realistic budget. The second budget will reflect the work performed by the resources. When you perform budget analysis, you often will extract this second budget from the project management software and then incorporate it into the spreadsheet.

Action 6: Identify Which Groups and Organizations Will Be Involved

Get out an organization chart and a piece of paper. Draw two vertical lines about one-third and two-thirds of the way across the page. Write down the organizations on the left and their roles in the project in the middle. Write down how important their involvement will be in the project in the right column. Define a role for almost every organization. Any that you omit can come back to haunt you. Include outsiders as well.

Action 7: Determine the Methods and Tools to Be Employed in the Process Improvement Project

In many projects people begin the work and then select tools and methods as they go. The homeowner, doing repairs around the house on the weekend, is an example of a person who starts a project and ends up running to the hardware or lumber store many times. Use two sets of methods and tools, one for the actual work and the other for the project. This is important since it validates the schedule and budget estimates. It also forces you to identify where you have holes and gaps at the start.

Action 8: Identify the Areas of Risk and Associate Them with Milestones and Tasks

Risk can arise from a number of factors. You may not know what is needed to produce the milestone. Perhaps the organization has never carried out this sort of work before. You may have to rely on unknown internal staff or external contractors to do the work. The milestone may be more complex than first perceived. Another factor is lack of definition of the tasks. Sometimes you just don't know what is an acceptable milestone. New technology and lack of direct control are other sources of risk.

Label the milestones that obviously have substantial risk. Now attempt to define some additional, more detailed milestones within each of these. If you can divide a major milestone into smaller milestones, you might be able to reduce the risk, or at least isolate the risk to smaller milestones.

From the work so far, you can start with the list of issues that may impact the project as defined in the project concept. Use the list of issues at the end of the book in the last chapter as a start. With the list in place, scan the tasks in the plan. Identify any tasks to which an issue pertains. Label the task with the issue. You now know these tasks have risk. Go through the list of tasks. You will find some that have risk. For each task that has risk, go to the list of issues and find the associated issue. There are two situations you will face in addition to matches. First, there will be issues that have no tasks. However, these issues are valid. Therefore, tasks are missing. There may be tasks that are risky but have no associated issues. This means that you have missing issues.

This action is valuable in validating the tasks so that you can feel that your plan is complete. It also helps you to identify tasks that have risk and the source of the risk.

Action 9: Refine the Schedule and Budget

Refine the estimates of budget and schedule. If they don't change, you are either a good estimator, or you have missed something.

Action 10: Identify the Project Manager or Leader

Think about candidates for managers for the project and for the subprojects. Identify several alternatives, if possible. Think of availability and the potential of not having them throughout the project. You will need a backup plan for a project leader as well.

Action 11: Identify and Establish the Project Team

In this initial stage of the project, identify a few key people that you need for the core of the project team. Decide how many team members you will need, then determine who you will choose to be the other team members by evaluating skills and knowledge. You can use the results of your budgeting and scheduling effort to help you here.

Action 12: Develop the Detailed Process Improvement Project Plan

You now have the knowledge to develop the tasks of the plan.

1. For each subproject enter the milestones and the resources that you identified. These are in two separate lists.

2. Now define the tasks that lead up to each milestone. See a detailed explanation following. You now have a work breakdown structure with a list of tasks. Go down to the detailed level for the initial phase of the project. Keep the tasks at a more summary level for later parts of the project (several months out to the end of the project).

3. Establish dependencies between tasks.

4. Assign up to 4 or 5 resources per task. Don't attempt to be complete in terms of all possible resources. Each resource should represent a job function or type of facility or equipment. Don't attempt to name people or individual components at this point.

If you are using project management software, you now have a template.

5. Estimate the duration of each task and set the start date of the project (if not already determined by the dependencies). Make sure that the tasks are assigned to be undertaken "as soon as possible." This will provide the greatest flexibility. The schedule will unfold.

6. Assign the quantity of each resource for the tasks.

7. Analyze the schedule and make changes by changing duration, dependencies, resources, and starting dates.

Save the file at the conclusion of each action. In this way you can go back and begin again if needed. Do not fill in the detail later in the project. You are going to have the project team members do this later so that they will be more involved and committed to the project.

Major disagreements or issues may surface during these actions. The project may not get off the ground. This is not a cause for despair. It is better to know at this stage that the project won't work than to find out when the project is underway and money and resources have been consumed.

SETTING UP TASKS

Here are some suggestions for setting up tasks so that they will be easy to use and work with.

- Keep the task description simple—less than 30 characters.
- If the task name is compound or complex, split the task.
- Start each task with an action verb.
- Use a field in the project database for responsibility for the task. This is different from resources since the person responsible may direct resources in the performance of the work.
- Each detailed task should be from 2 to 10 days long (shorter tasks mean too much detail; longer tasks mean that the task is too general and cannot easily be monitored).
- Use standard abbreviations wherever possible (e.g., Dev for Develop).
- Number all tasks in an outline form (e.g., task 1100 is the first task under task 1000).
- Establish categories of resources (personnel, equipment, facilities, etc.).
- Try to avoid using the individual names of people—put a job title in abbreviated form instead.
- Keep resource names to less than 10 characters.
- Use a field in the software to indicate which tasks have substantial risk (e.g., a flag field that is either yes or no in value).
- Use task outlining and indenting.
- Group the tasks with appropriate milestones.

- Label milestones as such (e.g., "M: Foundation completed" and "M:" indicates a milestone).
- Use a field to put in the name of the person or organization accountable for the task.

The reason for short names and abbreviations is to have more readable GANTT charts and reports. The numbering of tasks makes it easier to follow later when tasks are added or changed. Resource categories are useful in filtering and reporting by type or category. Most software has the capability of customized fields in the database. The flag to label tasks as risky allows you to extract only these tasks for evaluation and review. You can also define all paths that pass through these tasks. Define any of these paths to be a management critical path. The reason for not having names as assigned tasks is to provide flexibility if assignment changes for individuals, but the same person is performing the task. The reason for the use of a separate field for accountability is to distinguish between who is accountable and what resources are required. These are not the same.

Each project review has a single purpose. In the first review, give others just the scope of the project and the lists of tasks and resources. This gets them accustomed to the terms. In a later review, discuss the completeness and focus of the scope of the project.

During the next review, show the dependencies with the tasks, without duration or dates in the schedule as yet. The purpose of this review is to ensure that the relationships are correct.. The third review is to show the tasks, dependencies, and assigned resources so that people can agree on what the key resources are for each task. Leave some blank to generate interest.

If you wait for everyone to participate and join in the steps presented, you are likely to be disappointed. Take the view that the developer of the initial plan and the project manager should be proactive. Take a crack at carrying out all 12 actions. You will then have a working plan that consists of lists of items, the budget, and the project plan. This will accomplish several things. First, you will gain confidence in the schedule. Second, you will be more focused when you ask for reviews or input on the plan. Third, you will be more organized. Therefore, you will be more likely to be successful.

It is sometimes a challenge to get started, even with the steps and suggestions provided. If this is your first experience in project management, start by doing some of the steps for an existing project where information is available. This will help you get familiar with the pattern of this analysis.

PLANNING THE TRANSITION FROM THE PROCESS IMPROVEMENT PROJECT TEAM TO A LINE ORGANIZATION

Even though this is the start of the project, plan now for the eventual transition of the project from the project team to an operational line organization. This is important, since a project may be successful up to the transition and then fail.

Here are some things to include in the planning:

- Identify the organization that will be responsible for the results of the project.
- Work with the organization to determine several people who will be responsible for day-to-day operation.
- Plan a limited role for these individuals in the project before the transition to get them committed and involved in the project.

If the scope of the effort is small, go through all the steps anyway. Later, if the project expands or if problems arise, you will already have at hand formal project management methods and tools.

PROJECT DOCUMENTATION

Obviously, documentation depends on the size and complexity of the project. You can justify the time spent on this documentation on the grounds of managing risk and for marketing.

The minimum needed for a very small project is a task list. No formal schedule is needed.

Here is a list of items recommended for complex and large projects:

- A project plan for the overall project
- Detailed project plans for each subproject
- A list of initial known issues for the project

- A description of interfaces between subprojects
- A description of the roles of organizations in the project

Remember that most of these do not live on and are not maintained. The key exception is the project plan.

A basic guideline is to adopt a zero-based approach. That is, start with no documentation assumed. Then justify each document that is needed. This will help ensure that the project will generate the minimum amount of documentation.

DO YOU HAVE A WINNING PLAN?

After you have developed the working plan or the initial version of the plan, evaluate it yourself. Be your own worst critic. Put the plan aside for several days and work on other activities. When you reopen the plan, ask the following questions:

- Are the objectives and scope consistent?
- Is the scope reflected in the range of tasks?
- Is the strategy borne out in the tasks?
- Have you identified the areas of risk?
- Have you defined the key resources?
- Have you associated tasks that carry risk with the list of issues?
- If you were assigned the job of attacking the plan, what would you see as the major weaknesses?

MANAGEMENT PRESENTATION AND COST-BENEFIT ANALYSIS

Involve management through informal presentations of the project concept. In this way management gains an understanding of the trade-offs involving purpose, scope, roles, and issues. This will make things easier when you seek the review and approval of the project plan.

The development of the project concept and then the plan using a collaborative approach involves more personnel time—higher personnel costs. This is compensated for by faster approval of the project plan and the existence of a common vision of the project as work progresses.

KEY QUESTIONS

Does your firm follow an established sequence of steps in developing project plans? If so, are these clearly distributed and supported by training?

How are small projects handled differently from large projects in your company? What happens to projects that are in the middle?

If you were to develop a new project plan, what guidance, templates, and other support are offered in your organization?

In what areas of project management are your company's greatest strengths and in what areas are the greatest weaknesses?

EXAMPLES

Monarch Bank

Monarch started with the project plan. The project concept was assumed to be known. This turned out to be false. After the project got underway, issues started to appear. Misunderstandings surfaced repeatedly. Finally, it was decided to stop the project and go back and define the project concept. After that, things settled down. However, time was lost.

TRAN

TRAN spent several months in the development of the project concept. The political purpose was to develop consensus among management and staff. Management grew concerned about the time and effort without a plan. In retrospect the team probably started on the plan during the final stages of the definition of the project concept.

Stirling Manufacturing

For Stirling Manufacturing, the detailed process improvement project plan was developed first without the earlier eleven steps. This presented problems in marketing the plan since management was not involved in the development of the plan and sometimes resented the plan being thrust upon them. Ideally, plans should be developed so that people will become interested and committed.

A better approach would have been to develop parts of the plan, get it reviewed, revise it with feedback, and continue with the steps. In the end this would have saved time and reduced misunderstandings.

GUIDELINES

- **Build a plan with great detail on the near-term tasks but less detail for tasks that are further out in the future.**

  This will allow for flexibility in working with those future tasks. Also, project team members will then have the opportunity to participate and fill in details as the project progresses. On the other hand, if you build a detailed schedule for the entire plan, this schedule will have to be revised often, based on actual results. It may be too restrictive and may lead to disruption later.

- **Take a large project and divide it into phases.**

  In a given phase, identify the major tasks and milestones to see if you could increase effort and move tasks up in the schedule.

- **Consider how much time you have to spend on updating the plan when you design the plan.**

  If you design a complex and detailed plan, you will have to spend more time updating the plan. For example, if the lowest level of detail is two to three days, you can update the schedule twice a week. If you go down to tasks of one day or less, you may have to update the project daily.

- **Look at the project's external appearance to learn about the past and present of a project.**

  Examine the project from the outside. What are the perceptions of managers outside of the project? How has the planned budget and schedule tracked against the actual? Have people left the project? Why?

- **Use a chart to create a picture of the project.**

  A project can be thought of as an eight-dimensional figure—project plan/schedule, project manager, management, user, staff, purpose, scope, and methods/tools.

  Construct a bar chart or a radar chart with each bar or line signifying one dimension. You can use this to compare different projects in each of the eight dimensions. Charts such as this give a picture of a project without plunging into detail. You can also consider alternative purposes, scopes, etc. for the same project.

- **Start projects based on a fiscal year to avoid resource conflicts.**

  If your project begins at the start of a fiscal year, the project has to compete with other projects for attention and resources. If possible, begin three months after the start of the year with funding that was approved for the start of the year.

- **Avoid getting sidetracked by the process of a project.**

  When you consider the relative hardships of long projects and large projects, the more difficult is the long project. A long project can transform the project team into a pseudo line organization. Watch that the team does not get caught up in the process of the project as opposed to the actual work.

- **Remain sensitive to the environment throughout the project.**

  The environment of a project was covered in the second step. The project not only must be planned with these factors in mind but also assessed during the life of the project for changes in the environment.

- **Understand what not to do in a project.**

  Start the project with tasks that you know have to be performed. If you start adding tasks that might be needed, you could escalate the project cost and work. You will divert attention from the important tasks.

- **Hold one person accountable for each detailed task.**

  If you have to identify two people for a task, then split the task into two parts.

- **Minimize documentation.**

  In a project you can devote your time to doing either project work or to administrative tasks. Documentation is an administrative task. It may be necessary to produce the documentation. However, working on documentation may mean spending less time on the project itself.

- **Analyze risks at the start of a project.**

  This reinforces doing extensive analysis and planning prior to and at the start of projects. If you understand the risk areas, then you can give them proper attention.

- **Choose longer elapsed time over greater effort.**

  If you ever have an opportunity to choose between more time and more people, choose the time. Also, introducing more resources will likely impede the project. If you are offered more resources, do not accept these at face value. You may discover hidden costs in the politics of procuring the resources.

ACTION ITEMS

1. A first possible step is to evaluate a plan with which you are involved or familiar. Use the guidelines discussed earlier.

2. After doing this evaluation, sit back and try to determine what could have been done at the start of the project to head off the problems.

3. Now look over several projects and attempt to define the objectives, scope, and strategies for the projects. Create a table in which the rows are the projects and the columns are objectives, scope, and strategies.

4. For a simple project, develop a template using the following steps:
   - Identify 10 to 15 highest level summary tasks.
   - Identify the same number of major milestones. Put these into a task list. You now have a very high-level work breakdown structure.

- Identify dependencies between all tasks and milestones. Note any cases in which you are having trouble deciding if there is a dependency. Later, you will be able to determine such dependencies when you create more detailed tasks.
- Now, for each major task, write down the detailed tasks. Put these under the summary tasks.
- Identify five key resources for the project. Assign these to the detailed tasks.

You have now created a project template.

5. Take the template you just created and add more detailed tasks for the work to be done in the next month. Define the duration of all detailed tasks. Determine the starting dates for all detailed tasks that do not have predecessor tasks. You have now created a schedule. Flesh out the tasks one month in advance on a regular basis.

CHAPTER 4

THE PROJECT MANAGER

CONTENTS

4

THE PROJECT MANAGER

PURPOSE AND SCOPE

The purpose of this chapter is to explore the most significant parts of a process improvement project manager's duties. Administrative responsibilities will be examined. However, your success will rest on your ability to focus on objectives and scope, to deal with people, to address issues, and to analyze and demonstrate leadership, so these attributes will be emphasized.

The chapter covers not only principal activities, but also situations with which you are likely to be confronted. The time scope extends from the start of a project to the completion. Sometimes you are thrown into the middle of an ongoing project. This situation will also be covered.

END PRODUCTS

Because this chapter centers on a person and role, there are not the standard end products. However, in process improvement some targets can be set as behavioral end products such as the following:

- Widespread acceptance and consensus of the improvement project concept
- Solution of issues, problems, and opportunities associated with process improvement
- Ability to organize the delivery of quick hits (see Chapter 2) for process improvement simultaneous with work on longer term improvements
- Ability to implement and measure process improvements

RESOURCES

The key resource is the project leader. It is useful to have several project managers to share the duties of the improvement project. Having two project leaders may create coordination problems, but these are offset by many benefits, including the following:

- Two project leaders have different perspectives. This is valuable in dealing with the mixture of tactical and strategic concerns.

- There is so much to do and manage in a process improvement project that two managers can get more done in parallel.

- Two managers give the project a backup if one of the managers is transferred or leaves the project. Momentum is not lost.

- In a process improvement project, you tend to work with many different people with a variety of personalities. Two different people are more likely to work with these varied audiences.

In a traditional project this often is not necessary since the project is simpler, has reduced scope, and a more modest objectives.

APPROACH

One might say that a project manager's role is to implement and complete the improvement project. However, this is the narrow version of the scope of an improvement project. A wider view is to work towards leaving a project management process in place for people to use after the improvement project is completed. This is important because once you start on process improvement and get results, you tend to want to continue improvements.

At the heart of the role of project manager is the focus on achieving the objectives of the project. A look at past projects reveals key attributes of a project manager. Many successful project leaders share the following:

- Problem-solving capability to identify and to resolve issues associated with the project

- Steadfastness to see the project and tasks through to completion

- Ability to work successfully with the project team, management, and other employees and outsiders

In process improvement projects, these skills are called upon repeatedly. An additional ability beneficial to process improvement is that of maintaining perspective and managing the scope of the improvement project.

Notice what is *not* on the above list: being clever or being a technical genius. Notice also that the characteristics described above can be developed. Project leaders are not born, they are made. Most successful project leaders grew into the role by necessity. Even if you are not a project leader, you can use the material in this chapter to build your skills and prepare for the time when you become a project leader.

People sometimes fail as project managers because they never clearly define their role. A project manager who embraces the role in a broader sense can create a more aggressive approach to the entire project, while a project manager with a mindset of a narrow role may be defensive and weaken the project. Obviously, in process improvement the choice of the project manager is critical.

PROJECT MANAGER SELECTION

Unfortunately, many times the choice of a project manager is made on an ad hoc, spur-of-the-moment basis. Often, the people are selected based on availability and a general experience fit with the project. In projects that are routine and of low risk, this will probably work. This fails, however, if the project manager underestimates or misunderstands the risk and exposure involved in a project as is the case in process improvement.

What is a better approach for selecting a manager for a process improvement project? Here is an organized method:

- Have managers maintain a list of people who appear to be potential project managers and update this annually. Scour the organization to find these people. The benefit of this list is that it gives management a reference point from which to begin.
- When the process improvement project surfaces or is being considered, round up all other project ideas that are likely to

turn into projects in the next three to six months. Identify the degree and source of risk in each project. Sources include organization coordination, systems and technology, and external organizations. Construct a table where the rows are the projects and the columns are the areas of risk. In the table, rank each project according to the specific area of risk on a scale of one to five where one is low, or no risk, and five is very high risk. This table indicates what skills you need for each project to minimize risk.

- Take the list of project leader candidates and add the names of project managers who will be available during the period. Construct a second table in which the rows are people and the columns are areas of risk. Enter a one to five in the table, based on the degree to which the person can deal well with that type of risk. This shows the most suitable areas for each candidate to handle.

- Now you can compose a third table of project leader candidates (rows) and projects (columns). The entry is the extent to which each person is suited to the specific project. Note that you cannot just put the previous two tables together. The table here reflects knowledge and familiarity with the project as well as with handling risk.

- Select two candidates for the improvement projects based on their sensitivity to managing people, their interest and knowledge in business processes.

Errors in this approach come mainly from misunderstanding the process improvement project and its risks, not from misunderstanding the people. Often, there is insufficient analysis of the project before a project leader is selected.

PROJECT MANAGER RESPONSIBILITIES

Consider Table 4-1. The columns are the phases of a project from start-up to after project completion. These are common to process improvement and more usual projects as well. The three rows are for major duties, administrative duties, and background duties. Major duties are where you should spend the most time. Administrative

Table 4.1: Duties of a Project Manager

Type\Project Phase	Start of Project	During Project	End of Project
Major Duties	• Define objectives and scope • Define the project plan • Market the project	• Identify and address issues • Monitor the actual work • Make decisions and do marketing • Interact with line managers and team • Review the project	• Construct lessons learned • Support placing project members • Find a new project
Administrative Duties	• Set up the project files	• Update the project status • Perform a budget vs. actual analysis • Revise schedules and budgets	• Clean up and store project files • Document lessons learned during the project • Follow up on any loose ends in the project • Create a final budget vs. actual analysis with assessments of variations
Background Duties	• Conduct casual marketing of the project and plan • Line up staff for future work later in the project	• Track what is happening on other projects that have interdependencies with yours • Exploit common ground, issues, and opportunities with other project leaders	• Build ties with other project leaders • Apply lessons learned

duties are overhead tasks that are necessary. Background duties are things that you can do to help yourself be a better project manager. At any given time, have several of these activities in process with one getting primary attention. Give primary attention to the major duties rather than to administration. Also, gradually work at improving yourself through the background duties.

Major Duties at the Start of the Project

Define Improvement Objectives and Scope

This is a high priority. If you accept the objectives and scope you are given without analysis, you may find that they do not fit together. You typically have a chance at the start of the project to provide input on the objectives and scope. Use this time wisely. Having two project managers allows for different perspectives from which to work with the objectives and scope.

Define the Project Plan

Take the time to develop the project plan carefully. Typically, the first few attempts are not very flexible or complete. You will need time to think about risk and the impact of risk on the plan. Start early.

Market the Project

Even if the project has been approved, it has not been sold to everyone. Process improvement is often resented because people fear that their positions will be lost or change negatively. Focus on what is in the project that appeals to the self-interest of the organizations and individuals involved? By doing marketing and sales, you force your-self to consider the project from points of view other than management's and your own.

Major Duties During the Project

Identify and Address Issues

Keep on this subject constantly. Many process improvement projects can be seen as a continuous stream of issues and opportunities. If you let up, you risk the entire project. Act as a constant problem-solver. Look for issues. Make sure that the issues that have been resolved do not resurface under a different guise.

Monitor the Actual Work

Go out and actually see what is going on in the project. Do not take people's word for it even if they are good and truthful team members. By visiting them while they are working and showing an interest you also show that you care.

Make Decisions and Do Marketing

You have to do marketing to convince someone that the decision is needed, that the timing is important, and that the form and structure of the decision are correct. In process improvement, you must gain support of the actions that stem from the decisions.

Interact with Line Managers and the Team

Keep line managers informed of what is going on in the project and how their organization is contributing.

Review the Project

This is not a background task. Actively set aside time for analysis and perspective.

Major Duties at the End of the Project

Construct Lessons Learned

As the project winds down, develop a list of lessons learned with the tips provided. These demonstrate the added value of the project to the organization, as well as showing that you really do care about more than the single project.

Support Placing Project Members

Long before the people return to their line organizations or go on to other projects, help market them to ensure that they get positions using the strengths that you have observed during the project.

Find a New Process Improvement Project

Even if you are wildly successful, your next project will not often materialize automatically. Market yourself by volunteering for other work. Don't be stuck on one project. Show that you are interested in several projects.

Administrative Duties at the Start of the Project

Set Up the Project Files

This means not just paper files, but also electronic files, templates, forms, and all of the support required for the project. If you take the time to do this with care at the start, you will save yourself grief and problems later.

Administrative Duties During the Project

Update the Project Status

Keep track of status of the project and keep management informed. Don't assume that if you tell one manager, other managers will be told. Inform people one-on-one of what is going on.

Perform a Budget vs. Actual Analysis

Get in the habit of routinely looking at the budget so that you constantly know the status of the budget.

Revise Schedules and Budget

Administrative Duties at the End of the Project

Perform these tasks at the end of the project:

- Document lessons learned during the project.
- Clean up and store the project files.
- Follow up on any loose ends in the project.
- Create a final budget vs. actual analysis with assessments of variations.

Background Duties at the Start of the Project

Perform these background duties early in the project:

- Conduct casual marketing of the project and plan.
- Line up staff for future work later in the project.

Background Duties During the Project

As the project progresses, track what is happening on other projects that have interdependencies with yours. This will allow you to exploit common ground, issues, and opportunities with other project leaders.

Background Duties at the End of the Project

At the end of a project, attempt to build ties with other project leaders. Also try to apply the lessons learned.

Project Manager Status Checks

Use the following checklists to take status checks throughout the project.

Checklist for a Project Manager

- What results are you getting in terms of quick hits and the long term improvement?
- How much time are you spending in project administration vs. profit management? Is the balance good or does it need adjustment?
- What is the actual state of the work in the project right now? What are the problem areas?
- Do you communicate informally with upper management on the project? Do you need to communicate more often?
- List the key issues that remain unresolved. How long has each remained so? What is the age of the oldest unresolved issue?
- Is the project plan and schedule up-to-date? If not, what areas need to be brought up-to-date?
- Do you communicate with members of the project team one-on-one frequently enough?
- What is covered at meetings? Do the meetings last too long? Are the meetings rushed?

Your team members will benefit from periodically evaluating their own work on the project, also. Use the following checklist with your team members. Discuss with them areas that need to be improved, either with more effort on your part or on theirs.

Checklist for a Team Member

- Do you have an adequate picture of the overall project status?
- Have you taken care of issues assigned to you for analysis and resolution? Are you unsure about how to proceed with any of the assigned issues?
- How much time are you devoting to the project vs. other work? Is the balance good or does it need adjustment?
- Are you using the methods and tools of the project correctly and effectively? Do you need more training?
- Do you volunteer to do additional work?

- Have you had any problems getting along with the project leader?
- Do you communicate what is going on in the project with your line manager?

THE IMPACT OF TRENDS

The basic role of the project manager has not changed through the years. Some trends have made the work easier and some have made it harder.

Here are some trends that have affected the work of the project manager:

- Availability of software for electronic mail, data bases, groupware, and project management has eased some of the administrative and communications aspects of the project.
- Corporate downsizing and reorganization have made projects leaner and more accountable, making projects more challenging.
- The availability of new technology and project successes has increased management expectations for process improvement.
- Improvements in technology and their business impact have increased pressures for projects to succeed.
- Resources have to be shared among projects and with non-project work, creating a coordination challenge.
- Fewer resources are dedicated to an individual project, producing a management challenge.

These points especially apply to process improvement because people you need for process improvement are also required for daily business work for the enterprise to survive.

Overall, projects are more challenging than they were 20 years ago due to tight schedules and limited resources. The upside of this is that in many organizations you can more readily advance in the organization by succeeding with a project. The trend is moving toward more projects and, consequently, toward more project managers. Projects appeal to management in many organizations because of the accountability and visibility. As one manager said, "Projects can generate revenue; line organizations generate costs."

SECRETS OF SUCCESSFUL PROJECT MANAGERS

Here are some of the most common characteristics of successful project managers:

- **They have ties with the people involved in the business processes at all levels.**
- **They know what is going on in the project at any time.**

  They are ready to answer any reasonable question about the project from anyone. This will show that you are in touch. It will show the team that you care.

- **They work on communications with line managers.**

  Stay in touch with the line managers who are responsible for your team members. This way, they will know about the contributions of their people to the project and will be less likely to remove them from the project.

- **They are aware of the trade-off between the needs of the organization and the needs of the project.**

  Many times both the project and organization have a common interest. However, sometimes a decision is made one way for the organization and another way for the project. When you press for a decision, point out this trade-off so that all involved can see how the decision will affect the project if they decide in favor of the organization.

- **They can address resource allocation among multiple projects dynamically.**

  A modern project manager must often compete for resources for the project on an ongoing basis. This is true even if the project is recognized as critical.

- **They are able to evaluate and criticize themselves.**

  Be your own worst critic. However, also pat yourself on the back when you succeed. That is part of the evaluation.

- **They have a sense of humor.**

  Look at the humorous side of projects. Consider how ridiculous all of the red tape and bureaucracy are. Dilbert cartoons often point out the absurdities of organization life and sometimes give a humorous view of project management.

- **They work with project team members one-on-one to understand their needs and frustrations.**

  This includes working with the people who are part-time players in the project as well as with your core team. It may be casual conversation away from the project.

  Treat the team members evenhandedly. This is difficult since certain people at any given time are more critical to the project than others. Also, some people in the project may be taken for granted. When the pressures of the project build up, this continues. The project manager is the one who can most easily get such people recognized in their own organizations or with management.

- **They are always on the lookout for ways to improve the project and the environment of the project.**

  Listen to the team members for their ideas. Solicit suggestions as to what could be done to improve the work. Don't mention budget or schedule. This will just increase pressure. Ask the question, "Do you have any thoughts on how the work might be accomplished in a better or easier way?"

- **When decisions are made, they act immediately.**

  Prior to the management decision, map out a plan of action assuming that the decision goes the way you anticipated. Be ready to act when the decision is made. This is not just to show action. You wanted that decision; you had said how important it was. If you sit on your hands after you have the decision, you may lose credibility.

- **They become adept at the methods and tools.**

  The purpose of this is to be self-sufficient. You do not want to have a critical deadline come up and then have the person on whom you depend on be unavailable. While you cannot be an expert, you should know enough about most tools to get by.

- **They practice project fire drills in the planning.**

  Be ready for emergencies. This will also help you deal with the unexpected. For example, you show up for work on Monday and a manager comes in and says that someone is being pulled off the team for a high-priority task. Or management asks you to determine whether and how the project could be accelerated. Think through these and similar scenarios and formulate plans, both to have the plans ready for possible use and to practice thinking through problem situations.

WHY PROJECT MANAGERS FAIL

Here are some common reasons for failure as a manager of a process improvement project:

- **The manager does not stay in regular contact with the people involved in the process.**

  You have to be in almost constant contact with managers and employees who are working with the processes you are attempting to improve.

- **They avoid being involved in the actual work of the processes.**

  This is a sure ticket for trouble. You risk losing touch with both the work and the team. Also, if you roll up your sleeves and do some of the work, the team will respect you more.

- **They try to micromanage the project.**

  This can irritate the team members. The project manager might cruise the area where the work is being done and direct people in the smallest task. People notice the project manager's presence and start to ask, "Doesn't this person trust us?" or "Why can't we do the work ourselves?" Instead, delegate tasks and then follow up on tasks that have risk.

- **They attempt to deal with issues one at a time without analysis.**

  As will be discussed in a later chapter, issues tend to link together. Some issues may continually resurface due to political factors. Sit down and analyze these issues and then attempt to resolve a group of them at a time.

- **They leave project administration alone or delegate it.**

  Administration is downplayed compared with other work, but you still should do the reporting and analysis of the project yourself. If you rely on others, you may not be able to answer questions when asked casually by managers in a meeting or in the hallway. Any hesitation may be viewed as a sign of weakness.

- **They spend too much time schmoozing with upper management rather than spending time on the project.**

  The more time you spend with management, the less time you have for the project. It is a zero-sum proposition. Balance your time. Also, do not wear out your welcome with management.

- **They spend excessive team meeting time on status.**

  Get status one-on-one before the meeting. Use the meeting time to address issues and opportunities.

- **They become obsessed with how many tasks have been completed and the percentage of work completed towards a milestone.**

  If this occurs, you are becoming a bureaucrat. A milestone is only complete if you validate that the work is of high quality and fulfills its purpose. Percentage complete means nothing if you cannot validate it.

- **They leave issues, especially old issues, unresolved.**

  Issues left unresolved tend to fester and get worse. On the other hand, you might want to allow an issue to mature until you understand its ramifications.

- **They make too many changes at once or minor changes too often to the project schedule.**

  This can irritate team members because the project then appears to be adrift. Make several changes at one time with an umbrella reason for the changes. Then leave it alone for awhile.

- **They become focused on either the tools of project management or the tools used by the project.**

  Tools are often technology-based. They are impressive and captivating. Don't be sucked into this trap. Tools support a method. Pay attention to the method. Let others worry about the tools. Your main concern is whether the tools support the method and are being properly used, not the internal workings and features of the tools.

MANAGEMENT PRESENTATION AND COST-BENEFIT ANALYSIS

It is cost-effective to have two people managing a process improvement project. Work gets done faster and decisions and actions seem to be more effective. Of course, they can be managing other work as well.

EXAMPLES

Monarch Bank

The initial project management role was filled by an IT manager and a lower level business manager. This did not work because the business manager was intimidated by the IT manager. A higher-level business manager replaced the earlier manager and the project succeeded.

TRAN

At TRAN there were two project leaders for process improvement. One was a business project manager and the other was an IT project manager. This approach turned out to be useful. The business project leader could deal with people more easily and knew the business processes. The IT project manager, on the other hand, had the knowledge of the current systems and the new technology.

Stirling Manufacturing

Management in Stirling Manufacturing firm knew that the coordination of a project at multiple locations and headquarters required excellent human relations skills. They also knew that they wanted someone with experience and knowledge of operations. Ideally, they desired technical knowledge for networking. The final selection boiled down to three candidates. One was technically oriented and had carried out smaller network projects in corporations. A second had extensive experience in Asia, had rapport with surrounding offices, and was reasonably experienced within systems. The third had worked on non-technology projects with the divisions while lacking technical knowledge and systems experience. Fortunately, the managers met and discussed where the risk was greatest. They agreed that the organizational and human relations side of the project was much more complex and important than the technology behind the network, even though the company had not implemented such a network before. They chose the two people with people skills and technical knowledge.

GUIDELINES

- **Check out a project before joining or taking over.**

  If you are considering volunteering for a project or are a potential draftee, do some scouting about the status of the project. Ask some basic questions about the issues, status, and past events in the project. Then you can answer the important question, "How will I make a difference and contribute to the project?"

- **Play many roles, but not that of a specialist.**

  If a project leader is also a specialist, the team has to consider the leader as having two non-complimentary roles—leader and expert. This can lead to confusion when issues are being addressed. In some cases, the project leader should consider suppressing knowledge of his or her expertise to the team and center attention on leadership.

- **Learn about yourself from the way you manage a project.**

  A project applies stress and presents a variety of situations to you. You then respond. Sit back and review what you do. How are you holding up? Use the scorecard presented earlier.

- **Motivate the team throughout the project.**

  Projects are not for sprinters. They are for marathon runners. Coping with issues over time and dealing with management and organization are constant challenges for the project manager. The key here is to avoid being overwhelmed and to motivate the team throughout the project.

- **Control your administrative time.**

  This reinforces the earlier discussion of duties. Gather the information you require to accomplish these tasks along with a list of things to do. When you are not likely to be disturbed, sit down and dedicate yourself to the work.

- **Re-evaluate the project often.**

  Concentration refers to giving attention to issues, resources, and work. However, unless the project is short, if this is your major activity, you may be tripped up on some underlying problem or issue that you had ignored or not thought about. This means that on a regular basis, you should sit back and think about what is happening in the project overall.

- **Drive the work.**

  Don't just monitor the work—drive the work. This includes the work of all consultants and contractors as well as internal staff. This also reinforces the benefits of a team approach.

- **Be clear on what is wanted.**

  Project managers who are vague in directions will receive vague results.

- **Early in the project, establish how you will work with other project leaders and line managers to share resources.**

KEY QUESTIONS

What are the best attributes of project managers in your organization? What are the worse attributes?

Does your organization have a standard approach for becoming a project manager or remaining as a project manager?

How are project managers evaluated in your organization? Do the criteria involve motivation of staff, addressing issues, and dealing with crises?

ACTION ITEMS

1. Assess some project leaders around you in terms of the questions and key strategies in this chapter. What common attributes do the project leaders possess? How did they become project managers? Are most of the project leaders hired from outside?

2. What is the process in your organization for becoming a project manager and improving project managers? What training and professional development are provided to the staff or to people who are involved with projects? Is training offered on management as well as on administration and use of tools?

3. If you are not a project manager, consider a project for which you would like to be the manager. What are currently active issues and problems? What could you do about these?

4. Assess the state of the project management process in your organization. Are standardized templates and procedures in use? Are projects with different levels of risk managed differently? Are differences based on size, cost, or duration?

5. For the project you defined in Chapter 1 and expanded in Chapter 2, assume that you are the project manager. What challenges do you think you will face as the project manager?

6. Evaluate yourself in terms of the following:
   - How much exposure do you give team members in reporting to management?
   - How much time do you spend individually with team members vs. group meetings? Spend more time individually.
   - Do you involve team members in addressing issues? Or, do you present the issue and the recommended action for their feedback? This gets at the heart of the question to what extent the team is involved in decision-making.
   - How do you inform the team of project changes? Do you change the schedule and assignments each time some new item emerges? Or do you implement larger scale changes?
   - Do you know how the team members will react to an issue in advance? How much time do you spend thinking about what the team will think?

CHAPTER 5

THE PROCESS IMPROVEMENT
PROJECT TEAM

CONTENTS

5

THE PROCESS IMPROVEMENT
PROJECT TEAM

PURPOSE AND SCOPE

The goal here is to examine some of the key questions and issues related to managing a project team. Within this goal, the purpose is to help you assemble and maintain a cost-effective team. The scope includes both large and small improvement projects as well as projects that either are short or extend over a period of years.

END PRODUCTS

The major end product is to have team members who are effective in supporting the team and the process improvement project. Getting the right team members who know the business processes, have an open mind for change, and are creative is important too.

RESOURCES

Briefly consider the wide range of skills and knowledge that you will need to have available for the process improvement project. First, you want to have junior people in the business departments who are eager and interested in change. Second, you will want some involvement by senior business employees who are familiar with the business rules and exceptions of the processes. You will also need to involve business managers at different levels. Some, at lower levels, have process knowledge. Others, at higher levels, have the power to assign people and handle issues.

In IT you will require analysts who are familiar with the systems currently supporting the business processes. Then you will need others who know the architecture and technology. IT managers will be needed for issues and resources.

Others you may want to join the team are the following:

- Vendors of the new software and technology
- Internal auditors who can participate in reviews and validate benefits and the approach
- Consultants who will help in the process improvement project

APPROACH

Traditionally, a project team was formed and remained intact for the duration of the project pending any crisis. Once people were assigned to the team, they stayed on the team. The project team was given necessary resources and was held accountable. This often meant resources were dedicated for an extended time—even during periods of idleness or lack of activity.

This approach has changed over the past few years. Business complexity, downsizing, and mergers have contributed to the fact that few people understand the new technology and have in-depth business knowledge. They probably will not be dedicated to and consumed by a specific project. These factors have also increased pressure on the capable people employed in a company.

In process improvement projects, the project may extend over many months. At different points in the project different skills are required. You are likely to have a wide- ranging cast of people in the project.

The changing nature of projects has impacted the team. People are shared among projects. Many team members must also perform their line organization duties. Now more outsiders are involved—consultants, suppliers, partners, and customer firms involved in projects. The projects are more widespread geographically. Also, technology has enabled team members to communicate in a wider variety of ways with faster speed. This chapter addresses the new team environment.

Forming a project team and then managing it are often cited as two of the most important parts of project management. Yet, these are often the weakest links in the project and contribute to project problems and even failure. In process improvement you have to review the project team constantly to see which skills and knowledge are missing and what individuals on the team you no longer require.

When Should the Team Be Formed?

Some have said the improvement team should be formed as soon as possible. However, you must know the requirements and schedule of the project. Prior to management approval, contact a few people to determine their level of interest in the project. Choose people whose work habits and patterns you are comfortable with, who have skills that you think you will need, and who perform tasks well.

Here are two examples of what can go wrong.

Example: Banking

In a large banking project, the team was formed early. It consisted of ten people. The project scope and direction were set. Work was started. Within a week it became clear that there was not enough work to keep ten people busy. Rumors started flying about waste. Some team members worked on other assignments. Morale started to sink. The project had to be reconstituted with a smaller number of people. Time and money were lost.

Example: Aerospace

In a case involving aerospace, the plan called for staffing to be built up. The project manager feared that if he did not hire the people according to the plan, the budget of the project would be cut. Instead of preparing a revised staffing plan, he hired the people and the same problem occurred as at the bank. Time and money were lost.

In general, it may be better to hire slightly late rather than early. If you are slightly late, the pressure to get the work out can give a healthy motivation to the team.

Team formation will continue to change throughout the project. Different needs will arise and requirements will change. Teams today are very different from the teams of 20 years ago. You are unlikely to be able to keep a large project team intact. Your team will resemble a play or movie in which the cast changes as the plot progresses. Here are some suggestions regarding timing:

- Identify requirements for a small core of the team that will continue in the project. Get these people on board early in the project.
- Determine requirements for other team members, but add them to the team as you go. Get team members as late as possible to minimize the drain on their time, increase flexibility, and reduce costs.
- Develop the mindset that most team members will be working only part-time on the project doing specific tasks.
- If the requirements of the project are fuzzy, delay forming the team. Wait until the project objectives, requirements, and schedule become clearer.

How Many Should Be on the Team?

Keep the core of the team small—usually no more than two to four people. Why so small a number? First, it is difficult to attract good people to projects, given all of their other commitments. Second, it is easier to manage a smaller number of people.

Other specific reasons for a small core team are the following:

- The small core team is easier to coordinate.
- It is possible to devote more individual attention to the team members.
- The members will feel more accountable since the team size is small.
- The chances of having underused resources are reduced.

In Stirling Manufacturing, the team started with three people and kept this number for six months. As the system moved into implementation, more part-time people were acquired for installation and training. The total team at its peak was more than 20 members.

Watch for these disadvantages of a small team so that you can compensate for them:

- Any person who leaves the core team leaves a big gap to fill.
- Small teams can be more difficult to manage if the members do not get along with each other.
- In some organizations, power flows to larger projects with more team members.
- What if you take over a team and it has too many members? After you take over the project, start moving some of the people to a temporary status. When people leave the project, don't rush to fill the slots. Let attrition take hold. Morale might fall, but you can compensate by reassigning the work and getting rid of less critical tasks which can be deferred or eliminated. This might be a good time to review the project structure for excess tasks.

Who Should Be on the Team?

The core of your team should be people who have good general skills, but who have a specific skill area that will be required in many phases of the project. They should have good, but not in-depth knowledge of the several business processes to be improved. The remainder of the team will consist of part-time and temporary members who enter to perform a specific task or set of tasks and then exit.

An insurance firm had a project in which the project manager was an insurance executive. He felt weak in his knowledge of information systems. He then staffed the team with systems people. However, it later became clear that the team had too many IS members and suffered from a lack of people with insurance experience. The project manager had to do double or triple duty by filling in for several team members. The manager had to train the entire team in insurance procedures. The team was not as efficient as it could have been due to lack of diversity.

Here are some questions to consider when choosing people to make up the core of the project:

- Where are the areas of fundamental risk and uncertainty in the project? This is where you want help.
- Are the people interested in process improvement? Do they see problems in the current processes and the need for change?

- What are the types of tasks that lend themselves to a "jack-of-all-trades," generalist type of person? You want one person like this who is flexible and can be given a wide range of tasks.

Notice that you did not need to ask what technical or business skills were significant. The skills will become evident over time and they will change. However, if you know in advance that a specific business or technical area will have a major role, then at least indicate this to management. Do not even attempt to get someone committed to the project full-time, since it's not likely this person would be released for such a period. What you want is to have them work on the project intensely for a specific shorter period.

Obtaining Team Members

Make some initial informal contacts to determine availability and desire. The next step is to approach the managers of your candidates. If the people you seek are very good, their managers will be reluctant to let them go. Also, people will be hesitant to leave a secure line position or another project for a more uncertain future in your project.

How do you cope with factors such as these? First, describe to management what makes your project interesting and important. Second, indicate what steps you have taken to ensure that only a reasonable amount of risk exists. Finally, be willing to settle for part of an employee's time. If people join the project team, become interested, and understand that their work is critical, they sometimes become full-time on their own.

You will seldom get all of your first choices for a team. Rather than settle for mediocrity, consider leaving a position unfilled. This offers an opportunity to use volunteers as the project takes off later. Base this decision on how crucial the missing role is at this time.

A project offers the opportunity for project team members to gain exposure with management. This often offers employees a greater career opportunity than they would have in a line organization. This appeals to the self-interest of the team members. Use this approach to attract junior staff to the team.

Temporary team members enter the team to perform a specific set of tasks. When their task is completed, they are either released or they may perform other work on the project. These people can be contract workers or employees. Many times today you deal with contract or consultant people on projects. In one large government project, more than 75 percent of the total team was composed of non-employees. How can this be managed effectively? Employ the old strategy of divide and conquer. That is, manage the work by task area. In the government project, any given area had only one or two contract people, which made it easy to track and manage the work.

Temporary team members must be given an understanding of the beginning and end of their work at the start of the assignment. It is here that milestones must be well defined. Lack of clarity is an invitation for overrunning the project.

Instead of recruiting the top workers, go after more junior people at the start of the project. If you choose team members who are critical to their line organization and other projects, you could cripple their other work, especially if you use them full-time. Also, early in the project you don't know exactly what you need. Thus, it is better to recruit junior workers for a limited time. This gives you greater flexibility and a chance to evaluate their fit with the project. It allows you to buy time so that you can return and ask for additional people on a part-time basis later.

Training the Team

First, consider what training in project management should be given. Each team member needs to understand your methods for resource allocation to tasks, for identifying and resolving issues, and for using computer-based tools in a consistent way.

Second, the team members should become thoroughly familiar with the work in the business processes. They should spend a number of days learning and performing the current processes.

Third, they should understand the methods to be used in process improvement. These should be reinforced through the initial project work to identify Quick Hits.

Managing the Team

A key to managing the process improvement team is managing the project issues. The work on project issues can be thought of in terms of individual tasks and joint tasks. Joint tasks are those which involve multiple members of the team. Some people favor individual tasks for accountability. Others recommend that you use team meetings and team effort to do work. An ideal position is to balance the two extremes. Have people spend much of their time on individual work, but also employ group discussion and meetings to address and resolve issues.

When managing a team, get in the habit of holding issue meetings. These are much more important than status meetings or general project meetings. When the issue meeting involves a specific tool or method, use the meeting as a way for more seasoned members to discuss their views and experience.

Get feedback and suggestions from the team. Ask each person what he or she needs and what would be helpful to carry out the work. If an individual provides information, be prepared to act on ideas or problems. Do more than just thank team members for their views. Get back to them with specific actions. Test new ideas. If you use someone's idea, give the person credit.

How should you assign work to people? Some managers assign a few specific tasks to each person—like piecework. They think that this approach will keep a person focused. However, this can lead to boredom. Instead, assign groups of tasks that must be addressed in parallel. At a given time, a person will work on one of these tasks, but he or she will work on all of the assigned tasks over the period of time, such as a week or a month. An example of this method is found in a computer operating system. An operating system works on foreground (high priority) tasks as well as background (lesser priority) tasks. Help employees balance their time between foreground and background tasks by using the issues meetings to clarify which tasks are very important to the project.

In the case of people who bring up personal problems, if possible move them to a flexible work schedule to free them up for a few weeks to address the problems.

Keeping Team Members

Managers sometimes use bonuses, gifts, and lunches to keep team members motivated. These are fine as onetime fixes but may be ineffective in long-term projects. People tend to expect these as part of the job. Incentive value is lost. Another imperfect method is constant praise. If you keep telling people they are doing a good job, praise will eventually have little impact.

Here are some ideas for managers that will work to keep team members involved for the long haul:

- Get people interested and involved in the processes and the people who do the processes. They will then feel an obligation to see the work through.

- Involve people in the implementation and resolution of issues. Give the group specific praise for the issue. This shows that you value results and contribution over just hard work. They become more committed if they see that their role is important.

- Minimize the hassles of project management. Help the team members by meeting with their management when needed. Reduce status reporting to a minimum.

- Keep the project team informed of upcoming issues. Give them some insight into the world of project politics. This will capture their interest and give them some idea of what is going on in the bigger world.

- Try to keep a sense of humor.

- Give examples and war stories of past projects to show perspective.

- Keep the administration of the project low key and invisible. If you keep stressing administration, you will lose the team's respect.

- Never compare your project with any other specific current project. However, you can compare your project with other projects generally. Stress why your project is different.

What do you accomplish by doing these things? First, you convey to the team members how much you value their contribution and how much you want to have them involved in the project. Second, you provide them with a view of what you do as a project manager. This will tend to increase understanding. Many team members who have never been project managers mistakenly categorize the job as administration.

Solving Specific Team Problems

Observation over the years shows a number of problems that recur again and again in different types of projects. Here is a list of these, with suggestions on what to do when you encounter them.

Problem #1: You have absorbed a team member you do not want.

Upper management may stick you with a "turkey." What do you do? Instead of acting in a way that will show your attitude, look at the problem in a positive way. Determine the person's strengths and assign a noncritical set of tasks. Involve the person in meetings on issues. If this person proves to have valuable skills, continue to assign tasks and increase the responsibility involved in the tasks.

Problem #2: You have to replace someone.

Focus on having team members produce some milestone every two weeks. This will build momentum for the project and morale. If team members attempt to stretch the work out, get into the detail and narrow the scope of their work. Convey a sense that the project is changing and in transition. This is easiest to do with a part-time member of the team. Replacing a full-time member is a major issue. Divide up the member's work among a number of part-time people. This will avoid the team member resenting an individual replacement.

Problem #3: You have an enemy in your camp.

This is the team member who reports what is going on to managers and staff who are hostile to your project. This is very dangerous. How do you counter this? First, work to disseminate correct information to all team members, including those who are hostile. Second, establish direct contact with the line manager to whom the problem employee reports and have regular meetings to go over the project. Third, make the effort to meet with the employee and find out the source of these problem symptoms and get them resolved.

Problem # 4: A team member is not what you thought.

You thought that a certain team member was someone who really knew the technology and systems that were to be used in the project.

But it turns out that the team member lacks in-depth experience. Alternatively, they may not know the business processes. If this happens, what can you do? Cover the missing skills. Look for a part-time person who can perform the work. Try to have the team member work with this new person. If this fails, consider moving the team member to other tasks.

Problem #5: Two or more team members don't get along.

This is encountered often. Keeping the team small prevents some of this because there are fewer combinations of human relations. However, it can still happen. You want people to be individually responsible for work, then get together to work on issues. It may be that hostility surfaces at these meetings. Don't gloss over this or ignore it. Take a direct approach. Here is one: "We know that some of you don't get along and we recognize that this is part of human nature. This project is not going to solve problems with interpersonal relations. However, we have to tolerate each other to some degree to get the project completed. So let's make the best of it." In the meetings don't take sides on a personal basis. Keep the focus on the issue. Another action to take is to assign a task jointly between the two members who do not get along.

Problem #6: People become burned out.

Deadlines are tight in many projects today. Resources are limited. The same people are called upon to sacrifice their personal lives and work overtime and after hours. What you can do is take an active role in managing the overtime and extra work. Do not allow it to continue for an extended period. People will start to disappear. Absenteeism will increase. Productivity will plummet. Intersperse periods of heavy activity with forced periods of normal work. Do this even if the schedule has to suffer. As the manager, consider what can be done with the structure of the schedule to make up for the time. Build sympathy for the team with management so that they are aware of the heavy contribution being made. A rule of thumb is that the periods of heavy work should not exceed one or two weeks. Then there should be a two-week period of normal work.

Problem #7: Team members want to work on more interesting, but less important, project work.

If you force team members to work 100% on the important work, they will become resistant and will not work at all. Instead, go to them individually and ask what percentage of time they would like to spend on each activity. For the interesting work assignments, define precise, deliverable milestones that can be measured.

This problem can sometimes be headed off by assigning a range of work at the start or by making weekly assignments.

Problem #8: Work is reassigned.

During any substantial project period, issues arise and changes occur. The project team must be flexible in responding to these new demands. At the start of the project, indicate to the project team that assignments can be changed. The direction of the project may change. Indicate that you will warn people of impending change as much as possible within the bounds of your knowledge. Also, inform team members that you will have fewer, larger changes instead of many small changes. Many small project changes or continuous change can unnerve the project team members and make them feel that the project is adrift.

Problem #9: The fate of the project rests on the shoulders of one employee, who is overwhelmed with critical tasks.

This problem is common and often occurs in cases where only one person has certain critical technical or business knowledge. This occurred, for example, in a natural gas distribution firm where only one person knew how the gas distribution system at a plant was designed and why.

Can this problem be prevented? At the start of the project, ask yourself what critical business and technical knowledge will be needed. Then try to find several people with these skills.

However, it may still happen that one person is critical. What do you do? Sit down with the person and indicate the bind the project is in and that his or her knowledge is critical. Ask the team member what help can be given by others. Ask what else is required to facilitate the job. Your objective here is to have the team member participate in working out a solution, based on the team member's unique knowledge and background. You can assign junior team members to work on tasks with senior team members. This apprentice approach has been successfully used throughout history.

Problem #10: Management wants to change the project team in the middle of the project.

Management wants to remove a key person from your team. How do you respond? First, anticipate that this might happen when you are selecting team members at the start of the project. Assume the worst—that a member will have to leave at a critical time. Plan ahead by having team members do critical work in the early stages of the project, if possible. Second, when the request comes in, don't argue. Instead, develop a constructive transition plan.

Problem #11: Staff productivity is low.

Ask yourself why the staff is not productive. Go beyond the emotional and political areas. Consider what else they are working on in the project. Consider competing projects as well as non-project work. Also, consider whether they have the entire set of skills needed to do the work. They may be trying to learn and to do the work at the same time. Spend time with the staff to find out what is going on. Your last resort is to restructure the work and narrow the tasks that they work on. Identify more near-term milestones.

Problem #12: New skills need to be taught to the team.

Don't feel that you have to train everyone at once. The effect would be to lower productivity overall. Instead, have two people learn the tool or skill. Then have them apply it immediately after they are trained. Set up a meeting in which they give their lessons learned to the rest of the team. If people know that the skill will be used immediately, they will absorb more during training. If they know that they will be discussing it with the team, they will be motivated to master the material and present it clearly. The learning curve for the other team members will then be reduced.

Problem #13: The subteams have difficulties.

In many projects, several people on a team are assigned to work on a specific set of tasks together (forming a subteam). These efforts often get off to a rocky start and have to be redirected later.

Here are some suggestions. First, get the members of the subteam together. Go over their roles in the subteam. What will each person do? Who has overall responsibility? How will they work together? Why were they put together? All of these questions should be asked and answered. Then get the subteam back together when an issue appears involving the subteam. Use these meetings as opportunities to observe and ask how the subteam is working.

Problem #14: Task interdependence delays work.

The result of one person's task is required by another before he can begin his work. This is a recipe for trouble. Head this off in advance, if possible, by trying to eliminate these strict dependencies. If you must have dependencies, ask team members to plan what to do if another member is late. Get together with the dependent team members. Ask what one member can turn over to the other now so that he can start his work. Have them work together to become familiar with what the other is doing. If one encounters an issue, get the other involved in the process of resolution.

MANAGEMENT PRESENTATION AND COST-BENEFIT ANALYSIS

Team members should be involved in management presentations. This applies to the lowest level people in the business departments as well. This gives them visibility and also provides an opportunity for you to give them credit.

By insisting on full- time team members in a process improvement project, you not only hurt the project itself but also negatively impact the business department because it has to scramble to find replacements. What will help is releasing people from the project as soon as possible and employing junior people from business departments as much as possible, as they can be more easily replaced by the departments.

KEY QUESTIONS

Do you have the right cross-section of people on the team now?

If you could reform the team, what would you do?

Have you identified what skills you require in the future?

What has been the impact on the business department of having its staff on the project?

Does your organization provide any rules, guidelines, or suggestions on roles and duties of team members on projects?

What is the mix of full-time and part-time team members on projects? Is an effort made to keep the size of the core team small?

Are lessons learned shared within the team on a project? Are they shared between project teams?

EXAMPLES

Monarch Bank

Monarch employed a wide range of different people in the process improvement project. It was found that people who could think of new process procedures were not good at implementation. Similarly, different people were needed for training and procedure detail.

TRAN

Due to the political nature of the project, it was decided to involve as many business employees as possible—actually far more than necessary. The reason was simple. Each person who became involved in the project became a project supporter. The more people you involved in the project, the more supporters that you had.

Stirling Manufacturing

With a very large process improvement project, Stirling Manufacturing required a project strategy for implementing the new system and processes. The project manager identified a management steering committee of six managers, only two of which were from headquar-

ters. Part of their assignment was to work on a strategy for communicating between the busy people involved in the project.

The enemies of the new project were the current professional
schedulers who felt threatened by the changes coming. To disarm
these critics, two of the junior, more capable schedulers were put on
the project team. This had the benefit that potential criticism could be
diffused ahead of time. Also, the team had a chance to turn around
some of the hostility.

GUIDELINES

- **Look for achievement, rather than experience, when choosing team members.**

  You receive a resume from a candidate with seven years of
  project experience on five projects. All projects were completed. The candidate looks good on paper, but remember:
  Project experience does not equate to project wisdom and learning. Find out how the person changed over those five projects.
  Some people repeat the same errors again and again. Also, the
  projects may not have had crises, so the candidate existed in a
  sea of calm.

  It is not the number of projects or the years of experience that
  are important. What counts is the demonstration of achievement
  and the ability to deal with issues.

- **Consider apprenticeship.**

  Junior staff are often intimidated by senior staff. Most projects
  and firms have no apprenticeship program where junior people
  are assigned to senior staff. The apprenticeship idea does work
  and should be considered. To handle this, consider sharing of
  ideas and experiences, as well as apprenticeship. Asking senior
  people to talk about a particular tool or method is a way for the
  sharing of experience and lessons learned.

- **Consider asking for only part of someone's time.**

  The people assigned to projects are often those with the fewest
  current duties. When a line manager is asked to assign someone
  to your project, he or she might first ask who is available,
  instead of figuring out who is the best person for the work.

Remember, many line managers will get little credit for work on the project. If you ask for only a part of someone's time, you might get a better person than the one most available.

- **Involve as few organizations as possible.**

For each organization involved in a project, the project leader and team must spend time and energy communicating with the organization. As you add organizations, the burden grows. It grows faster than a straight line since you have cross effects between organizations that you will have to consider.

- **If you inherit the wrong people on your team, make the best of a bad situation.**

Have you ever wondered, "How did these people get on that project?" You might attribute it to project change or just bad luck. Sometimes line managers put the least experienced and least valued people on the team by intent. If you inherit this, don't spend too much time or energy fighting it. Instead, try to make the most of the situation.

- **Provide an orientation for new team members.**

It would be ideal for any new person to receive a briefing on the project at the time of joining. This is often not accomplished, however, for many reasons—too much work, deadlines, the person already knew people in the project.

Orientation can be very beneficial. It can move the person into the right perspective. It can reduce the learning curve. It prevents the new member from plunging in and trying his best with misdirected efforts. The person may then need to be redirected, which wastes time and money.

- **Before choosing a method, think about the skills needed.**

Any method presumes that the people using the method have certain skills. This applies to basic language skills as well as to complex production systems. When you are considering a method, think about what type of person can successfully use it. If the method requires a star player, and you have few stars, the method is elitist and inappropriate.

- **Assign responsibility, then give team members the latitude of defining how they are going to work.**

  Many project managers direct their team members like line managers directing hourly employees. How much time was put in? What was the hourly output? In most projects this is a portent for disaster. Managing the team by the clock will yield presence, but probably not results. Instead, be flexible.

  In one project, a team member worked on the project on weekends. She participated in meetings and worked at a slower pace during the week. This worked out well since it fit her lifestyle. The team was able to accommodate this.

- **Hold one person accountable for a detailed task.**

  Some managers like to assign a task to several people. They write on the project management form or in the software all of the resources involved in the task. The first problem with this is that you can never identify all possible resources required for all tasks. Second, the manager is not differentiating between assignment to the work and responsibility for making sure the work gets done. This act of delegation is very important. Assigning responsibility to one person is best.

- **Clarify team roles.**

  Do not assume that an experienced employee knows what his role is when he is assigned a task. Define the roles of each team member in front of the entire team. This will minimize misunderstandings later.

- **Eliminate excessive project team communications.**

  Excessive communications among small groups can waste time and impact a team's effectiveness in a negative way. Watch for this to occur especially in long projects and in projects in which the team is more isolated.

- **Recognize that the risk and importance of a project lie in more difficult work.**

  Some people prefer to work on easy tasks to build volume. This is human nature. Be aware of this and tolerate it to some extent. The dividing line occurs when team members spend too much time on these small tasks at the expense of the larger tasks. To gain control, ask team members how their critical work is doing. Never ask about the small tasks. This will indicate that the reward structure favors the critical tasks.

- **Avoid polarization of a project team.**

  This can be a by-product of untreated issues. If you leave a critical issue unresolved, it may fester. People individually and collectively share their opinions. The team starts to polarize around the issue into opposing camps.

  Spend time in issue meetings on discussing the issue rather than the solution. If you are correct in analyzing the issue, then the solution usually is more direct. If you don't take any action after several meetings, the team senses a lack of management. If the issue awaits management approval for action, say so. Move on to other issues. Don't beat one issue to death.

- **Avoid giving financial bonuses and rewards for work.**

  This can backfire. For example, a software firm was missing deadlines for development. Financial bonuses were awarded to the key people on the team who were working on the critical tasks. Others saw what was happening and felt that their work was not valued. They slowed down in the hopes of getting a bonus. The project fell apart. The firm collapsed and was acquired by another firm. The software product never made it to the marketplace.

- **Make a place for etiquette on a project team.**

  Many people are sensitive to what is said about them and their work. In a project meeting and within the team, this is especially true, since the team members will be working together constantly. Etiquette and politeness have homes here.

- **Vary project meeting dates and times to increase the level of awareness.**

  Routine weekly or biweekly meetings can lure team members into complacency. Often, the timing of a meeting does not fit with the issues at hand. At other times, a lack of issues encourages team members to revert to small talk. Dump these meetings, as they are generally a waste of time. Consider more frequent meetings when there are many issues and less frequent meetings if things are calm.

- **Do your own project analysis.**

  Some managers delegate project administration and analysis tasks to a team member. They don't want to be bothered by doing such mundane work. This can have several unfortunate side effects. First, the team member becomes more knowledgeable about the project than the manager. Second, the other team members lose respect for the manager. The managers should perform most of the project "what if . . .?" analysis themselves and then involve team members in reviewing and commenting on the results.

- **Take no credit for yourself.**

  A manager who takes all of the credit for the work of the team is eventually a one-person project team. Word will leak out that this is being done. People will mistrust the manager as someone who is trying to get ahead by using the employees in the team. Give credit to everyone. Take credit only for getting issues resolved. Take no credit for the solution or its implementation. Be content with the credit that will come with the results of the project.

- **Review test and evaluation results to raise morale.**

  Most projects have milestones that have to be tested and evaluated. Many project managers lose out on a good opportunity here. They downplay this effort to concentrate on the development or design. But testing and evaluation are very important. They show the team what is passing and what is failing. They also provide a forum for sharing lessons learned. If the test results are negative, in an issue meeting you can go over the reasons for this and how this could be prevented in the future.

- **Focus on progress.**

  Treating staff like children will produce amateurish results. When a manager badgers staff members for status and for work results, he or she is like a teacher who checks students' work every day. What is the alternative? Since people are working toward milestones for their tasks, give attention to what has been done in working toward a milestone. What will come next? This provides indirect pressure on the person to get the work done. Also, you will obtain status by listening to a team member's statements in regard to how the work will be used.

- **Don't ask what you should have done; ask what you should do.**

  Don't waste time looking back except to gain insight for the future. Learn the lesson from the past and then apply it to the future. Don't dwell on the past.

- **Work together to build a common vision.**

  Doing work individually results in the whole being only the sum of the parts or worse. Underlying this point is the conflict between individual and group work. This will be an issue for centuries to come. It is probably a good idea to have a mix of both types of work to develop a common vision of what has to be done as well as to encourage individual initiative.

- **Build a team that long outlives the project.**

  People often gain experience and knowledge from projects. You learn how the business works and how tools and methods are employed. In addition, you can gain friends and form relationships that continue after the project is completed. You can also build on lessons learned.

- **Keep the managers of team members informed of project work.**

  Almost all team members are based in line organizations. When the team members come into your project, they still report and have contact with their line managers. They will likely return to this manager after the project is over. The project manager should treat the line manager as part of the management overseeing the project. This is true even if the manager has no direct tie or interest in the project. You still want to point out the value of this person to the team.

- **Keep in touch with team members who exit the project.**

  Drop by to see team members who worked on a project for months and now are no longer involved. Find out how they are doing. Let them know how the project is going. If you throw a party at the end of the project, make sure that they are invited. Tell management about the credit they deserve for their work.

- **Beware of team members who are very hard workers.**

  Everyone tends to think of hard work as positive. It is, if it goes in the right direction. A team member who works too hard and fast can go in the wrong direction quickly and far. They can become burned out.

- **Detect indirect resistance by team members through observation.**

  People who do not agree with you often show this through physical appearance and body language. They may look down at the table. They don't look you straight in the eye. They are noncommittal when you ask for their opinions or commitment. They are often silent in meetings. They do not seek you out to discuss problems and issues.

- **Consider involving in the project as many people as possible from one department.**

  Widespread involvement will mean greater support and understanding of the project and its goals. It will also increase support for project results.

- **Work to prevent a project stampede.**

  When projects run into trouble, rumors start to fly and people express the desire to leave the project. You may view this as similar to a cattle stampede. How do you turn a stampede? In the western plains, the technique was to move the herd into a circle and then get them to calm down. It is similar in project management. Calm the team members by identifying a series of issues and questions in the project. Focus on these issues and not on the politics. Since most stampedes have a political origin, this often does work. You also may consider more drastic measures, such as replacing one or two team members.

- **When people disagree, depersonalize the situation.**

  People who disagree strongly in a project can harbor this hostility throughout the project. The project and the team are hurt. How do you deal with this? Never allow emotions to get out of hand and personal. Instead, focus on issues. Indicate that many different and acceptable approaches, tools, and methods are acceptable. Also, never announce that one side of an argument is a winner. This will just make the other side angry. Instead, think about how the solution can be presented as a compromise.

- **Mediate in external organizational conflicts.**

  Every team member on a project brings baggage into a project. Team members also bring the position of their home organization into the project. If two groups do not get along and one person from each group is assigned to the project, problems are likely to arise. What should you do? Get the people together and acknowledge the conflicts. Indicate that the project is a different entity. Reinforce this if necessary.

ACTION ITEMS

1. For the project you defined in earlier chapters (or a project selected as an example), identify the team members and their duties. Separate these into core team members and part-time members. Assign responsibility for the detailed tasks of your schedule. What skill areas are you missing? Where do you have gaps? The answers to these questions will provide information on the additional people you will require for the project.

2. If you are currently involved in a project, take this opportunity to assess the project team in the following areas:
   Do some members of the team have too much to do while others are not busy? This is a sign that the project team was not thought through or adjusted for workload.
   Have you had many part-time members on the team? How are they treated? Is too much time spent getting them on board and later getting them to leave?

3. Sit down with the current schedule and task plan. Compare it with the first approved version of the plan. What are the major differences? How many differences can be attributed to changes generated by team members?

CHAPTER 6

PROJECT RESOURCES AND FUNDING

CONTENTS

6

PROJECT RESOURCES AND FUNDING

PURPOSE AND SCOPE

The purpose of this chapter is to help you reach the following goals. You should be able to:

1. Define resources required for a project.
2. Determine the budget for the project.
3. Schedule all aspects of resource management.
4. Acquire the necessary resources.
5. Determine when to release the resources.

The scope of the chapter encompasses all of the resources identified for a project. Activities range from defining needs to acquiring the resources and then deciding which resources to retain.

END PRODUCTS

The end products are whether you obtained resources and funding support, rather than reports.

RESOURCES

The resources referred to in this chapter are the project leaders for process improvement as well as the staff and management involved in the process improvement project.

APPROACH

Process improvement projects may require many types of resources at different times. Critical resources cost money, affect multiple projects, and require meticulous planning in deployment and use. If you hold on to resources too long, you risk overrunning your project budget. You may also be denying the resources to others. If you are late in receiving resources, you may fall behind schedule. If you fail to obtain suitable resources, the project can be slowed and quality compromised. If you are not politically astute or careful, you can get the wrong resources assigned.

To think of managing all resources across the entire project life cycle is overwhelming. Instead, center your attention on resources in each of the categories that are scarce, significant to critical tasks, or especially importance to you.

Here is a list of questions you can pose when considering a resource. If you answer yes to any of these, you are looking at a resource you will want to manage.

1. Is the resource directly critical to multiple tasks?

2. Do multiple projects require the same resource?

3. Is the resource scarce and difficult to procure or to build?

4. Is the resource complex to use or to apply?

5. Is the resource part of a kit or collection that is critical to certain tasks?

6. If the resource is a person, does the person possess significant skills and knowledge?

7. Are resources being used and shared with non-project work?

Surprises are bound to happen during an improvement project of substantial duration and scope. Resources that are needed through procurement may take longer to receive than anticipated; people are not available when you want them. To prepare for these contingencies, go back to the list of issues in the project concept and estimate what the impact would be of the issues not resolved quickly.

Action 1: Determine What Resources Are Needed and When

When the process improvement project plan development plan was developed, generic resources were listed in the project template. More detailed resources were defined and associated with the detailed tasks to generate the specific schedule for the project. The information in the project template will provide the basis for what you are going to do in this chapter.

Consider each of the four types of resources:

- **Human resources**

  First determine if the people and skills are available internally in your organization. If they are, you may have to attract their interest and then negotiate for their participation. If you recognize that you require external support due to technical or engineering skills or specific knowledge, then you will be involved in the procurement process.

- **Equipment**

  Consider commonly available tools and parts as well as any exotic equipment that may have to be specially constructed for the project. Include software as well.

- **Facilities**

  Consider both general facilities, such as office space, and specific facilities, such as test facilities or special storage areas. Included here are utilities, telephone, parking, and other support associated with the facilities.

- **Supplies**

  Consider supplies that are chargeable to the project or which are unique to the project.

The extent to which equipment, facilities, and supplies play a role in a process improvement project depends on the industry. In manufacturing, equipment, supplies, and test facilities are often scarce and have to be allocated among projects. Computers and communications typically are considered equipment, as is software.

Equipment and facilities require more management attention than staffing. In many cases, equipment and facilities have to be set up. The equipment may have to be calibrated. Staff may have to be trained to use the equipment. Support may be required during use. When the tasks have been completed, the equipment and facilities have to be moved or reconfigured.

In all cases in which procurement is involved, be sure to define and place procurement steps in your schedule. The lead time for resources can be 90 to 120 days if you have to generate a Request for Quotation or Request for Proposal, receive and evaluate proposals, and negotiate with the selected winner.

Resource consideration fits in with financial management of the project. Many cases of budget overruns result from keeping resources too long, having resources lie around unused, and mismanaging the resources during the work. In your budget planning, allow for some of these events.

Action 2: Establish the Budget for the Project

Begin with estimating the easy part of the budget. This usually includes facilities, equipment, and supplies. These can be estimated from previous experience. Save for later the more difficult part of the budget, which is to determine the personnel resource requirements. Then carry out the following tasks:

Task 1: Use the project plan to develop a first cut at resource requirements. Get a resource spreadsheet view within the software. The rows are the resources and tasks and the columns are time periods. Export this into a spreadsheet for easier manipulation. Now look at the summary totals for each resource by month. Do these make sense? Are they too low? Often they are. Don't adjust the numbers in the spreadsheet. Instead, go back to the project plan and project management software and modify your resource loading on the tasks. You may even encounter missing tasks. Continue doing this until you are satisfied that you have the major resources.

Task 2: Now take the spreadsheet from Task #1 and add the resources for facilities, supplies, and equipment by task area. This will allow you to determine when you will be needing these resources. Another approach is to include these as resources in your project plan.

Task 3: You are now reasonably close, but you probably want to add some slack or padding to the budget for safety. Do this in the spreadsheet. If you do it in the plan, there is a problem in that the schedule will probably be too unrealistic.

Even though you may be tempted simply to create a spreadsheet and put the budget items in, avoid this because the plan does not match up to the budget overall. Moreover, the budget will not match up to the requirements of when money is needed. If you link it to the plan, you have not only obtained a more credible budget, but also a more credible plan.

Budget for large and multiple projects using a bottom up approach. That is, start with subprojects or individual projects, then aggregate these to get an overall picture.

Action 3: Create Project Oversight

Unless your improvement project is small in budget, resources, and time, you should have management oversight for the project in an organized way. This will provide a basis for dealing with issues and opportunities as well as a communications mechanism for management relations. It is best to consider a small steering committee. This will be easy to create.

Many managers are already overworked and overcommitted. It will be difficult to attract good managers. Look at the project and determine which departments are going to be involved. Go to the departments manager with high level tasks and milestones identified. Indicate the reasons they should be interested in the project. Point out that the committee will meet only for major milestone review and for issues that could not be solved at lower levels. This will show that you respect the various demands on the employees' time.

After getting some interest, hold your first informal steering committee meeting. Give the members of the committee an overview of the project and budget. Present the list of issues from the project concept. Do not ask for any decisions. The initial meeting should take no more than one hour.

Action 4: Integrate the Resources in the Project Schedule

When you have identified the resources needed, schedule the following tasks in your plan for each resource:

Task 1: Determine and document specific resource requirements.

Task 2: For internal resources acquisition—

- Identify resource candidates and determine their availability.
- Negotiate for internal resources.

For external resource acquisition—

- Prepare necessary requests for external procurement in terms of schedule, duration, and requirements.
- Procure external resources.
- Negotiate for external resources.

Task 3: Prepare resources for use in the project after acquisition.

Task 4: Determine the release date for each resource.

Task 5: Prepare the resources for release.

Task 6: Release the resources.

Task 7: Follow up on open items after resource use.

List these tasks in your schedule for each type of resource, even those that are not readily available, to avoid missing tasks as the project progresses.

Adding all of these tasks to the schedule serves a political purpose as well as an organizational one. Management will be aware of the effort required so that they can provide support if the procurement hits a snag.

Action 5: Define Your Resource Strategy

This may sound like a vague step. However, most of the problems encountered in getting resources can be traced to a lack of thought and consideration early in the project. Don't assume that just because the budget was approved resources will automatically be assigned. These are two different steps involving decisions.

What should be your resource strategy? The first part of a strategy is to concentrate on resources required over the next three-month period. This will get you started. Don't ask for resources further in the future. Commitments may be meaningless since you have yet to show results.

During the first few months, the improvement project should show results as initial milestones are achieved through quick hits. Momentum will build. With this progress you can move to the next part of the strategy. With results in hand, approach management after the first month to seek approval for resources in the next four to six months. Time frames are flexible, depending on the specific project. Continue with this pattern. You deisre a rolling commitment based on continued results. This is much easier to accomplish than wholesale commitment at the start of the project. Management will also feel more comfortable because they will have greater control.

At this point, establish priorities for trade-offs. Will you accept a less desirable resource as a trade-off for lower cost? Are you willing to forego the resource when you want it in order to obtain the desired vendor? Get your priorities straight now.

Prepare for positioning the project in terms of the techniques needed in negotiation and whether you get access to the best resources. Do this by answering the following questions:

- **Who is responsible for the resources that you require?**

  Find out both who has direct responsibility and who has political responsibility.

  For internal resources, begin contacting managers who control the resources at the start of the project or very early in the project. If you fail to do this early on, you will upset the plans of these managers when you require the resources, you will upset the plans of these managers.

  For external resources, contact purchasing to determine the process for acquiring the resources, the various steps, and the schedule. Start building rapport with the staff in purchasing.

- **What other projects and work are demanding the same resources?**

  Remember that your project will be going on for some time. If your plan calls for a resource from the second to the fifth month of the project, consider any project that requires the same resources from now until the end of the sixth month or longer. Allow for slippage.

What are the benefits of the project to management and their organizations after the project is completed? What is their self-interest in giving you the resources? What are their objectives and goals?

You may already know people in upper levels of management. If possible, sound them out on the potential problems of getting the resources. Maybe they can introduce you to the managers of the needed resources, so you do not have to make a cold call.

Action 6: Win the Competition for Resources and Complete the Procurement

With downsizing and rightsizing, many organizations do not have spare people, equipment, or facilities lying around. You may have to compete with other projects for resources. If you are the manager of the key project in the company, then you get priority. However, this is clearly the exception even for process improvement. The general situation is that you head up one project among many and the world will not end if the project is not completed. How do you compete?

Resources

A first guideline is to make sure that you have developed a realistic minimum requirement for resources. Tell managers that this estimate is truly a minimum and is realistic. You will have to be willing to negotiate for resources. Be ready to trade off.

A second guideline is to employ the project team as part of a sales force to obtain the resources. This approach is preferred to appealing to upper management to force a line manager to release equipment or people to you. That approach will breed hostility because you have removed the resources from the control of the line manager.

A third guideline is to follow your resource strategy. Aim at incremental commitment. You will tend to attract more support and resources with the momentum of success.

Procurement

Provide purchasing or the line manager with the resource requirements, a copy of the project plan and schedule, the specific tasks that you desire to be performed, and the milestones or end products that you seek from the resources. Indicate how the tasks affect the overall schedule. The more information you provide, the more comfortable the managers and staff will be in trying to help you. The more vague you are and the less information you provide, the less likely timely cooperation and support will be. Nail down your agreement in a memo of understanding that can help resolve any problems later.

During procurement, be available to help. Respond quickly when it is time to participate in the following tasks:

- **Preparation of the statement of requirements or statement of work to be included in the Request for Proposal**

  This statement should specify what goods and services are to be provided, how they will be used, the end products expected, the schedule, and how the resources will be managed.

- **Participation in answering questions at bidder's conferences**

  The purchasing agent has no detailed knowledge of what you are trying to do. He or she will pass questions and inquiries back to you for response. Timely, accurate, and complete responses are called for.

- **Review of proposals to do the work or provide the goods**

  Provide resources for this review. It may involve you having to search out staff to review these with you. When you select the winning proposal, always line up several backup vendors in case the later negotiations do not succeed.

- **Support in vendor negotiations, if needed**

  In most cases, the purchasing agent does not want you involved. However, be on standby in case there are problems or additional questions.

Action 7: Plan for the Transition of Resources into the Project

If you are bringing people on board, establish some kind of orientation for the improvement project. Don't expect people to jump in without some sense of priorities, tasks, and the project plan. Never assume that they were prepared or briefed by their own management in advance. Cover basic issues such as where they will work, how they will access the building, what telephones are available, and how parking will be handled.

If you are moving equipment in, make sure the necessary support (utilities, space, support staff, etc.) is in place. Many times equipment arrives on time just to sit on a loading dock for several weeks because the organization was not prepared to receive it. The transition also may include personnel being trained in the use of the equipment.

Facilities can present challenges. Visit to see if the facilities are ready for your use. If additional work is to be performed to get the facilities ready, who will manage the work? Who will do the work? Who will pay for the repairs or cleanup?

Action 8: Transition the Resources into the Project

This is the actual transition into the process improvement project. It is possible that you may find problems immediately with the resources. The right people were not sent. The equipment does not work. The facilities have power problems. If this should occur, contact purchasing, management, or the vendor. Stop using the resource. Do not use the person on the project. Do not employ the equipment. Do not move into the facility. Usage can be interpreted as acceptance.

Action 9: Determine When to Release the Resources

Even as the resources are beginning to be employed in the project, define how and when resource usage will stop. Make sure that this is in your schedule. Develop a turnover approach for the release of the resources. In most cases this can be a simple checklist. Never allow the core project team members to accept these temporary resources as permanent. Also, reinforce the temporary nature of the work with the people who are brought into the project so that there will be no misunderstandings.

The release of resources should be announced to the project team. For people, you will want to debrief them and get their lessons learned. For all resources, obtain feedback from the project team on how the resources could have been put to better use and the lessons learned.

In your budget analysis, consider what percentage of the time the resources were effectively used. This can help pin down any budget variances. It can also bring home to the project team the cost for resource waste.

If you have an opportunity to release a resource without significantly harming the project, then do it. Remember, the fewer resources you have in general, the better.

HOW TO COPE WITH CHANGING REQUIREMENTS

Here are some reasons that the resource requirements on a particular project may change after the project begins:

- **You find new information as you progress in the project.**

  This may alter the resources needed.

- **Management shifts requirements or direction.**

  Management decides on new requirements that the project must address. This can change the nature of the project entirely, including which resources are suitable. Changing requirements may occur in software systems, engineering, or marketing projects, for example.

- **A change in resources results from external information.**

  A competitor is about to introduce improved processes better than the ones you are building in the improvement project. Your team is sent back to the drawing board for a new product. This may mean new resource requirements. Another external source of change is government regulation. A rule can change, impacting the underlying assumptions of a project. The same is true with new technology, which may replace technology currently in the project. This change may call for different staffing and skills.

- **You have alterations in timing of requirements and the amount or extent of the resource needed.**

HOW TO TAKE ADVANTAGE OF RESOURCE OPPORTUNITIES

An opportunity in this context occurs when a resource that is potentially useful to the improvement project suddenly becomes available. To take advantage of this situation, do the following:

- Keep an eye out for resources at all times. Alert managers and your project team that you are always looking for resources— "A few good people."
- When you hear about potential availability of a resource, analyze your plan to see what benefits you could reap from this. Also, assess the financial impact on the project.
- Be ready to sit down and negotiate for the resources immediately. Cut a deal.
- Put the additional resources to work immediately. You will not only appear organized, but you will also attract more opportunities later.

MANAGEMENT PRESENTATION AND COST-BENEFIT ANALYSIS

You will have to make several presentations related to the resources selected as well as for the budget. In showing which resources you obtained, be prepared to answer the following:

- How are the resources critical to the process improvement project?
- How will resources be managed that are required for normal daily work and other projects? Your answer should show sensitivity to the needs of the organization.

In presenting the budget relate each budget item to the processes and the impact on the improvement project if these items were cut from the budget. Indicate how the budget is conservative by showing, if you can, some comparisons with other improvement projects you have found in the literature.

KEY QUESTIONS

How long do people stay on projects in your organization?

Are efforts made to release resources as soon as possible?

Do your projects have resource strategies?

Are efforts made to get management to commit resources too early? Are many resource changes needed? Is there often a mismatch between the resources you have in the project and those that are needed?

EXAMPLES

Monarch Bank

At Monarch there were waves of process improvement and systems implementation. Each implementation then required resources for maintenance and support. This presented a challenge in resource allocation because the same people needed for the current process improvement project were also needed for maintenance and operations.

TRAN

The project manager at TRAN found that high priority projects did not receive resources when needed. However, lesser priority projects did have the resources. What was wrong? No method was in place for assessing the resources on a project at any given time, so it was difficult to redirect resources between projects. Large, priority projects had project leaders who considered resources individually and did not work together.

Stirling Manufacturing

At Stirling Manufacturing, people in remote locations began to charge their time to the project without the leader's knowledge. The project leader could not be in many different countries at once. A subproject leader was appointed in each geographic location to handle administration and coordination. This shows that even with the Internet and rapid communications, it is important to have local control.

GUIDELINES

- **Identify at the start as many resources as might be needed.**

  The more comprehensive your list, the lesser the chance you will be surprised later with a new requirement. Review your resource list once a month and update it.

- **Develop a transition strategy.**

  Not only must you have a good understanding of the resources required, but also you must be able to transition resources skillfully and take advantage of opportunities. You must be able to come up with creative substitution approaches.

- **Seek incremental commitment from management.**

  Don't request too much over too long a period. Also, keep management up-to-date on the project and maintain interest in the project.

- **Make sure that your approach to resources is integrated.**

  Consider resources in groups necessary to perform and support specific tasks. This is an integrated approach. If your approach is on the basis of individual resources, you will be more likely to miss some resources. You will also lack focus during negotiations.

- **Think, plan, and take small actions when a resource is added.**

  Often this is wiser than precipitous, decisive action. Employ the new resource on a trial basis to see the results. If the resource is a person, for example, and you take decisive action and hand over a task area to the new resource, the person may fumble around for weeks and hurt the project.

- **Do not treat all projects equally.**

  Equality produces mediocre results. In considering resource assignment the first thing to discard is fairness. Projects have different levels of importance and benefits. No two are alike. Therefore, it doesn't make sense to treat them the same.

- **Keep infrastructures small.**

  Every project has an infrastructure. Included are files, methods, policies, procedures, and tools that are used in the project. In addition, projects have a project manager, a project organization, and project support. It follows that many times more infrastructure means more control and structure. More structure may mean that decisions and action in the project take longer. Smaller infrastructures are more efficient. The Romans were able to build large aqueducts in months with a small, organized team. The aqueducts were well built, many lasting for more than 1500 years.

- **Take on and manage some unsuitable people to contribute to a project's political success.**

  In an ideal world, you could assume that only the best and brightest will participate in your project. In real life, you run into mediocrity. Also, your project may be the place a manager unloads an unwanted employee. Your first reaction might want to fight it, but at what cost to the project and your career? Keeping that team member may be politically beneficial. Look over your project and see if you have any slack where this person could do some useful work.

- **Structure the work so that you will not need the best people.**

  Large projects stall under internal competition for resources. Even large organizations may have only a few highly experienced and qualified people. In your plan never assume that you will get the best.

- **Work with fewer resources.**

  Can you do the work with less in terms of resources? This is one of the questions you should always ask during the project. Ask it yourself before someone asks you. In an era of downsizing and efficiency, making do with less is essential. Remember, fewer resources means less to manage. It is also true that smaller projects get more done than large projects due to less need for coordination and a simpler chain of command.

- **Do not try to hold on to resources.**

    Do not hold on to resources that are not being used. You will become known as a person who hoards and wastes resources. Later, when you make new requests, you will be more likely to be turned down.

- **Understand why people are motivated to be on a project.**

    It is important to understand why someone is on a project. Obviously, many possibilities exist—attention, risk, the desire to do something different, the desire to learn, etc. Even if a person is assigned to the project and has no choice, you can still probe for what that team member would like to get out of it. What do you do with information? You use it to your project's advantage. Structure the project so that the work gets done and people get some of what they want. It pays off.

ACTION ITEMS

1. For the project you developed in the first chapters, make a more complete list of people, equipment, and facilities that you require on the project. For each category of resource, identify the manager or vendor who can provide the resource. Identify alternatives to be used if the selected resource is not available.

2. Using the information from the list in Question 1, develop a GANTT chart in which the tasks are resources arranged or sorted by type. The schedule is the time that the resource is needed. This GANTT chart is a useful tool to help you plan resource transitions.

3. Return to your project plan and insert the resource-related tasks that were identified earlier in this chapter.

CHAPTER 7

PROJECT MANAGEMENT
METHODS AND TOOLS

CONTENTS

7

PROJECT MANAGEMENT
METHODS AND TOOLS

PURPOSE AND SCOPE

The purpose of this chapter is threefold. You will be able to:

1. Define a method and tool strategy.
2. Define new methods for project management that take advantage of modern and emerging tools.
3. Provide guidelines and tips on how to use the methods and tools.

The purpose of this chapter is *not* to tell you how to use a one-person project management system. This information is available in dozens of books and manuals.

The scope of the effort extends beyond project management software. It also includes the Internet, Web, intranets, groupware, database management, electronic mail, and other software. The goal is to help you be successful through more effective and innovative use of modern methods in conjunction with network and software tools.

END PRODUCTS

When you think of project management tools, you tend to think of GANTT charts and project management software. Project management charts are definitely end products for presentations and updating the project. However, you also have as end products the tracking, collaborative sharing, and presentation of issues and lessons learned associated with the process improvement project. In addition, a process improvement project often must be divided into smaller, more manageable projects. Thus, the range of end products for process improvement tends to be broader than for a standard project.

RESOURCES

Given the scope of a process improvement project, you will be paying attention to collaborative methods and tools. This means that you should involve a substantial number of people in IT, business units, and staff organizations. There may be conflicting tools in use today in your organization. Involving more resources can help in a move to standardizing on a set of methods and tools.

APPROACH

A method is a technique, process, or procedure that supports project management.

A tool is something that supports the implementation and use of the method. Typically, this means software tools. Other tools include presentation aids and facilities. Manual filing systems are another category of tools. Tools shape methods and vice versa.

The arrival of PCs and project management software changed the tool landscape, but did nothing for methods. Even though maintaining schedules was less tedious, the overall methods still focused on a single scheduler or manager doing the work.

Three generations of project management software can be distinguished:

- **First generation**

    These were tools based on mainframe computers. The scheduler obtained updates to schedules based on a batch-processed turnaround report that the scheduler distributed. The scheduler collected the updates and input the data into the computer. The computer produced batch reports that the scheduler then analyzed. Errors were corrected through additional input. With the "final" reports in hand, the scheduler then distributed the reports along with a new update sheet.

    Problems with this process became apparent. First, by the time managers received the information, it was out-of-date and virtually worthless. Second, managers had to create their own schedules to address their own analytical needs. Nevertheless, impressive graphs and reports were produced. You could walk into a planning or conference room and see a PERT chart that covered all of the walls in the entire room. Thousands of tasks were printed courier font of size 10—virtually unreadable, but impressive.

- **Second generation**

  With the arrival of PCs, early, crude software became available. These software tools allowed limited drawing capabilities, little analysis, and were very restricted in terms of the number of tasks and resources. Individual managers could produce simple GANTT and PERT charts. Since the mainframe project management systems continued to be run, the end result was often confusion between the two systems due to incompatible information. Those of you who have been around for awhile may remember VisiSchedule and MacProject.

- **Third generation**

  With advances in PCs, people finally were given industrial-strength PC project management software. Microsoft Project and Symantec Timeline were two of more than 20 such packages. This generation of software tools led to the demise of the mainframe project management systems for many organizations.

  However, while the tool changed, the method often did not change. There was still the scheduler who worked now at a PC. While this was an improvement, the underlying problems persisted. Project managers continued to manage their schedules. Multiple schedules abounded.

  The requirements of project management are for methods and tools that support sharing of effort and collaboration in scheduling. While tools changed, their new benefits were largely mitigated by lack of change in methods. Organizations failed to have an effective strategy to allow project management to use new methods to take full advantage of the newly available tools.

- **Fourth generation**

  People are now finally starting to see the emergence of collaborative software tools. These are software products that extend project management across a network and allow updating, scheduling, and issues to be addressed in the network with aspects of groupware and electronic mail.

  Still missing are the methods to use such tools. That is going to be a major focus of this chapter. What will happen if firms adopt the software, but not new methods? They will fail to realize the benefits of the tools. Without new methods, things will probably be worse than before the new software was adopted.

BENEFITS AND PITFALLS OF METHODS AND TOOLS

A method provides a standard way of doing something. This is particularly important in organizations in which people undertake multiple projects with different people. If everyone does something different, there will be chaos. This can also happen with tools, although with less impact.

Beyond the benefits of standardization, common tools and methods can provide a company with a rich source of information from projects and from lessons learned. Incompatibilities, on the other hand, reduce this capability.

A third benefit of standard methods and tools is predictability. People know how to behave and how to use the methods and tools without additional training. They can come up to speed faster for the new projects.

Watch for these potential pitfalls with the use of methods and tools:

- If the methods and tools are not synchronized, benefits are reduced.

- People tend to be dazzled by a new tool. They adopt it without thinking of the method. Everyone adopts it a different way. Chaos reigns.

- People can become too comfortable with a set of methods and tools. Without thinking, they apply the methods and tools to projects of all sizes and shapes. The result is overkill and small projects become swamped with overhead and process.

- People resist new methods and tools.

A WINNING STRATEGY FOR USING METHODS AND TOOLS

You need a strategy that achieves the following goals:

- The first goal is *scalability*. That is, you want to be able to apply the method or tool to small as well as large projects. Also, plan for use with single or multiple projects.
- The second goal is *collaboration*. You want the method or tool to be compatible with having multiple people work with it in the same or different projects at the same time.
- *Modernization* is a third goal. You want a strategy that will accommodate new methods and tools in a smooth manner.
- *Measurability* is another goal. You want to be able to measure the effectiveness of the method or tool so that you can be assured that you are employing it effectively.
- *Formulating lessons learned* and improving at project management over time are also major objectives.

A practical general strategy is to have a standard set of methods and tools that address the goals above for all projects. Beyond this, supplement with additional methods and tools for specific classes of projects (e.g., very large projects, projects with specific customers). The strategy would also include processes for capturing and using lessons learned and experience. A regular measurement assessment process can improve the strategy.

WHERE AND WHEN METHODS ARE NEEDED

Here is a list of method areas to address in the plan and suggestions for each area:

- **Setting up the schedule and plan initially**

  The method should include a project plan template (see Chapter 2), along with lists of tasks and resources. Guidelines in the form of a step-by-step process should be given. The review method for the first version of the schedule should be identified.

- **Analyzing and improving a schedule**

  Support this with guidelines and examples. In addition, the availability of an "expert" helps. Look at the wording of tasks, split up long or compound tasks, reduce dependencies, and perform a specific "what-if" analysis.

- **Updating and maintaining a plan**

  Support this with a formal method in which the plan and the detailed project plan and schedule are maintained on a network at all times so that they are visible. Update plans at least twice per week. Label detailed tasks as either not started, in process, or completed. Summary tasks that are a rollup of several detailed tasks will have a percentage complete based on the detail underneath.

- **Modifying and changing a plan**

  Changing a plan in a significant way in terms of schedule, resources, and deliverable items should require management approval. Changing task structure and assignments without impacting the schedule in a significant way does not require such approval. Support this policy with a detailed set of procedures on modification and updating.

- **Addressing issues and communicating within the project team**

  Draw up a common and standard set of procedures for handling and tracking issues. These can be supported by guidelines on how to identify issues. Also provide lists of issues.

- **Communicating and working with people and organizations outside of the team**

  Communications is often a matter of style. Many different project managers have many different styles. Without intruding on personalities, provide information on what organizations outside of the project can expect from the project team.

- **Assessing benefits, costs, and risks associated with a project**

  Have a standard set of rules for defining benefits and costs for each project. Don't deal with fuzzy benefits. Deal only in tangible benefits. The same philosophy applies to costs. How costs are applied to a project is unique to the specific project as well as to the organization.

How do you select methods? Consider what other companies have done. Examine large and complex projects that were successful. This will give you ideas about methods. You should also be able to expand on the methods presented in these chapters. Here are more specific guidelines:

- **Consider a statement of method that uses everyday language.**

  A method that employs arcane words is too much work and effort without the additional payoff. People will not use the terminology anyway since it is not familiar.

- **Pick all methods at the same time.**

  For each of the method areas listed earlier, identify a specific method. Then sit down and determine how someone would work with the total set of methods. Or, do they overlap so that their use becomes counterproductive?

- **Evaluate scalability and flexibility.**

  Here is a test. Choose three projects of different sizes. These can be in the recent past or present. Next, choose several projects that are very different from each other. Apply the method to all of these. How do they scale up?

EFFECTIVE PROJECT MANAGEMENT TOOLS

The fourth (most current) generation of project management tools provides some or all of the following:

- Standard project management features

- The capability of sharing of project information, a plan, and a schedule in a network

- A means to delegate tasks in the project to staff

- A way for staff to update management and communicate with management regarding their tasks

- Consolidation and tracking of all work

Such a software package combines a database of project information, project management software, electronic mail, and groupware. It offers the benefits of an integrated approach for tools. It is simpler than having a grab bag of tools.

First, establish the team. Second, establish the process improvement plan on the network with the tool. If such a tool is not available, assemble a unified set of methods that draws upon specific tools. Integration is provided through the methods and not the tools. Take every item in the plan and define the procedures and tools. You could then expand on this with specific guidelines for small, medium, and large single projects, as well as for multiple projects.

The manager and team members can now work together with methods for identifying and resolving issues. They can track progress and identify areas of risk.

What tools would you employ if the integrated tool were not available? Here is a list of tools and the procedures they define in carrying out project management tasks.

- **Project management software can have data resident on a network to allow sharing of the files**

  Establish the basic project plan on the network with the baseline plan (agreed upon plan), the actual results, and an estimated plan for the future. They can add more detail to their part of the plan. Encourage people to review and update their schedules once a week and maintain their own tasks. The danger is that people make mistakes, so save the file frequently during the week.

  The project plan has fields for the person responsible, whether the task is management critical or has risk, and the issues that pertain to the task. These are put in individual text fields associated with a task. These fields are then searchable.

- **Electronic mail software supports attaching project files**

  Electronic mail can also be used as a vehicle for sharing and routing information. The limitation of electronic mail is that it lacks the database elements of groupware. It is freeform, which will cause problems later when you want to do analysis. It is often better to use the electronic mail within the groupware to add structure.

- **Groupware or a shared database tracks issues and action items**

  Groupware allows you to carry out a dialogue for managing a specific issue or updating the plan. Groupware has been employed for several international projects. It was found that the elapsed time to obtain decisions and resolve issues is cut by more than 50 percent.

  The issues database contains all of the information pertaining to an issue or opportunity. The database is stored on the network so that people can update the issue information. Data related to status, assignment, resolution, description, category, and tasks that relate to the issue are all in the database. You can now put the issues and project plan together. You can search the project plan, filtering the plan to obtain only those tasks that relate to an issue or are dependent on other tasks. Alternatively, you can search the database for all issues pertaining to a specific task. Establish a similar database for both lessons learned and action items. If you employ standardized templates of high level tasks, the results are even better, since anyone who employs the template can access the lessons learned for specific tasks.

- **A spreadsheet can be used for project analysis**

  Spreadsheets can help overcome some of the limitations of project management software. Most project management tools allow you to assign costs through resources. You can input standard and overtime rates and vary the calendar for specific resources. Some project management packages support earned value work and financial calculations. However, this is often too inflexible. Establish a table of data from the project database and then export the table to a spreadsheet. The spreadsheet can then be manipulated and analyzed to obtain cost and resource reports.

- **Internet links allow access for remote managers, customers, and suppliers**

Methods and tools can cover about 60 to 70 percent of what can arise in a project. The remaining percentage, based on human behavior and communications, should not be ignored. A major benefit of the methods and tools lies in freeing up time to address these other things. In project management you need time for establishing rapport with people, negotiating, fact finding, and making decisions. Methods and tools can make the project run more smoothly but they seldom reduce overall time and resources. There is a trade-off between the learning curve and the efficiency gained from the tool or method.

What does the future hold? It is evident that the tools are becoming more supportive of collaborative work. This bodes well for project management. It will eliminate some of the concern that people have for using project management. As it becomes easier to do, you will be able to use the tools for smaller projects. The use of the Internet provides standards for data sharing between firms and supports compatibility. Thus, you should see more effective projects between companies. In fact, it is not unlikely that more projects will be generated due to the availability of tools. The availability of collaborative tools will also mean good project managers can take on more work if their time is freed up. This should encourage more parallel effort.

There is a downside to using methods and tools. If you lack good methods and discipline, these tools can lead to more disorganization. Mistakes can multiply, since communications are faster and the results of work in a plan or database are instantly capable of being viewed by many people. It is a case of the good getting better and the worse deteriorating.

Tool Selection

Begin with the common PC tools that are in place in your organization. The first principle is to eliminate tool candidates that are incompatible. Next, try to use what the company has already purchased. You don't want to fund a major infrastructure software and hardware project out of your project budget. Since there is typically an office suite, electronic mail, database, and a groupware set of approved software, your choice is often limited as to which project management software you will use.

MEASURING THE EFFECTIVENESS OF CURRENT METHODS AND TOOLS

Before you replace or renew methods and tools, assess what you are have been using. Are the current methods effective? Are the tools you are currently using effective? What are the major problems you are having today? Can you measure what results are being obtained?

Here is a list of what you might look for in assessing your current situation:

- How many different schedules exist? Are they being tracked for the same work? If there are many, then a common effort will reduce redundancy.

- Are many project meetings consumed in getting exact data on the status of a project and resolving discrepancies between different plans? If so, then issues are not being addressed.

- How long does it take for an issue to be resolved after it has been identified? If the answer is "Too long," time is probably being wasted while people spin their wheels waiting for decisions.

- What comments do people make concerning the current process? Solicit and collect comments from team members.

IMPLEMENTING NEW METHODS AND TOOLS

As preparation for initiating the new methods and tools, answer these questions:

- How will exceptions to the general methods be addressed? Will people improvise, or are additional procedures necessary?

- Will the methods and tools be applied to all projects? If so, how will they be retrofitted onto existing projects? Who will pay for the learning and familiarity time? How will they be applied to very small and very large projects?

- Who will serve as the tool expert? Will this person be involved in training others? Is the expert going to be easy to reach when help is needed?

- How will the methods and tools used be monitored to ensure proper use? What constitutes proper use?

Here are three actions to use as you implement methods and tools:

- Start small. Begin on with several small projects. Learn from these projects to build lessons learned and guidelines. Document and use these guidelines and step up to new projects.

- Build a project with multiple parts and do a cross-project analysis. This demonstrates the added benefits of standardized methods.

- Analyze and perfect the methods and tools. This way, many more people will be able to use the revised methods and tools successfully.

Here are a few words of caution:

- Keep management fanfare and endorsements to a minimum to avoid bad feelings.

- Do not implement the approach on existing large-scale projects that are far along. This will slow progress as people attempt to use the new tools and methods.

- Test methods and tools so that you have experience with them before asking others to implement them.

The Cost of Implementation

Implementing modern collaborative scheduling is neither inexpensive nor easy, possibly involving hundreds of people and requiring a tremendous time commitment. Using a multi-phase implementation approach will help by spreading the cost over a longer period.

Some of the major cost elements are as follows:

- Hardware, software, and network upgrades
- Application software licenses
- Training and documentation costs for the new tools
- Staff time in learning the new methods
- Management time to measure and evaluate the new tools and methods
- Potential customized software development to provide additional features
- Conversion effort to move current schedules and data to the new tools

Once you implement the methods and tools and have used them for a time, you are ready to move into another part of the evaluation. Since tools support methods, focus on how people are using the methods. Also examine evidence that the tools are being used. Have team members discuss how they are using methods and tools.

Here is a list of questions you can ask:

- Is there consistency between projects? This refers to structure of the plans and whether they follow similar templates.
- Can you assemble an overall schedule composed of the detailed schedules? Will it make sense?
- Have the project managers identified issues and are these being addressed?
- Is there a table of issues vs. projects to see what different projects have common issues?
- Are people asking for help in using the methods and tools?

PROBLEMS AND OPPORTUNITIES

Even with analysis, organized planning, and necessary support, problems arise with the implementation of new methods and tools. Here are some common problems encountered, along with suggested remedies.

- **Resistance to new methods and tools.**

  This is natural since some team members may have used the previous methods and tools for years. Concentrate on winning over the younger staff members who are less resistant. As project leader, be a strong advocate of the new methods and tools through the processes of tracking the project, resolving issues, and maintaining communications.

- **Complaints that the new methods or tools take too much time.**

  Review how the team members are using the methods and tools they are complaining about. Hold a meeting specifically to address how to use these. Have team members demonstrate how these would be helpful.

- **Resistance to formal methods and tools.**

  Perhaps you are asking for more detailed methods and tools than the team members are accustomed to using. To counteract this attitude, show the team members that the more formal methods and tools free up time that can be better spent dealing with issues.

- **Team members raise new ideas on how to do project management.**

  Don't discard these. Try to get them reviewed and, if feasible, adopt them. This will show that you care about your team members and their ideas. And, of course, exceptional ideas can come from any team member.

- **A new release of software appears.**

  Team members are enthused and want to use it. Always be ready to carry out a pilot effort to evaluate new tools. Retain project information on an old project and use this to test the new tool. Always consider possible hidden costs of using something new.

MANAGEMENT PRESENTATION AND COST-BENEFIT ANALYSIS

Consider preparing an evaluation report of current methods and tools and circulate this to lay the groundwork for introducing change. Here is an outline for such a report:

I. Introduction—purpose and scope

II. Overview of current project management process, methods, and tools, describing what is being done today

III. Issues with the current methods and tools.

List the issues and describe their impact on the organization and projects. Use specific anonymous comments from staff.

IV. Summary—the cumulative impact of all of the problems

KEY QUESTIONS

Do you have a standard list of methods and tools for project management in your organization?

How has the list of methods and tools changed over the past few years? Is there a formal method for updating and replacing specific methods and tools?

Does your organization employ or endorse software tools that are network-based in which sharing of information is supported?

EXAMPLES

A Retailing Example

A retail firm had 12 different projects going on simultaneously. The firm was trying to do process improvement. It was trying to implement EDI, store point-of-sale, conduct video training, perform scanning, and handle management controls, all at the same time. While all the project leaders followed the same method, they used a total of four different project management software tools. They also set their schedules and plans up differently so that it was impossible to get an overall picture of what was going on. One project failed, which had the domino effect of dragging down two other projects. When the firm attempted to standardize its tools, it was too late.

Stirling Manufacturing

With the wide geographic distribution of manufacturing, the lack of uniformity in methods or tools in projects is no surprise. As long as managers performed and projects were on schedule, no one perceived a need for standardization. The use of the wide area network changed all of that. A major subproject was assigned to evaluate, select, and implement project management methods and tools. Specific tools used included project management software, electronic mail, database management systems, and groupware. To support the standard tools, project templates were created and stored on the network.

Nevertheless, team members continued to show resistance. Compromise carried the team through a transition period. Only new projects were to use the new software.

A lesson learned here is that methods and tools are intimately related to politics, power, and organization. A second lesson learned is that it is prudent to select one site as a pilot for the other remote sites. This approach can be successful if project managers recognize the autonomy and self-interest of each location.

GUIDELINES

- **Compensate for the inexperience of a project manager.**

  This inexperience tends to be reflected in two major areas. First, the project manager cannot provide perspective on the status and direction of the project, since the project is new to them. Second, the project manager has a difficult time sorting out which issues are important and how issues are related.

  Assist a new project manager in developing the plan and setting direction. After that, monitor how the issues in the project are being addressed.

- **Look over all of your tools and methods to see how they fit or conflict.**

  Methods and tools conflict in different ways. They can require duplication of effort. They may require you to do manual work to take the results from one tool to another. Different tools may not support the same level of detail.

In such a conflict, often one tool or method will dominate and the other fall into disuse. Which wins? It may be the easiest to use. It may be the one that is politically correct. It is not necessarily the best or most complete. This means that you have to keep a close watch on conflicts as they arise.

- **Base management directives on reality.**

  A manager may attend a seminar and become a believer in a certain tool. The manager spreads the word that the tool will be used. But if planning for integration is not performed and follow-up or enforcement is neglected, the tool will not be used. The manager's credibility may be jeopardized.

- **Do not add a new tool or method in the middle of a project; this will generally slow progress.**

  If a project extends for more than a few months, it is subject to the "tool of the month" syndrome. This occurs because there is a seller of the new thing. Management may feel that it may make a difference. If someone says to you, "why not try it out?" Beware, there are hidden costs. You first have to divert resources to understand it. Then you have to use it. You have to fit it in with everything else.

- **Test the method first when using a pilot project.**

  Pilot projects cannot easily test both methods and tools concurrently. After the method has been tested, then people in the pilot project will have many specific ideas on tool requirements. If a pilot project attempts to test the tool and the method together or the tool alone, then the focus of the pilot is on learning the tool. Guidelines for future use of the tool will be missing, since the method was not validated.

- **Do not ignore gaps in tools.**

  A tool gap may occur when you have to manually load data from one tool into another. Another gap occurs when you have to perform manual work because there is no tool. A gap results in more manual effort and is more prone to failure and frustration. This increases the pressure on the team since each team and manager must cope with each and every gap. This can lead to sharp falls in productivity and accuracy of information.

- **Look for interfaces between new tools.**

  When a car is modified for a new air conditioner, it is often the case that the team does not think adequately of all of the interfaces with the engine. An example of bad design occurred with a car where the entire air conditioner had to be disassembled to service the engine. How about that—a $500 tune-up? It is the same with tool interfaces. Interfaces include data, procedures, and human interface. Data may not only have to be converted but changed to fit the next tool. People don't want to hear this. They want to test drive the shiny new tool.

- **Assign an expert to every tool.**

  Even simple tools require someone who will watch to see that the tool is being used properly. Remember that the job of the expert goes beyond answering questions. It is also to see that the tool is being employed properly and that the expected benefits of the tool are obtained.

- **Allow for the uncertainty inherent in projects rather than adhering to excessive use of formal methods and tools.**

  Projects are part science but also an art. Along with the element of uncertainty, projects involve emotions, feelings, and politics. Projects cannot be reduced to a science by quantifying them and then applying formal rules. Quantitative methods have a value, but this value is limited.

- **If someone pitches a new method or tool, only believe that it works when it works in your project.**

  A method or tool depends on the project and its environment for its success. It is working when you see it work, not when people say it is.

- **Gain proficiency in tool or method use through experience rather than through study.**

  Suppose you buy some home accounting software and set it up on your machine. After an hour you get bored. You decide that instead of sitting at the computer, you'll read the manual. That helps, but you will not understand and retain what you are reading unless you go back to the keyboard and try it out. Reading about a method or tool is not as effective as hands-on experience.

- **Look over all of your tools and methods to see how they fit or conflict.**

  Tools and methods can conflict in different ways. They can require duplication of effort; they may require you to do manual work to take the results from one tool to another. The tools may not support the same level of detail.

  When two methods or tools conflict, it is not always true that the best one prevails. The victor may be the easiest to use. It may be the one that is politically correct. Keep an eye on potential areas of conflict and take an active part in resolving the conflict in the way that most benefits the project.

- **When considering a method, think about what type of person can use the method.**

  Any method presumes that the people using the method have certain skills. This applies to basic language skills as well as to complex production systems. If the method requires a star player, and you have few stars, the method is elitist for the small group. Missing skills may mean failed methods.

- **Train close, but not too close, to the time of implementation.**

  If those trained do not use what they have learned, they will gradually forget. Six months later you will have to retrain. Conversely, if training is done right before a major use, this can cause people to feel pressure.

- **Understand how methods work together.**

  Learning one method is relatively easy, involving only one set of procedures and experts. But when you use several methods, problems occur. You have to rely on documentation and procedures written by different people for different purposes. Be sure to fill in the linkage. Make sure people understand how to move between methods and tools.

To be effective, use methods consistently and frequently. If you use the method in different ways, you are less likely to develop proficiency and skill, since you are just adapting. House plants are frequent victims of this. People neglect them, then pay too much attention and overwater them.

- **Avoid resource leveling.**

  A method that is supported in many project management systems is resource leveling—don't use it.

  Resource leveling is when the project management software attempts to solve overcommitment of resources by moving tasks around within the boundaries of slack time. This is a good idea and feature in principle but it is not practical. In many systems, you cannot undo the leveling. Watch for this feature in your software and compensate for it. Use manual resource leveling in which you move tasks and changes are reflected in a resource graph.

- **Imposing some tools may mean other subversive tools are used in the organization.**

  Market methods and tools to staff and managers based on appealing to their self-interests. If upper management declares everyone will use a tool, people will pay lip service to the tool, but they may not actually apply it to basic procedures.

- **Avoid overtraining.**

  Overtraining in tools can lead to inertia. You probably have seen this many times in larger organizations. Rather than no training, the organization errs on the side of too much training. People can become so bored and disinterested that any desire that they had to learn the tool is dissipated.

- **Calibrate your tools.**

  Calibration means that the parameters for using the tool and interpreting results are in place. An example of a need for calibration is when you implement a statistical software package that has three levels of difficulty. The proper calibration depends on the level of experience and knowledge available on your team.

- **Focus on results, not process.**

  Do not become so entranced by a method that you forget what its purpose is.

- **Track both effort and elapsed time.**

  This difference is subtle. Elapsed time is typically the duration of the task. Effort is the total number of hours that are being allocated to the task. If no resources are assigned to the task, these are the same in the software. Elapsed time is affected by the calendars and work periods that are employed.

  For example, if three people work 20 hours on a task, the effort is 60 hours. The elapsed time, assuming one shift of work per day, is 2-1/2 days. However, if they work a shift and a half with overtime, then the elapsed time is less than two days. Be sensitive to the effects of changing calendars and schedules when effort and elapsed time are calculated.

- **Use electronic systems in support of project management.**

  If you attempt to use manual methods, the fast pace of the project may outstrip your ability to cope with the project. Also, electronic systems provide visibility of information. Set in your mind what you want the role of the project management software to be. For example, you may want to use it for reporting and for presentation to support analysis.

ACTION ITEMS

1. Evaluate your current methods and tools. Begin with the list given earlier in this chapter. In the first column, write each area of project management. Write down the method used in each area in the second column. Write down the tool used in the third column.

   Next, make a list of issues and problems that you have observed with current project management methods and tools. Put these in a row in the first column of a second table. The second column of this table should contain the area of project management from the list. A third column can contain the impact of each problem.

The first table shows what you have; the second indicates the gaps.

Area of PM	Method	Tool

Issue	Area of PM	Impact

2. Define what tools you would like to have to use with the software your firm already owns. Again, you can use a table. In the first column, list the tool areas. In the second column, give the proposed tool. The third column is for the current tool. The fourth column can contain the benefits of transitioning to the new tools.

3. Estimate the cost and time to implement a new set of tools. Write down answers to the following questions:

   - How many PCs will have to be upgraded for the new tools?

   - Will the network have to be upgraded?

   - How many people will have to be trained in the new methods and tools?

4. In your project defined earlier, identify the methods and tools you would like to use. Compare this to what your organization employs. What advantages are offered by those you would like to use? What are the limitations of the company's methods and tools not selected?

PART II TWO

UNDERSTANDING
THE BUSINESS

CHAPTER 8

STEP A: ANALYZE BUSINESS GOALS AND DIRECTION

CONTENTS

8

STEP A: ANALYZE BUSINESS GOALS AND DIRECTION

PURPOSE AND SCOPE

With the general purpose being to understand the business, you will work on finding more specific objectives that can be linked to business processes. For example, if you want increased profitability in general, identify the areas of the business in which this is possible. Going beyond this, seek to identify groups of processes that will serve as candidates for process improvement. You will look for groups because most processes are interwoven and usually revolve around a major process that crosses multiple functions and divisions or departments.

The scope in this first step is broad and includes all aspects of the enterprise. It also includes both the past and future, as well as the present. By looking at the past, you can see which business issues and objectives remain.

END PRODUCTS

The major end products are business objectives and issues that represent a major focus of the business, as well as comparison tables that tie the information together. You will look beyond short-term or quarterly financial goals to intermediate and long-term goals.

RESOURCES

You will be performing this step on your own. However, you will want to involve managers through data collection to determine business objectives and issues.

APPROACH

You are seeking a logical grouping of processes. You will not only select processes but you will also support your choice against a backdrop of all processes and their importance to the business. To find this, you first need to understand the business. In this first step you will answer the following questions:

- What are characteristics and trends in the industry?
- What are the driving factors for the business? What are the goals of the firm?
- Where does the firm make money?
- Where does it lose money?
- What critical processes should you consider?

Answering these questions correctly will help you select processes that have impact on the business, rather than processes that are meaningless. Choosing the most appropriate processes is crucial, because changing the focus of the process improvement effort after it starts is difficult, if not impossible.

Action 1: Understand the Basic Business

Read up on your organization in magazines, periodicals, and the financial press. What do outsiders say about your company? What do they list as its strengths and weaknesses? Who do they mention as competitors? What challenges does the firm face? What is said about your firm now as compared with two or three years ago? Use the Internet or CD-ROM databases in libraries to search for articles. See Chapter 10 (Step C) for more details.

Consider the politics of the business. Where is the center of power? What recent organizational changes have taken place? How secure are the people in power? To what extent does their management interest lie in specific business processes?

Examine stable areas of an organization. Why are they stable? Is it because their processes and workload are stable? Is the stability hiding inefficiencies? Hidden issues may lie underneath the stability. If an area appears stable after you have considered it in depth, move on to other processes.

Culture plays a strong role in business. Try to answer are the following:

- Does management encourage and reward teamwork? Process improvement is a team project. If the culture supports a mentality of every person for himself, you will have another barrier to overcome.

- Are problems and situations openly addressed? The answer to this will point to the appropriate manner in which issues should be addressed during the project.

- Are employees encouraged to develop new ideas and to think for themselves?

- Does management empower employees to make decisions and suggestions? If the answer is affirmative, process improvement ideas will be contributed by the staff involved in the process.

- What happens if people take risk? Is there any recognition or punishment? Process improvement involves political and process risk. If risk-taking is discouraged, the odds of success are lessened.

- Are people open with information or do they try to keep their knowledge to themselves? Many process improvement projects depend on the sharing of information and an open process.

Your goal is not to change the culture of the organization; it is to learn what you are up against.

Action 2: Identify Previous Attempts at Improvement

Tied to culture is the desire of the organization to improve itself. Over the past 20 years, many management improvement approaches have been tried in organizations. The following is a partial listing of sample management approaches.

- **Vision of the organization**

  This is a popular device to get a common framework and understanding of the focus of the organization. If there is a vision, it is tangible or fuzzy? Could it fit a hundred other organizations in different industries? Does the vision reflect reality? Do actions support the vision, or does the vision simply hang on a nice frame in the visitor entrance?

- **Analysis of the industry and competition**

  This is an increasingly popular method. Talk to the people who perform this analysis. Find out if they are satisfied with the actions taken. Ask whether the analysis translated into action or remained passive information.

- **Alliances with customer and suppliers**

  This does not apply to all industries. Some companies, however, have found such alliances beneficial in terms of quality improvement, electronic linkage, product design, and industrial practice. Finding out about alliances may provide clues to which processes are the most important.

- **Benchmarking**

  Does your firm do benchmarking? Does it look for good practices and then fit them into the organization? Does the firm benchmark, then do nothing with the results? Benchmarking will help in measurement of processes and can assist in identifying critical processes.

- **Organization streamlining**

  Has your firm attempted organization change without improving processes? Have management layers been reduced? To find out, dig out old organization charts and compare them to the current version.

- **Assessing management's commitment**

  Look at what the organization has attempted in terms of the following:

  —Using the value chain

  —Carrying out quality management programs

  —Retreating to core competencies

  —Undertaking efforts to reduce cycle time

  —Empowering employees and organizing them into groups

—Embarking on new technology (such as multimedia and groupware)

Look at management's response and attitude toward these techniques. What was the level of commitment? Did failure make them more reluctant to try new methods? This is the reality with many ideas that are oversold and overpromoted. Expectations are unrealistic.

Ascertain the areas in which management is willing to make changes. Alternatively, you might ask, "If you had the money and the time, what would you change?" Try to get management to address a process. If organization or infrastructure are mentioned, say "Which processes would you improve by doing that?" If management cannot come up with anything, the project should be considered for cancellation.

As a last question, ask why the managers didn't consider popular methods.

Action 3: Determine How Your Company Addresses Innovation

Organizations approach methods differently. Some are "innovators." They analyze a method, then try to implement it and achieve results. "Followers" attempt to implement changes but may not have the will to follow through for major benefit. They may achieve some benefit and then stop. "Dabblers" make up a third group. A dabbler investigates many methods, but they never carries out change. Dabblers sometimes initiate pilot projects, but never reach full implementation.

A fourth category is "resisters." Resisters are led by people who distrust methods. They watch methods come and go and become cynical. They concentrate on basics.

Process improvement can work easily with the first three groups. The fit with innovators is obvious. With followers, it will be the job of the project team to carry out the project and get benefits. There will be less management support. Resisters are an interesting group. Because they realize the importance of the basic business, they are more receptive to change.

The most difficult organization type is the dabbler. Often, dabblers do not take process improvement seriously until they feel threatened.

They require a trigger to activate a serious attitude toward process change. It is often best to explain first what will happen if they continue their current path. If they are still not serious, consider ending the project.

Process improvement focuses on process; it is not anchored solely in the infrastructure, the technology, or the organization. This is a primary reason some companies have been successful and it is why many organizations attempt process improvement. Your understanding of the type of organization to be improved will help you choose the appropriate approach.

Action 4: Collect Information

First, gather as much data as you can by passive means. Utilize organization charts, vision statements, long-range plans, policies and procedures, and some external information on the company and industry. Passive information is readily available with little effort. Use the information to help generate interview questions.

Data collection should not take a lot of time. The project clock is ticking. You will have an opportunity later to collect detailed information. Some who prefer detail find this frustrating, but it is in this step that you get the big picture. You will relate everything that follows to the understanding of the organization obtained in this step.

This information will provide suggestions for processes. It will aid you in Action 5, when you collect information for processes, infrastructure, and organizations.

Action 5: Identify Candidate Processes

You have gained an understanding of the business. Now define candidate processes for later evaluation and selection for process improvement. Table 8-1 lists processes that apply to different industries. You might consider some of these to start.

Your goal is to identify 20 candidate processes. An organization might have more than 250 processes, depending on the definition of the scope of the processes, making it important to narrow the field of candidates. Choose at least 20 because it is easier to choose at this stage than to add in the future.

Table 8-1:
Sample Processes That Are Key
to Specific Industries

Banking

    Installment loans

    Credit cards

    Leasing

    Savings

    Checking

    Real estate loans

    Commercial loans

    Foreign exchange

    Letters of credit

Insurance for various products (homeowners, auto, liability, flood, commercial, etc.)

    Application processing

    Claims

    Account servicing

    Accident investigations

    Billing

Retailing

    Sales

    Inventory

    Shipping and receiving

    Warehousing

Accounting

    Accounts receivable

    Accounts payable

    Payroll

    General ledger

Human resources

Manufacturing
   Order entry
   Order processing
   Inventory
   CAD
   Assembly
   Warehousing
   Customer service

Transportation
   Reservations
   Inventory
   Parts
   Equipment scheduling
   Operator scheduling

To begin to identify and narrow the field of processes, ask the following questions:

- Which processes appear to cause management problems?

- Which organizations appear to cause management problems?

- Which processes appear to be important in generating revenue or consuming large quantities of resources?

- Which processes cross the most organizations?

- Which processes have not been analyzed or modernized?

- Which processes appear to have the highest cost in terms of people and infrastructure?

- Which processes entail the highest volume of work? Which have the most transactions?

- Which processes produce the most rework and highest error rate?

- Which are the processes about which you know the least?

Ask the same questions about the computer systems and infrastructure that support the processes.

A good first step in downsizing is to figure out the process candidates for elimination. When examining a process for consideration, examine the possibility of elimination. What happens when you eliminate a process? Which other processes can pick up work that is necessary?

Consider processes that interface with suppliers and customers as good candidates for analysis. Customer and supplier processes are external processes that tend to link directly to revenue and cost. Thus, they make good candidates.

The fact that a big consulting or accounting firm has analyzed a process does not mean it is a poor candidate. A previous analysis that indicated that an area is not fruitful does not mean that you should avoid it. Perhaps the previous study did not focus on process improvement. The analysts may have had a different point of view. Enough time may have passed to merit reconsideration.

Technology and Infrastructure

As another approach, look for processes addressed by specific technologies. For example, image technology is a candidate for use in insurance claim and application processing. Electronic data interchange (EDI) is the electronic transfer of structured information between organizations. EDI can facilitate ordering, invoicing, shipping, and receiving. Technologies and their producers obviously identify and market their products to specific applications.

Interview Maps

You also may want to map the people interviewed (rows) vs. the processes (columns). Place an X in the table if that person mentioned the process as a concern. If you have a row with no entries, ask why this is so. You also could sort the rows by management levels as well as by organization.

Literature

Literature is another source of process information. Look in magazines and other printed material for information about leaders in your industry, which processes are regarded as excellent, and what other companies have improved.

Action 6: Summarize the Chosen Processes

You now have a list of individual processes to consider. To understand these more fully, prepare a brief summary table. The first column contains the list of processes. The second column contains characteristics of the organization; the third column contains characteristics of the infrastructure.

Creating such a table has several benefits, beyond support of the grouping of processes. First, people can review the table quickly. Second, it provides a basic understanding of processes at a high level. Third, the table will eventually help you select and market the chosen processes.

Action 7: Build Comparison Tables

Building these tables allows you to analyze the processes prior to a detailed evaluation and selection. The tables serve to validate the identified processes as well as the business objectives. They also help to explain what you are doing by displaying it in an organized method. These tables appear quantitative but are actually quite subjective. Enter a number from 1 to 5, depending on the degree to which the column is an issue with respect to the row (1 is lowest; 5 is highest). For example, if row A and column 1 is low, the column is not an issue of importance for the row. If it is high, process improvement should pay some attention to it. From the information gathered, you can build the following tables:

- **Business objectives vs. organization**

  The rows are business objectives as defined in the data collected. The entry in the table is the degree to which the organization supports the objective. Organization includes the major divisions and departments. Table 8-3 gives the table for the banking example, along with some comments explaining the scoring.

- **Business objectives vs. the identified processes**

  The rows are business objectives; the columns are the business processes that you have identified. The entry is the degree to which the process impacts the objective. See Table 8-4 for the banking example.

- **Business objectives vs. infrastructure elements**

  The rows are business objectives and elements of infrastructure are columns. The entry indicates the degree to which the infrastructure contributes to the business objective. See Table 8-5 for an example.

- **Business objectives vs. issues/opportunities**

  In the information you have gathered are certain key issues. This table reveals the degree to which resolving the issue or taking advantage of the opportunity supports the business objective. See Table 8-6 for the banking example.

MANAGEMENT PRESENTATION AND COST-BENEFIT ANALYSIS

You will likely be providing management with informal presentations on what you have collected so far. Show the comparison tables to get management's reaction and feedback. This accomplishes several goals. First, you are establishing a pattern of looking at concrete information in the form of tables. Second, management is becoming involved and more interested.

What should you expect from top management? At this point they should be able to give you feedback on your initial ideas through the interviews and tables. However, don't commit to specific processes at this point. You don't have enough specific information. A false start with a direction change can be deadly. Watch for managers who are enemies of process improvement to give out false signs and set traps.

By considering the issues that are raised in this step, you can start to make out potential substantial benefits. However, if you have to discuss costs and benefits, do so by pointing to the *potential* without getting pinned down to specific figures. Indicate that more data will become available in subsequent steps.

KEY QUESTIONS

What are the objectives and direction of the business? Make a short, specific list. If what you write applies to many organizations, it is too general.

What are the lessons learned from your assessment of the past? If these are either too general or too specific, you are less likely to use them later. Note each lesson learned and identify the impact on possible processes.

EXAMPLES

Monarch Bank

For Monarch, these were the objectives:

- Improved customer service
- Increased profitability
- Increased market share
- Reduced losses and charge-offs
- Improved efficiency in operations
- Increased staff satisfaction

Monarch Bank had a variety of problems in its credit functions, including credit cards; leasing; and installment, commercial, and real estate loans. These functions are shown in Table 8-2. The columns are processes for each of the products: application processing, servicing, payments, collections, and charge-off. This table shows how 25 processes can be generated.

Table 8-2 also shows sequencing of implementation. Some of the processes at Monarch Bank were distributed and some are centralized. The infrastructure included a variety of automated and manual systems. Note the level of detail shown here. This is important to support detailed process improvement analysis.

Table 8-2:
Processes for Monarch Bank

In this comparison table the processes are mapped against business functions. This table can show the similarity in processes across functions and can help in getting management support by showing how process improvement experience can be reused. The numbers show the sequencing of implementation.

Function/ Process	Application Processing	Servicing	Payments	Collections	Charge-off
Credit card	1	2	3	4	5
Installment loans	6	7	8	9	10
Leasing	11	12	13	14	15
Commercial loans	16	17	18	19	20
Real estate loans	21	22	23	24	25

Tables 8-3 through 8-6 are comparison tables.

Table 8-3:
Monarch—Business Objectives vs. Organization

This comparison table maps business objectives and organization. It is used to zero in on the parts of the organization that should be given the most attention.

Objectives	Lending	Commercial Lending	Real Estate
Service	2	4	2
Profitability	4	3	3
Market share	3	2	2
Losses	5	4	2
Efficiency	4	3	3
Staff satisfaction	1	3	2

Comments: Lending is very competitive and depends on volume. Commercial lending depends on individual relationships. Real estate is relatively stable. Examples of the basis behind the ratings: Servicing is being done adequately in lending (rating of 2); losses are a primary concern in lending due to volume (5); staff satisfaction is less important in lending and real estate than in commercial lending due to limited customer contact.

Table 8-4: Monarch—Business Objectives vs. Processes

This table relates the processes to the business objectives and aids in the selection of which processes to consider in evaluation and selection.

Objectives/ Processes	Credit card					Installment loans				
	1	2	3	4	5	6	7	8	9	10
Service	2	4	3	3	2	2	4	2	3	1
Profitability	2	1	1	3	4	3	1	2	4	4
Market share	1	1	1	3	1	3	2	1	1	1
Losses	4	1	2	4	5	2	2	3	5	4
Efficiency	3	3	3	4	4	4	4	4	3	3
Staff satisfaction	3	3	2	3	2	2	2	2	3	2

	Leasing					Commercial loans				
	11	12	13	14	15	16	17	18	19	20
Service	3	4	2	2	2	3	3	3	4	3
Profitability	2	1	2	4	4	3	1	1	3	2
Market share	3	2	1	1	1	3	3	2	3	2
Losses	3	2	3	4	4	3	2	1	4	2
Efficiency	3	4	3	3	2	4	3	3	4	2
Staff satisfaction	2	3	3	2	2	2	1	1	2	3

	Real estate				
	21	22	23	24	25
Service	2	3	2	3	3
Profitability	2	1	1	3	4
Market share	3	1	1	1	1
Losses	2	2	1	3	3
Efficiency	2	2	2	3	3
Staff satisfaction	1	1	1	2	2

Comments: It appears that real estate has fewer issues in terms of meeting the objectives than the other areas. Staff satisfaction appears to be lower in priority than addressing profitability and losses.

Table 8-5:
Monarch—Business Objectives vs. Infrastructure

This table relates the infrastructure to the business objectives. It reveals what parts of the infrastructure are most important to achieving the business objectives.

Objectives/ Processes	Facilities	Computer Systems	Communications	Information
Service	2	3	3	4
Profitability	1	3	3	5
Market share	3	2	1	3
Losses	2	3	2	4
Efficiency	3	4	4	4
Staff satisfaction	2	3	1	4

Comments: Four parts of the infrastructure are cited as examples. *Facilities* refers to physical plant and interior facilities. Computer systems and communications are considered separately because the network condition is sometimes an issue. Information refers to data being used and stored manually and in computers. Facilities appear to be less of a factor on business objectives than the computer systems and quality of information.

Table 8-6:
Monarch—Business Objectives vs. Issues/Opportunities

This table ranks issues with respect to business objectives. We will use this to identify which issues are the most important to address in reengineering.

Objectives/ Issues	Market-share data	Internal performance data
Service	4	4
Profitability	4	4
Market share	5	2
Losses	2	5
Efficiency	2	5
Staff satisfaction	1	1

Both issues relate to the availability of information and cover internal and external availability.

TRAN

Business objectives for TRAN, developed from observation, included:

- Improved customer service
- Better availability of transportation
- Increased efficiency
- Better management reporting and control

Triggered by technology, candidate processes were those major ones in which automation could substantially improve effectiveness. Because the entire organization lacked significant automated support, major processes across the organization were considered. Table 8-7 lists major processes. The major parts of the organization are accounting, payroll, human resources, operations, customer service, and route planning. The planning group does route planning while operations does short-term route adjustments. Purchasing involves accounting and operations. Payroll involves accounting and operations. Operations performs customer information support.

Refer to Tables 8-7 through 8-11 for tables generated by TRAN.

Table 8-7:
TRAN—Processes

Major Process	Description
Accounting	
General ledger	Old system that is being replaced
Accounts payable	Old system that is still useful
Accounts receivable	System unique to TRAN
Payroll	Much effort to keep this process and system up-to-date; unique to TRAN
Human resources	Paper-intensive, old; interfaces to payroll
Operations	
Purchasing	Recent package system in which process was built around system
Parts inventory	5-year-old process and system
Equipment records	Manual and some PC automation
Driver scheduling	Very old system; over 50 percent of effort manual
Customer service	
Customer information	Manual process using maps and schedules
Customer complaints	PC-based system along with paper forms
Route planning	Newest system based on GIS (Geographic Information Systems)

Table 8-8: TRAN—Business Objectives vs. Organization

This is the comparable table for TRAN for four major divisions.

	Operations	Finance	Personnel	Planning
Service	4	2	3	2
Availability	4	1	1	1
Efficiency	4	3	3	2
Control/rpting	4	5	4	4

Comments: Overall, operations has the most urgent needs with respect to business objectives. There is a general need for management information and for efficiency. This chart indicates which organizations may need attention and will help in setting priorities.

Table 8-9: TRAN—Business Objectives vs. Processes

Four sample business objectives have been mapped against four processes as an example.

	HR	Customer complaints	Purchasing	Payroll
Service	3	4	3	5
Availability	1	2	2	4
Efficiency	4	2	3	3
Control/rpting	4	3	3	3

Comments: Not all of the processes have been included, due to space limitations. Note the importance of payroll.

Table 8-10:
TRAN—Business Objectives vs. Infrastructure

This table was used to indicate that more than computer systems had to be addressed.

	Facilities	Computer systems	Communications	Information
Service	2	3	4	4
Availability	2	3	3	3
Efficiency	2	4	3	3
Control/rpting	1	5	4	3

Comments: Facilities are not a major issue. The old computer systems impact multiple business objectives.

Table 8-11:
TRAN—Business Objectives vs. Issues/Opportunities

This is a subset of the actual table prepared for TRAN. There were seven business objectives and over fifty issues.

	Improved scheduling	Better tracking	Reduced overhead
Service	4	4	4
Availability	3	2	2
Efficiency	4	4	5
Control/rpting	2	3	3

Comments: Improved scheduling means improving the scheduling of the vehicles. Better tracking refers to the ability of departments to get hold of information. Reduced overhead means reducing clerical and overhead labor in departments.

Stirling Manufacturing

Stirling Manufacturing had the following objectives:

- Reduced production time
- Improved quality of manufactured items
- Better utilization of staff
- Improved knowledge of status and plans
- Increased management control

The issue at Stirling was how to improve the manufacturing processes. Analysis revealed a number of candidates, including scheduling, and design. Table 8-12 gives a complete list. Look through this list to find processes that directly impact the manufacturing and assembly performance.

Table 8-12:
Stirling Manufacturing Processes

This list of processes served as the basis for process improvement projects at Stirling. The focus is on those processes that support the design, manufacturing, and testing of finished products.

Computer aided design: Modern system and process

Requirements and specifications tracking: Pertains to all parts of the products; older process, but still functions; does not support just-in-time

Project management and scheduling: Which product gets what resources; inconsistently applied across all business areas; manual with old computer process

Engineering drawings management: Newest process

Inventory of parts: Adequate process given limited range of parts

Inventory of finished goods: Complex, manual process since this includes semi-finished parts

Problem identification and tracking: Largely manual process with some personal computers

Testing and integration support: Manual process

MRP (manufacturing resource planning): Automated but process requires substantial manual intervention

Costing analysis: Older computer system supports process that does not reflect actual manufacturing process

---

Both issues relate to the availability of information and cover internal and external availability.

Refer to Tables 8-13 through 8-16 for examples of Stirling Manufacturing comparison tables.

Table 8-13: Stirling—Business Objectives vs. Organization

This gives an example of manufacturing in which the organization columns pertain to specific divisions which produce subsystems, which are then assembled.

	Subsystem A	Subsystem B	Assembly/test
Production time	3	3	4
Quality	2	3	4
Staff utilization	4	2	4
Knowledge	4	3	5
Control	2	3	5

Comments: It is clear that assembly and test is a major area. Note that only two subsystem areas have been included. Knowledge of what is going on is a major issue across the organization.

Table 8-14: Stirling—Business Objectives vs. Processes

This table ranks the importance of each of three processes to five
business objectives.

	Scheduling	Production/mfg	Assembly
Production time	4	5	4
Quality	2	4	3
Staff utilization	3	2	4
Knowledge	5	2	4
Control	4	3	4

Comments: Assembly is a major concern as a process. Scheduling is
only slightly less of a concern.

Table 8-15:
Stirling—Business Objectives vs. Infrastructure

This table indicates the importance of information to Stirling.

	Facilities	Computer systems	Network	Information
Production time	2	2	3	4
Quality	2	2	2	4
Staff utilization	2	3	1	3
Knowledge	2	4	3	4
Control	2	3	2	5

Comments: This table shows the concern for information in the
infrastructure. Facilities appear to be adequate.

Table 8-16:
Stirling—Business Objectives vs. Issues/Opportunities

This table reveals the importance of integration to Stirling.

	New technology	Integrated mfg	Integrated control
Production time	2	5	5
Quality	3	5	4
Staff utilization	2	3	3
Knowledge	4	3	3
Control	4	3	5

Comments: *New technology* refers to client server computing and wide area networks as well as new manufacturing software. *Integrated manufacturing* refers to the linking of all processes involved in manufacturing. *Integrated control* includes planning, project management, and tracking.

ACTION ITEMS

1. Identify three business objectives applicable to business processes. For each, indicate which goals are relevant from the following list. Keep the wording of the objective simple.

   1—Increase sales

   2—Handle higher volume of work with same resources

   3—Reduce overall operating costs

   4—Reduce staffing

   5—Reduce infrastructure and capital costs

   6—Streamline processes

   7—Realign power between the enterprise and the divisions

Objectives:

1. _____

   Goals: _____

2. _____

   Goals: _____

3. _____

   Goals: _____

2. Identify ten business issues that apply to business processes. For each, indicate what will likely or possibly occur if the issue is not addressed. These business issues will be related to process selection and other parts of process improvement later.

	Issue	**Implications**
1.		
2.		
3.		
4.		
5.		
6.		
7.		
8.		
9.		
10.		

3. Construct a table in which rows are organizations or divisions and columns are key business processes. In the table indicate the importance of the process to the division on a scale of 1 to 5 (1 is not important, 5 is very important).

Organization/
Process

4. Construct a table in which rows are elements of infrastructure and the columns are key business processes. Indicate the importance of the infrastructure to the process on a scale of 1 to 5 (1 is not important, 5 is very important).

Infrastructure/
Process

5. Relate processes to each other in the following table. Rows and columns are processes. The entries in the table can be any combination of the following: I–share infrastructure, O–share organization, IN–interface with each other, C–share customers, S–share suppliers, SY–share systems.

Process/
Process

6. Relate the business objectives to the business processes in the following table. Each entry is 1 to 5 (1 is not related, 5 is highly related).

Bus. Object/
Process

CHAPTER 9

STEP B: SELECT A GROUP OF PROCESSES FOR IMPROVEMENT

CONTENTS

9

STEP B: SELECT A GROUP OF PROCESSES FOR IMPROVEMENT

PURPOSE AND SCOPE

Your purpose is to select a process group from the processes you have chosen and get management approval.

The scope is governed by the business goals and issues uncovered in Step A.

END PRODUCTS

The basic end product is your assessment of the processes in terms of groups. You will recommend a specific group of processes for process improvement. You will also indicate why other groups and processes are less attractive for improvement at this time. Your selection will be supported by tables and graphs.

RESOURCES

In this step you want a great deal of input. You do not want to be accused later of showing favoritism to one process or another. Gather input from many people, but do the analysis and build the comparison tables yourself. That will position you better to explain, modify, defend, or present the information.

APPROACH

In this step, you will carry out the grouping process whereby you define clusters of related processes. You will then choose one group for process improvement. You will be considering selection based on factors such as politics, process stability, investment required, potential benefits, and long-term direction. You do not need to avoid taking on processes that are politically active and sensitive—as long as you know about this in advance. Being taken by surprise is a cause for failure.

You will need criteria and trade-off analysis to choose among the possibilities. You will want to select a group of processes in which the following is true:

- Sufficient commonality exists between processes in the group.
- A difference can be made in a reasonable time.
- The new processes will be stable enough to provide benefits.
- Major unknown political risk is avoided.
- Work with the first set of processes paves the way for addressing another group.

Recall that you have chosen 20 processes. You can group by function (such as servicing or collections). You can group by organization (such as credit card or installment loan). Neither of these groups addresses risk. You can group the processes with greatest risk, regardless of business function and organization. This is recommended, because management wants an approach that will address all of the major risk areas. Leaving one or more untouched leaves management feeling exposed. Within some of the processes there are subprocesses and related smaller processes.

Determine what to recommend for the processes *not* selected. Are they next in line? Are they to be untouched? If so, for how long? How do they fit into the picture? This differs from other methods that concentrate on the winners of the analysis. You are concerned with the "process portfolio," a group of processes.

Action 1: Define the Boundaries and Interfaces of Processes

Look at the list of 20 processes that you generated in Step A. Where does one process end and the next begin? How do processes tie together? The answers to these questions help to determine whether a process belongs to a group or not. Some ways two processes interface are as follows:

- **One passes work instructions to another.**

  One process depends on another for procedures and information. This is the strongest type of process linkage.

- **The two share of information.**

  One process feeds information to another. The second process is therefore highly dependent on the first.

- **One depends upon the completion of the other.**

  A process cannot begin until the previous process is completed. Of the three, this is the weakest link because it depends on an occurrence.

  Many other variations are made possible by combining any two of these factors. If there is a strong relationship between the content of one process and another, consider those processes together.

  Two processes do not have to interface directly. They might relate to each other indirectly through infrastructure, organization, and resources. Some examples are as follows:

- **They share hardware and network.**

  Both processes operate on the same infrastructure. Changing one process could impact the performance of the other process. If you change a process to increase network traffic, you impact network performance. If you increase the number of users or extent of use, you impact traffic.

- **They share facilities.**

  Two processes that inhabit the same space will impact each other after one of the processes changes.

- **They share equipment.**

  The processes may conflict over specific equipment. Different equipment and levels of equipment may be necessary following process change. If the same staff is to operate both sets of equipment, problems will arise.

- **The same people perform both.**

    Changing one process may be counterproductive to the other process.

- **They impact the same supplier or customer.**

    Changing one process may mean that the external organization now must work with two entirely different and incompatible processes.

When you consider a process, identify those processes that are *tightly linked,* meaning that any significant change (requiring a project and management approval) will affect the performance, cost, or requirements of the other process. Processes that are *loosely linked* should be considered separately. Loosely linked might mean, for example, that while different groups perform each process, both groups report to the same manager.

You might also consider a process by examining the impact of changes made, to see if there is any effect. For example, suppose you eliminate process A. Will process B be affected? If you move process A outside (outsourcing) or change organization or infrastructure (rightsizing), what will be the impact on process B? Assessing some potential impacts helps to determine groupings.

Action 2: Group the Processes

Using the list of 20 process, generate a process group. Some criteria for generating a group include the following:

- **Customer-based or supplier-based**

    Group all processes that touch the customer. In retailing, you could consider point-of-sale, bar coding, and other processes together in a retail store. In banking, you could group all branch-operated processes. This grouping has tangible criteria, but critical internal processes may be ignored.

- **Supplier-based**

    Group all processes that interact with the same suppliers. These processes could be those associated with ordering, shipping, and receiving.

- **Function-based**

  Group all processes that perform the same function. This is one of the safest groupings, but it will probably make the project more complex by spanning multiple organizations. In banking, this could be all servicing processes. In insurance, this could be all claims processes.

- **Organization-based**

  Group all processes that the organization operates and manages. In banking, this could include all credit card processes. Note that the placement of processes in organizations may be the result of politics rather than logic.

- **Technology-based**

  Group all processes that use the same technology. The same hardware, software, or network can serve as the basis for technology-based processes.

- **General manager–based**

  Group all processes under the direction of a high-level manager. Most organizations have many layers of management. Thus, a high level manager may oversee a number of organizations. Note that this grouping leaves you open to the charge that the project is too narrow.

- **Financial performance–based**

  Group all processes that lose money or incur too high a cost. In the banking example, these could be processes that have substantial losses.

- **Business objective–based**

  Group processes which support a specific objective. Be careful not to use too general a business objective.

- **Competition-based**

  Group processes that are keys to competitor success.

- **Issue-based**

  Group processes that generate the most complaints.

You can sometimes use a graph (as in Figure 9-1) to clarify the reasoning behind the grouping of processes. Note that while you may not have precise numbers for each axis, you can estimate. Figure 9-1 shows two group alternatives (A and B). The eight axes cover the dimensions of process improvement:

- Number of organizations involved
- Number of high level managers involved
- Number of users in departments affected
- Number of buildings impacted

Figure 9-1: Example of Two Possible Process Groupings

This graph compares the two process groups against various criteria. It shows the two groups in many dimensions of resources.

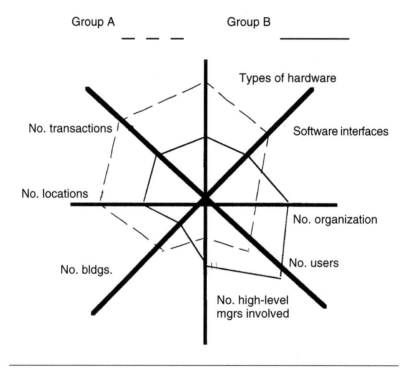

- Number of cities or locations
- Number of transactions
- Variety and number of types of hardware
- Number of software interfaces

A major process serves as the center for both groups. Group A is technical in nature. Many infrastructure changes will be involved because the processes in the group span a wide scope of infrastructure. Organization is the center of Group B. With more people, organizations, and managers involved, there is more complexity than is found in Group A. Keep this diagram to show comparisons between groups.

Alternatively, you can use a bar chart in which each group has a set of bars, and each bar corresponds to a specific axis.

Another guideline for constructing a group is to include some simple, related processes in which rapid benefits may be demonstrated. Rapid prototyping will be discussed. If the process is complex, try prototyping the user interface and general new method (within the processes) on a simple process. You are encouraged to pilot a process.

To the group of basic processes add smaller processes within departments and general purpose processes. Some examples of subsidiary processes are the following:

- Processes that supports letter generation or faxing from output of the primary processes.
- PC-based processes that use information generated by a primary process.
- Electronic forms or electronic mail that link to a process.
- Groupware that performs a supporting role to a process.
- Manual steps and processes that are extensions of a process.

These secondary processes are important because they fill out the picture and contribute to the overall benefits of process improvement. Ignoring them could, perhaps, lead to a new process that is worse than the replaced one because it is more awkward and cumbersome. By including them, you might achieve earlier improvements.

Too Many Processes in a Group

If too many processes are involved, infrastructure changes may bog down the project. You may be slowed down if too many organizations are involved. Look over your choices again. It is inefficient to group processes that are more different than alike. If the process group is still too large, stretch out the project and raise the level of risk and exposure. Also increase the number and extent of reviews, status meetings, and coordination efforts.

Action 3: Build Comparison Tables

Process Group vs. Process Group

Be able to discuss how process groups are compatible and supportive of each other. Two groups are supportive if one naturally leads to another. Groups are not supportive if they require different organization or infrastructure. Two groups are neutral if they have little in common. Construct a table with entries on a scale of 1 to 5 (1 is incompatible; 5 is highly compatible).

Later, when groups are ranked, and sequencing is established, this table will provide assistance and support.

Process Group vs. Technologies

The rows represent the process groups. The columns stand for technologies that you currently use or have a strong desire to use in the future. The entry is 1 to 5, based on the degree to which the technology is involved in the process group (1 is not at all; 5 is very dependent). You are concerned with the technologies on which the processes will depend when improvement is completed.

This table determines similarities between groups in terms of technologies. If you were later to select two groups that used incompatible or separate technologies, availability of people and money might prevent you from completing the task.

Process Group vs. Infrastructure

The rows are process groups; the columns are key infrastructure elements. The entry is 1 to 5 based on the degree the process group will depend on the specific infrastructure element (1 is irrelevant; 5 is critical).

This table is important because it reveals which process groups would benefit from investment in a specific infrastructure component. Where money is limited, this can be a determining factor in sequencing process groups behind a leader.

Process Group vs. Organization

The rows are as before; the columns are the major organizations involved. This table shows patterns. All process groups might fall in the same organizations. There would be several possible explanations for this. Perhaps you have not done your homework and should return for more processes. Alternately, one organization might be in disarray.

How do you obtain data to fill in these tables, when you have not yet performed detailed data collection and analysis on each process group? Base the tables on the interviews and data collected in Step A. In a perfect world, you would analyze all groups and then do the selection. Time, resources, and management pressure do not permit such luxuries.

The tables define the groups and set priorities between groups in a way that is logical, complete, and credible. The columns assist in your evaluation.

Action 4: Determine Two Winning Groups

In the previous step, you constructed tables of business objectives vs. processes, organizations, infrastructure, and issues. The issues table points to which objectives are important. The organizations and infrastructure tables indicate which are critical to key business objectives. They help in your later analysis. Here most of your focus is on the process table. This table indicates the degree to which the key business process in each group supports the business objective.

Evaluation Criteria

Define the criteria to use for performance, internal, external, and the process improvement project itself. A useful and fast technique is the development of a strawman set of criteria (such as the ones listed above). After seeing the graphs, people may then suggest additions and changes.

If process groups are different, instead of the traditional approach, take the following steps:

- Develop additional comparison tables for each group. These include process group vs. process group, process group vs. technologies, process group vs. infrastructure, and process group vs. organizations. (See Action 5.) These additional tables, along with those from Step A, will support the analysis.
- Determine conditions under which each alternative would win in the competition. Review the tables from Step A.
- Proceed by process of elimination. Eliminate all groups that do not strongly support major business objectives; those that remain will all meet a business requirement.
- Rank the remaining groups in each of the following categories on a scale of 1 to 5:

  Performance

  —*Revenue and cost*   The degree to which changing the process group will result in increased revenue and reduced costs (5 is great benefit)

  —*Competitive position*   The impact of the process changes on the competitive position of the business (5 is great benefit)

  Internal

  —*Organization*   Impact of changes in the processes on the organization structure and head count. Note this overlaps savings (5 is great positive impact).

  —*Infrastructure*   The effect of process changes on the infrastructure in terms of making the processes more responsive and effective (5 is great impact)

  External

  —*Customer*   The degree to which the process changes improve and enhance the relationship with customers

  —*Supplier*   The degree to which the process changes improve and enhance the relationships with suppliers

Project

—*Risk*   The overall risk in the project (inverse ranking here, 5 is low risk)

—*Elapsed time and overall effort required to carry out the process changes*   (Use inverse ranking here; 5 is low effort and short time)

You could substitute different criteria, but try to cover the same four areas.

You are now able to construct a graph similar to that in Figure 9-1. The axes of the graph are the criteria.

• Identify two different process groups that are winners, depending on which criteria are important. Alternatives are significant. They offer a way of dealing with involvement, commitment, and politics.

• Develop a scenario or model of what the business would look like if the changes each of the two process groups were carried out separately. This model is a representation of how the new process would work. It does not include details of infrastructure or organization.

Conduct the Evaluation

For each process group, write a list of bullet items that describe how you think the process group fares with specific criteria. This supports the defense of your later recommendation. Next, assign the numeric value to each criterion. The first graph you will show is Figure 9-2. This shows the rankings for each of two process groups A and B. This can sometimes be confusing due to overlap, so there is another chart, Figure 9-3, which combines all criteria in each area and assigns an overall rating.

The analysis of these charts should indicate two process groups that are most promising and one that is preferable.

Action 5: Define a First Scenario

With these two process groups identified, there is still further work. You want to be able to give a presentation and generate support. You need to show the audience how the new processes will work after the

Figure 9-2: Example of Process Groupings Evaluation

This graph, while similar to Figure 9-1, aids in the evaluation of groups using various criteria.

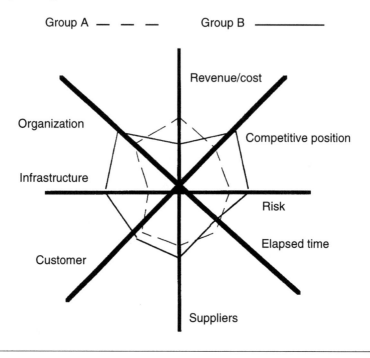

completion of the project. If you give people an idea of how the completed process will function, you will inspire belief in the benefits and analysis. To do this, create a scenario, which is a model or description of how the new process would work. You will refine the scenario created here later, when the new process is defined.

Action 6: Document the Selection

You will probably have to develop a report to support your selection of the process. In some cases, you can manage to avoid this effort and launch the next stage of the process improvement project through marketing and explaining the comparison tables and the scenarios.

Figure 9-3: Example of Combined Criteria Evaluation

Combining criteria into categories gives an overall evaluation of two or more groups.

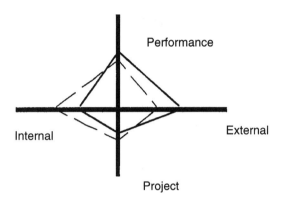

However, if you must write it up, minimize the amount of text. Avoid technical terms. Stick to terms commonly used in the business. Develop your exhibits first. These should be comparison tables and the steps involved in the existing and new process. Also, develop the project plan for the next stage of effort. This material can feed your presentation helping to ensure that presentation and report are consistent and mutually supportive. This will also save time.

Action 7: Begin to Identify Quick Hits

You want to identify quick hit opportunities that can be implemented in the short term as well as working on longer-term process improvement. Potential quick hits can come from processes that were rejected in terms of long-term improvement. In fact, this relieves pressure and prevents the dissatisfaction of people who wanted other processes to be selected.

MANAGEMENT PRESENTATION AND COST-BENEFIT ANALYSIS

After you have developed the scenario, construct the project plan as discussed in Chapters 1 and 2. You will be seeking approval for an assessment of external practices and technology and a detailed analysis later of the recommended process group. You are not yet asking for money to implement the plan. This is an important point, because the effort and cost here are far less than that required for implementation. You may even seek and get approval on a casual basis without a formal meeting.

Potential Management Issues

You are likely to run into several management questions and issues. Some of these are the following:

- **Assurance of the choice of process group**

  Accepting that management may perceive risk and uncertainty in a process improvement project, it is natural and important to reassure them. In addition to providing them with the analysis results and the plan, indicate what will happen if there is no action. (You will address this in the step on marketing.)

- **Concerns about processes that will not be improved**

  What will happen to the other processes? It is wise to develop an overall strategy for them. You have looked closely at strategies for organization and infrastructure, while little effort has been spent looking at what makes money and incurs cost—the business processes. Placing a business process in the context of an overall strategy is a good way to reassure people about the future of a process. Included in such a strategy are replacement, improvement, elimination, and rightsizing.

- **Concerns about staff and organization during the improvement process**

  Two actions should be taken to calm staff fears, which always arise. The first action is to have a project plan and documentation that focuses on improvement. This reveals what you will be doing. Second, write your approach with a focus on benefits that relate to saving paper, simplification, and better control. This can be part of the plan.

Management will begin to get concerned about costs, schedules, and benefits. Discussing the benefits is possible from the comparison tables. To discuss costs, gather costs and schedules of similar projects in the past. These may not fit the current situation exactly, but they will give management an idea of relative size. Management support here can be measured in terms of their interest in the project. Is it growing? Do they want more detail?

KEY QUESTIONS

How do you know if you are on the right track? Look at the process groups you have identified. If you made changes to a group, how would the organization and processes benefit overall? If you deleted a process from a group, what would be the impact?

Another test is to assess the level of interest in the project at the start of this step and at the end. The level should increase. It is in this step that you want to capture people's interest and imagination.

EXAMPLES

Monarch Bank

Monarch incorporated 30 processes. Several groups were defined as examples. The collection group (Collections) consisted of all collection systems across all products. The charge-off group (Charge-off) was defined in the same way. A third group consisted of processes that required substantial improved financial results (Financial): Collections, charge-off installment loans, credit card collections, and credit card application processing. A fourth group consisted of commercial lending (Commercial). This resulted in overlapping groups. To each group was added the letter generation, manual files, and customer contact processes for those processes.

Each of the four groups was a winner: Collections—performance; Charge-off—loss control; Financial—profitability; Commercial—political. Note the last one. Include a group of processes that corresponds to a politically potent organization. Failure to consider this may be costly in the future.

Comparison tables were then created. In Table 9-1, over half the entries are blank because the chart is processes vs. processes. Note that commercial has little in common with the others. Also, note that charge-off relates to collections because it follows collections in the natural flow of business.

Table 9-2 identifies four technologies: Distributed systems, client-server, electronic data interchange (EDI), and database management systems. Distributed systems are appropriate to several because charge-off, application processing, and collections can operate on separate computers linked to a mainframe computer. Due to flexibility requirements, client-server computing is appropriate for commercial.

Three elements of infrastructure appear in Table 9-3 (building location, network access, and proximity to the check processing area of Monarch). The network is important for three out of four groups. The others are less significant.

Table 9-1:
Process Group vs. Process Group for Monarch

This table shows the similarities between process groups. This helps show management which groups can be delayed for later improvement.

Process/Process	Collections	Financial	Commercial	Charge-off
Collections	–	3	2	4
Financial	–	–	1	2
Commercial	–	–	–	1

Table 9-2:
Process Group vs. Technologies for Monarch

This table reveals how the various process groups depend on technologies.

Process/ Technology	Distributed systems	Database management	EDI	Client- server
Collections	5	3	1	2
Financial	4	2	2	3
Commercial	2	5	3	3
Charge-off	4	2	1	3

Table 9-3:
Process Group vs. Infrastructure for Monarch

This table indicates how the process groups depend on the infrastructure.

Process/Infras	Network	Building	Proximity to check processing
Collections	4	2	3
Financial	4	1	2
Commercial	4	2	1
Charge-off	2	2	2

For external evaluation, the criteria was to retain the customer but replace the supplier with public image. The project criteria was risk and elapsed time. With the evaluation criteria defined, the graphs in Figures 9-4 and 9-5 could be constructed. These show that financial and collections are the two major groups. The tables indicate that they share some processes in common. Also, it is evident that charge-off can take advantage of the investment made to support these other groups.

Table 9-4:
Process Group vs. Organization at Monarch

This table can show impacts on multiple organizations of specific groups.

Process/ Organization	Installment loan	Credit card	Commercial	Real estate
Collections	3	3	2	3
Financial	4	3	1	2
Commercial	1	1	5	1
Charge-off	4	4	3	2

The scenario for Monarch's financial processes group focused on having online systems across areas of installment lending, credit card, and charge-off. In the development of the scenario, first the existing process was verified with the staff, along with the verification of associated issues. Next, the general new process was defined. The staff then reviewed this information. After the staff signed off, Monarch could proceed with the new process.

TRAN

At TRAN, processes were grouped by organizational function (operations, accounting, personnel, etc.). TRAN did not have the similarities of function that exist at Monarch, where processes could be grouped in terms of technology (for example—dependence on old computer systems). As with Monarch, additional processes were added, such as work based on electronic forms.

The process groups for TRAN were operations, processes that share the network, processes that share operations data, and accounting. The infrastructure included the network, mail system, and facilities. Technologies included wide area network, client-server computing, and fourth generation language.

Figure 9-4: Evaluation Graph for Monarch

This graph shows how various process groups compare on multiple dimensions.

Financial ━━━━━

Collections ─ ─ ─ ─

Charge-off ── ──

Commercial ────────

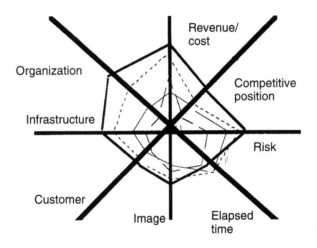

The two highest ranking groups were operations and the processes that could share the wide area network. This was due to the condition of the existing processes in operations and to the requirement for widespread connectivity in TRAN.

The scenario at TRAN emphasized the benefits of connecting all parts of TRAN with a network. With the network assumed, you can then give several examples of transactions. Three are a human resource transaction involving a performance review, a purchasing example, and the handling of a detour on a route.

Figure 9-5: Summary Evaluation Graph for Monarch

This graph can be used at the beginning of a management presentation, then supported with more detailed graphs and tables.

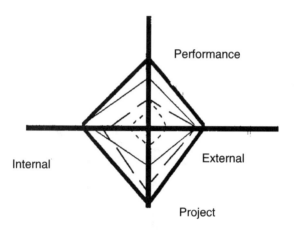

Stirling Manufacturing

Stirling Manufacturing focused on improving manufacturing performance. Processes could have been grouped that way. Another alternative was to group by management control (for example, processes that would contribute most to improved information and control). Another possibility was grouping processes by each area of the business.

At Stirling Manufacturing, the process groups were scheduling and project management, integration and testing, the processes of two organizations, and integrated manufacturing. Technologies included client-server computing, database management systems, access to databases, and EDI.

The two highest ranking groups were scheduling and integration and testing. Several parts of the scenario defined a new general scheduling process and explained how problem tracking would work in the new process.

GUIDELINES

- **Always focus effort on critical business processes.**

  Processes with immediate management interest can consume your focus. It is also easy to be sucked into a technology pit. Keep your focus on the key processes—those that contribute to revenue or have major costs.

- **Concentrate on processes that cross organizations and are not within a department.**

  Within a department, processes tend to have fewer benefits (due to the restricted scope of the processes). Taking on a process over several departments allows you to deal with a family of processes within those affected departments. Your work will have a larger impact.

- **Focus on processes that are stable. Long-time existence usually means that improvements are possible.**

  Stability helps in several ways. First, the process has been in use for some time. If you improve it, the new process will likely be there for some time so that you can recover the costs of your project. Second, the process probably has ad hoc ways of handling problems and issues. These give you process improvement opportunities.

- **Focus on processes that contribute to revenue, as they are often more important than those that contribute to cost.**

  Processes geared to revenue tend to be externally driven due to pressure from customers. Internal processes that are administrative are more difficult and less visible. Fixing a process that relates to revenue will tend to show faster business results.

ACTION ITEMS

1. Write down three critical processes. For each, identify what other processes could be grouped with it, based on the criteria in the chapter. Indicate the reason for including each in the group.

Also, indicate the strength of association on a scale of 1 to 5 (1 is weak affinity, 5 is strong affinity).

Key Process: _____

	Related Process	Reason	Association
1.			
2.			
3.			
4.			

Key Process: _____

	Related Process	Reason	Association
1.			
2.			
3.			
4.			

Key Process: _____

	Related Process	Reason	Association
1.			
2.			
3.			
4.			

2. Indicate the strength of relationship between organizations and candidate process groups using combinations of the following codes: O–organization owns the process group, U–organization uses the processes, I–organization is involved in the processes, N–not involved. This table helps to select the process group and

identify groups that impact multiple major divisions. Use the process vs. organization table from Step 1.

Organization   Group

3. Construct a table of process groups and systems and infrastructure in which the table entry is the extent to which the specific system or infrastructure element applies to the process group on a scale of 1 to 5 (1 is no relation, 5 is very dependent). This table indicates the scope of the infrastructure and systems you may have to change in business process improvement.

Process group   System or Infrastructure Element

4. Construct a graph like Figure 5-1 for your two main process group candidates. Alternatively, you can construct a bar chart in which each process group has a set of bars—one for each attribute.

5. Assess the degree of strength between the processes in a group. Construct a table in which the rows are the processes. The columns are organizations involved in the process, automated systems used in the process, issues involved in the process, condition of procedures and policies, volume of transactions, network, and infrastructure.

6. Compare your top two processes by isolating the key process in each group and comparing these with each other. Then correlate this with the group comparison of the previous steps.

CHAPTER 10

STEP C: ASSESS THE COMPETITION AND INDUSTRY

CONTENTS

10

STEP C: ASSESS
THE COMPETITION AND INDUSTRY

PURPOSE AND SCOPE

The primary objective in gathering external information is to obtain external information about the processes you are considering or have selected. This will support your efforts in developing a new process.

END PRODUCTS

Major end products of assessing the competition and industry are as follows:

Comparative tables   Specific tables will provide a good summary for management.

Graphs and tables on selected data   Use a few graphs or charts in your reports for clarity.

Comments and highlights on processes, issues, and use of technology   These comments should apply to the specific processes selected rather than to the business in general.

Database of source information   This will be useful in the long term as you move through the organization with other business process improvement projects.

Files of information providing more in-depth information than the database

RESOURCES

Initially, identify those who should become involved in a competitor and industry assessment. Verify that they can help you, then formulate the questions in some detail with them. This will encourage their participation and, ideally, their commitment.

Here are some categories of resources:

- **People who have outside contacts**

  Look to marketing, sales, and human resources. However, don't limit yourself to these departments. Consider the example of a major drugstore distributor. The company distributes drugs and other items to drugstores and retailers. The company managers decided to use employees as part of the intelligence and marketing effort. After the employees delivered the products, they reviewed the shelves not only for the company's products, but also for those of competitors. This information was sent back to the company. This effort contributed to the company's success.

- **Employees who have reputations as gurus within the company**

  These are people who know what is going on through reading and contacts. Identify these people early. Establish regular contact. In a bank, one collections supervisor belonged to several professional groups and had a wide range of contacts. He was not a star performer but he had a great deal of experience and was respected in the industry. Involving him in the process improvement not only helped the project, but gave him the recognition that he deserved.

- **People who can help you do the legwork on the project**

  Look for people who are inquisitive, are good problem solvers, and have outside interests. They may be avid readers, collect articles, and enjoy detective work and problem solving.

- **Suppliers and customers**

  Build up relationships with suppliers and customers. They can provide information on the industry and competition. Even if the information is not detailed, you will get their perspective. Suppliers and customers will tell you how the firm and selected processes are viewed and what they like and dislike.

- **Outside consultants**

   Firms offer industry-scanning services. Because they are not giving advice and direction, their liability is limited. But be careful. They may sell the same information to your competitors. Hire individuals as opposed to large firms; individuals provide accountability and access to a senior person with contacts.

APPROACH

Why Go Outside for Information?

Although most of your business process improvement effort will draw heavily on a company's internal processes, infrastructure, and organization, you should know what the industry and your competition are doing. You don't want to find out, after spending thousands of dollars on a new manufacturing process, that everyone else has leapfrogged you. For example, the founder of a major microcomputer firm invested some of his money in a company that made a programmable remote control device. His ego was such that he did not even consider the marketplace. After spending millions of dollars and building a prototype, he and his staff visited an electronics show. To their astonishment, they found many remote controls more sophisticated than his available there. He closed the company shortly thereafter. Thus, you collect information to avoid surprises.

There are also proactive reasons for collecting information. First, you may get ideas on how to do something better. Second, you might find out how to implement a new technology with less effort. Third, you can set standards that will have to be met. The changing nature of competition is another factor. Global competition has received much attention. You should know about new products, methods, and markets apart from your traditional base of business. Companies that do not have this knowledge sometimes find themselves locked into heavy competition.

Benchmarking

Benchmarking is a process for evaluating products, services, and business processes of an organization. It can be internally or externally based. Many view benchmarking as a continuous process that can improve business. There are several types of benchmarking, including the following:

- **Type 1: Internal Benchmarking**

  If an organization has several divisions in different locations that do the same or similar work, internal benchmarks can usually be determined. For example, profitability of divisions is one financial benchmark. Internal benchmarking is useful, but it lacks comparison to outside standards.

- **Type 2: Direct-Competitor Benchmarking**

  Another type of benchmarking considers only those competitors that sell to the same market segments. Retail firms and computer firms are two examples. One problem with this type of benchmarking is that it can be difficult to collect data on competitors in an ethical manner.

- **Type 3: Function Benchmarking**

  Function is the basis for the third type of benchmarking. It entails comparing your company to the leaders of specific functions. For example, if you want to evaluate customer service, warehousing, and logistics, find the best firms in each area and compare yours to theirs.

Benchmarking can be done on a continuous basis or on a one-time basis. In business process improvement there is less interest in continuous benchmarking than in working on a specific business process improvement project with deadlines and budgets. To save time, look only for information that pertains to your processes.

Benchmarking can support business process improvement in many ways: It can provide input for a planning process; help to determine forecasting; and be used to compare products and processes, derive new ideas, and set reasonable goals.

Why Don't Firms Go Outside More Often?

One reason firms don't engage in benchmarking more often is inertia. When you focus externally, you must cross a mental hurdle. People may question the value of the effort, as there appears to be no tangible internal product. The "not invented here" syndrome compounds this. If people didn't do it themselves, why should they consider it, just because some other company did? Most projects and activities focus inward on short-term requirements. Gathering external information tends to support long-term goals. Also, those who feel threatened by competition may prefer not to know more about it.

Additionally, people may not know how to go about collecting and analyzing information. It appears to be a formidable task when starting from ground zero. There is no model to follow. When you start collecting information, people may change the focus, which can make it a frustrating moving target.

The Nature of Competition Today

Most large companies have full-time staff and outside consultants doing competitive and technology assessments for their own and related industries. Numerous surveys and magazines offer comparisons and examples. In a recent survey, more than 450 magazines were found to carry such comparisons.

Wal-Mart is considered by many to be an example of a successful firm that has leveraged its investment in business processes to increase market share and profitability. Wal-Mart is somewhat unique because it addressed multiple processes at the same time. It addressed warehousing, ordering, receiving, sales, stocking of inventory, supplier relations, and accounting. Wal-Mart's purpose was to accelerate the flow of goods through its retail channel to the customers. By buying more goods at a faster pace, it obtained better prices and had a greater impact on suppliers. By selling more goods, Wal-Mart increased sales per square foot. The result is not only greater profitability, but the ability for Wal-Mart to expand rapidly into new areas by using the infrastructure and organization associated with its new processes.

Many other retailers have studied Wal-Mart to attempt to learn from this example. These firms, however, are not always successful.

One reason is reluctance to embrace so much change. For others, ingrained culture and rigid organizational structure prevent change. One firm lost more money after installing point-of-sale, electronic data interchange (EDI), and other technologies. The key is not technology but it is the process, and the firm did not change the process.

There are several lessons to be learned. First, you cannot ignore a successful company such as Wal-Mart if you are considering similar processes even if you are in a different industry. Second, these leader firms set standards and patterns of business. To ignore them is to risk disaster. Third, it takes more than simply installing some changes and technology to achieve success.

Communication of Findings

There is a tendency to tell people about your findings, especially when the data contradicts a previous position. Don't be tempted. You are unlikely to be successful if you attempt to copy and apply what you find directly to you. Also, avoid applying a solution. Instead, start building the following:

- Examples of success that have appeal and interest to people in your company
- Lessons learned about key issues relevant to your firm
- Statistical graphs and tables (even if they are only partially complete)

Action 1: Identify Information to Be Collected

Think of data collection as resembling a sieve or funnel. Start by collecting a wide variety of information related to the processes. Over time reduce the information that you actually use, while retaining and organizing the data you collect.

What information do you want to collect? Following is a list based on five common groupings. Note that this list is extremely ambitious. It is difficult to obtain some of the detailed information. In this situation, you must be willing to set your sights high and be satisfied with less. If you continue to collect information, you will gradually become more efficient and obtain valuable information.

- **Industry segment level**
  - —Financial health of segment
  - —Industry segment leaders and why they are in authority
  - —Trends in use of automation and technology
  - —Ratios and statistics for industry

- **Specific company**
  - —Financial information—revenue, costs, etc.
  - —Trends in the company
  - —Leading achievements
  - —Leading issues
  - —End products and services— features, cost, quality, variation, availability
  - —Customers and their perceived strengths
  - —Suppliers and their relationships
  - —Leaders and their characteristics
  - —Organizational structure, change, and status
  - —Infrastructure and its change and status
  - —What the company perceives as its strengths
  - —Specific process-related thrusts and strategies

- **Process**
  - —Process organization, distribution, centralization, and roles
  - —Changes in the process
  - —Degree of integration between processes
  - —Automation supporting the process
  - —Technologies that support modern versions of the process
  - —Perceived importance of the process to the firm and industry segment

- **Technology**
  - —Extent of specific technology in industry use
  - —Reported experience with technology
  - —Issues in implementing and using the technology
  - —Integrating the technology into the process
  - —Age of technology

—Competitive technologies and vendors

—Vendor characteristics

- **Country**

  —Leading companies by industry in country

  —Financial and demographic data and statistics

  —Specific laws and culture factors impacting processes

Examples of Data to Collect

Following are some examples of specific information that you might collect, along with potential sources:

- **Market share by area**

  Total unit sales and dollars (Annual reports and industry surveys)

- **Profitability**

  Return on sales, equity, and assets (Financial reports)

- **Product**

  Type, style, color/variety, warranties, price, discounts, quality—rework, yields, and errors (Magazines on products and marketing)

- **Research and development**

  Costs, cycle time, cost vs. revenue focus (Annual reports and magazines directed toward research)

- **Automation used by a company**

  Technical magazines using the company as an example

- **Labor**

  Cost as percentage of sales, work week and overtime, productivity—unit and revenue, mix of workers

- **Organization**

  Head count, layers, turnover (Outside reports with some information in annual reports)

- **Human resources**

  Benefits, bonuses, training (Human resource surveys)

- **Capital**

  Depreciation, lease, fixed asset turnover, maintenance, cost of capital (Standard financial reports)

- **Service**

  Complaints, response time, delivery speed, availability, order entry (Industry statistics)

- **Manufacturing**

  Outsourcing, EDI, JIT, locations, automation (Industry surveys)

- **Sales**

  Advertising, signage, promotion, sales force (Some financial data in annual reports and marketing and advertising magazines)

- **Information systems**

  Costs, head count (Surveys of industry use)

- **Policies**

  Depreciation, debt, dividend, financial, accounting, tax (Included in annual reports)

Action 2: Identify Sources of Information

National and International Firms

In order to search for appropriate firms, expand your horizon beyond local companies. Consider the following:

- **End products and customers**

  Who makes similar products? Who addresses the same type of customers?

- **Industry**

  Who is in the industry (*industry* is interpreted in a broad sense)?

- **Location**

  By regions of the world, who are leading firms with similar processes?

- **Suppliers and distributors**

  What can you learn from suppliers *to* you and customers or distributors *from* you?

Much has been written about the global environment. Information on foreign firms is widely available today. Contacts are frequent. The tide of information tends to stress the similarities around the world. However, exercise caution when selecting firms to consider in your assessment.

The international dimension adds complexity in the following ways:

- **The nature of the global corporation is more complex.**

  Structures of coordination, control, and organization differ widely. These differences are based on the environment of the countries in which a firm has a presence; they are also part of the outgrowth of the organizational culture.

- **Different industries place a different degree of importance on specific business factors.**

  Examples of these factors are flexibility in operations, control of risk, customer relationships on a global basis, supplier relationships, the extent to which the products are global, and joint resources and operations. Thus, comparing internationally across industries can be difficult.

- **The culture, regulations, and business environment of the country are reflected in information collected.**

  These factors have a major effect on the usefulness and applicability of the information.

Passive Sources

Libraries and computer networks are two examples of passive resources. In the past, libraries were often viewed as being limited in information, but with the advent of the Internet, web, networks, and CD-ROM databases, libraries with such resources can access much more data.

If you start your search at a college or university library, start with industry surveys and annual reports. Here is a partial list of items to consider:

- **Company-specific**
  - —Annual and quarterly reports
  - —Form 10-K (includes five years of information)
  - —State corporation filings, such as articles of incorporation
- **Government**
  - —Industrial Outlook, Department of Commerce
  - —National Technical Information Service (NTIS)
  - —National Institute of Standards and Technology
  - —State government records
- **Industry-specific**
  - —Trade groups (e.g., American Petroleum Institute, American Bankers Association)
  - —Encyclopedia of Associations
  - —World Guide to Trade Organizations
  - —Moody's various industry manuals
  - —Standard and Poor's Register of Corporations
  - —Business Rankings
  - —Registers of specific industries (e.g., manufacturing, energy, banking, and retailing)
- **Consultants and advisors**
  - —Nelson's Directory of Investment Research—investment analysts
  - —References of consultants and professionals

These resources can be found on the Internet or in the library. For specific industries, contact the relevant federal and state agencies that regulate or oversee them.

Look for periodicals and magazines that are good resources. A list of business-oriented publications can be found in the Appendix. The magazines *Information Week, Datamation,* and *CIO* offer surveys of firms and highlight leading firms in different industries. One article provided a ranking, total employees, total information systems employees, the information systems budget, the percentage involved in business process improvement, and the percentage involved in client-server computing for 500 companies.

Begin your search for additional publications with the following sources:

- CD-ROM periodical indices and summaries of articles in technical and business areas
- Business Periodicals Index
- Standard Periodical Dictionary
- Willings Press Guide for international sources

CD-ROM sources are particularly useful because they support key word searches and you can print out summaries. Also, they are usually free. Updates appear on a quarterly or annual basis.

After you have exhausted the library resources on your own, consult the reference librarian about specific questions. He or she may have suggestions about sources available at other libraries or different ways to online indices of libraries.

Online sources on the web may contain the most easily accessible information. However, you have to conduct a search of many sites to find useful information. Access references and articles through Internet or commercial online services. There are many different online databases. It takes quite a bit of time to find information and to become experienced in quick searches, so consider this only after you have exhausted library sources.

You might then move on to international information. Contact United Nations agencies, the Department of Commerce, securities brokerage houses, the International Trade Commission, or your city's Chamber of Commerce.

Active Collection of Information

Before you begin to collect data by telephone, electronic mail, and in person, organize the information you have already collected. Develop a list of specific questions for the active collection stage. Tailor these to specific companies and processes.

Begin with firms that are not direct competitors; for example, you might start with technology firms. Suppose that you have read an article about a success story in which a company used a specific technique or technology that provided benefits. Begin your information search by contacting the technology or consulting firm and see what information you can obtain. Explain that you are in the early stages of a business process improvement effort and that you are collecting information on business processes. Be sure to reference the article in your discussion. Ask the company's employee if he has a more detailed report. These people tend to be friendly, because you are a potential customer.

Once you have obtained sufficient information from these firms, begin researching suppliers and customer firms. Use employees from your company to obtain names of contacts. Again, the people you speak with should be friendly, because they already have an established business relationship with your organization.

The toughest source to tap is the competition. Contact names can be gathered through employees or through literature. When you call competitors, introduce yourself and state your purpose. Indicate that you wish no proprietary information. Follow up this call with a formal written request. Be sure to have internal management and your legal department review the letter. In your letter, focus on business processes. State that you are not interested in confidential product or manufacturing information. Follow up with telephone calls. This approach can also be used for other companies that are not direct competitors or companies that are in the same industry but in another country.

One approach is to enter an organization through a support organization, such as information systems, purchasing, or sales. People in these areas tend to be more open than people involved directly in production.

Visits to Companies

If you are fortunate, you will receive an invitation to visit one or more companies as a guest. At the end of the visit go over your questions and make sure you have the answers you need. Assume that you will not be able to return for some time. Follow up the visit with a thank you letter and an invitation for you host to visit you.

Visits provide not only an opportunity for direct observation but also a chance to meet with a variety of people in different departments. This gives you different points of view about the firm. Use these visits and contacts to establish a rapport with staff at the companies you contact. These contacts will be useful later when you have follow-up questions.

Caution about Sources and Information

Try not to jump to any conclusions from the information you have gathered. Some articles promote a product or technique. On visits you are likely to be shown the most favorable circumstances. If the company has problems or is very protective, your visit may occur when the plant is idle or running with little activity.

Example: Utility Company

Suppose that you work for a utility company and are worried about competition. Your industry is being deregulated, and you decide to investigate what other electrical and natural gas utilities are doing worldwide after deregulation. You decide to visit the library first. There you find standard financial and industry data and a range of technology initiatives tried by various firms. Next you contact other firms in the United States, which is relatively easy. The difficult part is finding the person in the company who could provide the information needed. Your initial contact is seldom the person with the information.

You collect and organize the information. The summary data is entered into a database. Once you print out the data, you can determine gaps in the information and the status of what has been collected.

Action 3: Organize the Information

Store and index articles using a simple alphabetical index of items and key words. Don't worry at this time about any duplications or ambiguity.

If you find information that cannot be copied, write it on standard notecards. You could enter everything into a computer, but this takes time and is inconvenient if you are in a library without a laptop computer or power outlet. Additionally, the process of data entry detracts from your focus on sources.

Use a computer to organize information once you have your notecards. Select multiple software packages for this task. Use word processing for standard text (as opposed to idea-type software), because eventually your report and findings will be prepared using word processing. Next, put tabular numerical data into a spreadsheet for graphics that you can later embed into the document. Enter information such as key quotes related to the subject, details of the sources, comments on trends, and notes on issues.

As you enter data, you will notice holes in the information. Start a list of data you wish to find. Keep this with you at all times. Contact the reference librarian as little as possible during the early stages of the data collection. When you have defined your list of items, you will be able to use the librarian's time most effectively.

Action 4: Detect Trends and Key Factors

Use the information to detect trends and key factors. Some of the major ones considered are the following:

- Process integration
- Emergence of dominant leaders in an industry segment
- Global firms with substantial consistent presence in different countries
- Centralized control and distributed responsibility
- Ability of suppliers to exert cost pressure on competitors
- Ability of customers to exert price pressure
- Ability of competitors to press advantage

Action 5: Develop Comparison Tables

From the data, build the following comparison tables:

- **Process Group vs. Competitive/Other Firms**

  This table displays in the rows the processes in the group you are considering. The columns are the names of various national, foreign, and international companies. Make the far left column your firm. The entry in the table is a rating of how you perceive the company is doing with respect to the process. Support this information and other tables by footnotes. Each footnote gives the source of the rating, a comment, or basis for inference.

- ## Competition/Other Firms vs. Internal Infrastructure

  This table has the companies listed in the rows. The columns can be a mixture of quantitative and descriptive information. For example, consider the following columns:

  —Investment in plant and equipment (rating of 1 is low and rating of 5 is high)

  —Cumulative investment in plant and equipment

  —Degree of centralization (rating of 1 equals highly centralized and rating of 5 equals highly distributed)

  —Industry rating of infrastructure through surveys.

  This table reveals the comparative investment that firms have undertaken. Footnotes could indicate specific projects that you have uncovered in the search.

- ## Competition/Companies vs. Information Systems

  The column headings in this table include information systems budgets, a mixture of information systems employees, a number of information systems employees, a ratio of information systems employees to total workforce, a ratio of information systems budget to sales, a ratio of information system budget to information systems employees, and a ratio of information systems budget to total workforce. This table reveals a comparison of information systems investment. If your firm falls at the extremes of the ratios, consider appropriate action.

- ## Competition vs. Industry Statistics

  This is a standard table drawn from industry averages. The columns include the industry measures. The entry is the value of the measure in terms of the specific company.

- ## Competition vs. Organization

  The columns in this table are characteristics of the organization, such as head count, head count trends, distribution of head count into production and support functions, and turnover.

- ## Competitors vs. Competitor Processes/Technologies

  This table should identify the key processes as columns. The ratings show how the literature and other sources rate the processes. Footnotes provide comments on sources and explain why they received the rating. For retail industries, consider using point-of-sale, EDI, Quick Response, scanning, dynamic store inventory, and supplier relationships. For insurance industries, consider using EDI, electronic funds transfer, distributed systems to agents, and business functions, such as application processing, servicing, payments, and claims.

You desire to make an impact on managers and staff, and these tables support a faster understanding. The competitive and industry information is intended to show shortcomings in the status quo and to generate enthusiasm about the business process improvement. If your firm is rated as a 2 and is the lowest in a row that has 4s and 5s, people will see the need for process improvement. Simple text may have little impact.

MANAGEMENT PRESENTATION AND COST–BENEFIT ANALYSIS

The costs associated with performing the external analysis include labor and access costs associated with obtaining and analyzing the information.

The benefits of the analysis come in reduced time required by the project. The analysis gives you a good idea of some of the business process improvement steps and actions that have proven to be successful. This saves time by eliminating the need for bad decisions and directions.

The analysis will impact the project in the following ways, once the project moves from analysis to future steps:

- **Costs**
  - —If the assessment provides positive results, there will be a desire to update it annually or at some periodic interval.
  - —The elapsed time to implement the new process is affected by the effort dedicated to the assessment. However, this time can be made up later by implementing the results of the assessment.

- **Benefits**
  - —The information gathered serves to narrow the focus of the business process improvement project and provide more

attention to the areas that will provide a competitive edge.

—The assessment provides information on tools and techniques that will reduce the cost of evaluating other tools and techniques (i.e., you can use proven methods).

—The measurements of the competition and industry can be useful later in measuring the business process improvement work.

When you present these tables, don't mix the presentation with information on processes and other activities. Tables tend to have a major impact, so don't dilute that effect with other information. In one situation, management was hostile regarding business process improvement. When management saw the tables and heard what was behind the numbers, they were transformed into supporters.

In developing the end products, circulate a draft of the tables and graphs with dummy or partial data and get people's reactions. You want them to become involved and understand what they will see later. When they finally see the end product, they will focus on the data. They may also suggest other graphs and charts.

Keep the number of graphs to less than 20 to prevent information overload. Keep a few good charts in reserve to use later, if necessary.

Focus on presentations, as opposed to reports. Reports tend to be dry and go unread. Put the chart on the right page and the text of bulleted highlights on the left side. This side-by-side presentation is effective. When presenting, use two overhead projectors.

The final presentation to management for the industry assessment can employ the following outline:

- Executive summary: Key findings and action items to pursue
- Purpose and scope of the assessment
- Comparison tables of the assessment
- Graphs and tables related to industry and competition
- Cost and benefit analysis

KEY QUESTIONS

What are the key points you have learned from the external industry assessment? From the information you have collected, choose an example or two that you could present to management. How do these examples apply to your processes?

EXAMPLES

Monarch Bank

Monarch started gathering external information after the process group was selected. External experience and competition, as well as internal factors, helped identify the process group and provided contacts for later work in the project. The information collected at the start of the project indicated that while some firms had made advances in collections, none had an integrated solution. This encouraged management because it showed that they were innovative in thought and that the idea went beyond an extension of what others had done. Five other banks were lined up who would share information on collections. This led to a mini benchmarking effort that continued for five years.

Petroleum/Energy Company

Using data from the American Petroleum Institute as a start, the Petroleum/Energy Company then collected additional data and created comparative tables. The information was used to support systems initiatives. When the company lost several offshore leasing bids due to poor technology, the information was employed directly to more than double the investment in exploration systems and processes.

TRAN

Survey information on other transportation districts was available, but this was of limited value to TRAN because of the similarity of the organizations. A new initiative was made to go beyond the industry segment and make comparisons based on best practice. This was successful because it provided management and staff with a new perspective and resulted in a change of spending priorities.

Stirling Manufacturing

Stirling's experience was similar to TRAN's. Using information from different firms in various industries, a model of the ideal processes and results was created for Stirling. This was an eye opener because it demonstrated how much improvement was possible.

GUIDELINES

- **Measure yourself not by the volume you have collected, but by the holes in the information that remain.**

  Use this very demanding standard to evaluate your work.

- **Subscribe to magazines that are free to qualified subscribers.**

  Hundreds of magazines available to people in various industries. This can turn out to be a steady mine of information. You will have to fill out a qualification form that indicates your potential as a customer to advertisers.

- **Things are not what is stated or what they seem.**

  Do not simply accept what you are given and write it down as fact.

- **An academic research approach to gathering information will take too long.**

  Don't look to corroborate all of the information. This is too time-consuming. Get going and gather more data on key issues and trends.

- **Use the information as a political tool during the assessment to gather support directly for change.**

  You are unlikely to effect change, but you can expect rising awareness of the issue. You will gain more support for the planning process as a by-product.

ACTION ITEMS

1. Develop a list of companies or organizations that are leaders in your industry nationally and internationally. Next, develop a list of firms that are innovators and examples for your critical business processes. You can use the literature to identify the firms and then access their annual reports.

   For each firm develop the following for the past three years:
   - Size of the firm in sales
   - Net profits
   - Capital investment
   - Earnings per share
   - Debt
   - Number of employees
   - Sales per employee
   - Expenditures on automation (if available)

   In the annual report, to what does the company attribute success? How do the company's business objectives match up to those of your organization?

2. Define categories for your data collection. Examples are specific business processes, types of computer systems, and industry type. A notation can have multiple categories or types. See the following item.

3. Prepare notecards with the following information:
   - Source—publication, volume, issue, date, pages
   - Title
   - Author
   - Type—category
   - Quotes or statistics
   - Comments

4. Prepare a table of process groups vs. firms. The entry in the table is the rating you give to that firm for that process.

PART III THREE

TECHNOLOGY AND PROCESSES

CHAPTER 11

STEP D: EVALUATE
TECHNOLOGY POSSIBILITIES

CONTENTS

11

STEP D: EVALUATE TECHNOLOGY POSSIBILITIES

PURPOSE AND SCOPE

Your goals in evaluating infrastructure are the following:

- Assess the current infrastructure supporting the process group.
- Examine opportunities for new infrastructure and technology using external information.
- Identify the changes that are most appropriate.
- Develop a scenario for a future infrastructure.

Note that, in parallel, you are examining the process in detail. If you complete the infrastructure assessment prior to the internal process analysis, you can revisit and refine it later. You are obtaining information on infrastructure while examining what competitors are doing (as discussed in the preceding chapter). Organizational issues supporting the process will be considered when you examine the process in detail (see the next chapter).

The scope of this step includes internal technology and infrastructure; potential new technology that may benefit our processes and is likely to be available; and technology and infrastructure used by competitors, other firms in the same industry segment, and other firms and organizations who are performing the same functions.

END PRODUCTS

The major results of this step are the following:

- **Comparison tables that assess the current technology and infrastructure and the potential of new technology and infrastructure for improvement.**

These comparison tables make a sharp distinction between the current infrastructure and the potential infrastructure.

- **A scenario for how new technology and infrastructure would work together to support the processes better than the current technology and infrastructure do.**

  This gives management and staff a picture of how the entire puzzle of technology and infrastructure can be assembled to help the process.

RESOURCES

You will rely on a variety of internal and external resources to perform this step. Internally, you will rely on technical staff to provide information about the infrastructure. Externally, you will rely on library sources, databases, vendors, and trade and industry information. You want to draw on a limited number of resources due to limited time. However, you want to allow people in the organization with technical knowledge to have input into the work.

APPROACH

Significant process change often depends upon modifications or enhancements to the infrastructure that supports the processes. A process exists within the infrastructure and depends on the infrastructure for its performance—availability, reliability, speed, cost, etc. If the infrastructure is shaky or is deteriorating, the processes can quickly deteriorate. Many people restrict their attention to technology. However, buildings, telephones, facilities, and other aspects of infrastructure often are equally important. In one project in a department, furniture changes and additional chairs were significant. Moving several groups to adjacent locations was also effective.

Infrastructure impacts the functioning and morale of an organization. If an organization is divided geographically, management and coordination are made more difficult. Similarly, specific problems with utilities can affect the organization's opinion about technology and its reliability.

Managers often separate the infrastructure from the process. They do not control the infrastructure, so they do not request improvements. Some managers treat infrastructure as overhead—the less spent on it the better. However, when the infrastructure inhibits the process, the impact may be severe. Morale may be low if staff members believe that poor working conditions reflect management's assessment of the importance of the process. When the smooth performance of the steps of a process is inhibited, there is an excuse for poor performance. You may have heard, "I was late with the work because of the problem in finding parking," or "The network was down so we couldn't do our work."

Intelligent changes to infrastructure can result in substantial improvements that are cost-effective, since the cost of the infrastructure change can be amortized across an extended period. The employees who perform the process increase their productivity. They also have fewer excuses for poor work. Physical bottlenecks and interfaces can be improved.

Pay attention to process impact when you make infrastructure changes. You can go overboard on infrastructure changes. You can paint, fix up, move, and build to the point of disrupting the process during this work. The process will not necessarily be improved.

Carry out changes to infrastructure with a strategy in mind. Otherwise, later improvements can undermine earlier improvements. A street system is a good example of this. A city will tear up and repave a street. Then, a week after the repaving, the street is torn up again for water main work. Of course, when the water main work is completed, the street will be patched, but it is never the same as complete repaving.

Technology

Technology is a central part of the infrastructure and will be discussed throughout this chapter. The obvious role of technology is associated with computers and communications, but technology encompasses much more. Many pieces of equipment have embedded technology, and technologies are associated with the nature of the business process. Computer-aided engineering, test equipment, vehicle repair equipment, and vehicles are just a few examples. As you have defined an overall infrastructure architecture, you can also define a technology architecture.

Technology categories include embedded technology (computers to make devices smarter), manufacturing and components, operating systems, hardware, database management systems, intelligent buildings, software development, client-server systems, data communications and networks, management issues, application software (several categories), image, decision support/artificial intelligence, GIS/GPS (Geographic Information Systems/Geographic Positioning Systems), and graphics/CAD. You can add and delete categories from time to time.

Any technology requires support. It may require operating support (it cannot run without help). It may need maintenance. Periodically, it may have to be upgraded (enhanced). The technology may interface and integrate with other technologies. It must be capable of being monitored, measured, and managed. As an example, consider an electronic mail system. It runs on a network. It must interface to the network, the network operating system, hardware, and the users of the software. It may require an interface with other types of software, such as other external mail systems. The network, of which the electronic mail system is now a part, must be monitored and managed. This example shows many interfaces and a degree of integration.

Technology moves through stages, from a raw product to a part of an integrated system. Table 11-1 presents a view of these stages. The location of the technology in the diagram often indicates whether it is complete and sufficiently mature.

Technologies can be classified into four areas. A technology is backbone if you rely on it constantly. Your business processes may find it essential. Your computer network or a manufacturing system are part of the backbone. Technology is considered as being niche if it fills a limited, very specific need for some amount of time. A specific desktop publishing system from an obscure firm is an example. A technology is marginal if its impact is limited (hence, so is its value). Premature technologies are those that lack support structure or completeness. The first hand-held computers (personal digital assistants) fit into this category.

Financial and operational characteristics of the firm behind the technology are important in technology assessment. So is the ques-

Table 11-1: Sequence in Technology

This chart shows how raw materials translate into finished products and systems. This chart can be used to explain the relevance and applicability of specific technology to processes.

Raw materials (e.g., chips, displays, antennae)

Components (e.g., disk drives, mother boards, radar)

Products (e.g., computers, radar)

System (e.g., accounting software, manufacturing software)

Integrated system and process

tion of whether the technology is part of the company's core strategy. Alternatively, is it just a niche product that later may not be enhanced or expanded? Is it the first in a series of products? If so, you may be at risk since the product line may be canceled if sales goals are not met.

Action 1: Collect Information on the Current Infrastructure

Begin by considering the current infrastructure. Always note the following:

- Physical location of all groups working with the processes
- Condition of their workplace in terms of space and specific location in a building
- How the process proceeds physically through the space

- The proximity of the managers or owners of the process to the process itself
- The current voice telephone system
- The current technologies in place and their structure and organization
- The condition of supporting equipment
- The support that the infrastructure receives
- The architecture—how the parts of the infrastructure come together.

As you gather this information, ask people what would be improved if the infrastructure were modified. You might also ask which improvement would be most helpful.

While this action may seem simple, it is valuable for the following reasons:

- The process depends on the infrastructure.
- Infrastructure, as compared to process steps, politics, and organization, is an area where money talks. That is, improvement can result from the expenditure of money.

The internal assessment provides a list of issues to be addressed and identifies the major infrastructure components relevant to the process.

Tips on the Internal Assessment

The infrastructure assessment is based on internal and external information. Pursue gathering information in both areas in parallel. To begin, make a list of infrastructure items that apply to the process today. In a typical organization, much of the technical infrastructure should exist in documents. Table 11-2 lists potential infrastructure components. For each relevant item you will want to know the following information:

- The current state in terms of operation
- The performance of the item

Table 11-2:
Examples of Technical Infrastructure Components

Within each category of infrastructure, the next level of detail is listed to help you define your architecture.

Mainframe/Minicomputer

Hardware type

Operating system

Online systems monitor and control software

Network utilities

Network management software

Database management systems

Fourth generation languages

Languages and compilers

Software development tools

Software configuration management tools

Security software

Wide area network

Transmission/cabling

Network operating system

Network utilities

Communication protocols

External communication protocols

Network management software tools

Network hardware (hubs, routers, bridges, etc.)

Network software

Test and monitoring equipment and software

Local area networks

File server hardware

Network operating system

Network cabling

Network protocols

Network utilities
Database server
Database server operating system
Network interface cards (NIC)
Client-server software

Workstation

Hardware
Network interface
Operating system
Microcomputer software
Client software

- Existing problems and issues that are known but have not been addressed
- Recent actions taken to fix or improve the situation.

This is a view of the infrastructure itself. Also look at what supports the infrastructure. You might consider some or all of the following:

- What is the recent history of work on infrastructure?
- What has been the extent of rework or failure to pass inspections and tests?
- How are priorities set for work assignments? Are priorities based on process or organization benefit?
- What is the process for requesting, approving, monitoring, and evaluating work?
- How has the level of work changed in volume and nature in the past two years?
- What outside management and support contracts are in place?

Gather this information by checking documents on file and, more importantly, by direct observation. When you are reviewing the process (as discussed in the next chapter), observe how the staff and process interact and depend on the infrastructure.

A two-step approach is recommended. First, observe the process passively. Second, interview people involved in the process. During interviews, ask what people would do about the infrastructure. People often take it for granted and have no ideas. Make suggestions, such as fixing up facilities or modernization. This will likely lead them to give more information.

Action 2: Determine Opportunities Regarding Infrastructure

Identify opportunities to improve infrastructure by looking outside the organization. Sources of information includes those identified in the previous chapter (competitors, industry surveys, literature). To these add visits to trade shows and contact with vendors. Opportunities range from new products and services, to systems and technology, to new methods for supporting a process.

Sources of Information: Magazines and the Web

Assemble articles and go through them. Include early articles so that you can see trends. You seek to understand how a technology works from a high-level perspective. Gather information on the advantages and disadvantages of a technology, as well as what competitors exist. Determine the state of the technology, whether it has potential for your organization, and the extent of its applicability.

Sources of Information: Benchmarking and Competitive Assessment

In the previous chapter you covered the steps in understanding the activities in the industry and how competitors carry out processes similar to ours. You not only can gain knowledge of what they are doing, but to what effect. You would like to have their lessons learned from a specific technology or infrastructure idea. Of course, this is very difficult to obtain because it represents proprietary information.

Consider approaching contact vendors who supplied the technology to the competition. Ask them for contacts for lessons learned in implementation and operation. This information is invaluable in reducing your learning curve and avoiding blind alleys.

The Role of Suppliers

In the past, the roles of the suppliers of the technology and infrastructure were limited to providing information and supporting their products through installation and operation. With today's more complex technology, this limited role is not practical. You rely on suppliers and vendors for technical information and support. To an extent, you also rely on their advice related to the appropriateness of their products to your situation.

Here are some of the tasks suppliers could perform to assist you in determining infrastructure opportunities:

- **Provide relevant technical information about the product.**

  Provide the supplier with sufficient information to judge which product version and information best fits your needs.

- **Provide references, lessons learned, guidelines, and other management type of information about the product.**

- **Participate to a limited extent in explaining how you could use their product in your processes.**

  This requires a general understanding of the processes and infrastructure.

- **Supply consulting support in determining benefits, issues in implementation, and determination of exact features required.**

  These roles can only be effective with information-sharing among suppliers and the organization. There is some risk that a supplier might use this information later, but in most situations the risk is minimal. After all, you will be changing the processes.

Action 3: Determine How Infrastructure Can Support Processes

Infrastructure support can take several forms. First, the infrastructure can provide the environment within which the staff performs the process. Buildings and furniture are examples. Second, the infrastructure can provide the means of performing the work. A telephone system is an example of this. Third, infrastructure such as a computer system can do some of the work in the process. Each of these increases the role of the infrastructure in the performance of the process.

Try asking what the ideal infrastructure would be. The answer you come up with will point to the ideal environment for the new business process.

Action 4: Narrow the Range of Alternative Technologies

To see the potential of specific technology, assume that the maximum effort and options of the technology are available and implemented within the process. Develop a technology assessment of the maximum that technology could do for the process.

Avoid technologies for which people emphasize standards. This may mean that there are no agreed-upon standards. The lack of standards or warring groups advocating different standards point to incompatibilities between different versions of the products. Two examples are EDI and the operating system UNIX. Both technologies suffered from a lack of standards.

Discard technology ideas that have some of the following characteristics:

- Only a few companies use the technology. Each candidate technology has a target audience. If a substantial number of companies are avoiding a technology ask why. Besides the potential existence of problems, this technology will give you few lessons learned.

- The technology or infrastructure will require too many resources for implementation.

- The new technology or infrastructure is counter to part of your architecture and standards that do work.

- The learning curve and time to gain proficiency are too long to be feasible.

- Integration with existing technologies and infrastructure is problematic.

Also beware of a new technology that is generating much excitement. Excitement is in no way equivalent to results. Look further than surface enthusiasm to see whether the technology would be effective in your company.

Group the technologies or infrastructure ideas that now remain. These groups will be useful because it is likely that you will want to select and implement more than one change. The groups will allow you to implement a set of changes over time that will improve the processes.

There are several ways to group technologies, including the following:

- Those that use the same area of infrastructure
- Those that will be supported by the same organization
- Those that impact the same processes or process steps
- Those that overlap with the same parts of the architecture

Action 5: Define the Infrastructure Scenario

To organize and structure all of the information gathered, develop a scenario. An infrastructure scenario should cover components, architecture, and support structure. Specify all of the major components of the candidate infrastructure. Include elements of the current infrastructure that remain and new elements in a candidate infrastructure.

Define how these components go together and how they relate to each other. This is the architecture.

The architecture must be supported. Specify the composition and organization of the support structure for the infrastructure and architecture.

To gain practice and useful information, develop a scenario for the current infrastructure. This will provide a useful means for comparing the effects of potential changes. Keep in mind that changing infrastructure takes time. Such changes require more than just planning, getting approval, and doing the work. Permits and permissions as well as legal agreements may be needed. These items tend to stretch out projects. Be realistic in your scenario about the extent of change that is practical in a limited amount of time.

Action 6: Map the Scenario Against the Current Process

Mapping the scenario against the current process will indicate relevance of the changes to the current process. (At this point, it does not indicate the true benefit. That will come later after you have developed a definition of the new process.) Note that you want to have an idea of the available technology and infrastructure for the new process. You will be embedding the technology and infrastructure in the new process. Here are two ways of mapping or developing the relationship:

- **Process steps vs. architecture**

  Specify what elements of the architecture support specific process steps.

- **Issues and problems with current process that are infrastructure-related**

  Will changes to the infrastructure by themselves alleviate some of the issues faced by the organization, relative to the current process?

Action 7: Develop Comparison Tables

These comparison tables will help in evaluating, selecting, and getting consensus on which changes to infrastructure and technology are most appropriate to your organization. The tables are based on the following variables:

- **Process group**

  The group was identified in Step B. This is the list of individual processes.

- **Current infrastructure**

  The elements are the key infrastructure components that have been identified as issues during the assessment.

- **Candidate infrastructure**

  Also developed in this chapter, this is the scenario of the new infrastructure.

- **Technology**

  This is the list of either current or candidate technologies.

- **Architecture**

  These are the components that hold the infrastructure and technology together.

- **Degree of automation**

  This is subjective; it identifies the extent to which individual steps in a process are automated.

These factors now can be employed to create a new series of tables. Table entries are on a scale of 1 to 5 where 1 is low and 5 is high. The tables are as follows:

- **Processes vs. Candidate Infrastructure**

  The rows are the processes in the group. The columns are the elements of the candidate infrastructure. Specific columns should include all changes. The entry in the table is based on the degree to which the infrastructure element supports the process. This table indicates the degree of process fit.

- **Current Infrastructure vs. Candidate Infrastructure**

  Rows and columns must contain corresponding elements. The entry in the diagonal of the table indicates the degree of change or improvement. The off-diagonal elements indicate the extent of compatibility (or difficulty of interface). This table indicates the degree of technology or infrastructure fit.

- **Candidate Infrastructure vs. Technology**

  The rows are the elements of the candidate infrastructure, and the columns are the new and old technology to be used. The table entry is the extent to which the infrastructure depends on the specific technology. What fits?

- **Organization vs. Infrastructure**

  This can be two tables—one for the current and one for the future infrastructure. The rows are the organization groups and the columns are elements of infrastructure. The entry is the extent to which the organization uses or will use the infrastructure. Identifying who uses what is valuable in marketing to see who will benefit from infrastructure changes.

- **Candidate Infrastructure vs. Architecture**

  The rows are the elements of the new infrastructure. The columns are the main components of the architecture. The entry is the degree of fit between the architecture and infrastructure.

- **Architecture vs. Technology**

  This is an important technical table. The architecture is the structure of the technology. The key elements of architecture (e.g., wide area network, local area network) appear as rows. The columns are the technology identified in the assessment. The entry in the table is degree to which the technology is critical to the architecture. (Or, which technologies are you dependent upon for success?)

Note that you can expand to additional tables as you consider the current process and formulate the new process. Whether you construct these tables is not important. What is important is that you compare the entities defined in the tables, because infrastructure changes cost money. Prepare a compelling argument so that you can obtain approval.

MANAGEMENT PRESENTATION AND COST–BENEFIT ANALYSIS

Keep in mind that you have been working on three interrelated activities—competitive and industry assessment, infrastructure assessment, and evaluating the current process and organization. In each area, the goal is not only understanding what issues and problems need to be addressed, but also what changes are possible and what benefits might accrue.

The presentation to management will focus on the potential for infrastructure and technology improvement. You want to get management excited about this potential. You also want management to understand the limitations with some technology that is premature or that has not proven itself.

Use the tables and scenario described in this step. You can add a list of benefits claimed from the infrastructure and technology, which is based on what others have cited. You can also add a rough estimate of costs, though you do not have sufficient information to supply detailed costs. Give costs in terms of the order of magnitude.

KEY QUESTIONS

Did you get your point across to management? Do managers understand the dependence of the process on the infrastructure? Do they understand what will happen if the infrastructure is not repaired, but the process is improved?

Do you understand why each technology issue is important? Have you found the root cause of the technology issues, or are you at the symptom layer? That is, if you fix the problems you have listed, is the problem actually fixed? To test this, construct a table in which the columns are issues, symptoms of issues, impacts on processes, and effects on processes if the infrastructure is improved. This table may be useful in your presentation to management.

EXAMPLES

Monarch Bank

The process group covered collections in installment loans and credit cards. Observations on the infrastructure supporting these processes were as follows:

- Collectors worked in individual offices where they could observe or help customers easily.

- The charge-off group and the collections group for installment loans were located in different cities.

- Staff members had available only a few terminals to check on accounts. They waited in line for access.

- The telephone system worked but had too few lines. Customers calling in often got a busy signal. Collectors attempting to call out were sometimes blocked.

- The architecture supporting the processes was weak, in that the systems did not work closely with steps in the process. Moreover, failure occurred in the interfaces between some of the parts (communications systems, for example).

These issues had not been fixed, because people took them for granted. Morale was quite low, and staff members had complaints
With these problems, the scenario for the future infrastructure needed to address a series of location, technology, and office-level infrastructure issues. The winning scenario consisted of the following:

- The organizations were first semicentralized and then centralized in one location. Semicentralization allowed staff to keep in touch with customers at a regional level. This interim configuration provided a smooth transition to the most cost-saving alternative—centralization.

- The charge-off unit was physically relocated next to the collections area.

- A more modern telephone system was implemented, along with specific features related to incoming call identification (ANI—automatic number identification). A voice response system was also added for incoming calls.

- The office layout was totally modified so that collections was performed in one large open area with conference/training rooms and management offices on the side of the room.

- New hardware, software, and network were identified and acquired to support collections and charge-off. The architecture appears as in Table 11-3.

- The information systems organization was distributed with staff permanently affixed to the collections area.

Tables 11-4 and 11-5 give two of the tables and comments for process vs. candidate infrastructure and organization vs. candidate infrastructure, respectively.

TRAN

Some of the infrastructure issues at TRAN were the following:

- The staff was spread across four locations. Most processes crossed at least two locations.

- There were no networks (local area or wide area). Data communication lines were limited. This, in turn, limited the number of terminals that could be used.

- All PCs were stand-alone, so each required a printer. A variety of software programs was in use. Each human–computer interface was unique.

Table 11-3: Monarch Bank Architecture

This is the Monarch Bank architecture after business process improvement. It indicates how processing is divided or distributed between mainframe and minicomputers.

Mainframe computer

Loan accounting

Demand deposit (checking)

ATM system

Accounting Place hold on accounts

Delinquent accts. Promise to pay current on bill

Minicomputer system/network

Collections-interface to mainframe

Collections- online system

Charge-off/recovery online system

Electronic mail

Voice Telephone

System

Workstation/telephone

Automatic dialing of customer

Routing of incoming calls to proper collector

Table 11-4:
Process vs. Candidate Infrastructure—Monarch Bank

This table rates some of the technology to the processes.

Process/ Infrastructure	Mini- computer	Voice telephone/ Dialing	E-mail	Link to Accounting
Inquiry	5	3	1	3
Initial collections	5	4	2	4
Collections	5	5	3	4
Charge-off/Recovery	5	2	4	5

Critical functions are the minicomputer for the online system and access to the host computer data. Having this in place, the functions with lower values come into play. The concept in this example of architecture is to indicate which of the infrastructure components are critical and which can be added on with limited cost.

Table 11-5:
Organization vs. Candidate Infrastructure— Monarch Bank

This table indicates how the infrastructure supports the organization within Monarch Bank.

Organization/ Infrastructure	Mini- computer	Voice telephone/ Dialing	E-mail	Link to Accounting
Collections	5	4	3	3
Charge-off	4	3	3	5
Skip tracing	4	1	5	3
Clerical support	4	2	4	4

Skip tracing here is the tracking down of delinquent customers. This example indicates that the online system and host access benefits all parts of the organization.

- The voice telephone switching system was ancient. Several locations were not tied into the switching equipment.
- Cabling in several buildings had been without inspection. It was unreliable.
- Facilities for the disposal of motor oil and cleaning vehicles were ancient.
- TRAN maintained five different vehicle types. Each vehicle required different parts, as well as mechanics trained for the specific vehicle type.

It is interesting to note that the problems in this example were not computer-related. Standardizing on fewer types of vehicles turned out to be a big money saver.

It was evident that TRAN required major changes. A number of small changes were formulated and evaluated. These failed because they did not yield major benefits. TRAN needed to change its organization culture; infrastructure changes were a means to support this transition. (See Tables 11-6 and 11-7.) The major infrastructure changes were as follows:

- Consolidation of all administrative units into one building, reducing the number of sites by three
- Establishment of local and wide area networks across TRAN
- Migration from proprietary obsolete mainframe hardware to an open environment (UNIX)
- Acquisition of software packages and tools for the network (electronic mail, electronic fax, electronic forms, and groupware)
- Downsizing of information systems and general services organizations and the outsourcing of a number of routine activities

Stirling Manufacturing

A review of Stirling's infrastructure revealed a number of problems:

- Some groups were located in distant, old buildings. The time required to move about in one building by elevator was excessive.

Table 11-6:
Current Infrastructure vs.
Candidate Infrastructure—TRAN

This table compares the current infrastructure to the candidate or potential infrastructure/

Current/ Candidate	Future locations	Network- based PC network	Future applic. systems	Future software tools
Current locations	2	1	3	2
Host based terminal network	1	1	1	1
Current application systems	3	2	3	2
Current software tools	2	2	3	2

The low values in the table indicate that the new architecture is significantly different from the existing architecture. A table such as this can help to explain to non-computer–oriented managers the extent of the changes required.

- One building had no convenient parking.
- The managers for the staff doing the process were located in a building four miles away.
- The data network supporting the systems was unreliable. It was typically out of service for an hour a day.
- Offices had not been painted for more than eight years and paint was peeling from the walls. Hallways were dimly lit.
- People who performed the process were spread across three floors.
- There was no conference room for meetings. Staff meetings to discuss process were held in small offices or in hallways.

Table 11-7:
Architecture vs. Technology—TRAN

This table ranks the technology in terms of the architecture for TRAN.

Architecture/ Technology	UNIX minicomputer	PCs linked to LAN	GIS data bases
Integrated wide area network	4	5	2
Open systems	5	3	2
Connectivity	4	5	3

Only a few parts of the architecture and several technologies have been identified. GIS (Geographic Information Systems) are used by a relatively small number of users so that their rating is lower. This chart can help show which technologies are critical to the architecture.

- The few microcomputers used in the process were more than eight years old. Secretaries, on the other hand, had the latest equipment.

- The software to support the process was so old and difficult to use that an expert was required. Data was always inaccurate and late.

The staff reaction was not unexpected. "They show how much they care by the condition of this building." "If they were interested in what we do, they would give us the tools to do the job." "They only care about their executive offices."

Stirling was faced with several insurmountable problems. It was impossible to move or make major changes to a manufacturing building. Minor changes and repairs were completed. Additional parking was created. Here are some of the technologies implemented:

- Extensive local and wide area network for 12 buildings
- Electronic mail for general communications

- Client-server system for management of work
- Groupware for tracking open issues

The effort was supported by extensive software training and support.

GUIDELINES

- **Be wary of just-announced technology.**

  Technology requires a support structure, which takes time to build. Seasoning is often necessary to work out its problems and errors. Time also allows users to gain experience. If a technology is too new or is complex, articles are necessary to explain what the technology is and how it differs from other products. Be cautious about investing in a technology that is featured in articles. Many of these articles are placed by the developers of the product.

  New technology finds its natural level through a combination of marketing and customer acceptance. As a technology emerges, the attention moves from definition and standards to guidelines on how best to use it. Organizations receiving benefits will start discussing the technology application and benefits.

- **To assess the benefit of technology, assume that you have to complete the process with no technology.**

  The benefit of the technology is often best seen when the process with and without the technology are compared. This emphasizes the benefits.

- **You don't need a deep understanding of the candidate technology.**

  The time and effort required to deal with the detail diverts you from important issues. Being involved in detail places you at the wrong level. You begin to think too technically about the technology.

- **Look for structure behind the technology.**

  Behind almost all technologies there is a structure. This structure is composed of the technology components, service, and support. The quality of a technology is directly related to the quality of the structure.

- **The largest hidden costs of infrastructure are maintenance and support.**

  Parts of the infrastructure become obsolete; other parts deteriorate with use and time.

- **Technology and new infrastructure should enhance, not replace, the new process.**

  It is important to place infrastructure and technology in perspective. Both support processes; neither replaces the process. Avoid the temptation to be diverted into interesting technical and infrastructure questions.

ACTION ITEMS

1. List the top five infrastructure improvements that would benefit the processes. This will help you focus on which changes have the greatest potential.

2. You have identified several candidate technologies. First determine how these technologies relate to each other. In the table below, write the technologies in the rows and columns. Since this table is symmetric, you only need to fill out half of the table. For each entry use the following codes: N–no connection; M–must have both technologies (row and column); B–beneficial to have both technologies, but not essential; C–conflict between the technologies so that you must choose.

Technology/Technology

3. What are the potential benefits of the technology to the group of processes you have selected? Construct a table in which the processes in the group are rows and the most promising technologies are columns. Use a 1-to-5 scale (1 is no benefit, 5 is essential). You will use this table as part of the effort to show people how important the technologies are.

Process/Technology

4. How do the technologies relate to the infrastructure and technology you already have? This is important because it will show you what you have ahead in replacement, conversion, and interfaces. List the technologies as rows, as before. List the key elements of the infrastructure as columns. Enter the following codes in the table: N–no relation, R–the technology replaces the current technology, I–interfaces are needed between the technology and this element of the infrastructure, C–conversion of data is necessary for the new technology. Note that multiple codes are often needed. If you don't know what to put in the table, you have just found areas where further data collection is needed.

Technology/Infrastructure

5. Which parts of the current infrastructure are causing the most problems? Construct a table of processes in the group (rows) and the infrastructure (columns). The entry will be either N (not applicable) or 1 to 5 (1 means the infrastructure is beneficial for the process, 5 means the infrastructure is a major problem for the process).

Process/Infrastructure

6. Assume that you have selected the best combination of technologies and that you are combining them with the current architecture to form a new architecture. It is useful to be able to explain the benefits of the new architecture for the processes. Construct a table in which the rows are the processes and the columns are elements of the architecture or new infrastructure. Place a number from 1 to 5 in each cell showing the benefit of the architecture element to the process (1 is low or no benefit, 5 is great benefit).

Process/Architecture

CHAPTER 12

STEP E: DEVELOP AN ENTERPRISE STRATEGIC SYSTEMS PLAN

CONTENTS

12

STEP E: DEVELOP AN ENTERPRISE STRATEGIC SYSTEMS PLAN

PURPOSE AND SCOPE

One of the purposes of a strategic systems plan is to provide direction for information systems activities for a period of three to five years. The following are more specific statements of purpose:

- **The plan supports architecture implementation for the new processes.**

  The strategic systems plan recommends specific actions and projects that will implement the systems and technology architecture. Changing hardware or upgrading networks benefits everyone and doesn't have a specific client or immediate benefits. The plan is needed to provide focus and priorities when changing the architecture.

- **The plan provides for prioritization of systems work.**

  Systems activities to support process improvement have to vie for resources with maintenance, enhancement, and other projects. The plan indicates the priorities for work in the organization that relate to systems support of business processes. If you set priorities without considering the plan, you are likely to end up with a series of incremental, small improvements that give no major benefit and will not be able to support the improved processes.

- **The plan generates identification of project opportunities that provide strategic advantage.**

  This is normally what most plans aim at-a list of project ideas that will give some benefit. A lesson learned is that the projects should add up to more than the sum of the parts so that you get leverage. The projects should span several years and make successively larger contributions.

- **The plan encourages supporter and facilitator of process improvement to build a common vision of systems and technology and their impact on the organization.**

  This is an important political objective of the plan: it is to act as a unifying agent for the firm. With a common vision, you can avert disrupting systems activities.

The scope includes the following:

- Hardware

- Network and communications

- Software

- Information systems staff

- Consultants and contractors

The time horizon is typically three to five years, although actions to support the plan begin immediately. The scope includes both the enterprise and major divisions and departments. Smaller departments that share common resources may be able to be bundled together.

END PRODUCTS

The plan provides recommendations and direction for systems and technology. What outputs are used by whom?

- **Resource allocation**

  The recommendations and action items from the strategic systems plan become competitors for resources with maintenance, enhancement, and new requests for resources and funding. This is resource management.

- **Business unit plans**

  The enterprise plan serves as the basis for constructing departmental plans. Business unit plans act to test the enterprise plan by applying it to individual business processes, systems, and business organizations. This will also demonstrate the benefits to be achieved from the plan. Business unit plans validate the company-wide plan and help gain commitment to the plan among business units.

- **Policies, procedures, and other non-resource actions**

  The strategic systems plan often will identify policies and procedure changes that do not require resources. Examples are changes in how resources are assigned, how projects are managed, or what software tools will be used.

How do you know if you have achieved your objectives and end products? Experience points to these signs:

- Management uses the terminology of the planning process, implying endorsement.
- There is discussion and support for implementing some of the results of the plan immediately without waiting for the next budget cycle.
- Implementation activity occurs before the plan is complete.

How do you sense trouble? Here are two definite signs of trouble:

- Management wants to finish the plan and then put it away on a shelf.
- There is no sense of urgency to present the plan.

RESOURCES

You and the team will play the key roles in the building of the plan. Team members will provide information, opinions, and reactions to elements of the plan. Team members can facilitate getting feedback on sections of the plan. You will convey recommendations and ideas to management and senior staff for their support and feedback. This is not only to get ideas for improvement but also to do marketing. If you have consultants involved at this stage, they can play a prominent role in plan presentations and reviews if management respects consultants. If not, consultants can still work in the background to develop the plan.

APPROACH

At the start you want to define systems issues, opportunities, and problems that the plan should address. At the end you want a set of specific systems project ideas, policies, and procedures that you can implement to support process improvement. Process improvement efforts often depend on systems and technology, which means that you will evaluate and adopt new systems and technology. Fitting the new with the current technology requires both a strategic systems plan and an architecture.

The inputs to the plan include the following:

- Systems issues, opportunities, and findings from the internal assessment
- Systems issues, opportunities, and findings from the competitive and industry assessment
- Current systems and technology and current architecture
- Systems issues, opportunities, and findings from the technology assessment
- Future architecture of hardware, network, software, and information systems

Consider Figure 12-1. Objectives address systems issues and opportunities. Objectives are blocked from reaching the issues and opportunities by constraints. Constraints can't be changed, so strategies to get around the constraints must be developed. Strategies have to be supported by specific ideas-action items. Action items consist of project ideas, policies, and procedures that can be acted upon.

A small number of objectives and strategies provide focus for the plan. These are what people will keep in their minds later. If objectives are fuzzy, numerous, or too specific, the maintenance of the plan will be more difficult.

Example

As part of process improvement, a company has the following systems issues and opportunities:

- Departments desire greater access to computer information

Figure 12-1

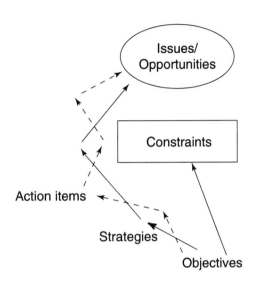

- There are opportunities to implement client-server computing
- Current business processes have been in place for more than 15 years with little change

What do these three issues have in common? On the surface, not much. But the company was able to develop an objective that addressed them all:

Implement a more effective systems approach that involves the business processes as well as the systems.

At this point, the company is faced with constraints, which is typical. There is limited money and staff. Current systems and business processes have to be maintained. These two constraints prevent attainment of the objective right away.

The systems strategy could include implementing a database management system and client-server system to fit the reengineering processes. This would yield many actions including the database design, and client-server systems. But it is important to select the appropriate tools and change the systems and technology architecture.

This example is fairly typical of a situation with many systems issues, constraints, and actions and a much smaller number of strategies and even fewer objectives. The above example of one objective is shown in Table 12-1.

Table 12-1: Example for a Single Objective

Objective: Implement effective approach for processes and systems

Issues:

Desire by management for information
Client-server technology is available
Current business processes are old and have had little maintenance

Constraints:

Available funds
Technology status and problems
Organization problems

Strategies:

Employ wide area networks and distributed functions
Jointly use both reengineering and systems efforts

Action items:

Client-server system implementation
Wide area network implementation
Reengineering project
Policy and general procedure modification

Note that while the topics are described sequentially, they should be addressed in parallel. That is, shortly after you start collecting information internally and externally, begin to build data in all of the categories at the same time. Results in one area can then be used in others. What you are attempting to do is build a set of interrelated lists that will then be put into tables. The tables and lists will form the core of the systems plan.

Action 1: Determine the Key System Issues and Opportunities

A system issue comes from a wide scope of factors, both internal and external. Nothing is off limits. An issue can often fit in one of the following categories:

- Shortcomings of current systems and technology
- Problems with the underlying system architecture
- Methods and tools relating to systems
- Shortcomings as compared to competition

An opportunity arises from a new or changed business or technology factor. Like issues, opportunities can come from internal or external forces. While new technology is a prime source of opportunities, other sources include the following:

- What competitors are doing
- Industry trends
- Changes in organization

An issue can be stated as a phrase in a structured way. This helps you to understand, market, group, and address issues. Consider the following statement.

Use Internet-related technology to improve customer service.

This statement, however, gives no goal. It identifies a very specific technology, but only a general business process. Add detail as follows:

Employ Internet-related technology to allow customers to communicate with you regarding product issues and questions, thereby reducing staffing requirements in customer service.

You can create tables with the system issues and opportunities. Here are three examples. In each table the entry is a number between 1 and 5 (1 is low, 5 is high).

- **System Issues and Opportunities vs. Organization**

  This table shows the extent to which an issue or opportunity applies to an organization. If you have a major organization with few issues, you probably have missed some issues. Do your issues cluster around overhead staff departments and not line divisions? If so, this is a sign of another problem.

- **System Issues and Opportunities vs. Business Process**

  Here indicate the degree to which issues and opportunities apply to major business processes. If this table has low values, you are probably missing some issues or don't understand the issues.

- **System Issues and Opportunities vs. Impact**

  Identify benefits in general from taking advantage of opportunities and from solving issues.

  After this analysis, you can decide to:

- Move the issue to being a constraint if you feel that you cannot do anything about it. What competitors do can be a model for you.

- Logically group issues that touch the same organizations and processes in a similar way. For example, obsolete hardware, networks, and software can be turned into obsolete technology.

When you have worked through these analysis steps, you are ready to formulate objectives.

Example—Atlas Oil

Atlas Oil is a natural energy company that developed a strategic systems plan to support process improvement. Tables 12-2, 12-3, and

12-4 give the final tables in abbreviated form for Atlas Oil. (1 is low, 5 is high.)

Table 12-2: Issues and Opportunities vs. Organization

Issues and Opportunities	Refining	Retailing	Exploration
Corporate Structure	2	4	2
Need for more oil production	3	3	5
Lack of general information; information inconsistent	2	4	5
Improved distribution process	4	5	1

Table 12-3: Issues and Opportunities

Issues and Opportunities	Refining	Distribution	Sales	Production	Exploration
Corporate Structure	3	4	5	2	1
Need for more oil production	3	2	4	5	5
Lack of general information; information inconsistent	2	4	4	2	5
Improved distribution process	2	4	5	4	1

Table 12-4: Issues and Opportunities vs. Impact

Issues and Opportunities	Revenue	Costs	Flexibility
Corporate Structure	3	4	5
Need for more oil production	5	3	2
Lack of general information; information inconsistent	4	3	5
Improved distribution process	2	5	3

Action 2: Develop Overall Objectives

An objective is a directional and timeless statement. An objective that is too vague to have meaning will lead to failure. Here is an example of a good objective:

Implement improved integrated business processes.

Note that the focus is on business processes. In a systems plan, this means that you want systems and technology to give strong support to the business processes.

The first word is *implement*. This is stronger than invent or develop. It means getting results and having the changes implemented.

The next word is *improved*. This means better, but better is a relative term. Indicate a standard as well as a means of measuring whether you achieved any improvement.

The use of the word *integrated* implies that you would like to have business processes not just talking to each other through an interface, but integrated. This means that the processes overall will be more efficient. However, you also want to integrate systems and technology with the processes. You can extend this further and indicate that you desire that organizations be more integrated with their processes. Note that these expansions and observations help to lead you to strategies that will support the objective later.

The sample statement above demonstrates the possible structure of an objective.

- The action verb (implement) indicates that the objective should be carried out.
- The noun (business processes) focuses on some particular aspect of the business or business activity.
- An adjective (improved) specifies how you are to meet the objective.
- An adjective describes the benefit to be achieved (integrated) along with measurement.

Applying this to the example yields the following:

Implement business processes that are integrated and automated so as to reduce operations costs.

Here is another variation of the example:

Install new technology that supports the integration of systems and technology for reduced personnel time.

In this statement the scope has been suddenly narrowed. First, the word implement has been changed to install, which means to make available. Second, the word improved has been deleted and made more precise. Third, more terms that explain the role of technology have been inserted. The scope has been narrowed to systems. No reference is made to organization, so you can assume that organization change is out of bounds.

These examples show that choice of words is very important in the plan. While you have many issues and opportunities, you will have only a few objectives. Choose your words carefully. Even if you know that management wants the plan to be "safe," do not water down the objective. Start strong and be flexible. For example, you might compromise by keeping the word implement in place instead of using the narrower version of the objective with the word install.

Why have objectives at all, if they are so broad? They act as centerpieces for systems activities, as well as for the plan. Activities performed by the systems organization that are not part of the plan should fit within the plan. Objectives also enable management to "just say no" to proposals that deviate from the objectives. Without objectives you would be changing strategies every year in a reactive way as the projects evolved-a true bottom-up approach. Another reason for objectives is that in defining them, you are forced to think things through on a larger scale. Defining objectives gives a rare opportunity to consider systems and technology on a broad scale.

Categories of Objectives

Classify objectives as to whether they fit in the following categories:

- Business organization and roles
- Business processes
- General mission of information systems
- Information systems organization and roles
- Architecture of information systems
- Hardware
- Networks
- Software
- Policies and procedures of information systems

Example—Atlas Oil

For Atlas Oil, the initial systems objectives before the development of the plan were the following:

- Be responsive to business needs.
- Implement new technology based on tangible benefits.
- Provide efficient support to meet user requirements.

These objectives are general, vague, and timeless, though they may sound reasonable. Be responsive to business needs means that the business needs must first be stated. Often, they are not. Responsive can be equated to reactive in a positive way. However, it is still reactive.

The second objective emphasizes tangible benefits. This means that each new technology must yield these benefits. However, most architecture-related projects and work relate to the entire business. They produce long-term benefits but not short-term benefits. If you keep this objective and enforce it, you will adopt only piecemeal products that supply some immediate need.

The third objective, like the first, requires that user needs must first be defined. Efficient here can mean low cost. Cost is not the criterion in all cases. You might sometimes select the most expensive technical solution if it provides the greatest overall benefit.

The emerging picture is one of a reactive, cost-conscious maintenance organization that is not improving the business. Atlas Oil management had lost faith in systems to deliver. Information systems thought they were doing just fine. They were within budget and on schedule. However, they were working on the wrong projects and spending money unwisely.

After collecting information, management came up with the following objectives:

- Employ systems and technology to position the company more effectively for exploration of oil.
- Support the streamlining of refining and distribution processes.
- Implement new technology that would provide a competitive edge to gasoline retailing.

These objectives are much more specific and in line with the business. The first implies aggressively supporting seismic research and exploration. The second provides for system integration and streamlining. The third calls for integrated, state-of-the-art technology for retail sales. As a result, the plan contributed toward the establishment of sales of food, soft drinks, and other personal items. The profits from these exceeded the profits from gasoline. These objectives were mapped against the categories presented, as shown in Table 2-5.

Table 12-5: Atlas Oil Objectives

Category/objective	Exploration	Refining/distribution	Retailing
Business organization and roles	X		X
Business processes		X	X
Information systems mission	X		X
Information systems organization		X	
Architecture	X		X
Hardware	X	X	X
Software	X	X	X
Network	X	X	X
Policies/procedures		X	X

Note the overlap and complimentary nature of the objectives. They support a more proactive role for information systems.

Table: Objectives vs. Issues and Opportunities

You can now create a new table of objectives vs. issues and opportunities. In this table again insert a 1 to 5 in each space, depending on how strongly the objective could address the issue or opportunity (1 is low, 5 is high). As stated before, the rating system is subjective. In thinking through the table, you will be able to validate the objectives and increase your understanding; Whether a specific table entry is a 3 or 4 is not that important. Another benefit of the table lies in its indications for consolidation. Suppose that you had six objectives for 50 issues and opportunities. By using the table you can see which ones cover the same issues to the same or similar degree and this will enable you to narrow down the objectives.

Action 3: Identify Constraints

A constraint is an immovable object (for now) that blocks the short-term attainment of your objectives. When you think of constraints, money and restricted funding will come to mind. However, these are just one type of constraint. Other categories of constraints include the following:

- **Technology gap**

  The technology to support the objective is not mature or even available. You may not be able to bridge the gap. This occurs when an innovative product appears without supporting software.

- **Lack of standards**

  The technology exists, but the many different versions are not compatible. Plunging ahead will mean that you will likely pick a loser.

- **Physical location**

  Physical location of different offices, warehouses, and factories is a barrier that has to be accepted, whether it is global, regional, or across the city. Setting up a network in a country with little infrastructure is an example of a challenging physical location.

- **Existing technology**

  While you might like to exchange all of the existing technology for new, this is virtually impossible in a one-year period.

- **The industry**

  The nature of the industry defines which business processes are key. This is a constant.

- **Regulatory environment**

  Laws and regulations on a local, regional, national, and international level apply here.

- **Competition**

  You can choose your friends, but you can't choose your competitors, although you can be both responsive and proactive.

- **Mission of the business**

  The underlying mission of the business may be a constraint.

- **Union rules**

  Union rules and other similar agreements are constraints.

- **Standard company administrative policies**

  You must accept rules laid down by human resources as well as accounting and other departments.

- **Organization roles and organization structure**

  This is changing. Up to about five years ago, these were constraints and had to be accepted as sacred cows. Reengineering has changed this.

- **Information systems resources**

  This is a constraint in two ways. First, there is the total headcount. Second, there are the specialized skills of specific individuals.

Constraints prevent you from doing something or impose a burden. Here are examples of problems caused by constraints:

- **Technology gap**

  Prevents the implementation of certain systems

  Limits the potential benefit of some technologies

- **Lack of standards**

  Limits the range of available and usable technologies

  Restricts the business applications that can be addressed

- **Physical location**

  Increases the support costs of the remote site

  Makes the deployment of some systems costly

- **Existing technology**

  Limits use of new technology to what can interface with existing technology

  Consumes too much staff time in support

- **Industry**

  Restricts the range of applicable systems and technology

Imposes specific standards on interfaces (e.g., Electronic Data Interchange)

- **Available funding**

  Limits deployment of hardware, software, and network

  Restricts the extent of upgrading architecture and core technologies

- **Regulatory environment**

  Restricts available technology

  Imposes the burden of compliance on software

- **Competition**

  Sets priorities on what systems are needed

  Imposes a selection of specific vendors and products

- **Mission of the business**

  Limits what business processes can be supported

  Sets priorities over information systems activities

- **Business policies**

  Defines how new technologies can be obtained

  Increases cost and provide structure for acquisition

- **Organization roles**

  Imposes specific interfaces that increase systems efforts

  Limits the extent to which reengineering is possible

- **Organization structure**

  Restricts cross functional systems

  Does not support integration

- **Information systems resources**

  Constrains the deployment of staff due to specialization of skills among the staff

  Consumes resources in maintenance and operations support

Formulating a Constraint

As you did with issues and objectives, draw up a list of constraints. Start by looking through the list of issues and opportunities. When you generate the list of issues, you normally uncover some that you cannot change or address. Move these over to the constraint list.

Example—Atlas Oil

Here are three constraints listed by this company:

- Limited funding is available.
- Technical expertise and experience are limited.
- The information systems role is to be supportive.

Like the initial objectives, these are general. They should be more specific in terms of impact.

Here is a more detailed list of constraints:

- Limited staff knowledge of oil exploration methods restricts the extent of support possible for this area.
- Individual profit centers in the company mean that systems efforts are dedicated in each area, which limits flexibility.
- Competitive oil firms set priorities for systems activities.
- Management focus on near-term profits restricts investment in long-term architectural improvement.
- Industry pattern of software use limits which software can be acquired.
- Distributed authority among divisions limits the systems role to obtaining improvements.
- Dispersed locations increase support resources required.
- The mission of the business means that some supporting areas of the business will not receive support.
- Regulations by overseas and domestic governments increase the cost and effort required for systems.
- Existing technology consumes the time of experienced personnel.
- The current systems staff has limited knowledge in new technology.

Constraint Tables

Once you have drawn up a list of constraints, you can construct additional tables. Fill in the same rating of 1 to 5 in each blank in the table.

- **Issues vs. Constraints**

  This is a table to employ for validation of issues. The table entry is the extent to which the issue relates or applies to the constraint. This aids in refining and sharpening both issues and constraints.

- **Objectives vs. Constraints**

  This table shows the extent to which a constraint binds and applies to an objective. One use of this table is to see if you have real constraints that don't apply to any objective. If so, you may be missing an objective. Elaborating further, you can see which types of constraints are the most binding on the objectives. The table can show management how a constraint that can be changed impacts systems. In some cases this table can be used to obtain changes in policies. Remember that a constraint to you may be an issue to upper management, capable of being changed at this higher level.

Action 4: Define Systems Strategies

Objectives are directional goals. The immediate or short-term attainment of these goals may be blocked by constraints. If you just started listing project ideas and policy and procedure changes, you would lose your sense of direction in the plan.

How do you link a general objective to a specific project or policy? The answer lies in creating strategies. Strategies are more detailed and focused than objectives. They cover a period of several years.

Example—Atlas Oil

Returning to the Atlas Oil example, at least three strategies were required to cover exploration, refining and distribution, and retailing.

Consider one as an example showing how to devise a strategy. For retailing, the company began with the following statement:

Implement a retail network to support gasoline station operators.

This statement, however, is too narrow. The emphasis is on current operations. Make it more general. Also, the term network does not encompass the architecture or hardware. Design work and software development should be included. Implementation doesn't cover this.

The statement can be generalized and expanded as follows:

Design and implement a full function, flexible retail system and network that will accommodate current and future station operations.

This statement provides more detail and is more specific.

Strategy Categories

Here is a list of strategy categories and sources of strategies:

- Technology infrastructure (network, hardware, and system software)
- Application software
- Databases
- Internetworking connectivity
- Information systems staff resources
- Facilities and voice communications
- Business processes and procedures
- Service levels and performance

Several of these can then be combined into single strategies.
To devise a strategy, use this step-by-step approach:

- Step 1: Start with an objective and determine what would be needed in each of the above areas to fulfill the objective.

- Step 2: Repeat this for each objective. You now, in essence, have a table of objectives vs. the above categories.
- Step 3: Summarize or aggregate what you have developed for each category across all objectives.

For the format of a strategy, start with the action verb, followed by the area addressed by the strategy. End the sentence with the purpose of the strategy. Format helps managers and staff understand each strategy by itself.

Strategy Tables

You now have four elements of the plan: issues and opportunities, constraints, objectives, and strategies. With these four elements, you can generate three new tables. The same rules for the table entries apply.

- **Objectives vs. Strategies**

  This table is where you begin. It shows how the strategies cover all of the objectives. The entry is the degree to which the strategy could fulfill the objective. This table indicates to management where specific objectives lead. Use it in presenting the plan.

- **Strategies vs. Issues and Opportunities**

  You can actually derive this table from the one above and that of issues and opportunities. This table supports validation that the issues and opportunities are addressed by the strategies.

- **Strategies vs. Constraints**

  This table has more limited value. It tells you which constraints relate to each strategy. Use this table to verify that the constraints do not block the strategies.

Action 5: Propose Specific Planning Actions and Project Candidates

Planning action items are specific projects, policies, and procedures. In many methods, the plan ends with the strategies. For each strategy you will generally have many actions. Some may support a number of strategies. Your projects and ideas can fit in the same categories as strategies, since they support the strategies.

Here are some types of action items.

- **Projects**

  Standard systems projects design, build, implement, convert, or install a system. Projects encompass operational support, maintenance, and enhancement to systems.

- **Policies**

  These actions include change, addition, or substitution to an existing policy.

- **Training and skills improvement**

Here are some of the action items listed by Atlas Oil:

- Implement a VSAT satellite network. This enables all three objectives to be supported by providing an enterprise-wide network.

- Design and install a client-server system for gasoline stations.

- Change contracts and policies for gasoline station franchises.

- Hire new petroleum engineers and geologists who can work with the new seismic software and systems.

- Acquire databases and software to support seismic exploration.

- Define a business project plan for streamlining refinery operations.

- Investigate and acquire enhanced software for refinery operations.

These are only seven more than 85 action items. Note that these items are mutually supportive. Some are not totally systems related but are included to indicate how the action items link to the business.

After identifying the action items, estimate their scope, cost, risk, and schedule. Determine any interdependencies among the action items.

Action Item Tables

Here are more helpful tables that you can generate using a list of action items:

- **Strategies vs. Action Items**

  The entry is the degree to which an action item applies to a strategy. This table is critical because it reveals which action items together address each strategy. It also indicates how an action item can support more than one strategy.

- **Action Items vs. Action Items**

  The entry is the degree to which an action item depends on other action items. This table helps you to group the action items.

- **Objectives vs. Action Items**

  This table is derived from the tables of objectives vs. strategies and strategies vs. action items. A guideline here is to do it directly and then compare your results with that of combining the two tables.

- **Issues vs. Action Items**

  This is an interesting table since it closes the loop. That is, you started at issues and ended with action items. The entry is the extent to which the action item addresses and is relevant to the issue. This is a good test for management. If they seriously want to address an issue, they have to be serious about the corresponding action items.

The planning process should lead, as seamlessly as possible, to action. Get the initial actions going. You also want to pave the way for updates and implementation of the planning process on an ongoing basis.

Action 6: Build the Initial Plan

Step 1: Get organized.

Before collecting any data, set up files and decide how you are going to store and organize information. More specifically, address the following tasks:

- Organize paper files.
- Set up the software for organizing the data. You will want to establish a planning data base of the data you collect.
- Establish the format for your contact list.

  Specific the outline of the report and planning presentation.
- Design how you will provide written status reports on the project.
- Develop a project plan for the work.
  —Identify initial issues and barriers that you may encounter in your planning.
  —Develop a standard one description of the purpose, scope, approach, benefits, and end products for the planning effort.

Step 2: Identify information sources and begin to collect information.

The key operative phase here is "parallel activities." Here is an activity list for this step:

- Identify important competitors and search libraries and the Web for information.
- Determine applicable industry groups and associations who can provide information.

  Identify vendors and their web sites that might be useful.
- Search your organization for annual reports, previous plans, technical reports, presentations, memoranda, and other documents pertinent to planning.

Build your own network of contacts. Find people in divisions and departments who are interested in technology, business process, and planning issues. Draw them out informally on what they consider to be significant. Start making notes of what issues and opportunities they raise and what they are interested in.

Step 3: Sort and organize information.

Before reviewing articles, reports, and other documents, start sorting the information. Create a form that has the following items:

- Date
- Source
- Title
- Topic
- Area of plan to which it applies
- Comments (your observations)
- Description (or copy of material)

Use one form for each item. If you keep these separate, they will be easier to use later.

Step 4: Conduct in-depth data collection.

You have defined some preliminary issues, objectives, etc. Next, you will use this to get feedback and reaction from the people in your organizational network. Don't present anything on paper at first. That is too formal. Try out the ideas verbally. You might start with, "I ran across something that raised some questions." This will lead into a discussion of the issue. After you introduce it, sit back and listen. Then ask them for their ideas. Take notes and interact with questions such as the following:

- Did anyone try to do anything about this before?
- What could be done about it?
- Does this apply to other parts of the company?
- Has it gotten worse or changed?
- If you left it alone, what would happen?

Turn to positive ideas that might work. Suggest positive small actions. End the discussion on a positive note. Ask them what could be done and what would they consider to be ideal.

In addition to these meetings, widen your network of contacts. Make sure that you have contacts in each major division or department. Try to stay in regular contact with all of the managers in the systems department. Plan to spend time on the Internet and Web searching for information. You may want to download some Web pages and graphics into the planning documents.

Go to a major reference library. Prepare lists of sources and questions ahead of time. Describe your project briefly to the reference librarian. Follow up on each suggestion. If some leads turn out to be dead ends, do not be discouraged. These searches are sometimes referred to as "K out of N." That is, you are successful if K of the N suggestions work.

Give yourself an entire day for this part of the project. This will force you to keep looking even after you find information or get tired. What if you run out of ideas? Walk through the racks of magazines. Use the microfilm files to search for information via articles and annual reports. Do the same with Internet search and CD-ROM sources.

Step 5: Analyze the information.

With the information at hand, start building lists of the following:

- Planning issues and opportunities
- Objectives
- Constraints
- Strategies
- Action items and project ideas
- Recommendations for immediate action

Build the tables as you go. If you are unable to enter a ranking, you are missing information and knowledge. Try to combine tables to see if they make sense. That is, put the table of issues and opportunities vs. objectives next to the one that is objectives vs. strategies. Does the combined map of strategies vs. issues and opportunities make sense?

Step 6: Iterate the results.

Continue doing analysis and gathering more information. If you feel that you are getting burned out in one area, such as interviews, turn to analysis. Interviews are an external activity and the analysis is an internal, private activity—a good contrast.

Step 7: Build the initial draft plan.

With sufficient data in the form of lists and tables, you are prepared to build a draft plan. This will consist of lists of the planning elements as well as the tables. In building the plan, you will have to estimate costs and benefits. For the costs you will need help from technical staff in getting reasonable estimates. Raise their estimates to cover contingencies. For benefits, list the intangible benefits that provide no monetary value. This can help later to sway managers toward the plan. Tangible benefits can be based on headcount, increased sales, reduced equipment purchase, smaller facilities, etc. If you are in doubt as to the monetary value of the benefits, underestimate them or indicate rough but specific savings.

Step 8: Conduct a planning session.

With the extensive homework you have done, you are ready to have one or more planning sessions. Up until now you have obtained data and feedback from individuals. It is time to conduct a planning session to establish common ground and point of view.

In a planning session you will meet with a group of people who share organization membership or the same business processes. The session will last several hours. You will be acting in the capacity of moderator and note taker. In the cover memorandum, state that you wish to obtain feedback and additions, deletions, and changes. Circulate the planning lists with explanations ahead of time. Hold the tables back. Through their involvement, managers will acquire a sense of ownership of the plan elements.

Who should be invited to the session? Go to the managers involved and ask them to send people involved in the business process and real work. These people, while being at lower levels, will have direct, detailed experience with the issues. They will be able to contribute in several ways:

- They will be able to discuss issues and their impact in detail
- They will provide detailed examples of issues as well as new ideas
- They will be able to identify the benefits and impact if issues are solved

How should you conduct the session? After introductions of those present, describe the purpose and approach. A sample agenda is as follows:

- Introduction
- Discussion of issues
- Review of objectives and strategies
- Examination of action items and project ideas

In the introduction, describe the planning process without jargon. Emphasize results. Note that constraints are excluded from the agenda. Constraints are negative and are best addressed indirectly by asking why the objectives cannot be immediately achieved. Move constraints into issues to solicit reaction.

In the discussion of issues, present each issue and elicit opinions. Ask questions such as "Is this important?" and "What if we leave this one alone?" Throughout the session, use an easel to write notes on large sheets of white paper. Each new page of the flip chart should be numbered at the top. Post the notes around the room in sequential order. By the end of the planning session you will have generated 20 or more sheets. Make additional notes on paper as you go. Handling one issue after another can leave people bored. Liven things up by jumping to possible actions. Ask questions such as "If money were not an issue, what would you do?" You will run into political walls. People will be afraid to talk in the group. Once you sense this, indicate and label the political realities. You might say, "I realize that some of this is politically sensitive so we won't cover it here."

Technologies and technical terms may arise. People may not understand terms such as "client-server" or "intranet." Jump in and give a one-minute business definition. Highlight the importance of the term. Don't go into depth concerning the technology, as this will lose some of your audience and divert the discussion.

After each agenda item is discussed, summarize it for the group. This will not only serve as validation that you have the right understanding but also will help to create a common view of the subject. Have a short break before introducing the next topic.

Note that objectives and strategies are combined. Keep the presentation of these quite general. When discussing objectives and strategies, try to make them tangible by relating them back to issues. Use the same technique with action items. Relate them back to issues as well as to objectives and strategies.

After the planning session, expand and modify the material. You can now expand the description and impact of each issue as well as give examples. Do the same for other parts of the plan. Some of the basic tables can be inserted at the end of the document along with a summary of key relationships from each table. Add the constraints with the objectives. This is the first version of the plan. Note that it lacks descriptive text. This would divert attention from the tables.

Action 7: Refine the Plan

With some feedback already and your first candidate plan, you can perform more analysis and expose the plan for additional reactions. Refinement is more than just adding detail or making corrections; it means the building of an overall consistent plan fabric. That is, you want to ensure that all parts of the plan are linked and that you can identify tangible examples and impact.

Some questions to consider are the following:

- **Does the architecture support the plan?**

  Link each of the identified technologies to planning action items, project ideas, and strategies. If unsupported elements of the architecture cannot be justified, they should be dropped. One approach is to revert to the use of tables. The table of action items vs. architecture components would indicate, for example, which elements of the architecture (columns) apply to each action item (rows).

- **How do the issues apply to divisions and departments?**

  Build the table of issues (rows) vs. departments or divisions (columns). The rating in the table refers to the degree to which the issue applies to the department. For entries that are high in value, apply a further test. You should be able to explain more specifically how the issue impacts the department.

- **What if you do nothing?**

  Suppose you drop the plan and don't finish it, much less implement it. How will the situation deteriorate? Which issues will worsen? What will be their impact? Focusing on this question will help build support for the plan now and assist in marketing later. This is extremely important. Many people have become jaded by hearing about the wonderful benefits of technology that have never come true. However, if they are made to realize the downside of not changing anything, then they will become more interested.

- **When will an issue become critical? How stable are the issues?**

  These questions really mean, "When will the issue impact the performance of a critical business process?" Answers can point to priorities and also help in grouping issues, since if one issue worsens, other dependent ones will too.

- **If you were to spend no money on projects from the plan, how many and which action items could be implemented? What would be their impact and benefit without the projects?**

  This shows the limitations of not using money.

- **If you throw money at the plan but do not change policies, processes, procedures, or organization, then how far can the plan be implemented?**

  This will reveal the limited number of things that money can solve.

  - **If you eliminate all projects with the new architecture, how much of the plan can be supported with the existing architecture?**

  This points to the need and justification for the new architecture projects later.

- **What if you do the projects and spend money but fail to modify any policies? What benefits will accrue?**

  Tangible benefits often are attained only through the combination of action items. This discussion will also highlight the important policy changes. While you are discussing these, also ask for suggestions on implementation.

- **From the perspective of a division or department, if these actions and strategies are implemented, how will the division be better off?**

  This often touches a raw nerve in divisions that were promised much by corporate but received little.

- **What will the business processes look like and how will they be different with the action items being addressed?**
- **If you could spend any amount of money and have any level of resources, how many more planning action items would you generate? How much better off would the company be?**

  You can also group the action items around business processes and rank these by importance.

- **How will actions be implemented?**

  Discuss the answers to this question. When a participant starts to focus on details, try to steer the person out of the detail and into a discussion of the role of divisions, systems, and other groups in implementation.

Action 8: Conduct Informal Presentations

As you are going through Action 7, begin to present parts of the plan informally. During the data collection and analysis, you built up a sense of urgency for action. Now shift gears. Turn to the bigger picture, which can be difficult and challenging to grasp.

Presentations can be given from four perspectives:

- **Business unit perspective**

  The plan lists and tables are shown to be relevant to at least two key business units. This takes effort, since the wording of the lists and tables will be changed to show relevancy. The reward is that this perspective generates reaction, interest, and support. People will appreciate the time you took to prepare the material.

  Close the business unit presentation with a call for support when priorities are set to generate the project slate.

- **Company-wide perspective**

  Step back and extract the issues, objectives, and strategies. Have these ready for the presentation, to give the big picture. You also will be able to show upper management a summary of what you have done.

  From upper management you seek understanding and general support for the plan, but no money.

- **Business process perspective**

  Select two or three key business processes. Extract the elements of the plan that are most relevant to the business process. Be ready to discuss benefits and how the new process will work.

  The business process perspective is important because it shows the true benefits of carrying out the actions.

- **Technology perspective**

  This gives the architecture and plan parts that are relevant to the architecture. Use this plan with the systems managers and staff.

With the scope and structure of the presentations covered, turn to specific suggestions. Start with issues. With these you are starting on familiar ground. Then move to strategies. These are general but are indicative of direction. Next, move to action items and then to benefits. Finally, return to objectives to show the umbrella for the plan. Never start with action items; they are the punch line. Get the audience interested before you close in for the sale.

Follow up after the presentations with updated materials. This shows that you have taken what they told you to heart. Allow only a day or two to pass before incorporating the feedback. Ask people in what ways they would like to be involved in implementation again.

MANAGEMENT PRESENTATION AND COST-BENEFIT ANALYSIS

Present the plan one-on-one to key managers who have supported the planning effort. Encourage them to talk about the plan with others. They will know who will be supportive. Give them extra copies of the plan. Next, inform them of potential opposition and ask what their thoughts are on addressing this. You may wish to try different approaches with different managers before you hit on a style with which you are comfortable.

After these one-on-one presentations, ask the managers who the audience should be. Point out that political issues are involved and the sequencing of the formal presentations is important. Make presentations to divisions to build a ground swell of support. This makes the presentation to top management easier. Remember that the prize is not plan acceptance; it is implementation.

The planning document should consist mainly of lists and tables with limited text. Benefits and costs can be summarized in tables. Writing should be in a formal style but simple. Once you have the plan created, make sure that it lines up with the formal presentation. Many plans have run into trouble because it was difficult to relate the actual plan to the presentation. Once you have built up momentum and enthusiasm with the presentation, you want to be careful not to let everyone down by presenting a confusing report.

Circulate the plan draft to the managers to whom you made informal presentations. Have them answer the following questions:

- Do you feel politically uncomfortable with any part of the plan?
- What is the weakest part of the plan?
- What is missing from the plan?
- What area of the plan will be the most difficult to sell?
- Is there any part of the plan that you don't understand?

KEY QUESTIONS

What happens during the current planning process? What feedback is received? How are people selected for participation?

From year to year, are there differences in the approach to developing the plan? Are any lessons learned?

What are the steps that you follow in building an information systems plan? Are these documented or followed?

If you are in a large organization, does each division develop its own strategic systems plan?

What is the review process for the plan? What changes are made to the plan prior to its adoption?

How is the plan announced to employees?

When was the last time that the plan was updated? Was the update better than the original plan in terms of results?

EXAMPLES

Monarch Bank

Monarch developed a strategic systems plan very early in the process improvement effort. They realized that in banking the core of their work would involve their systems. The current systems were old and needed replacement so that they wanted to identify a stable direction prior to doing process improvement.

TRAN

TRAN thought that they could proceed with process improvement without having a plan. Management felt that a plan would slow them down. As they progressed on the project they found that there was confusion in direction due to indecision about what would be done about the systems. Some people were saying that the processes could not be changed because of the systems—they were treating it like a constraint. TRAN had to stop and go back and develop the strategic systems plan—resulting in significant delay.

Stirling Manufacturing

Stirling had a plan in place so that the effort in the process improvement effort was to validate that the plan and process improvement project were synchronized.

GUIDELINES

- **When you have doubts about specific items in the lists, move to detail.**
  Seek examples to verify the wording and content of the planning item.
- **Always have an example ready of every planning item.**
  More importantly, have an overall example that you can use to discuss the tables.
- **Build the tables as you go.**
  Don't wait until the end to create these tables. By creating them early, you will be able to find gaps in your understanding. This will aid in both data collection and analysis.
- **When seeking feedback, don't present the text.**
  Instead, present a table or list. Then discuss how the table was constructed. Ask people to add rows and columns and then to reevaluate the ratings in the table.

- **Don't rush to develop action items without the objectives and strategies.**

  You will then backtrack and create the strategies backward.

- **On action items, don't plunge into too much detail.**

  If you get bogged down, then you will miss a number of other action items.

- **In defining action items, make sure that you cover processes, policies, and procedures as well as project ideas.**

  Don't focus only on project ideas.

- **Periodically, set all of the tables aside. Go on to other tasks. Then go back and review them different ways.**

  For example, one time start top down with the objectives. Another time work back from action items. A third time start with issues and constraints.

- **Although the actions had to be mentioned in sequence, address them in parallel.**

  This will not only save time but will also allow you to build consensus faster.

- **During the development of the plan, be visible, but low key.**

  If people ask when the plan will be completed, indicate that action items must be approved and implemented.

- **Even when the work gets you down, be enthusiastic.**

- **Continue to build up examples and endorsements from people at the bottom of the organization.**

  These help to get your points across.

ACTION ITEMS

1. Learn how to define individual issues, objectives, constraints, strategies, and action items. Write these five headings on separate pages. Take the issues page and start writing all of the issues of which you are aware. Don't bother yet combining and grouping. Next, go to the page on objectives and write one objective. See how many issues this addresses. Go back and forth between issues and objectives. Now refine and structure both lists. Build the table of issues and objectives.

2. Look at the list of issues. See if the list triggers constraints in your mind. Go over the categories of constraints and list at least one constraint for each. Build the table of objectives and constraints.

3. Go back to the objectives and get out the categories of strategies. Try to develop strategies for each objective within the categories. Map the strategies against the objectives, and the strategies vs. the issues and opportunities.

4. Go to the strategies and the list of action item categories. Create a list of action items. Map the strategies vs. the action items. Ensure that you have defined more than project ideas.

5. Complete the other tables discussed to close the process.

6. Practice estimating benefits. Assume that a procedure is simplified. How would you estimate benefits? Do the same for a policy change.

7. From your knowledge of your organization, identify who would be your inner network of support for the plan. Who might be the enemy? Why would this be so? What countermeasures do you think would work?

CHAPTER 13

STEP F: DEVELOP DEPARTMENTAL STRATEGIC SYSTEMS PLANS

CONTENTS

13

STEP F: DEVELOP DEPARTMENTAL STRATEGIC SYSTEMS PLANS

PURPOSE AND SCOPE

The objective is to create strategic systems plans for critical business units involved in processes that will be improved. Note the word *critical*. You cannot develop plans for every business unit. The technology assessments and architecture are basically company-wide tasks and documents. It is the plan that is specific to the business unit. You will take all of the action items from the business units and corporate, then narrow the scope to what concerns a particular unit.

The scope involves all technology and systems that support the processes you are considering for the department. Recall that processes are interdependent. This means that the processes you are attempting to improve are likely to be interdependent with other processes. Your departmental strategic IT plan should include the systems and technology for these as well.

END PRODUCTS

While the major end product is the business unit strategic systems plan, you will add the following related end products:

- **The fit between the business unit plan and corporate plan must be addressed specifically.**

    How each supports the other must be identified. This includes the fit of the business unit plan with objectives of corporate, as well as the fit of the corporate strategies to those within the business unit plan.

- **The plans of different, but related organizations must be addressed.**

You need to ensure that there is consistency of plans between business units that share business processes, interface with each other, or support each other. If you ever want to attack a plan, get the plans of two business units and compare the two. You are likely to find inconsistencies.

In addition to the planning tables for the business unit that are analogous to those of the corporation, there are several additional planning end products. These tables include the following:

- Issues and Opportunities of the Corporate Plan vs. Issues and Opportunities of the Business Units
- Objectives of the Corporate Plan vs. Objectives of Business Units
- Strategies of the Corporate Plan vs. Strategies of Business Units
- Action Items of the Corporate Plan vs. Action Items of the Business Units

Each of these four tables contains as the general entry how the corporate element applies to the specific business unit.

There are also tables for specific business units, such as the following:

- Mission of the Business Unit vs. Objectives of the Business Unit
- Mission of the Business Unit vs. Strategies of the Business Unit
- Mission of the Business Unit vs. Action Items of the Business Unit

Each of these indicates how the specific planning element supports the component of the mission of the business unit.

Taken together, these tables serve to cement the business unit IT activities to those of corporate. You could also create tables that relate elements of the plan between several business units.

RESOURCES

Several alternative approaches will be presented. By employing some people from the business unit, you will be able to count on them buying into the process and taking over the updates of their plan after it is completed.

With respect to obtaining people for the team from the business units, experience has taught that you want to let this evolve naturally. In order to get more complete information, you may have to obtain information from people beyond the team because of the need to find people with specific technical knowledge.

APPROACH

To reduce the time and impact on process improvement, consider developing the plans in parallel at both the business unit and corporate level. As you collect information, create and update the lists and tables for both business unit and corporate plans. Share all of the information of a unit with that business unit. Do the same with corporate.

When you are ready for the sharing of information, arrange a meeting for people from both the business units and corporate. At the meeting present the issues, objectives, strategies, and action items of each. Do not compare or map any of this in the meeting. At the end of the meeting, hand out a complete list and set of tables to all attendees. Ask them to look it over. Get back to them individually to get their comments and changes. Also, mention that you will show the interdependencies of the planning elements at a later meeting.

Why does this approach work? First, it protects the business units and corporate from each other. Second, everyone trusts you—even if people don't trust each other—because everyone has shared information with you. Third, by not revealing the information in advance, you prevent people from trying to use it for their own self-interest and career, thereby sabotaging the trust people placed in you.

After the creation of the plan comes the setting of the project slate and the ongoing planning. You will want different business units and corporate to form alliances to back action items that are of common interest. How can you weld the common bond? Have them get together with you to hammer out project plans and implementation approaches. Define the roles of the business units and corporate in implementation.

Consider the ongoing planning because the department plan is a valuable contributor to the process improvement project. For the ongoing planning, begin to move the maintenance of the planning data to the unit and the corporate coordinators. For Stirling Manufacturing and TRAN, planning databases were established on respective wide area networks. This database establishes joint ownership between the business units and corporate.

Specific situations and cases must be addressed because each requires a different approach. Case 1 and Case 2 are based on whether the corporate plan does or does not exist. Case 3 concerns multiple business units.

Case 1: Develop the Business Unit Plan when There Is a Preexisting Corporate Plan

Action 1: Extract material from the corporate level plan.

Start with the corporate plan and extract lists and tables of issues and opportunities, objectives, constraints, strategies, and action items. Do the same for the assessments and architecture, if they exist. If these items are not available or are embedded in text, you will have an interesting exercise in extraction. The existing plan may be full of problems, but it was endorsed by management and should be considered first.

Action 2: In parallel to Step 1, define business issues, processes, strategies, and objectives.

This action is a key to success, as it not only saves time but also provides focus. You are going to take the work from the previous steps and use the resulting tables. However, you may have to augment these for the department to be complete. Action 2 is performed as discussed in earlier chapters. However, take advantage of the narrower scope of a business unit. Start with the critical business processes. Then define issues that affect these processes.

Action 3: Integrate the results of the first two actions.

Build the business unit tables as defined in Chapter 12. Apply each item in the corporate plan to the business unit. Here are some specific guidelines:

- Create a table in which the first column contains the issues and opportunities of the enterprise. The second column is the interpretation of this to be relevant to the business unit. Use the categories presented earlier as a way to sort the items. Add a third column that indicates an example and comments.

- Objectives and strategies should carry over to the business unit without major changes. After all, they are general and directional. However, you may want to change some of the wording to create a good fit with the business unit. Your goal is to make the objectives and strategies relevant to those who are in the business unit so that they can associate and support it.

- Create a table for issues using the constraints and action items.

  You will find that in creating these tables, some items will not apply when they apparently should. Some important business unit items may not be reflected in the corporate plan. Note these in the tables.

At the end of this step you will have the core of a draft plan for the business unit.

Action 4: Develop the complete initial plan for the business unit.

Actions 1 through 3 provide you with credibility and a partial plan. At this point, put the corporate plan aside and follow the approach described earlier in developing the plan and fleshing out the initial plans for business units.

Presenting the plans at this stage is premature, since the business units have not yet had a role in developing the plans.

Action 5: Refine the draft plan.

The process is the same as before. You will be updating the tables that show the corporate and business unit items side by side. The elapsed time should be shorter since there are fewer people to see. However, you should involve the business unit staff here more heavily. A potential long-term business unit coordinator should emerge during this step or the previous one.

Case 2: Develop Plans for Multiple Business Units

At the heart of this case is the question, "Where do we start?" Begin with an overall strategy for how you would develop multiple plans in a cost-effective manner. Several variations of the following approaches have been used:

- **Bottom up**

  Develop the plans for each major business unit first. Try to ensure that these mesh and are consistent with each other. Then aggregate them into an overall corporate plan. This method works best in a company in which business units are autonomous and have little in common. You can build powerful tables in which the first column is the general objective or issue and each successive column is the wording of the item as it applies to a specific business unit. This almost forces the corporate plan to conform due to the overpowering evidence.

- **Top down**

  Develop the corporate plan with an eye to key business units so that, as you proceed, much of the effort can be used at the business unit level. While academically attractive, this approach requires coordination and sensitivity. It will also take longer to complete than the bottom up approach.

- **Hybrid**

  Start both bottom up and top down. Develop plans for two key business units in parallel with the corporate plan. This is the best approach if you have the time, skills, and resources. If you start this way and become overwhelmed, sacrifice the corporate plan and complete the business unit plans.

The hybrid approach is usually preferred. It gives you flexibility to move around in the organization if you run into obstacles, so that you can keep the momentum going.

In the rest of this section attention will center on the hybrid approach.

The Hybrid Approach

Action 1: Classify Each Business Unit.

Classify each business unit as to the level of the plan required and the similarities between it and other business units.

- **Level 0 Plan**

  The business unit that fits this plan can inherit the enterprise plan. This applies to small departments as well as to corporate administrative units.

- **Level 1 Plan**

  Use plans of major business units as well as the plan enterprise and adapt them to the business unit in this category. For example, if there are three manufacturing divisions and one is smaller, but somewhat different, it would be a candidate for Level 1.

- **Level 2 Plan**

  This is reserved for major business units of an organization that require their own plan.

You can later change your mind, but classifying each business unit now will get you started.

Next, group business units that have major characteristics in common. Here are three groupings:

- **Resources shared**

  Group business units that share the same physical systems and resources. Changes in systems would impact all business units in the group.

- **Business process shared**

  Group business units that perform steps in the same overall business process, making their fates interwoven.

- **Organization**

  Group units that report to the same manager.

316 **PART III:** Technology and Processes

Prepare a table that lists business units as rows. Those units at the top of the list are Level 2 clustered in the groups you have defined. Level 1 units follow. Level 0 units are listed at the end. The second column is the level of the plan. The third column is the grouping. The fourth contains comments as to why the units were given that level and grouping.

This table provides a very different view of the organization to management. It has even been employed as a tool to review budgets submitted by business units. If you are working with limited resources, restrict your attention to Level 2 business units. Sweep up the units at the other levels later.

For some of the other actions, the method is as before. Carry out these steps in parallel to the extent possible. Also, pay close attention to Action 6 because it centers on the consistency issue.

Action 2: Conduct an Internal Assessment of Corporate and Key Business Units

Action 3: Define the Current Architecture and Conduct the Technology Assessment

Action 4: Conduct Analysis to Develop a Future Overall Architecture that can Accommodate Both Business Units and Corporate

Action 5: Develop the Plans for Corporate and the Units Concurrently

Action 6: Refine the Plans to Make Sure that Corporate and Business Unit Planning Items Are Consistent

The above actions are important politically, besides being necessary in the overall planning process. You will ensure that business unit needs are being addressed in the plan. Bringing in corporate later, as opposed to earlier, is offset by showing them business unit plans. Finally, when you show the corporate plan to the units, you will also provide a summary of the plans of the other units.

More Coordination

The development of these plans involves delicate coordination and balancing. You have to balance your time between all of the business units. You cannot afford to let one unit feel that it is being short-changed. Keep management in corporate and the business units informed. Whenever you write about the plan or give status reports, carefully explain how you are doing the coordination and what levels are being coordinated. Show and discuss similarities and common ground.

As you move into other organizations, keep the business units you started with informed. Also, stay in touch with business units you have not started to work on.

Business units with Level 1 plans are a challenge. By the time you begin to work with Level 1 units, time is getting short. You cannot afford to give them Level 2 attention, but they should receive more attention than Level 0 units. Communicate with these business units by doing some limited data collection based on an initial set of lists

You will probably not allot much time to talk with Level 0 units. Beyond status and progress reports, you will want to create a draft plan for them with the lists and tables. You may wonder whether these business units will feel neglected. However, they are probably not used to the limelight and may now even feel flattered that some-one is giving them some attention.

MANAGEMENT PRESENTATION AND COST-BENEFIT ANALYSIS

After the above actions, there are two presentation actions.

Conduct Informal Presentations Within the Business Unit

Involve corporate in the presentation and review process. Indicate that the plan is the business unit's and that you have matched up the enterprise and business unit plan. When presenting plans to the enterprise, begin with the tables discussed in Step A.

Make Formal Presentations to Business Unit Management

Make the first formal presentation to the business unit management. Expand this within the business unit. This will help build solid business unit support and protect the plan. Then offer to make a formal presentation to corporate. If you did your homework in Action 6, they are already aware of the content. In the presentations, emphasize the emerging cooperation between the business units and corporate. Point out potential areas of further cooperation and mutual benefit.

The costs of developing multiple business unit plans are substantial but worth the expense. You cannot just take a plan from corporate or another business unit and modify it for a new business unit. Also, consider when you constructed the plan. You spent a lot of time in communications. You tried to build enthusiasm and support. These activities, along with the analysis, are specific to a unit. The approach of a parallel type of effort with a few key business units can help minimize cost and effort. However, it means that each year more work will be required to bring additional units into the planning fold.

KEY QUESTIONS

Do business units have their own strategic systems plans? Are these plans compatible with the enterprise plan?

Is there a systems planning process for any business unit? To what extent is it dependent on the style of the current division manager?

EXAMPLES

Monarch Bank

At Monarch Bank, processes crossed many departments. The task was to develop a corporate plan as well as division plans. Corporate was basically neutral on planning for systems except to insist on low-cost, economies-of-scale actions. There were 14 divisions of the domestic bank and seven of the international part of the bank. The approach was to classify each division based on size, profitability, and competitive position.

The next step was to address four related divisions in the domestic bank. Managers in the other parts of the bank were extremely skeptical that anything of value would come out of this effort. Therefore, it was decided early in the process to identify action items that could be implemented to show results and boost confidence.

A key lesson learned here was that you have to be politically flexible. A management shakeup occurred in one of these divisions in the middle of the process. The best technique to use when this occurs is to continue process improvement with the other units and immediately establish the planning process with new management. In this case, the self-interest of management was appealed to because they could take credit for the plan for their division. Having multiple divisions allowed risk to be spread out rather than concentrated.

TRAN

The management had been badly burned twice by planning efforts that went nowhere. As indicated earlier, the new method was proven in one division first. Success here was measured in enthusiasm of the division and the adoption and implementation of recommendations. Corporate management for TRAN then provided additional resources. However, because this division was a key operational division, it was felt that planning for the other divisions should await the implementation of the action items and projects by the first division. This was a wise decision because the availability of new systems and other changes impacted the planning process for the other divisions.

Stirling Manufacturing

As you know from previous chapters, Stirling Manufacturing had autonomous business units. Corporate had moderate strength. The first step was to clarify the role and goals of corporate. These results were then projected to divisions as constraints on division plans. One division of the three was addressed. This Level 2 division was part of a group that was formed based on business process. After this, a small Level 1 division was addressed.

This situation was distinct in a pleasant way. With the success in one division, other divisions wanted to copy the plan of the first division and then adapt the systems solutions to fit themselves. While some of the systems and processes could be adapted, requirements and issues specific to the divisions still existed. Therefore, the approach was to parallel implementation with the development of the plans.

GUIDELINES

- **Prepare a checklist to log how often you communicate with business unit and corporate people.**

  Monitor yourself so that you maintain constant and regular contact.

- **Think ahead about how to cope with volunteers.**

  What would you have them do? To avoid problems later, never turn away a volunteer.

- **Do not jump in and attempt to implement actions without thinking of the consequences.**

  Opportunities and targets of opportunity will arise during the planning effort in one business unit. Think about how your actions will affect other units. You will be drawing off effort from the other plans. People in other units will sense this and may become jealous. They may raise their expectations, thinking that you are going to spend the same amount of effort on them.

- **If you hit a wall in one unit, deal only with the business unit management.**

  Treat the business unit as a company. Do not attempt to go to corporate to get them to intervene.

- **Try to identify similarities through common issues and action items.**

  Investigate the architecture and see how the units would benefit from a common approach.

- **Use a two-pronged approach if a business unit does not implement or use the results of the plan after it has been completed.**

  First, make sure that you are implementing with another business unit. This will serve as an example of success and help pressure the other business unit to implement. Second, go to the business unit and volunteer to help guide the implementation.

ACTION ITEMS

1. List the business units of your company. Divide these into the levels discussed earlier.

   If you cannot decide on the category a specific business unit, you may not know enough about what this unit does.

2. Develop alternative groupings of business units based on business process, organization, architecture, and, perhaps, common suppliers or customers. Write the business units as rows of a table. Each column will be one grouping. Assign numbers to groups and enter these in the table. Do you see a pattern in which units have more than one characteristic in common?

3. Write down the advantages and disadvantages of the bottom up, top down, and hybrid approaches in planning. How would you rank these in terms of political risk, systems and technology advantage, and ease of management? Obtaining different rankings may show that you must make a conscious trade-off.

CHAPTER 14

STEP G: DEFINE THE SYSTEMS ARCHITECTURE

CONTENTS

14

STEP G: DEFINE THE SYSTEMS ARCHITECTURE

PURPOSE AND SCOPE

Systems architecture is important in process improvement because your new processes are dependent on the systems that you implement. To implement the new systems, you have to define a new architecture. The architecture gives you the structure and understanding to deal with the new business processes as well as the current processes.

The objective of this chapter is to help you define the architecture you currently have and also define the new one that will be implemented as a result of defining and carrying out the strategic systems plan. Methods will be examined that can define future architecture that will improve systems and business processes for your organization.

An architecture is crucial to the strategic systems plan and process improvement. The strategic systems plan identifies specific objectives, strategies, and actions that should be undertaken. Many of these relate directly to specific business processes. Others will relate to improvements in the architecture. If you develop the plan without considering the architecture, you are likely to base the plan action items on the current architecture. You will not get the full benefits of the effort if you accept this artificial constraint. You will likely require the new architecture elements to support your other non-architecture action items. Or, what is worse, new technology will be thrown in as it fits with specific action items. Action items will receive serious attention only if there is an overall blueprint for the future showing the benefits that the organization will receive from the investment.

END PRODUCTS

Evaluation of the Current Architecture

The first end product is an evaluation of the current architecture. Consider a simple example of architecture. Your PC at home, with the software, printer, modem, office support, and even you, constitutes an architecture. The components of the architecture are the following:

- Hardware-PC components, scanner, auxiliary storage, and printer
- Communications-telephone line, modem, cabling
- Software-operating system, office productivity, communications, games, etc.
- Personnel-you
- Support-room, desk, chair, supplies

To describe the architecture further, specify how the components are linked. The interfaces can be cable, manual, software, and hardware.

Answer the following questions:

- Do the components link together easily, or do you have to perform additional manual steps each time you run a different type of software? This evaluation will show you whether the architecture *integrates* well.

- Are the various software components compatible? Can you share information between software, or do you have to translate the data and then manipulate it into a form usable by the second software program? This evaluation will show how well the architecture interfaces.

- What is the *performance* of the architecture? How fast does the system work?

- Are you missing some components or parts? Do you need a backup device? Do you need a backup power supply? Could you use more software? If you are missing components, you have *missing pieces* in the architecture.

- Are you lacking some piece of technology that is not yet available? An example might be high quality voice recognition software. This is called an *architectural gap.*

- Is your hardware up-to-date? Do you have the latest release of the software? Are the suppliers of your components still in business? If the answer to these and other, similar questions is no, you have to ask, "Is the architecture facing *obsolescence*?"

The terms in italics apply to architectures of all sizes, from your computer at home to computer systems at large organizations.

Definition of the New Architecture

The new architecture, is characterized by the desired changes and improvements that you have identified. Define the components of the current architecture in the same way you did the current architecture. Define several architecture alternatives. Then perform an evaluation and selection process. Alternatives can be based on extent of change, level of funding, or some other criterion.

Comparison of the Existing and New Architecture

Compare the current and the future architecture to see how and the new is better. You can use this test before you buy a new computer for your house. A basic criterion is whether you will be running the same software with the new hardware. If so, you have to question whether it is worth the investment of your money and time.

If someone gave you $300 to improve your PC architecture, what would you spend it on? Here are some alternatives:

- Hardware—replace or upgrade to add function
- Communications—faster communications or communications with more functions
- Software—upgraded or new
- Personnel—training, books, magazines
- Support—more comfortable chair, additional shelves, better desk

Which of these has the most benefit? Using the approach presented in this chapter, you can look at combinations of improvements. You can make conscious trade-offs.

RESOURCES

As you develop the architecture, you can do some of the work on
your own. You can consult magazines and books, visit computer
stores to get opinions, and use the Internet to gather opinions about
technologies. The Internet also has useful information and prices.

While all of this information is valuable, it pertains only to the
technology. It does not directly pertain to how you would use the
technology and what benefits your company would derive. To find
this out, talk to friends and associates about new technologies they
have used and find out what they perceive as benefits.

To find out more about business systems, talk to technical systems
people inside the organization, experts outside, and reference sources.
Go to business departments and ask managers and staff what new
capabilities would provide in terms of function and benefit.

Here are some guidelines on meeting with these managers and
staff people:

- Ask consultants or internal staff specific questions related to
  trends of individual products and interfaces. Avoid general
  questions.

- Distribute articles and information you have gathered; note
  reactions.

- Provide an outline of questions or information so that you can
  incorporate responses and comments into the assessment in the
  format you have decided to use, rather than gathering information in random form.

Your role is to act as a coordinator to pull the information together.
You can use the vision and technical knowledge of others, but often
the critical factor is the translation of the systems and technology
architecture into business terms. What does it all mean? Your ability
to answer that question is the true value you add.

You also need a gatekeeper of the architecture. This person must be able to work with management and to understand technology in moderate detail. The gatekeeper serves several vital roles, including the following:

- Assessing new technology suggested after the plan is developed quickly and accurately
- Watching for new technologies that might be of use
- Supporting the generation and update of the strategic systems plan
- Working with suppliers to ensure that the organization receives adequate information and support

APPROACH

What Is a "Good" Architecture?

How do you evaluate an architecture? What are some characteristics of a "good" architecture? Look for the following qualities:

- You can easily add components to the architecture for new requirements without tearing everything apart. This is *flexibility*.
- When you use the technology and systems, they are ready 99 percent of the time. This is *reliability*.
- When something is wrong, it can be fixed quickly and the first time. This is *maintainability*.
- The architecture should be relatively easy to support. Finding new people to provide support should not be a major issue. This is *operability*.
- Components should be modular so they can be checked, repaired, and replaced without major work. This is *modularity*.
- There is direct benefit to the business processes. Technology with new features in itself is not enough. The new features need to provide direct benefit to the business staff as they do the work in the business process. This is *utility*.

Classifying Technology in an Architecture

Classify the technology using the following four categories:

- **Backbone**

  The technology is used all of the time and fits solidly in the architecture. Word processing software is an example.

- **Niche**

  The technology fulfills a unique need. An example is an electric three-hole punch.

- **Temporary**

  The technology is not ready, or really suitable, but you are willing to endure it to get some experience and benefit. An example is cheap speakers for your computer. You want to see if you like having sound with the computer before you invest in good speakers.

- **Out of Scope**

  The technology is interesting but irrelevant to you. An example might be an exotic scanner.

You are mainly concerned with backbone technology and systems. These will remain for a long time and provide support for key business processes. However, you might have niche systems (e.g., a treasury money market management system) for a specific need for one department. Temporary technologies are only of interest if the benefit balances the effort required to install and interface it.

Architectural Evolution

Another way to look at a system or technology is in terms of its life cycle. It emerges from being tested and is initially released to the market. Few supporting products are available. Typically, the product is rushed to generate a revenue stream. Then the product starts to mature. If it finds a market, additional components appear that interface and take advantage of the technology. If it is a bomb, it quietly goes into the dust bin of faulty technology. Initial versions of Personal Digital Assistants (PDAs) are prime examples of bombs. As a product ages, the suppliers come out with new, improved versions, intended to replace and cannibalize the earlier product. Today's PDA's offer many more features and interfaces with e-mail and software organizers on PC's. In Japan, the classic example is the Sony Walkman radio, which appeared in a new version every few months.

What happens when an architecture evolves?

- Additional features are put into the product to make it more valuable and useful.

- Interfaces are added to allow you to more easily integrate the technology with other products.

- The product may become easier to use.

- Third-party vendors add more products on top of the basic product.

As evolution continues, a new product or version will appear. Typically, this will cannibalize the existing product—forcing you to buy the new one. Third party vendors will abandon your product. Staff and potential employees will stop learning about the product and move onto new technology. Eventually, the vendor will stop supporting the technology.

Actions for Developing the Architecture

You have several dimensions for technology: type or category, classification (importance to business processes), and maturity. These can be put into a series of actions.

Action 1: Define the Current Architecture and Issues Associated with the Architecture

Make a diagram to define the architecture in your company. Examples are found in Figures 14-1 and 14-2, which give the current architectures for two of the example companies. In each case there is a diagram of major components. The diagrams are simple without fancy symbols so that managers can easily understand what is being shown. Figures 14-3 and 14-4 show how each company simplified

Figure 14-1: Current Simplified Architecture of Stirling

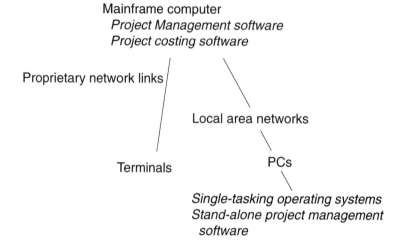

Mainframe computer
Project Management software
Project costing software

Proprietary network links

Local area networks

Terminals

PCs

Single-tasking operating systems
Stand-alone project management software

Parallel, duplicative work is going on at the PC and the mainframe. This causes not only redundancy but also confusion.

Figure 14-2: Current Simplified Architecture of Monarch

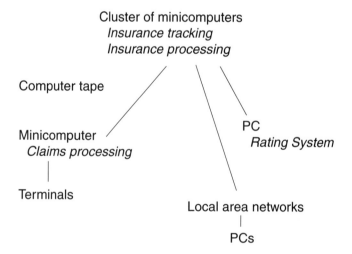

Cluster of minicomputers
Insurance tracking
Insurance processing

Computer tape

PC
Rating System

Minicomputer
Claims processing

Terminals

Local area networks

PCs

In this figure, the interface between the rating system and the processing system is manual. The interface between the tracking system and the claims system is by computer tape.

Figure 14-3: New Simplified Architecture of Stirling

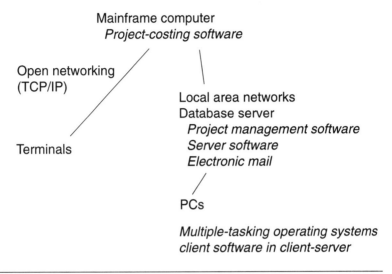

Figure 14-4: New Simplified Architecture of Monarch

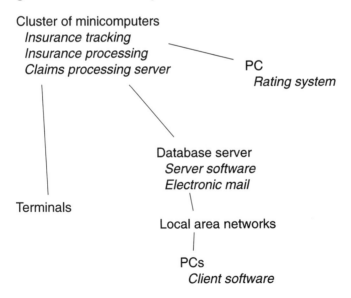

Here a client-server system for insurance tracking links online to the minicomputer system. The old claims system is replaced by a new package that runs on both the minicomputer cluster and the PCs (client software).

and improved the architecture. To develop this type of diagram, first define a list of the technology components in the architecture. Then create the diagrams.

Having a diagram of the current architecture provides understanding, but does not go far enough to highlight the problems with the current architecture. So the next part is to define issues. To do this, go out and uncover problems associated with specific technology and business processes. Then look for technologies that competitors use that you do not employ. You now a list of issues and potential opportunities that could improve the architecture.

To relate the issue to the architecture, you can use your diagram of the architecture and add a list of issues. Use arrows to link an issue to the components that give rise to the issue in the architecture diagram. This shows how the issues relate to the components.

A second suggestion is to create a table with rows of architecture components and interfaces and columns of issues. Place a number from 1 to 5 in the cells, indicating the degree to which the component contributes to the issue (1 is low and 5 is high). Alternatively, indicate the reason that the component contributes to the issue and impact of the issue on the architecture.

Examples of Architecture Issues

While the exact issues are unique to the company, often you can find a common thread. Look over this list and see how many of these apply to you.

- The existing backbone applications software is so old that maintenance is all but impossible.

- The backbone hardware and network are fragmented across many different hardware and operating system platforms, making integration extremely difficult.

- The network cannot support the communications traffic. Usually, traffic due to electronic mail, calendaring, electronic fax, and other uses of the network was underestimated.

- The software applications were bought or built at different times so that linking the data between systems has limited value.

- The current architecture worked when the company was smaller and less complex. The current architecture does not support the existing business environment. Departments have to institute workarounds to the architecture.

Action 2: Identify, Classify, and Evaluate the Current Architecture and Potential New Technologies

Now sit back and look at the current architecture. You have defined a series of issues. Which parts of the architecture create most of the issues? Use the tables that you created in the previous action. Are these parts that cause the most problems related?

In the previous chapter, the technology assessment identified promising new technologies. It is here that you take this information and apply it to the current architecture. Make a table. The rows are the current architecture and the columns are the new technologies. In the table, use the following codes:

- R—replacement
- E—enhancement or extension
- N—new

Now put the issues and the new technology together in a table. The new technologies can be listed as rows. The issues are placed in the first column. The second column contains the state of the technology in terms of maturity. The third column is the classification based on importance. The fourth and last column consists of the business impact of the new technologies.

You now know which technologies are of most interest. In Action 3, you will explore how the technologies go together with everything else.

Action 3: Develop Alternative New Architectures

You want to define alternative architecture and not come up with one solution. After all, what do you do if the architecture is unaffordable? There are different ways to define alternatives. Each alternative should embody a particular business strategy. This will give clarity of focus. Here are several strategies and their impact on the architecture.

- **Status quo**

  Continue the current architecture as the new architecture. New technology is ignored. Always have this one handy since you will have to defend change.

- **High tech**

  Assume that you will attempt to use all of the new technology and fit it into the architecture. This is likely to be impractical, but it is important.

- **Throw money at it**

  You can buy hardware, software, and communications, but you cannot hire more staff in this alternative. This might be able to handle capacity and performance issues, but it does not address structural issues and problems.

- **Throw support at it**

  Attempt to live with the current hardware, software, and communications. Hire people to make the current architecture better. This alternative might be attractive because you might be able to resolve some of the issues.

- **Maximum change**

  Attempt to devise the most radical change to the architecture. This means not only high technology but also wholesale replacement of the current architecture components.

- **Competitor and industry copy**

  Attempt to copy what was gathered from external sources and apply this to your firm.

- **Centralized control**

  Devise an architecture that maximizes central control. Stand-alone and separate computing will not be allowed.

- **Distributed control**

  This is the opposite of the previous one.

- **Defined by vendor**

  Select your favorite vendor or the one that is in your backbone. Have the vendor define an alternative for you.

Consider all of the alternatives. There will be overlap among these. Create management interest and involvement in the selection process. If they are involved, they are more likely to become committed. Once committed, they will be more likely to support the action items that pertain to the architecture. Remember, these architecture action items are going to be hard to sell because they do not result in short-term, tangible benefits. They are an investment for the future.

Action 4: Evaluate and Select the New Architecture

To understand how the architecture alternatives are different from each other, create a table of architecture alternatives vs. architecture alternatives. Half of the table will be empty because the table is symmetric. The table entry is the extent the two architectures (for the row and column) are different from each other.

To evaluate the alternatives, start with the criteria of a good architecture, then add business process criteria. Here is a sample list:

- Flexibility
- Reliability
- Maintainability
- Operability
- Modularity
- Risk to business process operation
- Cost
- Technical risk based on current staff knowledge
- Impact on key business processes in terms of benefits
- Impact on the current systems

After developing your list, build a table of alternatives as rows and the criteria as columns. In the table, place a 1 to 5, depending on the value of the alternative in terms of the criteria (1 is low, 5 is high). Don't compute a total score now. Instead, determine the two or three highest-rated alternatives. Rank these in terms of effort and change. By doing this, you will find an alternative in which you can gradually implement the new architecture. Also, watch for alternatives that will defer spending money and getting hardware until as late as possible, since hardware prices drop quickly.

Your ideal future architecture will likely have the following attributes:

- The backbone part of the architecture is sufficiently flexible to avoid gap filling, temporary technology.
- The backbone technology can meet business needs.
- With the architecture in place, almost all of the technical issues are resolved.
- Suppliers of the technology in the backbone are stable and provide products that can be easily inserted into the architecture.

Action 5: Define Actions and Projects Needed to Implement the New Architecture

After the selection process, don't rush out and present your findings to management. Take a look at what you have discovered and start building up ideas on implementation. Answer the following questions:

- What components will you have to acquire?
- What are changes to the architecture that will impact the business units?
- What staff and consultants will have to be hired?
- What technologies will you have to integrate and fill gaps for?
- What technical training will be needed to prepare for the new technology?
- What user training will be necessary?
- What conversion activities will be needed?
- What activities will have to be performed in terms of testing and integration?
- What is the sequencing of the projects and work?

Take the answers to these and build a general project schedule. You will then construct an initial budget.

Moving Toward the Ideal Architecture

Obviously, you are not going to be able to achieve the ideal right away. By the time you get close, state-of-the-art technology and the ideal architecture will change. Although you will never reach the ideal, keep it in mind and use it as a way to discard possible technologies. The ideal is a good tool for technology evaluation and dismissal.

MANAGEMENT PRESENTATION AND COST-BENEFIT ANALYSIS

With the thinking and work on implementation completed, you are now ready to face management and present your recommendations. However, you need to do more than show the old vs. new architecture. The architecture report to management should cover the following topics:

1. What are the issues with the current architecture from a business view? What is the current architecture preventing you from doing from a business perspective? How does the current architecture hamper your business activities?

2. What are the attributes and benefits of a good architecture? Stress the benefits of a new architecture for the business processes and the organization. Give examples of business processes before and after.

3. What are the new technologies to be used in the architecture?

4. How do you migrate to the new architecture? First, present the implementation plan; follow it up with the budget.

5. What are the architecture action items that management will be called on to support? This is the close of the presentation. Describe what management will have to support in the strategic plan to implement the architecture.

Addressing the five topics in this order will be effective. The first item is most effective in getting management's attention. Notice what is missing. You did not bore people with an arcane, technical discussion. Keep the technology discussion to a minimum in the third step.

Prepare for criticism by supposing that you were hired as a consultant to destroy the new architecture approach. What issues could you raise with management? Here are some potential areas of attack:

- The analysis did not consider some promising technologies.
- The analysis was biased toward one supplier or was too narrow in scope.
- The architecture does not contain much that is new. Stripped of the jargon and technical terms, the architecture contains little that is new.
- The new architecture will not benefit the business processes, or the implementation will take so much follow-up work that the architecture is of little value.
- The implementation of the architecture has not been thought through. Too many gaps exist. It is time to go back to the drawing board.

A major cost of developing an architecture involves personnel time. You also incur the cost of bringing in outside experts to review the architecture. Keep in mind that most outsiders have their own bias from their own experience and knowledge. You can deal with this asking them to justify their views.

The biggest potential cost is incurred when the entire planning process gets caught up in the architecture. What should have been treated as a sideshow suddenly moves to center stage. This means that the plan will have a technical bias and will not be responsive to business needs. Many technology projects will be proposed. But in the end, full implementation will have little business impact.

The benefits of defining the new architecture are evident in the discussion of the interdependence of the plan and the architecture.

KEY QUESTIONS

What are the components of the current architecture? Make a list and develop a diagram of the architecture.

What are the issues and problems with the current architecture? Map these onto the diagram you have created. You will likely find that you have omitted some components of the architecture.

Who is in charge of the architecture? What is the role of the business organization?

EXAMPLES

Monarch Bank

Monarch Bank had to implement a new architecture to support the processes being improved. The approach was to install a distributed client-server system and wide area network. The new architecture then linked to the existing mainframe computers in both an online and batch processing mode. In implementing the architecture, the major problem was in programming and testing the interfaces.

TRAN

The old architecture involved several incompatible minicomputers that had been acquired over a period of six years. New applications were impossible due to the limited capacity of the systems. Programming resources were divided and specialized. There were no economies of scale. The architectural alternatives included the following:

1. Modernize the current hardware.
2. Replace the current hardware with new, more powerful minicomputers.
3. Use alternative #2 plus a wide area network.

Alternative 3 was chosen for the following reasons. First, there were more than 150 PCs, some of which were connected to local area networks. The users wanted to be linked to the computer for data access. This supported the wide area network. Second, it was felt that since the project was so large, it was better to proceed to modernize the entire architecture at one time instead of stretching out the schedule. Today, there are more than 400 users and the architecture is being modernized again.

Stirling Manufacturing

Stirling used a mainframe and minicomputer for work scheduling and project management. The data and business processes were both faulty. It was realized that changing the architecture would go hand-in-hand with reengineering the business process of project management. The new architecture consisted of a wide area network along with client-server project management software. At one time, about 20 professional schedulers were using the old project management system. Today, more than 550 people are accessing and updating their schedules online using the client-server system. In the management presentation, the old process was linked to the old architecture. Changing one without the other was not feasible.

GUIDELINES

- **Avoid getting bogged down in each small, detailed component of the architecture.**

   Stick with the major components and the ones that relate to the issues.

- **Remember that the architecture is an overall blueprint.**

   The architecture is not a detailed parts list or a complete itemization of all pieces.

- **Early in the process, alert managers to issues that relate to an architecture alternatives.**

   As you define the alternative architectures, relay the issues involved to management, along with the corresponding parts of the architecture. This is a good way to pre-sell before the overall management presentation. Managers are ready for recommended change.

- **Always include the alternative of doing nothing.**

   Show how this will stop or degrade other parts of the plan in terms of new software and functions.

- **Construct an architecture out of components offered by competitors of the vendors you use.**

   This will give you a view of the pluses and minuses of moving to a different vendor.

- **Create an architecture out of non-legacy systems only.**

  This will indicate the dependency upon the legacy systems.

- **Identify what resources are required to support each part of the architecture.**

  If you had the ideal architecture, what would be the staffing requirements? What would be the benefits? Try to translate a good architecture into cost savings and revenue increases.

ACTION ITEMS

1. It is useful to be able to explain how the new architecture will benefit the processes. Construct a table in which the rows are the processes and the columns are elements of the new architecture. Place a number from 1 to 5 in each cell showing the degree of benefit of the architecture element to the process (1 is low or no benefit, 5 is great benefit).

Process/
Architecture

2. Create a table of problems as rows and architecture components as columns. Carry out the rating system described earlier in this chapter.

3. Generate three alternatives for the new architecture. Use some of the strategies discussed. For each alternative, identify the strategy, the components, and how they are linked.

4. In another table, map the issues vs. the alternative architectures, as discussed earlier in the chapter.

CHAPTER 15

STEP H: COLLECT INFORMATION FOR PROCESSES, INFRASTRUCTURE, AND ORGANIZATIONS

CONTENTS

15

STEP H: COLLECT INFORMATION FOR PROCESSES, INFRASTRUCTURE, AND ORGANIZATIONS

PURPOSE AND SCOPE

Your purpose goes beyond gathering data. You seek the best approach for implementation. You also want to build up a relationship of trust between the staff and yourself. Successful implementation rests upon the trust created during data collection. Of all of the activities in business process improvement, this is the one that you should do yourself. Do not delegate data collection.

The scope of the work includes the following:

- **Files**

  These are not just process and project files, but also files associated with the process, such as customer or order files. Additional files pertain to infrastructure and organization.

- **Forms and procedures**

  Consider both informal and formal (official) forms. An informal form might include copies of checklists.

- **The processes themselves**

  Direct observation and even participation in the processes are intended here.

- **Infrastructure**

  You can gain information through interviews, files, and direct observation.

- **Organizations**

  We want to gather information about the organizations involved in the processes. Political, personnel, and structural information can aid in understanding problems and issues.

- **Customers and suppliers**

  Under certain circumstances when the processes touch the customers and suppliers, contact them and observe their interaction with the processes.

  The scope may change, based on the information you collect. The work in this phase is adaptive.

END PRODUCTS

You want to achieve a detailed understanding of the process group that you have selected. You want to be able to perform analysis and develop the new or improved processes. You definitely do not want to return to collect more data again and again until implementation.

Here are some of the end products of a detailed understanding of processes:

- **Definition of specific individual steps in the processes**

  This is the technical core of the work. Level of detail is an issue as is the handling of exceptions. An exception is a variation of the business process to address a specific transaction.

- **Additional comparison tables that reach down to the detailed process steps**

  These tables follow from previous chapters.

- **Understanding of how infrastructure and technology either inhibits or aids the process steps**

  The support structure is key to change.

- **Understanding of the involvement of the organization and staff in the process**

  Attitudes toward the process, staff turnover, and supervision are important factors.

- **Determination of tactical issues addressed by the new process**

    If you develop a wonderful new process that is strategically correct, but it fails to address tactical issues for the staff doing the process, you fail.

- **Identification of the detailed changes attempted in the past**

    Lessons learned are always important.

- **Understanding of the politics and self interest surrounding the processes**

    What are people's opinions and feelings? What is important to them?

- **Ideas about feasible approaches for implementation**

    While you do not have a new process defined, you can think about marketing and implementation based on your knowledge of the environment.

- **Identification of immovable constraints**

    Where are the real boundaries of the process?

- **Established relationship with the staff involved in the process**

    Rapport and trust will make work easier and lead to successful implementation.

RESOURCES

You are concerned mainly with time in this step. The project may have a very tight schedule, and you do not want to take too much of people's time. Here is a fundamental rule: The more time you take from people, the higher you raise their expectations. Also, if you take up a great deal of someone's time, he or she may tell his or her manager that your work is impeding the process. Your project may stop right there.

Time spent doing the data collection should be limited. Most projects involve less than 20 days of direct data collection. But it may be is impossible to gather all of the data and see all of the people in this time. Another way to measure time is elapsed time. Elapsed time is three to four times what the collection effort takes, if you do all of the Action steps suggested in this chapter.

APPROACH

Critical success factors in process improvement are collecting data and interacting with people through interviewing and observing processes. While these factors are important in traditional projects, their stature increases in process improvement because of the following:

- **Process improvement tends to be political.**

  There is fear among the people involved in the process as well as in middle management and supervision levels. What you say and how you work can have a direct impact on whether the project will succeed.

- **Collecting data is the principle means of interacting with the staff and management involved in the business process.**

  Keep in mind that you are not only collecting data, you are also showing your confident attitude. During this phase of business process improvement you create an impression with the staff who will make your changes succeed or fail. Through the interaction you have the opportunity to get people involved and committed to process improvement.

While traditional methods of interviewing and data collection have value, a total approach is more efficient. Change and implementation are marketed at the same time that information is collected. Also, the detailed data collection effort discussed here is conducted in parallel with the infrastructure assessment and the competitive and industry assessment.

Here are some ways to gather information:

- **Observe the process or organization.**

  This provides direct raw data but could be misleading depending on factors such as the time of day.

- **Interview people.**

  This is the traditional approach. However, interviewing has its drawbacks. First, people can only tell you about things that they can remember. Second, their memory may be faulty. Third, people respond subjectively. Fourth, if several people are being interviewed at once, some may not speak up.

- **Use passive sources.**

  This is the search for information through libraries, the Internet, and archives.

  Given the significance of data collection , carefully plan, carry out, and follow up after each contact. Be up-to-date on the project at all times so that you can respond to questions. Consciously learn and take information in and continually add to your cumulative base of knowledge.

  On the surface this seems straightforward. You can read through the files, observe the process, and conduct interviews. Usually, there will have been previous studies. However, even with the blessings of upper management, you are likely to encounter the following problems:

- **Management may have already provided all of this information.**

  Prevent this reasoning from stopping you by doing substantial homework prior to interviews. Most often, the information provided was not very detailed. Often people are not asked how they would improve the system on their own.

- **Other studies exist, but no action was taken. How will your effort be different?**

  Prior to conducting interviews, you will learn about actions and items that were not implemented. It is important to discover the attempts, discards, and failures. These can be as important as knowing what worked. Be different. Don't promise them results. All you can honestly say is that you are going to make your best effort, and that you will need their support.

- **You are so dependent upon technology and the existing systems that you cannot improve the processes.**

  This is a rational excuse. The current processes may depend on old systems. These systems cannot be changed, so it follows that the process cannot be altered. Respond by expanding the scope to include changes in technology.

- **Top management may want change, but the managers you report to prefers the status quo.**

  Gather as much information at the bottom as you can and pay less attention to the middle. Middle management is, after all, remote from the action.

It is useful to get these issues out on the table at the start. You must be able to deal with them at the beginning of the activity. Whether you employ these or other methods of dealing with these problems, you will need to be overcoming barriers along the way.

Action 1: Develop the Plan of Attack

First develop a plan for the work. This helps you track your work and determine when you are falling behind. Also, the plan forces you to give structure and organization to the work. The plan of attack should include the following:

- **List of potential contacts and their profiles**

  A profile might include title, role in process, telephone, location, and any comments about their role.

- **Log of documents**

  As you collect information, you will see many documents, reports, and form. Log these. This not only helps in organization but will help you respond to questions later.

- **List of issues in the project**

  These are issues and opportunities that surface during your work. Give a summary title, date the issue appeared, short description (if the summary title is not sufficient), and references to documents or interviews. You might indicate identifiers to show importance and to whom the issue is of interest.

- **Approach to the work**

  This is a description of how you are going to go about your work. Include any methods and tools that you will employ. Tools might include the software you will use.

- **Task list summary**

  This is a list of tasks and a schedule for the tasks. Keep this task to less than ten items. You do not want to spend much time maintaining this. It is a road map that you can use to make the approach tangible.

- **End products**

  Describe each end product along with an outline and discussion of the use of the end product. Notice that the word *report* did not appear. End products in industry today are often presentations prepared with presentation software.

  View the plan as a living document. It is more than a checklist of tasks; it includes some of your key lists. Automate as much as possible. For the issues, use a spreadsheet or database to help in tracking.

Action 2: Set Up for Data Collection

Set up a series of databases or files on a shared network server. This will ensure that data is accumulated on a timely basis, that it is consistent, and that people share information. You can use any of a variety of software packages—database management systems, file systems, groupware, spreadsheets. Choose something that the team members feel comfortable with.

On the software, set up the following:

- **Issues database**

  This is a database of the problems and opportunities associated with the business process. Over time, it will be refined in detail. Use this to ensure that your new process will address these issues.

- **Contacts**

  This is a file of all contacts for the project. It includes positions, time of contacts, who contacted, and any pertinent comments.

- **Idea database for the new process**

  This is a database of ideas that are gathered from data collection. This will serve to generate the alternative scenarios or models for the new business process later.

- **Benefits**

  Have a file of benefits that can accrue with change.

- **Implementation considerations**

  This database includes ideas about organization, infrastructure, policies, and technology that impact the implementation of a new process. If these are not recorded, they could come back and haunt you later when you are ready for implementation.

Action 3: Review the Files on the Process

An early element of the project is to review the files on the processes. Having the information in the files can reduce the data collection and interview time. It provides the information needed to ask better questions. You also may be able to identify the players and their attitudes.

Here is a typical list of files and file contents:

- **Organization charts**

  You really want several versions of the organization charts. First, you would like the current organization for the company. This includes all groups, not just the ones involved with the processes you have selected. Next, you would like an organization chart from one to two years ago in order to see what happened to organizations and who moved up and down in the company. Some of these people may be critical in your effort. You will be using these organization charts as you consider the real organization (discussed below).

- **Departmental budgets (past, current, and projected years) for departments involved in the processes**

  Keep the budgets detailed so that you can determine how much effort the organization devotes to activities around the processes.

- **Annual internal and external reports**

  You want to know what people say publicly about issues, opportunities, and trends. The internal reports are those annual progress reports that divisions and departments might make as they summarize the year. Quarterly reports may be available as well. As with organization charts, get several years' worth.

- **Previous studies about business process improvement, quality management, and other efforts at change**

  These studies may be hard to find. If a company spent a lot of money on a study to improve itself and nothing came of it, the company may be embarrassed to have evidence of this available.

- **Reports on information systems, technology, and infrastructure**

  What changes and enhancements have been made? What was the basis for selecting the technology currently in place?

- **Procedures and forms related to the processes that you will be analyzing**

  Also look for information on procedures for using any automated systems that support the process. Ask to see old versions of procedures and forms, if they are available.

- **Internal memoranda and notes about the departments involved in the processes**

  Include any internal or external audit reports and findings, if these exist.

Note that personnel files have been excluded because these are confidential.

Where will you find these documents? At each step in your interview and data collection process, indicate that you want to save time and not ask obvious questions and so will need to access the files.

When you review a file, first write the document identification in the log. Make copies of important documents after you have reviewed the file. Return the original documents to the file. Inform staff members that you have returned the documents. Review the copies later in your office.

When you read the document, read first for content. Note the issue or subject that is being addressed. Note the person who wrote it, and the audience. As you review documents, look for references to other documents in the same file.

After reviewing a number of documents in a file, you can construct several document trees, which show the documents in time sequence. The length of the tree and how it ends are important. If there is no tree, the document went nowhere. The bottom of the tree is the last event. Was the subject identified at the top of the tree resolved at the bottom? Are there many stand-alone trees? This would indicate a possible lack of communication. The length of a tree can sometimes indicate the degree of interest in the subject.

Look for follow-up reports. Are there memos indicating the type of action to be taken with respect to the reports you have found? Or, is the file silent? If there is no follow-up, make a note to ask in interviews what happened.

In reviewing files, you are trying to answer some or all of the following questions:

- What are specific steps in the process? Which organization performs what steps?

- What is the condition of the process?

- What do people feel are the boundaries of the process?

- Who are the people who write about the process and what are their attitudes?

- What are the attitudes of organizations and managers toward the process?

- What are apparent issues regarding the process? How were issues resolved? Why wasn't there follow-up?

Sometimes, in collecting data, you will find files that are in poor shape or not in one place. In such cases, ask to see the forms. To review a form, consider the following:

- **What is the date of the form? Is there a number?**

  The date and number indicate that it is formal form. If it is undated, make a note to ask how long it has been in use. If the date is old, this may indicate that the process with respect to the form is stable; alternatively, it may mean that the form's use is infrequent.

- **Look at the layout of the form. Does it appear well organized?**

  Prior to computers, form design was considered an art and viewed as important. Today, it is less so. But fields on the form that group together should be adjacent.

- **When you view the process, ask to see several completed forms. How well does the form hold up under real use? Are there many handwritten notes and attachments to the form?**

  This indicates that the form is not serving its purpose.

- **Are there multiple copies of the form? Is the routing of these copies clear?**

  The copies can give you a trail for following a transaction in the process.

- **If there are instructions for filling out the form, try to follow these instructions. Are the instructions complete and clear?**

Action 4: Observe the Process

Experience shows that it is important to observe the actual process. This is true regardless of where the work is being performed. Review the documentation that you have on the process and the list of issues. Then contact the supervisor of the process either directly, if appropriate, or indirectly through a manager, and arrange for a walkthrough.

Start the walkthrough at the beginning. Many supervisors often have to give tours. You can differentiate yourself from the more casual observer by asking detailed questions as you go. For example, suppose that you are shown raw documents being received. Ask about the quality of the documents and forms. Ask for samples. Try to get permission to copy a sample of each type. Make detailed notes as you go.

Be aware that the supervisor is granting you a favor. By showing you around in the presence of staff, a supervisor appears to be endorsing what you are doing. A tour can take several hours. The supervisor is under pressure to return to work. Be sensitive to these factors.

Here are some situations you may encounter on the tour, along with suggestions on what to do:

- **For some reason, part of the process is not being performed.**

  This is a perfect opportunity to arrange for a return visit.

- **The process is too big and the tour is getting too long.**

  Cut the tour off at a logical point and arrange to come back when it is convenient.

- **The supervisor cannot answer your question.**

  Respond that you can find out later.

- **The process is not in good shape and the supervisor is embarrassed about it.**

  Show understanding and express that it is not the fault of the supervisor or the employees. Assure the supervisor that you understand that all involved are trying to make do with a difficult situation.

- **It is obvious that you are being shown only the best part of the process.**

  Don't try to get into other areas. Wait for another time to see more.

The meeting with the supervisor should follow the rules of interviewing discussed previously. Point out to the supervisor that if possible you would like to perform some of the work in the process. This means that you will have to be trained in the process. This is important because it can reveal what formal training and procedures new employees need. You will also learn who has the experience to answer questions and how exceptions are handled.

Later Visits to the Process

A basic rule is *do not disrupt the process*. Allow people to do their work. Once you start with recurring visits, plan on going to the process for a portion of every day. As you keep showing up, people will accept you. If possible, dress like the people who are doing the work.

Adopt the terminology of the organization with which you are working. Demonstrate respect for and affinity with the departments. Adopt some of their key words, phrases, and abbreviations and use them in everyday conversations. Recognize and respect the fact that every organization has its own jargon.

Observe the business process in periods of peak and calm. An "average" probably is a myth, but people can tell you what are the peak and slow times of the day, week, and month. Observe several examples of peak and slow times. Observe the workings of the process and the interface with the public or other departments.

If you are going to be trained in the process, behave like someone new to the process. Don't ask why something is done. When the trainer indicates some experience or lessons learned, show appreciation for this. This will show respect for his or her creativity.

As you perform the work after training, you will want to ask many questions. Save these up rather than posing the questions one at a time. Perform work in 15-minute increments. After each period, write down your notes and questions.

If you cannot be trained because of the nature of the process, you will need to proceed through the workflow and observe what people do. When there is no time pressure, you can ask questions and cover topics such as the following:

- How long have you been doing the work?
- How did you learn to do the work?
- What is most unusual type of work you have encountered? This will help you get at exceptions and shadow systems.
- When are there peaks of work? What do you differently at those times?
- How do you measure how you are doing?
- What happens when there is an error? How is rework handled?
- What do you think could be done to make the job easier?
- What are some problems with the current computer system?
- If you could spend money on anything, what would you do?

It will take many visits over several weeks to get answers to these questions. Here is an ambitious but realistic list of what you hope to accomplish:

- **Identify exception work and how it is handled.**
- **Identify shadow systems and procedures that employees use to do the work.**

    Gather as much detail on this as possible. It will be essential that your new process addresses both exceptions and shadow systems and procedures.

- **Draw people out for ideas on improvement and the history of what has happened with the process over time.**
- **Identify people who are energetic and eager for change.**

  These individuals can be of great help later during implementation and in marketing the new process.

- **Identify senior people who know the business rules of the process in detail.**

  These people will be invaluable later during the development of new systems and procedures.

- **Solicit ideas for improvement and give people credit for their ideas.**
- **Flesh out the issues that were identified at the start.**
- **Try to estimate in qualitative terms the benefits of changing the current process.**

If you establish trust with the supervisor and employees, you may be able to test some parts of the new process and procedures on several pieces of work. Prior to each visit, make a list of people and topics for follow-up, based on your notes and observations from previous visits.

After Observation

First, write a note to the manager of the supervisor to express thanks for the time given you. Then, as with interviewing, make notes after each visit. Update the following:

- Details on the impact and validity of issues
- Documentation of the current process in terms of business rules and workflow
- Ideas for improvements to the process
- Identification of key employees
- Comments on constraints and conditions you will face when you pursue implementation
- Comments on infrastructure

- Comments on organization
- Comments on technology and systems
- Comments on policies related to the business process

As with interviewing, the information should be structured and shared among the project team on a network disk drive.

After some observations, the team could attend a staff meeting and generate some ideas together. This can occur in a workshop mode. Also, you could show documentation on the current process and have people validate the steps. Avoid exotic flowcharts that are not easily understandable.

In reviewing the current process, start to get verbal reaction to issues and potential actions. Do this at the process level. If you do it generally, it will have little impact and you may arouse defensive instincts.

After reviewing the process, check back with the managers. Indicate that the time spent by their staff was helpful.

Action 5: Perform the Initial Process Analysis

As you conduct interviews and observe the process, you will be constructing some basic items for analysis:

- **Basic information flow for the process**

  You can use a graphics tool. You can also simply use a piece of paper with the following columns: step, description, who performs the step, infrastructure used, forms used, time to perform step, and comments.

- **Exception workflow**

- **Rework workflow**

- **Issues with a label tagging at which steps the issue is significant**

- **Rules used to do department work**

  In the Monarch example, this would include the collection rules ("if the account has never been delinquent and the amount owed is less than X, then....").

- **Input and output volume—peaks, average, low**
- **Observations on the process itself**
- **Steps taken to measure the performance of the process and control it**
- **Ideas of minor improvements (e.g., changes in handling of steps, changes in forms)**

  After some initial analysis, formulate some basic questions about the workflow. Get together an initial list of minor improvements as well. Return to the process and ask additional questions, both to gather additional information and to build up trust and a relationship with the people involved in the tasks.

Action 6: Consider the Process Boundaries

As you gather information and perform analysis, begin to identify and examine the boundaries of the process—where the process begins and ends. You must know about boundaries between departments within the process as well as boundaries with infrastructure, suppliers, customers, and other departments. Remember that many opportunities for improvement lie on these boundaries.

Here are some of the problems that might arise at the boundaries:

- **The input that starts the process is not acceptable.**

  Errors are already present at the start of work.

- **There is no measurement or control at the boundary.**

  There may be no quality assessment.

- **The infrastructure poorly supports the process so that the boundary with the process is flawed.**

- **Outputs of the process may not be measured or even known.**

  You hear about the transaction because of problems in the next department.

- **The surrounding organization must immediately reorganize the work to do anything with it.**

  By considering boundaries, you also are making a determination of whether you should follow up in other departments surrounding the process.

Action 7: Move to Other Processes in the Group

Ask the same questions and follow the same steps. You want to build a cumulative body of knowledge. Determine whether the issues in one process carry over to other processes performed by the same group or using the same infrastructure.

Also try to get ideas about which process and which steps would be the best starting points for implementation.

Action 8: Build Comparison Tables

Earlier comparison tables focused on the process level for analysis. This was all that was possible without detailed information. Now you can move down to the individual step in the process. You are attempting to identify which steps in a process deserve greater attention. Consider no more than ten steps per process so that you don't get entangled in too much detail.

- **Process Steps vs. Process Steps**

  Earlier you aggregated processes into a group based on common ground. Now you will consider similarities at the level of the process step. If you can identify similarities, when you define a new process, you can, perhaps, replicate some of the changes to other processes. You can also validate changes by assuring that they work across more than one process. The table indicates the degree of similarity between steps in the processes. For the rows, you will often only use the major process. The columns are the steps of each of the other processes in the group. In the Monarch Bank example, installment loan collections was the major process; leasing and credit card collections were other processes in the group.

- **Process Steps vs. Infrastructure**

  How does the infrastructure support the process? To answer this you progress down to the step level. The rows are the process steps; the columns are major elements of infrastructure. The table entry indicates the strength of support on a scale of 1 to 5. Alternatively, you could use the table to determine relevance, importance, and shortcomings of the infrastructure with respect to the process steps. This is an important table since it will begin to indicate where infrastructure improvements might make a difference.

- **Process Steps vs. Technology**

  This is similar to the preceding table. However, here you could put the existing technologies in as columns along with potential technologies that you identify in Step 4. Relevance and potential can determine the rating for the new technologies. Alternately, consider only current technologies and indicate the degree to which the technology adequately supports the process step.

- **Process Steps vs. Issues**

  In Step 1, you identified a series of business issues relating to business objectives. In this table, you are assessing the relevance of the issue to the step in the process. At first, this appears to be too much detail. However, if you find that there is no fit, question your choice of the group or the identification of the issues. In place of issues, you could select business objectives. For example, if a business issue reduced paper handling, you could rate each step as to the degree to which it is paper intensive.

- **Process Steps vs. Organizations**

  This table indicates which organizations perform what steps in the process. The table is very useful in showing the ineffectiveness or complexity in processes that cross multiple organizations. An example for charge-off for Monarch Bank appears in Table 15-1. The charge-off area is where loans, leases, and credit card accounts go that failed to be collected. Charge-off includes legal, accounting write-off, repossession, and sending the account to an outside agency.

  If you have a single organization, you could assess the quality or effectiveness of the organization in performing the steps.

You can modify all of these tables by applying weights to indicate the relative importance or some other weighting factor to the table and producing a new table. Use spreadsheet software, which calculates the new weighted tables based on different criteria. Consider employing weighting factors based on elapsed time of the work in the process, importance of the process step, and labor effort involved in

Table 15-1:
Example of Process Steps vs. Organization for Monarch Bank

Process Steps vs Organization	Installment loans	Credit card	Leasing	Charge-off legal	Charge-off accounting
Collections	X	X	X		
Prep for charge-off	X	X	X		
Review to determine action				X	
Pursue legal recourse				X	
Write-off account					X
Record on credit bureau file					X

the step. If you keep coming up with the same general relationships, this sensitivity analysis supports your findings in front of management.

MANAGEMENT PRESENTATION AND COST-BENEFIT ANALYSIS

Management presentations will be based on comparison tables, which will make clear the problems and potential for improvement with the current processes.

In terms of costs and benefits, you can define how much the current process costs in terms of the following, to build a sense of urgency for change:

- Money to perform and support the processes
- Rework and correction
- Problems in customer service and potential lost business

KEY QUESTIONS

Have you identified the interfaces between the critical processes and the other processes in the group and in the company?

Do you need to move a process into or out of the group.?

What problems would prevent the benefits of change from being realized if you improve what you have identified?

EXAMPLES

Monarch Bank

Because collection activity occurred over two shifts, it was useful to collect data during both shifts. Work in multiple shifts was the same. Different shifts could handle different transactions, different customers, and different orders. Upper management had a strong interest in improvement and wanted frequent updates on findings. With management interest high, an overall vision of a new process was developed. Details followed during later analysis work.

As is the case in many organizations, the true organization network rested on long-term, lower-level supervisors. These people knew the most and had the most ideas on what to do. Several newer employees also had ideas for automation.

A major issue that surfaced was the difference in collection approaches followed by different parts of Monarch Bank. This variation was a result of the nature of the banking product, but it was also due to a lack of procedures and training. Some interim suggestions related to training and procedures were helpful.

TRAN

The process of interest in this stage was the payroll timekeeping process for bus drivers. The key time for observance was 4:00 a.m., when many drivers appeared for work. By observing and talking with drivers, the project team gathered several useful ideas. The team also was able to learn how much automation the bus drivers could handle and use.

Resistance had to be overcome. People had been promised results in the past, but had been disappointed. Data collection was a continuous effort to gain trust and confidence. Management received feedback on the staff's attitude. It took a great deal of restraint not to raise expectations.

Another point of resistance was the old technology in place. It was clear early on that implementation must begin on the network and systems. Without these, major improvements would not be possible.

Stirling Manufacturing

As the work got underway, it was clear that Stirling had no formal process for part of the work. Actions derived from the shop floor supervisor. This was chaotic. Information was gathered on several variations of the process. After documentation, these were reviewed with senior staff to determine what was correct. This precipitated a major discussion about process, which helped reinforce the need to change and formalize the process. People were so busy, however, that no one had time to study and understand the entire process. At the end, the students of the process had the best knowledge and trained the staff members in how to do the process.

GUIDELINES

- **Stress simplification and paper elimination, not job elimination or process change.**

  When people ask what you are coming up with, focus on simplification of work and elimination of paper and handling.

- **Keep a sense of humor in considering processes.**

  Too often, people take everything seriously. Ask someone about the oddest transaction or piece of work they have experienced. This cannot only break the ice, but can useful later in giving examples of workflow.

- **Move among organizations as much as within.**

  If a process involves several organizations, make sure that you are visible in all of them. If you do not balance your time between groups, you may lose the support of the departments where you spend little time.

- **Ask people where they spend their time.**

  People will often describe a process and their role by importance of the process steps. Thus, they give more attention to
  review and control steps than collating or entering information.
  Find out where they spend their time. To improve the process,
  you must impact the way they spend their time.

- **If people seem to resist involvement, move to keep them
  informed; avoid isolation.**

  After meeting with a number of department employees, you
  may sense that some people do not want to talk about the
  process. They avoid your gaze. Do not leave them isolated.
  Seek them out and ask them what they think. If they are not
  talkative, bounce off of them some of the observations and
  issues that you have identified. Ask them if these are correct.

- **When someone suggests a change, ask yourself why the
  existing process exists in its present state.**

  Ask this person to tell you in his or her own words how it the
  change might be implemented. Do not question or challenge.
  You can learning three things—the new idea, what is important
  to the person, and language and terminology that may be new to
  you.

ACTION ITEMS

1. Because many of the processes cross multiple departments and
   organizations, it is helpful to construct a table of process steps
   vs. organizations. In the table, use these codes: P–performs the
   step, O–owns or is responsible for the step, E–involved in the
   step on an exception basis. Leave the space blank for no involvement. When you define the new process (in Step J), you
   will be creating the same chart for the new process with new
   steps. The two tables can then be compared.

2. Construct a table of exceptions and normal work (rows) vs.
   process steps (columns). How an exception differs from normal
   work and from other exceptions can be seen from the table.
   Place an X if that step is performed for the particular exception.

3. Which technology and parts of the architecture apply to each process step? Construct two tables. The first is for the current architecture and technology. The rows are the elements of the current architecture and the columns are the process steps. Then create a similar chart for the new technology and architecture. In the cells within the tables, enter the codes: C–critical, B–beneficial, but not critical, and N–not used. These tables show how technology or the lack thereof impedes the current workflow and how new technology can aid the process.

4. Relate the business issues defined earlier to the process steps to pin down how the process contributes to the issue. Note that if an issue cannot be associated with a step, it applies to the overall process, policies, or organization.

   Put the issues in the table as rows with general business issues at the top. For columns, enter the steps of the process first. Add more columns for policy, organization, and infrastructure. The entry in the table will be 1 to 5 (1 means that the issue does not apply to the step, 5 means that the issue arises directly from the step).

5. Organize the data in terms of the individual process step. Construct a table in which the rows are the process steps and the columns are sources of information. In the table are your major findings relative to the steps.

6. Set up an organized file for the information you have collected. Consider using the following tabs for the file:
   —Interviews
   —Direct observation
   —Reports
   —Minutes of Meetings
   —File notes
   —Other information

   Summarize the data according to the following categories:
   —Process steps
   —General process
   —Current automation
   —Shadow systems
   —Workarounds

PART IV FOUR

DETERMINING
THE NEW PROCESS

CHAPTER 16

STEP I: ANALYZE THE INFORMATION

CONTENTS

16

STEP I: ANALYZE THE INFORMATION

PURPOSE AND SCOPE

Following is a short list of goals that you want to achieve when you analyze the data:

- Understand how the current processes work.
- Decide on the issues to be addressed through the new process.
- Structure information to serve as the basis for developing the new process.

END PRODUCTS

The major end product is analysis results that support implementing new processes for each process in the process group mentioned earlier. More specifically, you will:

- Understand the current processes, their issues, and their problems in detail.
- Be aware of problems that will occur if the current processes are continued without change.
- Understand interaction among processes, organization, infrastructure, and business factors (as revealed in comparison tables).
- Develop an understanding of an approach for the group of processes.

RESOURCES

Other people should be involved in helping you with the analysis. However, it may be impossible to do a complete job with limited time and resources. One solution is to consider how much team time and effort you want to spend in each of the following analysis activities:

- Organize the process information
- Summarize the process information
- Document the process information
- Perform statistical and mathematical analysis, such as simulation of the process
- Conduct follow-up interviews to review analysis results and hypotheses
- Document the analysis results

You will probably want to use a software tool to document and analyze processes to save time and to support more analysis.

APPROACH

As you collect the information, you will organize, understand, analyze, and eventually present it. Your audience will include department staff, managers, and members of the process improvement team. In the previous five steps you collected information that includes the following:

- Business objectives and issues
- Details about the processes
- Details about the infrastructure and organization
- Ideas about potential technology and industrial practice
- Specific problems and opportunities related to the process

Here are some steps for a general approach to gathering the information:

- Understand the processes in detail and from different perspectives. Graphic tools may be helpful for this.
- Model, simulate, or describe the process in a way that highlights a specific issue or opportunity. For example, if there were a

shortage of CAD workstations, the analysis should indicate that this shortage of workstations is a bottleneck. You want to show the issues that exist and their degree of impact.

- Show the interaction between the process, the organization, and the infrastructure. After all, many issues and improvements will occur in these areas. Showing only the process sheds little light on organization.

Action 1: Document the Current Process Workflow

You will use work from previous steps. Take a piece of paper and turn it sideways (landscape). The organizations that work on the process will be the columns. Put these in the order in which they handle the transaction. In the columns, write a general description of the steps that each organization performs.

Recall that *organization* is a general term. It may include the following items:

- Title of person doing the work
- Person doing the work by name
- Organization and group involved
- Performance measures
- Staffing characteristics

An example of the chart is the bus operators timekeeping workflow for TRAN, Figure 16-1. Three organizations are involved in the workflow: the remote base, operations, and payroll. So, those three organizations are the first three columns.

In this case, the process steps are data capture and some editing; data entry of exceptions and review; and review, data entry, and error tracking. However, because errors are sent back to the base for correction and then reprocessed by payroll, two more columns were added at the end: remote base and payroll.

Now take separate pieces of paper for each process and write this at the top of the page. Create six columns on the page and use an abbreviation of the following as column headings:

Figure 16-1:
Bus Driver Timekeeping Workflow

This example shows the workflow steps across organizations. It helps reveal the complexity of a process.

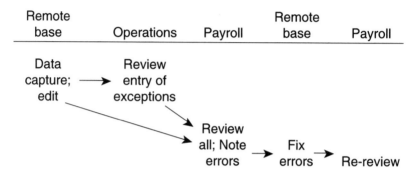

- Step number in the process
- Process step description in common language
- Frequency, volume, and time involved in the process step
- Who performs the step
- Automation and infrastructure to support the step
- Issues involved in the step

The infrastructure you should include depends on the specific process involved, but here are some suggestions:

- Online system or PC
- Network and other software (e.g., electronic mail, electronic forms)
- Computer reports
- Manual forms and logs
- Procedures and policies
- Files
- Location and buildings

- Mail facilities
- Telephone
- Office layout

Do not try to include all possible infrastructure items. Only include those that have an impact on the process. A test you can employ is to ask the question, "Does this item merely support the performance of the process step or does it impact the process step?"

Tables 16-1 and 16-2 provide two examples of process steps for the timekeeping process. The frequency, volume, and time involved in each process step are important if you want to estimate the cost of performing the process and assess improvements.

The simple column approach has several advantages. First, you can choose to look at the process in general or in detail. Second, you can aggregate the detail and move up to the process level. A simple chart with columns and text fields is all that you need now. If you want to create more exotic charts later, you will have the data.

When you begin to review your work, first check readability of the tables. Eliminate jargon or common language. See if the details in

Table 16-1:
Operations Review of Timekeeping

This is an important table in that it provides detailed information on the flow and problems.

Step No.	Description	Freq./vol./time	Who	Automation	Issues
1	Receive exception timesheets	Daily; 80/day; 15 mn	Clerk	None	
2	Sort in alphabetical order	Daily; 80/day; 30 mn	Clerk	None	Errors
3	Review each timesheet	Daily; 80/day; 2 hr	Staff	None	Labor intensive
4	Enter data into system	Daily; 80/day, 3 hr	Staff	Terminal	System is complex

Table 16-2: Payroll Review of Timekeeping

This is similar to the previous table. It is useful to divide the detailed steps into those performed by each organization.

Step No.	Description	Freq./vol./time	Who	Automation	Issues
1	Receive timesheets from base and Opns	Daily; 750/day; 15 mn	Clerk	None	Labor intensive
2	Sort timesheets in alphabetical order	Daily; 750/day; 2hrs	Clerk	None	Mistakes are many
3	Check each timesheet on system	Daily; 750/day; 4hrs	2 clerks	System	System is not easy to use
4	Manually write up error report	Daily; 60/day; 3 hrs	Staff	None	High-priced staff doing clerical work
5	Send report to Base; retain copy	Daily; 60/day; 2 hrs	Staff	None	Handling time high

each process cover its scope. Review your notes and make sure that the issues people raised appear in your tables. Look down the organization and infrastructure columns and see if they are complete.

Verify the steps with any written procedures. Staple the blank or completed forms and logs to the appropriate table in which they are referenced.

If you run across a process that is performed by only one organization, divide the process into logical segments based on control, different groups in the same organization, or a similar modular structure. Then proceed through the same steps.

Action 2: Reflect the Issues in the Process Workflow

You have identified issues during data collection. Now that you have identified process steps, make a table in which the columns are process steps and the issues are rows. Entries to the table will be comments on the issue in terms of impact on the process step.

Consider the impact entries from different views, ranging from the staff involved to managers of groups apart from the immediate organization.

Some issues may be quickly addressed. Take advantage of this opportunity. Prepare to suggest actions for the short term. As long as they do not undermine the process improvement, intermediate actions help the process and raise your credibility.

Action 3: Validate the Analysis

Preceding chapters identified a series of comparison tables. These relate business factors, the processes, organization, and infrastructure and show degree of relevance, importance, or a similar factor. Use the tables to validate what you have created in your analysis.

Action 4: Automate the Analysis

Automating the analysis will accelerate the process and will enable you to make changes and additions easily without recreating the entire chart. Another reason to automate is political. Use of the appropriate tool, and the inference that you know how to use it, gives you credibility as an analyst. Because you are a user of the tool, you do not have to spend time describing how it works in detail. Thus, you avoid being perceived as being excessively technical.

Roles of Software Tools

Wait until this step to identify software tools because your choice should be influenced by the type of data available and the level of detail. Keep your options open until you have collected sufficient information.

Software tools assist in the following:

* **Data collection management**

  As you collect data, you will need to find a way to organize it. Simple microcomputer database management systems are useful. They help you to extract and analyze information.

- **Enabling a better understanding**

  Any software tool that can help you understand a process and identify where you should collect more information is useful.

- **Analysis and modeling**

  Software shortens the time taken up by analysis and "what if" analysis. Modeling tools are useful.

- **Presentation**

  Presentation aids are useful for explaining workflow and process.

- **Implementation**

  Software tools aid the implementation of process improvement results.

Trade-offs and Tool Requirements

Tool use involves trade-offs. Before selecting a software application, consider the following questions:

- How long does it take to learn the software?
- How long does it take and what effort are required to become proficient?
- How is data entered?
- How are data and results extracted?
- What are the hardware and software requirements?

Be sure that you have the time to learn to use and work with the tools you select. Learning the software tool means that you are able to enter data, manipulate the tool, and achieve results. If the tool requires too much effort in input or output, you will probably not use it much, regardless of its ultimate value.

Categories of Software Tools

Following is a way to categorize software tools that can support your process improvement project:

Data Management

- **Database management**

  You can use an off-the-shelf microcomputer or network data-base management system or a fourth- generation language. These tools provide a way to organize data and to export selected data out into any of several common formats. They will assist in analyzing and reporting material.

- **Groupware**

  Groupware (e.g., Lotus Notes or Microsoft Exchange) allows you to build files and databases that are available to the project team. Groupware provides the glue for carrying this out. The advantage of this software is that it provides functions that are easy to learn. The disadvantage is that, if the software is not currently available in your office, it is unlikely that the process improvement budget can support the implementation of group-ware.

Analysis

- **Project management**

  When you think of project management software, you think about defining tasks and milestones to input into the software. However, you can also use the steps in a process when working with project management software. The software can then be used to check your understanding of the process. You can also try out different alternatives by changing tasks, relationships/ dependencies, resources, and durations. Use GANTT and PERT charts for analysis.

- **Simulation**

  Workflow simulation software allows you to enter the process steps and relationships into the software. You can now add durations, resources, and other parameters. The software results are the result of running the model with these inputs. The first run should be the current process, which can show its problems and validate your understanding of the process. Next, you can modify the process and rerun the tool. This step has several attractions: It is quantitative and can produce interesting graphic results. There is an issue of level of detail, which is addressed later. All simulation tools have mathematical assumptions that can restrict their use in the real world. Additionally, increased time is required to learn this type of tool.

- **Statistics**

  This software is both an analysis and presentation tool. There are now statistical software packages that provide interfaces to spreadsheets and databases. The packages offer a wide range of analysis capabilities, which were previously only available on large mainframe computers. They required extensive programming—a situation not unlike the early days of Internet use. Rapid analysis and exotic graphs are pluses, but you must understand statistics and the limitations on the methods in terms of their validity. Thus, this tends to be a tool for the specialist.

Presentation

- **General graphics**

  Standard presentation graphics software will support your presentations. You can paste in graphs and tables from spreadsheets and other software. Become proficient with it because you will use it frequently.

- **Flowcharting and diagramming**

  This software has free form and standard drawing templates. There is a range of drawing standards (some of which will be listed). This type of tool requires some specialized learning. If you use such a tool you may need to explain symbols and conventions in a diagram. The tool does not perform analysis. Basically, you enter the data, and it produces tabular and graphic results. Use this category with care as it can be time consuming.

Implementation of Process Improvement Results

- **Client server systems**

  This is a commonly used technology for implementing process improvements. The software runs on the microcomputer on your desk, and the server attaches to the network and operates a database management system. Business process improvement computing provides several advantages: flexibility to fit the steps of a process, ability to support all staff involved in the process, and capability to support change. There are disadvantages as well: interface to old legacy systems is difficult, software development can be a major effort, and the hardware and network investment can be substantial.

- **Document management**

  This category of software supports the scanning, indexing, and processing of documents. As a document proceeds through the process, the system routes and tracks each document image. This software has the benefit of reducing paper handling, improving document traceability, and automating more of the process than traditional software. But it is expensive. Some systems require specialized workstations. Storing the image and routing require substantial disk and communications resources.

  If you have very little money or time, start with the tools you have. Typically, you have standard microcomputer graphics, spreadsheet software, project management software, and database software. You may have access to electronic mail. Use the database management software to organize the data. Use the project management system for modeling. Rely on the spreadsheet for numerical analysis and some graphics. Use the presentation graphics software for graphics in reports and for presentations.

Application Software Solutions

Some of the newer application software is sensitive to workflow in a process, meaning that the software may provide for some or all of the following:

- Dynamic routing of transactions as the transaction moves between work locations in the process
- Support for forms so that there is less training
- Capture of the image of the document

- Performance measurement of the work being done to evaluate efficiency

Process Modeling Software

With process modeling software, the software takes as input the structure of the process. It describes each step in the process in terms of resources needed, time required, and any conditional relationships between steps. For example, if 10 percent of the items for reaching Step 5 require rework and are sent back to Step 4, the model reflects this.

The output of the model can provide statistics on units produced during a production period of the process, costs, resource usage, and bottlenecks. You can export output to a graphics or spreadsheet software package. The process models can be modified to see the impact of specific changes to the process.

This program appears to be very attractive. You put the information in and let the model do its work. But there are caveats. First, all models involve statistical assumptions on the distribution of arrival of work and the processing time. You may not know these. If you do not have a background in statistics, you may encounter problems. Second, if you use the results in a presentation, you will have to defend the model. Use this tool sparingly, if at all. It is best to use it for your own analysis.

Suggestions on Selecting Tools

When evaluating and selecting software, first identify requirements for tools and determine which tools are available. Then choose implementation software, which will be discussed later in the book. From the standpoint of tool requirements, ask yourself the following questions:

- **Would the tools be most useful in organization, analysis, or presentation?**

  Focus first on the pre-implementation tools, although your overall focus might be analysis. When you begin your process improvement project, you will spend a considerable amount of time coordinating people and tasks, obtaining support, and dealing with political issues, which will require a decent presentation tool.

- **Where does the greatest uncertainly lie, in terms of the information gathered? Will any tool help?**

  Tools should help to reduce uncertainty, which may mean collecting more data, so look carefully at the capability to do so.

- **How much time is available to learn the tool?**

  You must become proficient with the tool, because is dangerous to rely on someone else, especially at a critical point in the project.

Evaluate some highly rated tools in the preferred categories. Mentally simulate how you would use the tool. Ask the following questions:

- What are the data requirements of the tool?
- Is the data available?
- Do the examples and tutorial cases match your situation?
- Who is using the tool today (perhaps within your organization)?
- What is his or her experience?
- Is technical help available?

Find out if you can obtain the software on an evaluation basis. Set concentrated time aside to work with it. Do not try to enter your information. If you do, you will spend the evaluation period doing data entry. Instead, concentrate on interfaces, parameters of the software, output, and range of capabilities. Use the data that comes with the software.

Then return the software. If you keep it and don't use it, you will feel guilty and obligated to tinker with it. This effort represents wasted time—time you do not have.

A final thought on selection involves measurement. Devise a process to measure how much you are using each tool, what activities the tool supports, and the effort required in working without the tool.

Justifying Software Tools and Getting Approval

You have some factors working in your favor. First, a body of tools is probably available internally. Second, many software tools are not expensive. Third, many are available on a trial basis, and many packages offer extensive tutorials. However, you still must justify the tool.

Get the support of the team. This involves presenting the range of tools that you will be using to the team. Demonstrate the software and explain its use exactly. Also explain the team's role, if any, with respect to the tool. Explain the measurement of the tool's effectiveness. Solicit suggestions from the team. If one of the team members is an experienced user of the tool, ask him or her to give a testimonial.

To obtain management approval, be prepared to answer the following questions:

- What does the tool do?
- What are the labor and effort without the tool?
- What are the risks associated with the tool, and how you are going to mitigate them?
- How you are going to measure the tool in terms of effectiveness?

Hints on Implementing and Using the Tool

Once the tool has been selected, approved, and installed, you will need to implement it. To learn the tool, work with online tutorials and examples that come with the software. Copy the example and modify it to fit your process.

Diagramming Standards and Templates

A number of methods have been developed for diagramming and documenting processes. Some of these involve process steps; others involve data. It is important not only to decide which software tool you will use, but also to select the appropriate template. A *template* is a graphic representation of a set of rules developed by specific researchers as a standard. Some software packages offer multiple templates. Consider how much time needs to be spent in learning a template before choosing one.

Some popular diagramming methods are as follows:

- **Structure chart**

  Using a format similar to an organization chart, each level of the chart breaks down the process into subprocesses and the sub-processes into steps.

- **Data flow diagram**

  This technique tracks the flow of a transaction in the process. The data flow diagram explains each transaction path using specialized symbols. Content labels apply to the arrows connecting process steps and data.

- **Entity-relationship diagram**

  This diagram relates data entities, such as customer, product, or invoice. Connecting lines that have specific symbols and labels reveal the relationship between the entities.

- **Warnier-Orr diagram**

  At the left of a page is the process step. To the right is the sequence of items required to perform the step. Farther to the right is the logic to carry out the item.

- **Action diagram**

  This appears as pseudo computer code. At each step of indentation, more logic appears.

The above list is representative, not comprehensive. Some of the items overlap. To be complete, employ three types of diagrams:

- A diagram of the process, such as the structured diagram of the process
- A diagram of the data and relationships
- A diagram that relates process steps to the data entities

There are several benefits of using three types of diagrams. They are established methods and supported by software. The graphs can help you assess your understanding of the process. Once information has been entered into a model, changes and regeneration are possible.

The downside of this effort is the labor involved. You must develop very detailed information about the process for these diagrams to be complete and useful. If time is short, you may derive more benefit from spending time defining the new process instead.

MANAGEMENT PRESENTATION AND COST-BENEFIT ANALYSIS

Assuming that you have performed some analysis (e.g., a workflow layout of the process and validation of some of the issues in the workflow), you are now ready to receive feedback. Present the results informally. Set the stage for the analysis by first reviewing what you have done. Use the terminology of the departments who will carry out the process. Make a list of jargon, including abbreviations and acronyms, to help others who are not familiar with it.

Start at the bottom of the department and review the workflow step by step. Mark any corrections to the workflow as you find them. Return to the department with corrections. People should agree that you have represented the workflow accurately for both normal and exception work. Feedback at this time may give you more information about the process and issues.

Once the workflow steps are finalized, work your way up the organization. This becomes easier as you go along, because you already have feedback from the people at lower levels. Develop a five-minute summary of the workflow that you keep updated as necessary. Use this as the lead-in description of the process. To make it more relevant, indicate where issues lie in the flow.

Try to avoid formal presentations. Long, detailed presentations of processes can be tedious. Your audience may get the impression that you are a technocrat. Provide documentation of the process in detail in a readable form that your coworkers can understand. Not everyone will read this documentation, but you have given those who want to know more about the project the opportunity to go through it in detail.

KEY QUESTIONS

Have you defined the current processes in sufficient detail? Remember that you will be comparing the new process to the current process.

Have you identified all of the interfaces between the processes? Are these within the scope of change?

EXAMPLES

Monarch Bank

At Monarch Bank the analysis steps proceeded as described in this chapter. Interestingly, different people had varying and contradictory views of the process. Thus, an early benefit of the analysis was achieving agreement on how the process actually worked.

Additional tables were required to assess the impact of centralizing and semicentralizing the collection processes. There were two tiers of tables. The first tier showed the detailed collection process independent of performance location. The second tier indicated the multiple locations and pointed out problems with the distributed workload. The new process was defined in the same manner, to allow for a side-by-side comparison.

TRAN

More than 30 steps involved three organizations. Rather than start with this detail, steps were grouped into four areas: data entry and data collection (at the remote bus yard), review and input of exceptions (in operations), review and input by payroll, and handling of exceptions by the base staff and employee.

Next, the detailed steps were presented in a modular way in each of the areas. Issues, organization, and supporting infrastructure were reviewed with each step. This completed the review with the staff, and corrective information was solicited as well to gain their support.

For supervisors and managers, the first step was to indicate validation of the process workflow by the staff. This enabled the managers to focus on understanding, rather than validation. Then the big picture was presented. Next each of the four areas was identified. During the overall view presentation, flows between the areas were discussed and the issues were highlighted. This explanation solicited questions and led to the natural question, "What are we going to do?" At this time, some improvements were indicated and a general approach was outlined, but details were appropriately saved for later stages of the process improvement.

Stirling Manufacturing

At the heart of implementing the project management process in several business areas was the requirement of agreement on an overall template for the process. That is, there had to be agreement on a standardized set of tasks at a high level. Below this level, employees could insert their own detailed tasks. Tables were first used for this task. Later, the team used standardized diagrams because the engineering staff and managers were familiar with them. Next, process modeling software was employed to determine performance of the process. This suggested several internal process improvements. Although the use of the process modeling software was an additional tool and was not given highest attention, it provided the team with valuable feedback.

GUIDELINES

- **When downsizing, focus on managers and supervisors first.**

  If your analysis focuses on downsizing, consider the role of supervisors and managers in the process flow. Are they watching for quality and performance, or just doing direct, hands-off supervision? If their role is minimal, question their value to the process.

- **Do actual work in departments; do not always go back to your desk.**

  As your analysis proceeds, consider going out to the department and doing the work yourself, if possible. This will put you in closer touch with the process and will aid your analysis.

- **In deciding whether you have enough data, make sure you have been to every location and office.**

  If you have not covered all of the locations of the process, have you taken steps to ensure that what you are doing is representative?

- **Consider the evolution and deterioration of an untouched process.**

  In your analysis, consider what might happen over time if nothing is done; for example, experienced people can retire, computer systems become more complex to maintain and more inflexible, more work may be done on an exception basis, or process requirements will change. Create a set of tables to indicate the effects of time on the process.

- **Relate the organization to the processes in terms of roles and stakes (politics).**

  Roles in the process have been discussed, but now you should determine who has a stake in the success of the project. This is important in terms of getting changes approved. Stakeholders should also be part of the feedback regarding the analysis. Are the issues you are addressing important to the stakeholders?

ACTION ITEMS

1. What is the performance of the process? Performance can be measured in many ways. The focus here is on process level performance.

   Volume of transactions—total   _____

   Cost per transaction   _____

   Types of transactions   _____

   _____

   _____

   Number of transactions by type

Type	Quantity
_____	_____
_____	_____
_____	_____
_____	_____

Weighted cost of process by transaction type (apply the total cost to the proportionate volume of transactions)

Type   Quantity

_____   _____

_____   _____

_____   _____

_____   _____

_____   _____

Types of exceptions

_____

_____

_____

_____

_____

Volume by exception type

Type   Quantity

_____   _____

_____   _____

_____   _____

_____   _____

_____   _____

Weighted cost of normal vs. exception work based on volume

Type   Quantity
Normal, non-exception   _____

_____   _____

_____   _____

_____   _____

Types of errors _____

_____

_____

_____

Correction effort per error and number of errors by type

Type	Quantity	Effort
_____	_____	_____
_____	_____	_____
_____	_____	_____
_____	_____	_____
_____	_____	_____

2. Create a table in which the rows will be a list of the process steps. Between each step insert a step for waiting between steps. The columns will be a list of the normal work and the top three exceptions in terms of volume. Also insert in the table the times that you observe. This table will help you to draw graphs about where the time is spent.

Process Steps
vs. Work Type   Normal   Exceptions

3. Prepare the following graphs using the data you collected in this section:
   - Pie chart on the distribution of errors by type

- Pie chart on breakdown of total cost by transaction type
- Pie chart on distribution of exceptions
- Pie chart on breakdown of total costs of exceptions

You can also use the data you have collected to create the following trend lines on the chart:

- Trend line on total cost per transaction and volume of transactions
- Trend line on number of errors for each type (multiple lines on the chart)

4. Now you can proceed to the process step level. First, draw the workflow for the normal process and for high-volume exceptions. Place a piece of paper sideways (landscape) and draw a horizontal line to represent the total time that a piece of work or transaction takes to move through the process. Draw vertical lines at the two ends to mark the start and end of the process. Mark the proportional time for each step and for waiting between steps. You now have a graph showing how much time is spent on each transaction. Repeat this process for exceptions to create a tool for comparing the exceptions and for considering bottlenecks.

CHAPTER 17

STEP J: DEFINE THE NEW PROCESS

CONTENTS

17

STEP J: DEFINE THE NEW PROCESS

PURPOSE AND SCOPE

The purpose of this crucial step is to define and analyze the new process. The scope of the work includes defining alternative new processes or scenarios, evaluating the alternatives, and comparing the old or current processes with the new. Once these steps have been completed, you will be presenting the new process to management to gain approval for implementation.

END PRODUCTS

The key end product is the new process or scenario. You will also have supporting comparison tables and evaluations using information on alternative processes. These can be used to compare the old and new processes.

RESOURCES

In your attempt to develop new ideas, you will be discussing current processes and new ideas with the staff and supervisors involved in the current processes, as elaborated in the previous two chapters. You will also cover your new ideas or processes with them to get their input and involvement to ensure that your ideas and new process are realistic. This will also help in getting them to provide political support for the new process. Consider involving specific technical and audit staff to ensure that these areas are covered. In general, review the new process with many people several times; this will prevent surprises when you make your presentation to management.

APPROACH

Creative work and energy are necessary here. To make your work credible, consider a series of alternative processes before choosing one new process.

Action 1: Define the Dimensions of the Processes

Using the analysis you performed, define the dimensions of your process. Dimensions are areas of assumptions that are associated with the standard "how," "what," and "why." Different dimensions generate different scenarios. Experience has shown that you can identify the following nine dimensions, or areas of assumptions:

A. Process change

This dimension is self-explanatory and includes only those changes related to the performance of the work.

B. Organization

This pertains to the organization that owns the process. It answers the question of "who."

C. Infrastructure

This dimension is similar to the organization dimension in that it pertains to the infrastructure supporting the process. This answers "what" and "how."

D. Resources and importance

These are related because if a process is important, management will assign it resources. This pertains to "why" and "what."

E. Other organizations

This dimension includes groups in the same company as well as external firms and pertains to "who."

F. Other processes

This dimension includes any other processes that interface or share resources and support. This dimension answers "what" and "how."

G. Management

This includes all aspects of measurement, planning, and control. It pertains to "what" and "why."

H. Automation

This includes hardware, the network, software, and architecture.

I. Policy changes

This includes changes to policies that impact the process.

These dimensions are valuable because you need to consider a wide variety of options when generating alternative scenarios. Check yourself by considering alternatives in each of these nine dimensions. Multiple scenarios are often combined and integrated. Alternatively, a new scenario can be created out of the parts. One way to conduct a visual comparison of the multiple scenarios is to construct a graph that is formed like a star or asterisk. This type of graph is sometimes called a radar or spider chart. Each finger would represent one dimension. The point of each dimension is the degree of change with the particular scenario.

When you have done this for one process in the group, move to another similar one. Try to copy dimensions listed above over to the second process. Continue in this manner until you have covered each process in the group. Next, review all of the scenarios from different views. Consider them from the standpoints of organization, technology, management, and general infrastructure. Detect the issues, problems, and pluses of each process.

Action 2: Generate Scenarios

A *scenario* is a possible specification of the future process. It is a definition of a new process. A *scenario* is also called a *model*. Because you can design a new process in different ways, multiple scenarios are possible. In information systems, the scenario is the design of the new system and specifies all changes in processes, organization, infrastructure, resources, external organizations, other processes, policies, and control.

To be complete, a scenario should contain the following:

- Description of the process steps and how transactions flow through the process
- The organization and its relationship to the process
- The infrastructure required to support the new process under the scenario
- Interfaces with other processes, organizations, and customers and suppliers
- How the measurement and management of the process will be performed
- Commonality across multiple processes in the process group

For example, a scenario of the collection process for installment loans could involve the following dimensions:

- **Policies**

  Management specifies more stringent requirements for reporting and measuring delinquent accounts.

- **Organization**

  A single collection group handles all collection activities.

- **Other organizations**

  They specify automated interfaces and pass data.

- **Automation**

  Automation requires an online system that tracks accounts, interfaces to accounting systems, automatically dials customers, and automatically processes delinquent accounts.

- **How the new system will work**

  Delinquent accounts will be kept in a single queue. When an employee arrives for work, he will log onto the computer. The most delinquent account will appear on the screen. The staff member has a limited amount of time to view the information, then the system auto dials the customer. The employee enters customer contact actions and results into the system.

- **Control**

  The system tracks performance of collectors as well as monies paid by customers. More than 100 parameters in the system control its specific aspects.

When developing a scenario, make sure that others can visualize the new process. They must be able to compare the old and new process and see the differences between them.

Ideas for a scenario might originate in several ways. An interesting and creative way to begin is to consider the impact of drastic actions or triggers (called alternative actions and triggers) on the process and process group. These triggers lead to workable scenarios when considered in combination. Other alternatives can result from more traditional methods, such as bottom up, top down, and outside in.

Each scenario typically goes through revisions and additions in order to complete and address the entire process. Because you are dealing with a process group, you want to reduce overlap by combining individual scenarios. This is also important in terms of reducing implementation effort.

Using Triggers to Generate Scenarios

A scenario comprises combinations of assumptions. Considering different triggers can lead to scenarios. From a scenario you can derive a concept of how transactions would work in the new process. Do not attempt to group these actions. Instead, consider them individually. Each of these triggers arise from a combination of the nine dimensions. Each trigger is numbered. The triggers are shown in Figure 17-1 in terms of placement with respect to the nine dimensions. Note that these also overlap in some cases.

1. **Eliminate the process.**

   Before you do this, consider what would be the impact on the organization. What would replace the process? This trigger fits in the management dimension. It is an extreme step, but it is valid when applied to processes that are no longer useful.

2. **Place this process outside of the organization.**

   This includes outsourcing, which fits into the other organization dimension. This is a valid solution for generic processes that involve no organization-specific knowledge or competitive advantage.

3. **Starve it.**

   Deny the process resources for maintenance or enhancement. Without resources, the process will probably be eliminated.

Figure 17-1: Triggers vs. Dimensions

This chart shows the impact of triggers for change vs, dimensions.

Trigger/Dimen.	A	B	C	D	E	F	G	H	I
1	X								
2	X				X				
3			X	X				X	
4	X					X			
5		X			X				
6		X			X				
7							X		X
8			X	X				X	
9		X							
10		X	X	X					
11		X		X					
12		X	X	X					
13		X							
14		X			X				
15		X	X		X				
16					X				
17		X	X	X					
18		X	X						
19				X	X				
20				X	X	X			
21		X		X					
22		X			X				
23		X		X					
24		X	X						
25		X		X					

This fits within the resources and importance dimension category. Politically, this may be the best route for eliminating a process.

4. Merge it into other processes.

This might include dividing the process and placing its tasks and functions into other processes. This process fits in the other processes dimension. This approach is valuable in an organization that is not competently handling a process but is politically strong. Rather than confront the organization, move the process from under the organization.

5. Transfer it to another organization.

Transfer the intact process to another organization. Resources and some elements of infrastructure may accompany the transfer.

6. Throw people at the process.

By putting a large number of people to work on the process, you can uncover the non-resource bottlenecks in the process. This demonstrates the benefits of flexibility of a manual system.

7. Start with management measures and work backwards.

Management measures include performance measures and statistics reflecting the process. This is a variation of the "work backward from outputs" approach. In this case, you work top down (beginning with management) on the process. This alternative considers whether the process is significant. The process then feeds the measurement process.

8. Throw money at it.

Throwing money at a process often makes problems worse. Money brings new resources into the process. These resources are then incorporated into the process. Providing a resource with money is useful, however. It helps you set priorities for what the process requires. It also reveals problems that cannot be fixed by resources, which include policy problems, organizational issues, and interfaces with customers and suppliers.

9. Move data capture up in the process.

Data capture is internal to the process. It reduces paper handling and effort in the process. Since usually there are fewer errors at the front end, moving up data capture should be beneficial.

10. Copy the best competitor.

Use the information you gathered from observing a competitor (see Step C) and generate a scenario. This trigger reveals goodness-of-fit, but it never seems to fit exactly. Attempt to discover why and you will find some of the underlying factors that differentiate you from your competition. For example, TRAN was able to discover basic internal policy problems.

11. Outsource it.

When a company outsources, it hires outside vendors to do some or all of the work in a process. When considering outsourcing a process, first ask which processes and parts of processes are specific to the organization and which are generic. Examples of organization-specific activities include those that depend on company knowledge, procedures, and sensitive data. The outsourcing trigger is a good indicator of the degree to which the organization's processes are unique.

12. Downsize it.

Downsizing includes reducing resources. It also includes moving the computer system used in the process to smaller, more affordable computers. If downsizing appears to work, perhaps the problems with the current process are not structural. Remember, downsizing in an organization often leaves people at the bottom alone, as layers of middle management are eliminated. Therefore, it may have little impact on the process. Organization downsizing is faster than systems downsizing. If you are considering downsizing a process, consider all parts of the process evenly. Do not give too much detail or attention to the part being downsized; it will create a bias in your analysis.

13. Abolish the organization.

What if you did not consider the process? Instead, you just wiped out the organization. What would happen to the process? Who would carry it out? How would it be done? This type of radical trigger helps to define the boundaries of processes.

14. Split up the process.

Can the process be divided among surrounding processes? This tests your knowledge of the surrounding processes. It also tells you how strong the organization and infrastructure are for different processes. When you consider splitting up a process, you identify the core of the process that cannot be compromised.

15. Cut out the paper and forms.

This trigger assumes that all paper and forms in the process are questioned. Eliminating paper and forms supports the analysis of simplification, automation, and work elimination.

16. Automate all of the process.

Determine how much of the process can be automated. The parts that would remain manual are typically what is important. Automating the entire process is not feasible for most processes. Some areas that cannot be automated include those in which customer or supplier contact is important, complex and changing logic is involved, or management decisions are required.

17. Eliminate all automation and replace it with a manual system.

The process will slow down, but the automation hassle will be eliminated. Manual systems are very flexible. This trigger can help to identify areas in which flexibility and standard production are desirable.

18. Perform the process with different people.

The people who are carrying out the process may be the problem. If you could replace them, how long would it take to train new people? Are documentation and procedures sufficient to support the new staff? What part do personality and personal relationships play in the performance or lack of performance of a process? This trigger is important because many processes depend on key staff members who have worked in the organization for many years. A small core of people may be all that keeps the existing process going.

19. Move the process to suppliers and customers.

Not all processes are suited to this trigger. Processes such as order entry and accounts payable are appropriate. When you consider moving a process out of the organization, define the maximum that can be moved without loss of control. Even if you don't move it, you have at least defined the simpler tasks and those that are generic. A successful example of this has been in retailing; firms like Wal-Mart have taken this very approach.

20. Change the policies governing the process.

This trigger is tried by only a few. Policies are often taken for granted, yet they can be altered or dropped with the stroke of a pen. You want to be able to see the effects of policy change and elimination. This allows you to see the cost of the policy in terms of process. It also permits you to see how work may be simplified if the process is dropped. In one project, a savings of 30 percent of the staff was demonstrated. Federal government agencies have begun to do this in terms of eliminating and simplifying policies, but much remains to be done.

21. Break down the process.

Can the process be simplified by creating many smaller steps? By breaking down the process, you may be able to reorganize the work. This trigger can validate the simplicity of the process. If you can simplify the process, you may require a less specialized staff for handling mundane parts of transactions. In the Monarch Bank example, the collection process was simplified. The detailed process was broken down into finite chunks and reassigned. Lower level staff can now perform more of the work.

22. Open up information to all.

In some processes, people keep information to themselves, particularly when several projects or products compete for the same resources. By opening up the information, you depoliticize the process. You can see the impact of politics and hidden information on the process.

23. Have fewer people or one person do it all for accountability.

This is the trigger of the single point of control. If you consider having one person do everything, you see where the process is complex and where specialized knowledge is required.

24. Change the location where the process is performed.

This is an infrastructure trigger. The location where the work is performed is important to many processes. In the Monarch example, centralizing collections increased control and reduced personnel problems. It also flattened the organization. In other cases, moving processes closer to the customers was considered.

25. Minimize or maximize customer contact.

The customers perform as much of the transactions and work as possible. An ATM machine is a good example of this. On the other hand, when you maximize customer contact, you emphasize customer service. A service-oriented department store is an example.

These actions can be tested against the data and analysis that you developed in the previous chapter. You can build a scenario out of pieces of the results of the impact of actions.

Other Approaches for Scenarios

Other ways to construct scenarios are as follows:

- **Bottom up**

  Proceed from the bottom up. That is, take the information and detail from the previous chapter and try to improve each step in the process. This will improve steps but will leave the process structure intact.

- **Top down**

  Examine the process and create new subprocesses. Logically move top down in the process to the lowest level of detail. This gives you greater flexibility with the process but retains the boundary of the process.

- **Infrastructure architecture**

  This approach builds the process on top of the architecture that has been defined in Step G. This approach will reveal gaps in the architecture and the limits of the infrastructure.

- **Outside in**

  Consider the customer or supplier as you move inward to the process. This scenario leaves you with a clear idea of how the new process would work in interfacing. It gives less attention to the strictly internal parts of the process.

- **Organization-based**

  Begin by considering where functions in the process should be placed organizationally.

These methods have different benefits and will yield different results. The triggers and the above methods can be combined when generating scenarios. Remember that these are intended to get you thinking creatively about a process group because it is sometimes difficult to think of changes by yourself.

When you have created the scenarios, look at whether each addresses an issue. If you are not sure, reconsider the scenario. Also look at how a scenario addresses an issue. Be able to verbalize how the process will result in benefits.

Validate a scenario by changing the scope and constraints of the project. If the scenario is fragile and is changed frequently, or is easily replaced, it is probably not stable. Consider replacing it.

To ensure that your scenario is understandable, present it verbally to staff members who are knowledgeable of the current process but who are not technically literate. Take suggestions about how to reword the scenario for clarity. Keep process descriptions verbal as long as you can to get the most feedback. Once you write things down, they tend to be more difficult to change.

Action 3: Put Together Scenarios for a Process Group

After generating the scenarios for each process, distill out the support structure for the processes. For infrastructure and technology, define a list that covers all processes. Do the same for the organization, interfaces, and other items.

Requirements for support of the defined new processes are now present. What is missing are the changes required. Compare the existing process and the new process (as defined by the scenario). This comparison leads to a set of required actions and changes. Use a side-by-side list for the existing and new process. Table 17-1 shows the Monarch Bank's example for collections.

The comparison identifies appropriate actions that can be used as part of the implementation plan (see Step K). The comparison is also valuable during management review. If a manager does not want to spend money for a specific change, you can immediately map it into the area in the comparison table so the impact on the new process can be seen.

Table 17-1: Monarch Bank Collections

Part of Process	Current Process	New Process
System	Older, batch system with reports	Online system with queueing and performance tracking
Work control	Manually performed by supervisor	System assigns workload
Interfaces	Limited to installment loan system	Online interfaces to installment loan system, checking account system
Organization	Five tiers of staffing	Three tiers of staffing
Infrastructure	Multiple locations	Single location

Action 4: Test and Evaluate Scenarios

The following approach is both inductive and deductive. It can be iterated if you are dissatisfied with the new process. The actions can be performed quickly with the aid of the comparison tables and analysis. Only five to seven alternatives should be considered.

Action 4.1: Assess the range of alternatives.

You have a new process in mind. However, the details and organization issues are undefined. Focus on the same general process, but identify several alternative methods of support and organization. A wide range of alternatives increases your credibility with management.

Presenting several alternatives may be a good way to deal with political issues in process improvement. People may not want to make more involved changes unless and until they see the benefits. If so, start with one of the less drastic alternatives.

The range of technology alternatives may be wide while the organization alternatives are narrow. In this case, focus on the organizational alternatives and keep the technology alternatives fuzzy.

Action 4.2: Eliminate alternatives by comparing them with the current process.

Using the list of alternatives, you can determine whether any alternative:

- Is marginally better than, the same as, or worse than the current process.
- Requires a technology or infrastructure investment that is too great when compared to the benefits.
- Is possible only with major organization change that has been ruled out.

Do not eliminate rejected alternatives. Instead, keep them in mind to show management what could happen with fewer constraints.

You can use comparison tables similar to those of the previous chapters. Samples of tables are as follows:

- **New Process Steps vs. Existing Process Steps**

  Table entries indicate elimination, consolidation, change, or no action. This table indicates the degree of change.

- **New Process Group vs. Existing Process Group**

  Moving up to the group level, each row and column heading is a process. The entry in the table indicates the degree of change.

- **New Architecture vs. Current Architecture**

  This is the extent of change in the technology and systems between processes. This gives you an idea of the effort and time required for the implementation.

- **New Infrastructure vs. Current Infrastructure**

  This indicates the effort and time required for different alternatives.

Action 4.3: Associate alternatives into sets and compare the alternatives.

Choose a critical process. To evaluate alternatives, you can use comparison tables similar to those shown earlier, comparing the new process to the current process.

Define a set of alternatives based on a common infrastructure, technology base, or organization approach. Another set of alternatives could be based on online systems.

Here are some guidelines for grouping alternatives into sets:

- An alternative can belong to more than one set.

- Associating alternatives for different processes into the same set will often help in the evaluation.

- The sets of alternatives provide clarity and focus to the overall process improvement effort.

Action 4.4: Eliminate all but one set of alternatives.

To choose which sets to eliminate, look for those that involve great expense, infeasible organization change, unproved technology, or excessive time requirements for implementation of change.

Action 4.5: Select the desired alternative

Alternative processes in the remaining set will have common characteristics. If you have difficulty selecting one, you may want to generalize and combine them. This means a less detailed alternative but greater flexibility in implementation. To perform the final evaluation, use two detailed methods: comparison tables and process simulation.

Action 5: Build Comparison Tables

Comparison tables useful in final selection of an alternative are as follows:

- **New Process Group vs. New Architecture**

  This is the fit of processes to the elements of the architecture. A lack of fit indicates that limited benefits are offered by the new architecture.

- **New Process Group vs. New Organization**

  This table indicates the degree to which the organization changes support the new processes. Lack of fit indicates that the solutions to different processes may not be compatible.

- **New Process Group vs. Process Issues**

  This table indicates the degree to which the issues identified earlier are addressed.

- **New Process Group vs. Process Characteristics**

  This table indicates the degree of similarity between process solutions.

- **New Process Group vs. New Infrastructure**

  This table indicates the degree to which the new processes depend on the same elements of infrastructure.

- **New Process Group vs. Business Objectives**

  This table indicates the degree to which the new processes improve the achievement of business objectives.

You can use process steps as opposed to process groups to get a more detailed and refined picture. Again, if several alternatives appear to have the same scores in the tables, combine them.

Action 6: Simulate the New Process

Use software to input parameters that describe the process. The parameters of many simulation models are as follows:

- Each process step in terms of whether it is a process or a decision
- Duration of each process step and its statistical distribution
- Relationship between processes in terms of dependencies
- Arrival rate of units or customers into the system
- Cost parameters associated with doing work

Table 17-2 shows what should be considered when drawing up cost parameters.

The output of the simulation model is typically the output volume, the rate of output, the costs associated with the model, the busy and idle time at each step, and resource consumption and utilization.

Table 17-2: Sample Cost Elements

Listed below are areas of cost that you should include in your budget planning.

Infrastructure
Capital
Implementation of change
Office layout/furnishings
Facility moves—openings/closings

Staffing
Hiring/termination
Training

Process
Development
Training materials
Procedures
Policy development
Training in procedures
File conversion
Training in policies
Audit and control

Technology
Hardware acquisition/installation
Network acquisition/installation
Software tools and system software acquisition/installation
System development
Data conversion
Integration

Organization
Downsizing
Outsourcing

Infrastructure and organization change must be reflected in the parameters of the simulation. All simulation models make statistical assumptions. Verify that your situation meets these assumptions.

When you consider simulation, first construct and run a simulation of the current process. After validating this, consider the new process.

Action 7: Document the Selection

Create a flow chart of steps in both new and existing processes.

In the second step, show how the other processes in the group relate to the critical process. Comparison tables that reveal similarities are useful here. You also may wish to demonstrate how improving two of the processes results in synergistic benefits.

Prepare a list of the changes and improvements that are required in the infrastructure and organization to support the process improvement. To show why these are necessary, use some of the comparison tables that relate the process group to the infrastructure, automation, and organization. For backup and detail, prepare a table of process steps (for the critical process) vs. each of the changes and improvements.

Action 8: Match Types of Change to a Time Horizon

The time factor will be considered during strategy and implementation. However, at this point you may want to develop a table of the changes to be made (rows) and the feasible time horizon (columns). Short-term changes will involve procedures and process, intermediate changes will concern organization, and substantial systems changes will require a long term.

The table entry is the degree of feasibility for the specific time horizon. This helps provide realism and assists in defining resource requirements over time.

Action 9: Map the Resources Required to Implement Change in the Various Stages of the Process

Identify exact changes and list the resources that will be needed for each stage. This level of detail may show areas in which you need to rethink the new process.

Action 10: Develop a Functional Organization to Support the New Processes

In defining a new process, also define the functions to support it. Don't feel restricted by the current organization. Identify the roles and responsibilities that would best support the new process.

Action 11: Develop an Ultimate and Likely Unattainable Model of the Downsized Organization

Define a streamlined organization that will support the processes in your scenarios. This step uses the top-down approach and will give you a picture of how much improvement is possible.

MANAGEMENT PRESENTATION AND COST-BENEFIT ANALYSIS

The management presentation for the new process is crucial. It is discussed in depth later in the marketing chapter. Your presentation should follow this outline:

- Review the problems with current processes and need for change.
- List the benefits of the new process.
- Present the new process that won in the evaluation.
- Present other alternatives considered and a summary of analysis.
- Present recommended next steps.

Note that you reinforce the need for the new process first. Then, rather than bury people in details, describe the benefits of the new process. These should be readily apparent from the process step comparison. At this point, identify costs and benefits by type, but do not provide an exact amount. Wait for management feedback before you flesh out the details. Here are examples of benefits in the major areas you will want to cover:

- **Infrastructure**
  - —More friendly and productive offices
  - —More efficient offices
  - —More reliable telephone equipment
  - —Safer and more secure work place
  - —Lower maintenance
- **Staffing**
  - —Reduced numbers
  - —Reduced levels
- **Process**
  - —Less rework
  - —Lower error rate
  - —Improved sales
  - —Fewer returns
- **Technology**
  - —High cost technology replaced by lower cost technology
  - —Improved reliability
  - —Lower maintenance
  - —Greater flexibility to make changes
- **Organization**
  - —Fewer management levels
  - —Reduced support staff

Next show how the new process will alleviate the problems with the current process. Then describe in detail how this will work and present other alternatives. End the presentation by defining the next steps.

How you document the above work depends on the style of the organization and its practice. Base any documentation and presentation on the flow charts and comparison tables. Marketing and presentation of a scenario to management and staff are addressed in Step L.

KEY QUESTIONS

How does the new process compare to the old?

Are the improvements enough to justify the cost and effort as well as the disruption?

Do you understand the new process? Can you explain and address all of the interfaces? Can you respond to detailed questions? Explain the new process to people involved in the current process. Then have them feed it back to you using their own terms. Remember that eventually they will present the new process to management. They will be the ones who will actually be doing the work.

EXAMPLES

Monarch Bank

Group selection consumed a substantial amount of effort in the analysis. Next, the team turned to application of the strategy, which consisted of moving incrementally the process improvement one area to another. Definition of the steps in the new process took less time, because people disliked the old process.

Some surprises arose during scenario development. Initially, all scenarios involved automation and procedures. Roadblocks were encountered in getting the entire collection process to perform smoothly. The infrastructure element of location also kept recurring. Finally, organization issues were included. An entire new set of scenarios was developed, which later won approval.

TRAN

The scenarios at TRAN centered on the benefits of software and data being accessible through a wide area network. The team focused on the use of the network and its impact on processes. It was difficult to identify groups of separate processes due to extensive process inter-relationships. After the selection of the group, the number of subsidiary processes began to grow.

A surprise in the work at TRAN was the concern for the processes that were not changed. Because of this concern, development of an overall strategy for all processes required much effort. TRAN also showed the importance of fixing infrastructure and architecture issues. Analysis of different processes indicated that only limited improvement was possible without infrastructure improvements. This led to approval for action. Action stemmed from demonstration of what was possible in terms of improvements. Efforts to improve infrastructure had failed in the past because managers did not see the benefit or impact.

Stirling Manufacturing

Management agreed with the proposed scenario. While the scenario did not change the organization structure, it did modify the roles of individuals and their organizations. Wishing to reduce risk, management insisted that prototype and pilot projects be pursued. After success here, the project pace and resource pool could increase.

There were several surprises. First, the extent of hidden information was underestimated. Thus, the part of the process that focused on sharing information to reach decisions was the centerpiece of the presentation and the pilot project. Second, because this was a technology-oriented firm, they wished to avoid technology risk. This was the reason for both the prototype and pilot.

GUIDELINES

- **Consider the ripple effect from a change to a process.**

    Assuming you make the proposed changes, what effect will these have on subsidiary processes? Once you have a list of these, reconsider or rework the changes that will cause problems.

- **Avoid using a canned software package.**

    During this part of the project someone may propose acquiring a software package that appears to fit the requirements of the process. This is often too simple a solution for a complex problem. The process needs to be altered to fit the software and if this is never done, the software lies unused.

- **Design a new process that is self-sustaining.**

    Don't invent processes that require constant intervention and support. In particular, you want to avoid attracting political attention.

- **Make sure that people's habits and behavior fit in with the new process.**

  Do the staff members have the flexibility to learn new technology? Before you go to management with the scenario, test it on the employees and get reactions. Ask for specific responses to start. Ask, for example, how the new process compares to the current process.

- **Always consider possible objections to any new process or change.**

  Ask yourself why no one thought of the changes before. What is different now? What is unique about the new process? Answering these questions can help you to counter arguments against your changes.

- **Take into account what the new process will do to the existing power alignment between affected departments.**

  With a scenario defined and organization support determined, power typically changes. Some groups win and some lose. For example, as automation increases, the information systems group increases its power. Power shifts should be part of your review of the scenarios.

- **Be prepared to deal with rumors.**

  Rumors will spread as to alternatives being considered. You can counteract negative effects of rumors by involving people in the process of change. Ask people to review the scenarios. State that you welcome feedback and ideas.

- **Identify the natural allies and enemies of the new process scenario.**

  To determine this, think about the scenario from the point of view of the managers. Then consider what changes in organization and infrastructure are threatening to them. Work on positioning the scenario to appeal to their self-interest.

ACTION ITEMS

1. Decide who will do the work. For each process step, construct a table showing this information: P–performs the step, O–owns

or is responsible for the step, E–involved in the step on an exception basis. (Leave the space blank for no involvement.)

2. With the steps in the new process defined, construct a table of exceptions and normal work (rows) vs. process steps (columns). Place an X if that step is performed for the particular exception. How an exception differs from normal work and from other exceptions can be seen from the table. Compare this table to the table in Step H.

3. Decide which new technology and parts of the new architecture (from Step D) apply to each process step. The rows are the elements of the new architecture and the columns the steps for the new process. In the cells within the tables, enter the codes: C– critical; B–beneficial, but not critical; and N–not used. Now compare this table to the table in Step 5.

4. Determine which issues are addressed by the steps of the new process. Put the issues in the table as rows with general business issues at the top. Then for columns enter the steps of the process first. Add more columns for policy, organization, and infrastructure. The entry in the table will be from 1 to 5 (1 means that the issue does not apply to the step and 5 means that the issue is addressed by the step).

5. Compare two candidates for the new process. How are the processes different? The differences may involve policies, technology, infrastructure, or organization. In the rows, enter the policies, infrastructure, and organization involved. In the columns, enter the process candidates. The table entry is a comment that highlights the characteristics of the row and column. Make a second table that is a comparison of process steps. The rows are the process steps and the columns are the process candidates. The table entry is a comment about the step for that candidate.

6. For several alternatives, construct a radar or spider chart that compares alternatives in terms of the following: risk, duration of implementation, tangible benefits, overall benefits, estimated cost of implementation, organization change required, technology required, and size of implementation effort.

7. List the 25 process generator ideas as rows. In the second column, give the results of using these ideas. Comments and notes appear in the third column.

CHAPTER 18

STEP K: DEVELOP THE IMPLEMENTATION STRATEGY

CONTENTS

18

STEP K: DEVELOP THE IMPLEMENTATION STRATEGY

PURPOSE AND SCOPE

The implementation strategy identifies the scope of change in terms of organization, business processes, policies, technology, and infrastructure. It also indicates how changes in each of these areas combine into projects. The strategy identifies how you will realize the benefits and vision of the new process.

Here are some additional reasons for implementation strategy:

- **Scope**

  The broad scope of different projects cries out for an overall umbrella for process improvement. A vision can be difficult to relate to projects because the vision is general while the project is detailed.

- **Consistency**

  You must ensure that projects and efforts are consistent across the organization. This is the same as having groupings of projects under the strategy within the common vision.

- **Focus and sequencing**

  Focus is vital, especially with projects that can span a decade. The project can outlast some of the staff (as was the case with Monarch Bank). People must be aware of which projects are underway and of the sequencing of the projects. Focus will help prevent management from tinkering with the process improvement effort.

- **Flexibility**

  It is difficult to accommodate different technologies and lessons learned in a single project plan. By definition, a project plan addresses end results. Flexibility outside of the project plans can be achieved through the strategy.

In the case of Monarch Bank, the strategy was to employ new online systems. These supported collections and charge-off recovery for a range of bank products. Successive products paved the way for further consolidation. This wave was followed by transitioning into servicing and application processing for new customers. As new technology emerged, the strategy frequently involved retrofitting areas previously touched by process improvement.

Thus, the strategy is a relatively brief statement of the direction of implementation. Read between the lines and a number of additional factors are revealed. In Monarch's case the new online systems would require the following:

- Several waves of organizational change and consolidation

- At least two and possibly three waves of technology modernization

- Enforced stability between waves of change

- Integrated process, technology, and infrastructure change

The strategy should also include the following:

- **Phased approach in implementation**

  What are the general phases of work? For Monarch, this included phases of collections, servicing, and application processing, as well as expanding into leasing and other finance production.

- **End products associated with each phase**

  Where do you conclude each phase? Process and organization change as well as systems changes were indicated in this stage for Monarch.

- **Measurement approach to be employed**

  How will you know if the strategy is successful? The measurement criteria for Monarch were the tangible goals of productivity and reduced losses.

The scope includes all aspects of the processes, new and old, as well as the business, infrastructure, and organization changes. Many mistakenly include only the infrastructure and process change within the implementation strategy. People then get the impression that when these are completed, the project is finished. At that point it is difficult to rewrite the strategy and gain acceptance of the new version.

END PRODUCTS

The major end product is the strategy. As with the end products in previous steps, the strategy is supported by comparison tables. Make sure that the strategy is understandable and tangible to everyone. You will be referring to the strategy often to resolve issues during implementation.

RESOURCES

While you will be the major resource in this step, don't neglect to involve the managers and staff who were doubtful supporters. Getting them involved in the strategy will move them along from the concept of the new process to the reality of implementation. Don't wait until you have developed the plan, because the plan is detailed and there is a gap between the concept of the new process and the detail of the plan.

APPROACH

It seems obvious that an implementation strategy is useful, yet many organizations fail to develop one. Experience points to the following reasons for this:

- **Fear of revealing the total scope**

  It is feared that if the true scope of the change is revealed, management and staff will become hesitant and obstruct the projects.

- **Generation of enemies**

  The scope and strategy reveal the direction and depth of change across the organization and systems. Managers may collude and try to resist.

- **Impractical and unrealistic project**

  Painting a picture of an overall strategy may give people the impression that the project cannot be completed.

To address these concerns, focus publicly on a general vision of the future. Keep dates, timetables, benefits, approach, and other such detail in the implementation strategy in low profile.

Without a strategy, the process improvement project may succeed initially but ultimately fail.

Following are eight common reasons for failure in implementing change. Many of these reasons reflect the need for a strategy:

- **A sense of urgency for change is lacking.**

- **A vision is lacking.**

  The guiding coalition of management is lacking. The implementation strategy serves to reinforce the vision and make it feasible and tangible.

- **The vision is not communicated effectively.**

  A vision is vague. Most people prefer more tangible, action-oriented statements. Properly constructed, the strategy can assist in communicating the vision in a more palatable form.

- **Obstacles to the vision are not removed.**

  The implementation strategy can serve to point the way in identifying obstacles early.

- **Systematic planning for and creating of short-term wins is lacking.**

  The implementation strategy helps to provide sequencing of projects and indicate order of delivery.

- **Victory is declared too soon.**

  The implementation strategy serves to keep long-term goals in mind. It can head off declaring victory prematurely.

- **Change in the corporate culture is not achieved.**

  Sometimes, it is difficult to see how one project or a set of unrelated projects can change the culture. The implementation strategy can serve as the bridge between the vision and the culture.

Additional problems that follow from the lack of a strategy are the following:

- **Ad hoc changes in the process improvement effort occur.**
- **Vendors and individual managers may seek to fill the vacuum and take over the project.**

  Their own strategy can then support their own tactics.
- **Changes to the project may appear to be signs of disorganization.**

  A strategy that supports change and evolution produces less surprise when change occurs.
- **Without a strategy the project can become reactive.**

  Project leaders may spend too much time reacting to change and suggestions

Action 1: Define the Dimensions of an Implementation Strategy

Technology, systems, and process are dimensions that come immediately to mind. Organization, infrastructure, and measurement are also key dimensions. Your strategy should address each dimension. The omission of one or more may limit the scope and flexibility of a process improvement effort.

The implementation strategy is the road map and link between the vision and the detailed implementation plans. The dimensions of the strategy must match both the scope of the vision and the type and nature of the implementation project plans.

When developing your strategy, address the six dimensions in the following manner:

- **Technology**

  The ways in which technology supports the process change should be part of the strategy.

- **Systems**

  Address what will happen to the current application systems and new systems.

- **Process**

  Highlight policy areas to be changed in the business process, procedures, and policies.

- **Organization**

  Use general terms to describe change in this area

- **Infrastructure**

  This area absorbs most of the expense and project lead time, so give this area sufficient attention in the strategy.

- **Measurement**

  Define the criteria for measuring success.

You could view these dimensions as the rows of a table. Columns in the table are phases. The entry in the table is the strategy for that specific dimension and phase. Use a four-phased approach and define four phases as follows:

- **Phase I—Prototype new system, begin work on infrastructure.**

  In this phase initiate work on the system and the process and establish the infrastructure to support widespread deployment of the new process and system in a later phase.

- **Phase II—Pilot the new process and refine the system; complete the infrastructure.**

  In Phase II, complete the infrastructure preparation. It defines the new process in the context of the new system (the pilot). Test the combination of the two in this phase.

- **Phase III—Complete and implement the process and measure the results; begin organization change.**

  Following success in Phase II, spread the process and system through the organization. With this near completion, pay attention to organization change.

- **Phase IV—Complete organization change; begin the measurement process.**

  When the process implementation ends, implement measurements.

The entries in the rows and columns of the table consist of the projects appropriate for this cell. Figure 18-1 gives some comments and requirements regarding the table. Note relationships exist across rows as well as between columns. Also, in this strategy you address technical risk earlier and organization risk later.

Figure 18-1:
Implementation Strategy Table

This chart shows how the implementation strategy crosses the phases. It helps in showing management the overall implementation strategy.

Strategy/Phases Areas	Phase I	Phase II	Phase III	Phase IV
Process				
Systems	Projects in later phases should depend on those in earlier phases			
Infrastructure				
Technology	Since business process improvement is an integration process, projects in later phases should depend on projects across all rows			
Organization				
Measurement				

Action 2: Define Alternative Implementation Strategies

Many alternative strategies must be considered. They should address what to do and how to do it. Here are several types of alternatives:

Revolutionary Type of Strategy

In this approach, the strategy addresses change to many processes at the same time. For example, you may want to change the process and organization concurrently. This approach is typical in radical business process improvement literature. Revolutionary strategy has advantages, such as faster completion time and less general disruption over the entire time, but it also carries risk. One disadvantage is that the approach ignores the learning curve from an incremental approach. Also, with so much change, projects may get in each other's way.

Infrastructure-Based Strategy

Examples of infrastructure-based strategy are relocation, distribution of departments, and consolidation of functions. Process changes here take a back seat to infrastructure. Many business process improvement results fail as a result of some aspect of the infrastructure.

This is a viable approach for large projects, though it can delay benefits until infrastructure changes have been completed. The most common reason for using this approach is that the infrastructure is preventing the current process from functioning and is inhibiting the implementation of the new process.

Organization-Based Strategy

This is a classic implementation strategy. The approach is to change the organization first. With new managers and staff in place, attention moves to process. Like downsizing, this can force savings, but the cost may be high. Morale and productivity can suffer. People with a working knowledge of the process may leave. For people who are new or who remain, the learning curve may prevent any process improvement.

Incremental Mixed Strategy

In this strategy you gradually change the process and infrastructure. At a later time with sufficient implementation, you can attack organization issues. This approach offers the advantages of minimal or no disruption and little risk. The drawback is that results are achieved at a slower pace. In some large organizations, this may be the only viable approach.

A Deadly Combination: Revolution and Downsizing

An almost surefire way to fail is to carry out a revolutionary approach and combine it with downsizing. Morale will be shattered. People will begin to feel like disposable commodities. Organizational paralysis may occur. No one will want to take any risk, and even with involvement in the process, they lose trust through the chaos. This is especially true when you change processes across departments.

Action 3: Develop a Strategy

Use the tables constructed earlier to develop a strategy. Following are a series of steps to develop a strategy:

- **Create the rows of the table.**

  For the infrastructure area divide the work into two or three phases. Each phase should result in usable, tangible parts of the infrastructure. Keep the time period of each phase vague.

- **Move to systems and technology.**

  Now place the major development areas into the phases you have defined. The development areas include prototyping, design, development, conversion, testing, and integration. Development should finish in the last phase of the infrastructure.

- **Consider the process.**

  Overlay the process, policy, and procedure changes and their implementation on the phases. Completion of the new process should occur shortly after the system.

- **In the area of organization, you may wish to create a separate, later phase for organization change.**
- **Measure the current process in the first phase.**

   The new measurement process will be established in the last phase.

To enter activities across the phases in the table, work with each row separately. Each activity will probably consist of a small project. You now have a table of sectors of process improvement vs. phases. To check your work, first ascertain whether there are any dependencies that you failed to identify. To adjust dependencies, move activities between phases. Carefully review the tangible results achieved at the end of each phase and identify the benefits of each phase. Write these below each column of the table. In general, the more dense the table (the fewer empty cells) the more parallel effort is possible.

Next identify subprojects needed for each row activity. The projects and subprojects will become the center of the implementation plan.

Write the resource requirements at the bottom of the table, so that you can tabulate them.

You now have a general phasing approach for your elements of strategy. The nature of the activities you placed in each phase identified the "what" of the strategy. Enhance the strategy by providing a statement of how work will be done. Do this for each row and column. Table 18-1 presents the table for Monarch Bank. Row comments indicate the approach for each process improvement component. Column comments indicate the approach used to manage each phase.

Action 4: Evaluate Your Strategy

Your strategy will be tested and tried and may be changed during implementation. Examine how work in the rows and columns can be altered, or shifted, to respond to the pressure or crisis. Following are some examples of change and impact:

- **Reordering of process priorities**

   Reordering process priorities changes the rows for systems and for the process. There is typically less impact on the other rows.

Table 18-1:
Implementation Strategy Table for Monarch Bank

This version of the table is more description of the phases and the parts of the new process that will be impacted in each phase.

Strategy/ Phases Areas	Phase I	Phase II	Phase III	Phase IV
Process	Semicentral. manual process	Semicentral. automated	Centralized automated	
Systems	Development for semicentral	Enhancement for centralized		
Infrastructure	Establishment of semicentral facilities	Establishing of centralized facility		
Technology	Selection and acquisition			
Organization	New semicentral organization	New centralize organization	Downsizing	
Measurement	Measure current	Measure new	Measure new	

Notes:
- This more classic approach requires substantial infrastructure work.
- This example applies only to installment loans collections; collections for credit card and other products would have to overlay this for a complete picture.

Thus, you should be able to create a new table with reordered columns.

- **Speeding up the project**

  The goal is to conduct more work in parallel by moving activities to the left. That is, move activities from later phases to earlier phases. Do this for each row.

- **New technology**

  Implementing new technology causes a substantial change in one row and a ripple effect on other rows. For example, different technology might require different infrastructure or office layout. You may also change the new process.

- **Resistance**

  Substantial management or staff resistance to the new process may necessitate a change in the pace of implementation. You can do this by stretching out the duration of each phase or by adding phases.

- **Diversions**

  During implementation, you may be diverted into other new areas. This will add work to your rows within a specific phase. Use the table to show the diversion and the impact of a shift and delay due to the diversion.

- **Technology failure**

  When the technology on which you pinned your hopes and dreams has failed, return to the table and redo the technology-related row. Make adjustments to other rows reflecting the impact of the technology change. The table can reveal the impact of technology substitution.

Action 5: Define the Prototype and Pilot Activity

Define an initial version of the process, then develop the *prototype*, which is a working version of the system that lacks major databases and files. Functionality of the system is not complete.

You can test the prototype with department staff. You can use a demonstration approach. For example, you can employ an approach of continuous demonstrations. These were conducted for three hours a day, across a month in Stirling's case. Work can continue to enhance functionality. You can begin to flesh out the new process.

When the prototype has been tested and evaluated and is complete, it can be united with the new process and tested. This is the *pilot* activity. At the end of the pilot work, the system and process are together and ready for implementation.

Benefits of this approach are the following:

- The prototype tests the infrastructure and network.
- The prototype provides for tangible feedback from staff.

- The approach reduces the documentation required.
- The process has more meaning with the prototype system in place.
- Through direct involvement in the evolution of the prototype, staff and managers begin to feel that they have a stake in the outcome and they commit.

Some drawbacks are as follows:

- People may think of the prototype as the production system. This is a common problem with any prototyping approach.
- The initial work may take longer, due to the prototyping and pilot work.

Action 6: Test Your Complete Strategy

Once you have developed the table representing your strategy, use the following steps to test your strategy:

1. Check that the rows are complete.

   Each row represents the major focus of a component by phase. Make sure that these activities are clearly defined and complete.

2. Make sure that the columns are consistent.

   The columns, which show phases, have specific known dependencies. For example, elements of the infrastructure typically must be in place prior to installation of the new process and system. Looking at the entries in adjacent columns can assist in determining dependencies.

3. Make sure that the phase end products have been listed.

   What end products occur at the end of each phase? Are the business in general and process in particular improved?

4. Look for gaps.

   When there is a blank entry in a row with entries in the surrounding columns of the same row, you have a problem. You will lose momentum because you will have considerable dead time while work progresses in other rows. Consider moving entries around to eliminate such gaps.

5. Test strategy flexibility.

Mentally project the results of some of the changes covered. These changes affect rows and echo down columns. What happens to your table after these alternations have been carried out? If the number of columns expands, this may mean that the project is becoming more sequential, which is bad if you are trying to meet a deadline.

Action 7: Revisit the Comparison Tables

Carrying out the implementation strategy will produce the benefits defined in the comparison tables. Review the implementation strategy table. Define the benefits and results achieved for the completion of each column. Completion of the work in a column should yield benefits and progress toward the objectives. This is another test of the implementation strategy.

MANAGEMENT PRESENTATION AND COST-BENEFIT ANALYSIS

Presenting the strategy as a table will facilitate understanding. To gain support for the strategy, show how the column results support the comparison tables. Managers may pose various questions in the form of "What happens if…?" Answer these questions in the context of the strategy table. Show what happens when you change and reorder the table entries.

In the management presentation, also show alternatives. Two that you can frequently employ are a go-slow implementation and an accelerated strategy. These can be compared in the tables. They can also be discussed in terms of costs and benefits. Remember that the costs mostly relate to infrastructure and tend to be incurred in the early stages of implementation. The benefits that you present should include those that will be achieved as implementation stages are completed. You want an implementation strategy that yields intermediate results. If the benefits are at the end of implementation and the costs are at the start of implementation, you may have a major problem on your hands. It is important to discuss in rough terms cumulative costs and benefits over time. A graph showing the cross-over point when cumulative benefits exceed costs is useful.

KEY QUESTIONS

Can you explain your implementation strategy clearly and concisely? Can you explain why you developed an implementation strategy?

Have you tested your strategy by assessing the effects of change or crisis in the project on the implementation?

Are people using your implementation strategy in their documents, presentations, and conversations? If they are not, you likely have a problem in lack of acceptance. Alternatively, you may not have explained the strategy clearly.

EXAMPLES

Monarch Bank

After the new process had been defined at Monarch Bank, it was clear that the implementation plan would be very broad and extend over a long period. Because the implementation included more than 6,000 bank employees, crossed over 15 major systems, and affected more than one million customers, it would probably impact revenue and costs and involve considerable risk. New technology, projected for use in later phases, was still in the design stage at the start of the process.

Once Monarch Bank realized the consequences of change and the fact that benefits would be cumulative as implementation progressed, development of an implementation vision and strategy became more important. Factors in the vision were productivity gains, improved service, economies of scale in handling large volumes of data, reduced staff turnover, and a reduction in number of management layers.

Implementation strategy centered on changing one critical banking area. Then there was a pause to consolidate and measure the benefits. This period allowed the new process to be showcased and marketed to other banks. The pace of implementation quickened as similar functions were changed and automation spread to other areas of the bank.

Four phases were identified for the installment loan collection area. The first three phases moved the bank from a distributed collections activity to one that is semicentralized. The three phases were due to unevenness and inconsistency in the distributed data and process. Once regionalized, collections activities consolidated into a central site because the bank had established a standardized process and system.

The actual strategy was larger because it involved other banking areas. Additional collection areas were improved and automated between phases three and four.

The strategy in a table form gave management a clear understanding of the implementation of the new process.

TRAN

The chart for TRAN in Figure 18-2 applies to the consolidation of staff into fewer facilities. In TRAN's case, the bus scheduling system had to be operational prior to changing over to the new process. Systems and infrastructure work, however, were performed in parallel. The prototype and pilot were undertaken in Phase II.

Stirling Manufacturing

The strategy table appears in Table 18-2. The strategy followed the prototype and pilot approach as discussed. The method of continuous demonstration lasted two months. Seven versions of the prototype were developed. At each demonstration, a questionnaire was distributed to obtain feedback.

Insurance Company

An appropriate process improvement approach was developed for a large insurance company. The purpose was to implement a new process for insuring and servicing automobiles, homes, and mobile homes. The process included evaluating insurance applications, issuing policies, collecting premiums, and handling claims. The goal was to establish one consistent process that was valid for all types of collateral (autos, houses, etc.).

The company started with changing the homeowner's insurance area, but there was no strategy. As marketing opportunities surfaced,

Figure 18-2:
Implementation Strategy Table for TRAN

Phases Areas

Strategy/	Phase I	Phase II	Phase III	Phase IV
Process	Identify processes	Implement initial change ⟶	Implement stage 2	Implement stage 3 ⟶
Systems	System requirements	Design/ develop	Implement	Implement
Infrastructure			Set up of PCs/network	
Technology	Selection	⟶ Configuration/ acquisition		
Organization			Change payroll	Change operations
Measurement	Measure current process	Implement measurement for new processes		

Notes:

- Stage 1—payroll by exception basis implemented; stage 2—entry of exceptions at the bus bases; stage 3—coach operators enter their own data.
- In this example, little infrastructure change was needed.
- In the area of organization, the payroll area was changed first; operations was changed second.

management changed direction and priorities—five times in three years. The project responded to management each time. The entire project failed and was terminated. Costs were in excess of two million dollars and nothing was implemented.

Table 18-2: Implementation Strategy Table for Stirling Manufacturing

Strategy/ Phases Areas	Phase I	Phase II	Phase III	Phase IV
Process	Design and prototype	Pilot	Production	
Systems	Design/ develop	Refine		
Infrastructure	Bldg modification	Telephones		
Technology	Selection	Implementation		
Organization		Design	Implementation	
Measurement	Measure current	New meas. method	Implementation	

Notes:

• This approach emphasized the prototype and pilot approach. The other approaches also did this but were done in some cases within the same phase.

GUIDELINES

• **Base alternative strategies on policy and procedure and focus on the short term.**

• **Determine whether each entry in the table is a project or multiple projects.**

   Get rid of multiple projects in the table by splitting them into separate sentences or lists so that each becomes a project.

• **Use the strategy table for multiple processes.**

   To handle multiple processes, keep the strategy table and create additional rows for the other processes and additional systems. Typically, the infrastructure will apply to all of the processes so that it can remain as one row. The same is true for organization and measurement. This is also a way to evaluate whether your groupings of processes were correct.

- **Make sure that the early phases offer little risk in terms of organization and policy.**

  Management will often be reluctant to take major risks early in the project.

- **Watch for too many entries in one column.**

  This may mean that you intend to attempt too much in a short period of time.

ACTION ITEMS

1. Develop alternative implementation strategies using each of the following criteria:
   - There is no resource limit.
   - Very limited resources are available.
   - You are unable to change the organization during implementation.

   Define the phases of the implementation for each alternative. This will indicate the differences in focus and emphasis between the alternatives.

2. Determine if your strategy is complete by answering the following questions:
   - Are all resources covered by the strategy?
   - Does the strategy address interfaces with other projects and activities in the organization?
   - Does the strategy allow for contingencies?
   - How does the strategy appear from management and business unit perspectives?

3. Test yourself on what you would do if things go wrong or change. How robust is your strategy? For each of the following factors, indicate how you might respond in a way that is consistent with your strategy:
   - Management finds a new management concept and asks you to incorporate it within the process improvement project. The concept might involve reward structures, team methods, etc.

- Delays occur in the building of infrastructure involving the first departments in the implementation of the new process. Should you consider changing the strategy to implement with a different group?

- There appear to be delays in building and installing the software. Should you consider implementing other parts of the process without the automation?

- Management has decided that the project should be speeded up to get the benefits earlier. How would your strategy accommodate such changes?

- Management has decided to deny resources to your project. How will you slow the project down without ending it?

- As you start implementation, you find that an adjoining process has even greater process improvement benefits. What should you do? Should you propose redirecting resources or continue on?

CHAPTER 19

STEP L: MARKET THE NEW PROCESS

CONTENTS

19

STEP L: MARKET
THE NEW PROCESS

PURPOSE AND SCOPE

The purpose of marketing the project is not only to gain approval for specific actions but also to garner enthusiasm to move ahead and continued support as the project progresses. A long project will have many issues. To handle these, you will need not only sales skills but also an organized approach to marketing.

Successful marketing means that the correct message on an issue has been conveyed. For example, suppose you hold a project meeting. The meeting goes well. You resolve issues, and the new process looks as though it will work. However, most of the time in the meeting is spent in dealing with detailed workflow questions about how the new process might not address a situation in the same way as the old process. Later, someone asks one attendee how the meeting went. The attendee replies, "We spent most of our time on several areas in which the new process will not work." This is not the impression you want to create. You have not conveyed the benefits of the new process.

The scope of marketing is the entire project. Marketing includes damage control. Listen for rumors so that you can correct mistaken assumptions. If you do not correct misimpressions, they will spread. It will become increasingly more difficult to deal with the situation and confront issues. Damage control takes exponentially greater effort the longer you avoid dealing with it.

END PRODUCTS

The major end product is support for the process improvement project from business units as well as from management.

RESOURCES

Marketing is the responsibility of the entire project team, including the project leader. Participation and commitment are keys to success. The leader must bring up the subject of marketing and convey information. He or she must define people's roles so that expectations will be realistic. The entire team isn't going to become a sales force, but team members must be aware of the importance and impact of their statements, attitudes, and impressions.

APPROACH

Even with the many books and seminars covering the subject, business process improvement does not sell itself. Selling the concept is more complex than selling standard computer systems, quality management, team management, or many other topics. Here are some reasons for this:

- There is often no natural sponsor or specific department to champion process improvement.
- The processes may cross multiple departments, each with its own agenda.
- Process improvement involves a large process and requires time and effort; large projects are more difficult to market.
- Numerous points in the project require successful marketing. Failure with any one of these may doom the entire project.
- Improving the organization's and infrastructure's business process at the same time adds complexity.
- Time-honored policies and roles are difficult to change. Resistance can be both direct and subtle.

Failure to consider marketing is probably one of the leading causes of business process improvement failure. Marketing includes direct and indirect sales and marketing. When you conduct demonstrations, gather information, review results, and present documents and plans, you are in fact marketing. The care and attention given to marketing, sales, overcoming resistance, and meeting challenges are critical success factors.

Presenting a new process requires careful marketing preparation. When you come up with a new concept, you raise excitement and interest. If you are not careful, you risk raising unreasonable expectations. Marketing is also important because a process improvement project requires substantial human interaction. Therefore, there is always an opportunity for people to misunderstand. It is not enough to merely present results. Your attitude and your marketing follow-up will strongly impact success.

An example of a marketing misunderstanding occurred at Stirling Manufacturing. A large project spanned three years. During the first year and a half there were several pilot, small-scale process improvement projects. They were successful, but no one took the time to trumpet their success. Management, hearing nothing, moved on to other projects. This afforded political enemies of the project an opportunity to move in and end the project. A sure success became a classic failure because of a lack of marketing.

Consider the situation from management's perspective. A stream of new ideas continues after the date of project approval for business process improvement. They receive sales pitches from consulting, technology, and accounting firms. Everyone competes for attention and resources. Winning project approval is only the first step. You must keep on selling the project throughout the process.

In marketing, keep a low profile. High visibility for a long time will dilute your efforts and may create enemies.

Combine a low profile with a constant presence. Seek regular contact with managers and staff to give updates, to bring issues to the surface gradually, and to push for decisions. When people know what is going on in a project, they feel comfortable. They also feel a greater sense of participation.

Action 1: Get Project Approval and Kick Off the Project

Seek approval from middle management to begin a process improvement effort even though upper management has already endorsed the effort. You will work with and seek the support of staff and supervisors in the areas you will investigate. If these people are indifferent or lukewarm, you have little chance of success. Remember that endorsement of a general concept and approval of a project that may be expensive are two entirely different things.

Build up support slowly to catch the interest of departments. As you present the idea to management, stress process improvement. Do not claim huge benefits. Do not highlight expensive infrastructure changes or risky organization changes. You do not know enough yet to suggest and support changes of this sort. Your attitude should be, "We're going to make it better, but we don't know yet how much better." Your goal is that the project will begin in a low key. If you are too successful too soon, management may label the project as the salvation of the firm. In such a case, you will set yourself up for failure.

Here are some common obstacles to gaining approval, along with suggestions on how to surmount them:

- **The status quo**

  Defenders of the status quo may raise false reasons for rejecting your project. For example, if people tell you that they are too busy, they may be defensive or afraid of change. Reason with them that no time is a good time, so why not begin the project now? Address what will happen if the current process is continued. How fast will deterioration occur? Do not be alarmist, but indicate that changes will be more complex and expensive later. Create a table of deterioration. The table's rows consist of deterioration attributes and its columns of time periods, such as months or years. The entry in the table is the error rate or deteriorated value. Table 19-1 gives an example of a deterioration table for Stirling Manufacturing.

- **Other concepts and buzzwords**

  Two examples are *quality management* and *team management*. Point out that business process improvement has its roots in industrial engineering and work design. It is stable and can yield more benefits, if properly implemented.

- **Other business process improvement projects**

  Emphasize an aspect of your project such as near-term results, the fact that your project is more realistic, or the fact that you have more related experience.

- **The timing of other work (the long-range plan, the architecture, the big study)**

  While the subject of the big study is an issue, the arguments for going ahead are that the big study will not impact process

Table 19-1: Example of Process Deterioration Table for Stirling

This table shows how a process deteriorates over time.

Attribute	Year				
	2	3	4	5	6
% of people who have not been formally trained	10	15	30	60	70
% error rate	5	5	8	10	14
No. of types of exceptions	3	5	7	12	16
Increased size of system	110%	115%	125%	140%	155%
No. of people involved in process	45	48	51	56	62

improvement and that by the time the study is out, the process improvement will be underway and can employ any results from the study.

Make sure that, when people initially approve the effort, they have agreed on what to do next. After the decision and approval process, take advantage of the momentum generated by the approval to encourage continued participation. Begin to identify people to be team members.

Action 2: Market the New Process

Once you have approval to begin a process improvement project, your marketing efforts will shift to focus on the details of the new process. The new process will receive future support in terms of funding and politics if it is strategically important. so show management how the new process supports the vision of the organization.

As in other areas, market the new process to staff as well as to managers. If the staff members are supportive of the new process, management will also be supportive. Staff members should be able to articulate the reasons for and explain the new process. Otherwise, confusion will occur, because you are asking management to endorse a new process that is unclear.

Your first step in marketing the new process is to present the tables discussed in earlier chapters. These comparison tables clearly highlight the differences between the old and new process. Use the software aids that come with graphics presentation software to prepare presentations more rapidly and effectively. If the staff members participate in this work, they can help you explain the tables to management in an informal presentation.

In the presentation, first give an overview of effort and tasks performed. Call on staff members to explain the details. Then explain how this new process is better overall for the company than the current process. Use this same approach to present the new process to upper management.

Always present alternatives. This will indicate that you have done your homework. Also, alternatives can offer more palatable versions of the plan. For example, an alternative process may use no additional funds or involve no organization change. Employ staff members to present the details.

In getting people to accept the new process, one of your goals is that the people be willing to end the old process. One way to encourage this is to pose the question, "How should the old process be eliminated?" Ask people to think of all of the actions that are necessary to terminate the process. Also ask them to verbalize how they will know that the old process has been eliminated.

You are unlikely to achieve 100 percent acceptance of the new process. Focus on the key individuals who work with the new process and who will support and reinforce the new process after you have left. You cannot be around the process forever. When you leave, you want to be able to rely on key people to maintain the process.

If you fail to win approval for the new process, figure out why. Perhaps, your presentation was too detailed and perceived as overly complex. How were you turned down? Did someone devise a better way? Is there a less expensive version of the new process?

Success in new process approval means that you can move on and generate an implementation strategy. In parallel, you can also develop the plan and budget and a detailed list of initial implementation tasks.

Action 3: Market an Implementation Strategy

The marketing of the implementation strategy is a watershed activity. The previous efforts were tied to selling concepts. Now you will market practical plans. This sets the stage for support needed later, during implementation, when problems and opportunities arise.

The goal of marketing the implementation strategy is to show how the implementation supports the business vision and will actually install the new process. The marketing effort links the big picture and detailed implementation tasks.

The audience for this marketing step, as for the other steps, includes both staff and management. Employees who understand the strategy are better able to deal with change in the plan and alterations in direction. The strategy will also show managers how their employees are part of the implementation.

With the surfacing of the implementation strategy, processes and change are made more visible. This may increase resistance among people who perceive the new process as a threat. This is yet another reason for convincing people of the validity of the implementation strategy.

If you are successful in presenting the strategy, quickly follow up with the implementation plan. If you wait, you risk loss of momentum and a need to reintroduce the strategy. Follow up can also head off misunderstandings or confusion raised in the strategy presentation.

Action 4: Market an Implementation Plan

The goal of marketing the implementation plan is to stimulate involvement and commitment, rather than to obtain funding. You want people to volunteer to work on the project in order to avoid drafting unwilling participants. Your marketing of the plan should show people their roles and their importance to the project. You can indicate future challenges when you present the plan, but also show organization and an approach that is systematic.

The selling of the implementation plan is the selling of your management style and methods. Most marketing failures occur here. The impact of failure is substantial. Give the marketing of the implementation plan a great deal of attention. Be prepared to answer many questions.

In marketing the plan, present it informally to the people you want on the project. If the wrong people wind up on the team, the project is handicapped. Keep your presentation on a general level. Don't rush in with GANTT and PERT charts. Explain the scope of the implementation, what it means to the company, and the big picture. Then move to the detail of their roles in the project. Explain how these roles contribute to the overall project and why they are important. The closing argument is not an attempt to sign them up, but an opportunity to indicate that you are sensitive to their other commitments. Explain that you will use them part-time when possible. In this way you show respect for their time.

As you move from staff members to managers, the same approach applies. Appeal to their self-interest. Indicate that you are going to be making limited demands on their time. Also, indicate how you will be providing feedback and getting input from them.

The sign of success in marketing the implementation plan lies in the people you have lined up for the implementation. You can get all of the money approved, but if you start with unqualified or junior employees, you are headed for trouble that will be difficult to remedy later in the process.

Action 5: Market the Budget

In this marketing step you are attempting to show that you know how to manage the budget and are careful with resources. You want people to have confidence in you. Thus, in marketing the budget, you are also marketing your management skills.

The audience for the budget consists of three groups. The first is the staff in the project team. Staff members must understand the budget and areas of risk so they can help control the budget. Managers who keep their staff in the dark put their project at risk. How can a staff member understand whether a decision is important without some understanding of the budget? The second audience is vendors, suppliers, and customers. Outside firms must agree on the budget as it pertains to them. The third audience is management.

In your presentations, begin by identifying the areas of the budget that are subject to change. Concentrate on areas of risk. Remember, the infrastructure bears the greatest financial risk. Explain contingency plans that you have developed and how you are going to control costs. Don't spend a lot of time on parts of the budget that are large but fixed and known.

If you are asked how you will manage the budget, either directly or indirectly, the following approach may be useful. Highlight which areas of the project are not dependent on unknowns in the process and can be funded immediately. This removes them from the critical path. Areas of the budget that hinge on the outcome of the prototype and pilot of the process remain pending. This mixed strategy of commitment and control works. Also, by having areas of the budget uncommitted, you can gain power over vendors and push staff to achieve specific objectives.

Process improvement budgets can be very large when you add up all of the pieces. Divide the budget by phase so that you target incremental commitment and approval on a phase-by-phase basis. However, indicate that if you are successful, you will be seeking a specific sum overall.

Action 6: Provide a Project Progress and Status Report

In a status report you convey an impression of what is going on in the project. This is an important ongoing part of the marketing effort. The audience for status reports includes not only the direct management for the project but also the managers of your project team members. These people can pull the plug or discourage others. You want them to be supporters, so strive to keep them informed.

When you provide progress information to managers or team members, begin with a general view of the situation. This tends to calm people. Then move to the three topics that are often of the greatest interest. First is the budget. Has there been any change? If not, say so. Second, what events and milestones have occurred? Give a general report, not a blow-by-blow description. The third topic is that of issues. Zoom in on a few issues. To generate interest, build up each one in terms of importance and impact. Then indicate what actions are being taken. If you have identified several alternatives, present them. Stress that you are moving toward a decision on how to deal with a particular issue and that you will consult with them prior to making that decision. Do not ask for input or force decisions on how to solve problems. You are simply providing information.

Give progress reports frequently and informally. Do it on the spur of the moment in hallways if that works for you and those who need the information. Keep a casual tone. The audience feels that they are being kept up-to-date and will not have to ask you for status in more formal ways.

How do you head off negative reaction to status reports? Establish regular updates and progress reports. Go in early or stay late and make the rounds. People will trust you because of your tie with the project and because of the rapport you have established.

If you fail in marketing here, managers will seek you out with questions. If you are proactive, this should not occur. Furthermore, success means that managers will be willing to address your issues based on the relationship you have nurtured.

Action 7: Identify Issues and Resolutions

Issue resolution, including the marketing of solutions, is probably one of the most important aspects of managing a process improvement project. In these projects issues rise rapidly as you address major infrastructure, organization, and technical concerns. Your ability to deal successfully with issues will affect your chances for success in the project.

First, develop alternative solutions, as you did in Step 10 when you created a new process. What happens if nothing is done about the issue? What happens if you throw money at the issue? Whether or not you present these alternatives to others, this exercise will help you to understand the issue more clearly. Also determine if you have identified and prioritized issues correctly. Have you moved beyond identifying merely symptoms?

The participants in this marketing step are project members, department staff, and management. Participating in issue determination is enjoyable for many people. They begin to feel that they are a part of a team. Dealing with issues also permits them to participate in a limited way without devoting themselves full-time to the project.

Relate issues in terms of their source and nature, grouping them similarly to processes. Talk about why an issue has surfaced now. Is it due to urgency? Or is it because it is convenient for someone? What is behind the issue?

Address multiple issues through one or a series of decisions. Resolving issues one at a time through the project is too time-consuming.

Don't rush to announce solutions. To market solutions successfully, keep management informed as to which issues have been addressed. They can then join the bandwagon and support the resolution. It may be better to have a manager announce a solution. He or she can take credit for it and stand behind the enforcement of the resolution.

If you are going to let an issue alone, tell people why you have decided to do this so that they do not perceive you as indecisive and weak.

How do you define success? Did the resolution work? How do you know it worked? Did people's behavior change? Search for signs that the issue is returning in another form. Success occurs if, and only if, the solution sticks.

Action 8: Get Approval to Continue Process Improvement

Your last step is to be able to move to another process. The purpose is to continue the momentum of success to other processes. This does not call for formal marketing. If you have performed well, you will be able to start up the new project with management's informal approval prior to the end of the first project. Begin with a low cost analysis effort as you have done in previous chapters.

Do not abandon the first department and process. Straddle the two processes for several months while the first process shakes itself down. If appropriate, have the first department staff share experiences with the new department staff. Have the first staff demonstrate the differences between the old process and the new process.

GENERAL MARKETING ISSUES

Getting People's Interest and Keeping It

One important general marketing issue in process improvement projects that extend over a long time period is how to keep people's interest. Over the years, several techniques have been used, including the following:

- **Take a low profile and give out little information.**

  This approach will work for projects that will last less than six months. With longer projects people will begin to ask questions, so this approach does not work for long-term projects.

- **Take a high-profile, headline approach.**

  This technique is one pursued by a number of accounting and consulting firms. It works for awhile, but eventually people want to see tangible results. The pitch and crescendo of the headlines often tie only indirectly to the real results.

- **Gain different perspectives by viewing the project from various angles.**

  This approach works for long-term projects. Concentrate on detailed procedures in order to involve people in details of the process. Then shift attention to infrastructure and technology. Next, concentrate on policies. These were not brought up for discussion previously and they open up a new view of the process. Finally, address organizational issues.

To transition between two perspectives, show the links between them. Use issues as the mechanism to present different perspectives.

Self-Evaluation

Here is a list of questions to help you assess marketing results:

- Do you have regular contact with managers and staff members in which you convey information on the project? Do you have an open line of communications with managers and staff members?
- Is the list of issues being tracked and managed?
- What is the tone of the project team? Are there emotional ups and downs? Is there enthusiasm for the project?

Marketing through Documents

Be careful when using written documentation for marketing. Positive projections and statements have a reputation of returning later to haunt you.

When you document, be factual. Avoid emotional prose. Avoid tacit threats in terms of deadlines. If you want a decision, indicate that you and the team await the decision. Do not describe the dire results that will occur if there is no decision. Document status, issues, and budget in a regular pattern. Establish a format, so that readers will not have to cope with different structures. Use short words and keep your writing dispassionate and to the point.

Marketing through Presentations and Meetings

This is a favorite way of marketing. When you present in person, you can express passion and emotion. There is give and take. You can elicit commitment. Another advantage is that, while the multitudes are using Internet and electronic mail, you are using personal contact. Keep the electronic mail in the background as support.

Decisions

Major decisions need to be made by management. However, routine decisions should involve staff members and managers. Involvement in decisions increases commitment.

Your objective is not quick decisions. Decisions are a matter of timing and circumstance.

When a decision needs to be made, first lay the groundwork. Present the issue. Review it several times, along with alternatives. Communicate with those who are affected by the decision as well as those involved in carrying out the decision. Here are some strategies to pursue next:

- **Break large decisions into smaller chunks.**

  Smaller decisions can be addressed at lower organization levels.

- **Do nothing.**

  Err on the side of inaction. Being too much of an activist and pushing for decisions may alienate management.

- **Don't force an issue.**

  If you force an issue, you will likely lose support for a decision.

- **Consider marketing to the people around the decision-maker.**

  Attempt to achieve consensus. Watch for signs that you have antagonized someone. Follow up and see if a little more effort can win over this person.

When a significant decision goes against you, this can affect the momentum of the process improvement project. People begin to question management's desire to continue the project. That is why decision-making should be your highest priority.

Once you have a decision, take action immediately. Have an implementation approach ready for launching when the decision is made. If you delay, the force behind the decision abates. People wonder, "If it was so important, why hasn't there been any action?"

KEY QUESTIONS

Are you learning the lessons from the previous activities? Are you getting better? Or are you making the same types of mistakes?

If management has changed, has your marketing approach been modified?

EXAMPLES

Monarch Bank

In the case of Monarch, the key marketing event was presentation and sale of the new process and vision. Once the managers and staff understood this, they offered their support. Demonstrations and presentations by department staff showed progress.

TRAN

Because of the nature of TRAN's organization and charter, substantial marketing was involved at each stage. This required widespread involvement. Knowing that formal decision-making caused problems and delays, Tran moved to the informal method of decisions by consensus. There were very few decision-making meetings. Decisions were disseminated through staff meetings.

Stirling Manufacturing

Experience with manufacturing and distribution firms indicates that much of the marketing lies in implementation. At Stirling, therefore, the focus was on implementation. The marketing of the implementation strategy was combined with the plan. With their marketing still underway, implementation was begun. It was felt that only a parallel approach would succeed in mitigating staff cynicism toward new processes.

GUIDELINES

- **Involve people in minor issues and questions.**

  Examples are the location and number of cable outlets for workstations, status and other codes for a new process, and policy and procedure statements. This will help you develop a sense of what people are thinking.

- **Continue to spend time with the staff performing the steps in the current process.**

  This time helps to maintain rapport and pays off both in support and reduced training later.

- **Sell change and stability at the same time.**

  Make people comfortable by linking to the past. Excite them by linking to the future.

- **Line up support at each level.**

  While improving business processes, you cannot afford to rely on only one person. Seek broad-based support at different levels. While this requires a major initial effort, the approach pays dividends later in reduced effort.

- **Use the trial balloon approach for issues to reach decisions.**

  Casually float proposed solutions of issues to generate reaction.

- **Keep a marketing log of contacts and results.**

  Consider building a marketing log for a week. Each day write down what you have done from a marketing perspective. If several days go by with no entries, set aside time for marketing in the near future.

- **Follow up after decisions are made.**

  Make yourself available, both before and after decisions are made. Ask those involved if there is anything else they would like to see performed in the project.

ACTION ITEMS

1. For each marketing step identified in the chapter, list two or three people who are critical to the decision-making. Then look across the lists and find the two or three people whose names appear most frequently. This helps define your marketing audience over time.

2. For each decision area identify two reasons people could oppose a decision. Determine what factors could be behind each reason.

   Decision:_____

   Reason:

       1. _____

       2. _____

   Factor behind reason:

       1. _____

       2. _____

3. Maintain a list of the managers in Action 1 with whom you have talked.

   Include the following information:

Manager	Date	Subject	Comment

Analyze these contacts over time and identify any gaps where you have not maintained contact.

CHAPTER 20

STEP M: DEVELOP THE IMPLEMENTATION PLAN

CONTENTS

20

STEP M: DEVELOP THE
IMPLEMENTATION PLAN

PURPOSE AND SCOPE

The implementation plan has several objectives. It is obviously the blueprint for carrying out changes. Second, it helps to reinforce the business process improvement effort by supporting the strategy. Third, the planning effort is a major way to engender support and gather momentum for implementation.

The fourth objective is political. In your plan, line up project team members by working with their management. This shows management that the business process improvement project is serious.

These objectives are in addition to the standard reasons for developing a plan—to track work and progress.

The scope is comprehensive and includes all parts of implementation, including infrastructure and organizational change related tasks. The more detailed and encompassing the plan, the better.

END PRODUCTS

Each business process improvement project is unique and end products will vary by project. Develop a general project plan template and suggestions for individual areas of the plan. The general template for implementation consists of the following:

- Prototype of the system
- Pilot project of the new process and system
- Infrastructure (non-technology)
- Technology infrastructure
- System development

- Integration and testing
- Data conversion
- Process policies, procedures, and training materials
- Organization change
- Training and installation
- Cut-over to new process

The content and detailed activities of each of these are covered in detail in Steps 14. Attention is on the plan in this chapter and the phases of the project are defined.

RESOURCES

Since implementation is a planning activity, you might be tempted to do it yourself, but this is not a good idea. Up to a point, the more participants you have the better. You will give them task areas and they will supply detailed tasks and schedules. This will help in them understanding the overall plan and committing to dates.

APPROACH

Business process improvement projects fail in implementation when they are planned and managed like traditional projects. To be successful, you must understand these differences and their eventual impact on the business process improvement project.

Business process improvement planning differs from traditional planning in the following ways:

- **Scope**

  The scope of the business process improvement project is wider, involving organization, systems, process, procedures, and changes between organizations.

- **Politics**

  Business process improvement is politically more sensitive and volatile than a traditional project. Hence, the structure and wording of the project plan and tasks are more important.

- **Coordination**

  Business process improvement requires more people, which involves more coordination because there is a higher likelihood of confusion in the roles and responsibilities of people and organizations. Also, many people have never carried out a business process improvement project and will need proper guidance.

- **Subprojects**

  Many traditional projects are set up as a single project. Business process improvement projects are different. They usually involve a number of interdependent subprojects, which may be done in parallel.

Business process improvement projects differ from other projects in that business process improvement often involves multiple, successive projects. Standard projects that have a specific scope tend to fall into patterns. Each business process improvement project tends to be different. Methods, tools, and lessons learned in one project can be applied to the next, but the actual process, political, and organizational situation will be different.

Implementation—An Opportunity for Attack

When you begin to plan the implementation of the business process improvement project, people may begin to try to sabotage and terminate the project—before it really begins. Here are four common lines of attack:

- Lack of project organization. No detailed implementation plan exists.

- The plan is incomplete, missing infrastructure tasks.

- The plan may reveal a hidden agenda. Downsizing was not proposed, yet it is evident in the task lists.

- The project manager and team lack experience, so the plan may be incorrect or incomplete?

Heavy, successful initial activity can mitigate such attacks before they become serious. Before proceeding further, define known and potential project enemies. Target those people as possible members of the project team. This entails risk. These people can create issues within the team and may attempt to undermine the project with their management. However, excluding them offers greater risk.

Action 1: Define the Phases

Since a business process improvement project will take a long time to complete, partitioning the project into phases is a natural first step. Each phase should include demonstrable and tangible results. If you were to line up what you have achieved at the end of each phase, you should be able to discern a cumulative momentum of change.

Breaking down the project into two phases (e.g., process and group) is one approach, but there are other ways. Instead of two phases, you could associate a phase with a department. In this case, each phase would be completed once the processes in each of the departments have been improved and implemented. This approach is useful when you must address a number of smaller groups.

You can also define phases based on infrastructure, geographical location, and technology. For example, you might improve each office and consider the phase complete once the technology in a location is implemented. The next phase of the project would be to implement technology in a new location. This procedure is used when deploying new processes and technology across store chains.

Whatever approach you choose, new tasks should be added to later phases as the scope expands in order to link work between phases.

Action 2: Determine Major Milestones and Subprojects within a Phase

Each phase must be divided. Approach this top down to ensure consistency across the plan and to make sure each subproject fits with the implementation strategy. Rather than deal with tasks, define key milestones in each phase. Once you achieve the set of milestones, you will know that the phase is complete.

Using the two-phased approach discussed earlier, you could define sample milestones as follows:

- **Prototype**
  - —Definition of prototype completed
  - —Initial prototype ready
  - —Stable prototype achieved
  - —Completed prototype
- **Pilot project**
  - —Pilot project defined
  - —First pilot project results obtained
  - —Second version of pilot project ready
  - —Completion of pilot project
- **Infrastructure**
  - —Completion of building plans
  - —Approval of building permits and approvals
  - —Completion of foundation
  - —Building inspections of specific subsystems (e.g., electrical, water)
  - —Completion
- **Technology**
  - —System and network architecture defined
  - —Cabling and data communications completed
  - —Installation of hardware and system software completed
  - —Architecture is application ready
- **System development**
  - —Design completed
  - —Development completed
- **Integration and test**
  - —Test scripts completed
  - —Integration starts
  - —First systems test
  - —Integration completed
  - —Testing completed
- **Data conversion**
  - —Definition of conversion approach completed
  - —Completion of programs for automated conversion

—Manual conversion starts

—Conversion ended

- **Process policies, procedures, and training materials**
  —Outlines of all materials completed

  —Policies reviewed and approved

  —Training materials tested and completed

  —Procedures completed

- **Organization change**
  —New organization and details approved

  —Reassignment of staff and managers completed

- **Training and installation**
  —Training started

  —Training completed

  —Systems installed and tested with converted data

  —System ready for cut-over

- **Cut-over**
  —Cut-over of system

  —Cut-over of process

  —Cut-over of policies

Action 3: Define the Detail within a Subproject

You can now define a subproject and the detailed schedule for a subproject. Start by defining the next level of detail within a subproject. Assign each area to a team member. Your political goal is to involve team members in the planning process, and by so doing, to build commitment. Provide the team members with an example to indicate the level of detail needed for the plan. Before they start, hold a group meeting; attempt to get consensus on a list of resources. This will serve as the resource pool for all of their projects.

Each team member should now develop detailed tasks and task dependencies and assign specific resources to tasks. This is the "what" and "who." The duration and dates ("when" and "how long") will come later. This omission is intentional. Doing it all at one time is too much and team members may manipulate tasks to meet schedule dates.

Assign resources carefully. Assume that the tasks are in an outline form in which lower level tasks fall under and within summary tasks. Assign the person who is responsible for the task area to the summary task. Assign only critical resources to the detailed tasks under the summary. Consider people, facilities, and equipment. Do not include resources that are overhead or that are plentiful. Also exclude common support roles. By doing so, you will have a small, manageable set of resources for each task.

Early involvement of the team not only heads off future problems, but also gives team members an opportunity to see the overall plan. If you wait to involve people during implementation, it may be too late. With no active participation in the planning process, team members will need you to spend more time explaining the project. Another problem that may arise is that staff members may revisit changes, which is time-consuming and unproductive.

Assume that you know the "what" and "how." To review these with the team members, begin by showing them how their tasks roll up into the overall plan. You are now acting as a schedule integrator. Here are actions to take before you ask them to assign dates and durations:

- If the schedule is on a software program, run a "what if . . .?" analysis to schedule copies of the team members' work. Suggest possible changes. Don't force them to make the changes; these are only suggestions.

- Describe the difference between duration and effort. For example, if a task requires four days and a person is assigned half-time, the duration is four days while the effort is two days.

- Make sure that team members do not force dates when they put in the detail. Suggest that each task be scheduled as soon as possible to provide flexibility.

- Have team members update their own schedules. Track the changes.

Action 4: Develop Schedules for the Process Group

When addressing process groups, you may find that some organizations support or perform multiple processes in a group. The following are suggestions in handling development of the schedules in the group:

- Groups concerned with one process can be treated as suggested above.

- Support groups that support multiple processes will need separate infrastructure schedules for all processes in the group. Place summary tasks in the appropriate schedule.

- Begin with the schedule for a critical process in the group. Then split out the work for the infrastructure and technology that cross processes. Develop these schedules next for all processes in the group. Then return to the processes with the summary tasks.

Action 5: Analyze the Plan

Steps in analyzing the plan include the following:

- **Add milestones where management decisions will occur.**

  This highlights the subjects that management will review. It will be important and useful during the review of the schedule. Assign management as the resource to these milestones so that you can later pull them out and highlight them.

- **Look for dependencies you can eliminate by parallel effort.**

  Try to have consistency in dependencies so that most links are between tasks and milestones at the same level of the outline. This will make managing the schedule easier.

- **Find all tasks assigned to a specific resource type.**

  Do you require this resource in each of these tasks? Is the resource crucial to the task? Review tasks with the largest number of different resources and determine why they are assigned so many resources.

- **Review the wording of the tasks.**

  Is the wording of a compound task complex? If so, consider dividing up the task.

- **Edit the schedule so only summary-level tasks are given.**

  Assuming inevitable changes to the schedule, are these summary tasks complete and stable?

- **Build a glossary of terms.**

  Include the definition of each resource and its role, as well as what constitutes each major milestone.

  Extract separate subschedules for each involved organization that is providing resources.

  Answering the following questions may prompt further changes:

- **Is too much being demanded of an organization over too short a period?**

  If so, review each resource assignment and the extent of involvement in each task.

- **Does the schedule contain gaps when an organization is not involved?**

  If so, is this politically acceptable? You may want to keep people involved and up-to-date. If you have heavy use intermingled with periods of dead times for some resources, you may have a problem. If people leave the project and are reassigned, how will you get them back? Loss of contact means increased overhead as you bring them current.

Plan ahead for schedule changes. Use the outlining feature of the software. You want the high level of the schedule to be the same despite changes. Detailed tasks can vary. This will allow analysis and comparison of the planned or baseline, the actual, and the "what if…?" schedules.

Once the analysis is completed, return the schedule parts back to the team members for revision. Volunteer to help if they request this. Attempt to get a final plan after two or three iterations of changes.

Assessing Risk

To mitigate risk, develop a list of assumptions related to the schedule. These assumptions often relate to the conditions of the facilities, the technology learning curve, the condition of existing data and use in conversion, and training time required. Project risk often occurs in integration. Consider setting up a special task group within the team to develop the integration tasks. You may wish to have someone on the team serve as the integration czar.

Evaluating the Plan vs. the Strategy

Here are some tests to apply to your strategy:

- **Does the implementation plan yield tangible benefits at each stage that support the strategy?**
- **Are the stages consistent and cumulative or are they separate and unconnected?**

  The phases of work in the plan should show that as time progresses, you are moving closer to fulfilling the strategy.

- **Are political, technical, and managerial issues spread out during implementation?**

  Spread the issues and risk associated with the strategy throughout the implementation plan. If they occur too early, there may not be enough available information.

Action 6: Complete the Other Parts of the Plan

Indicate the method of change control in the implementation plan. Tracking and relating issues to the processes and to the tasks is another important part of the planning process. While these points are in the strategy, it is the plan that tends to be used by more people.

Action 7: Analyze Schedules for the Process Group

Assemble the individual schedules in a single project for analysis. Along with the specific suggestions mentioned earlier, do the following:

- **Filter all schedules by the same resource area.**

  Then combine the filtered schedules. This will provide an overall pattern of resource demand by area.

- **Ensure that the schedules for the infrastructure and technology fit the work on the processes.**

- **Proceed by adding coordination, testing, and integration tasks between processes in the group.**

  Put these in a separate schedule because there is a risk that they will be buried in the individual schedules.

  Figure out how coordination will be performed across the process group. How will changes and schedule slippage be implemented?

Action 8: Show Your Plan to the Team

To complete your plan, show it to the team. This is part of building team spirit and enables the team to visualize the big picture. To give the members a feeling of progress, show both the first and last versions of the plan. You can then comment on the positive changes to the plan.

In this team meeting, ask the team members what they got out of the effort. If they were to do it again, what would they do differently? This is the first conscious effort to establish a pattern of recording lessons learned. At the end of the meeting, indicate that you are going to make any last changes needed and present the plan to each of the team member's managers with the team member present.

MANAGEMENT PRESENTATION AND COST-BENEFIT ANALYSIS

During the work on the plan, stay in regular contact with management. Give out the list of phases, subprojects, and milestones. Provide copies of the resource pool. At this stage, you are seeking passive understanding. You have not provided the dates, but if you wait to give out the entire plan, you may encounter more problems. Management will be more likely to revisit task definitions.

When you present the initial materials, ask who should review the work. This will yield a list of potential reviewers who are highly regarded by management.

Prior to reviewing the plan with the team, provide management with a summary high-level schedule for additional feedback. You are seeking major concerns, not approval. If concern is expressed about the schedule, indicate that you will review it and see what can be done.

Management Presentations

You will be making presentations to each manager before you present the plan to the highest level managers. The presentations are intended to resolve as many questions at as low a level as possible.

Materials needed for the presentations include the summary schedule, the detailed schedule, the implementation strategy, the detailed subschedule that uses the managers' resources, and a summary of resource use over time.

The sequence of presentations is important. To gain experience and sharpen your skills, first schedule some of the groups that are only peripherally involved. Later, make the presentation to the main owner of the key process. After this presentation, make any revisions and return to the first groups. Their support will be key. Next, go on to other groups. You can finish with departments with lesser roles.

Tell your presentation audience members that they can bring others. Begin the presentation with the management summary. Show the detailed schedule next to indicate how much work went into the effort. Drill down to the subschedule. The person on the team responsible for the tasks should describe them and make any necessary comments. After the presentation make any changes and go on to the next department.

If you have been successful in the individual presentations, the main management presentation will be easier. For the major presentation, start with the summary of the tasks. Then present the management decision points. Emphasize management's role and possible decisions. If this goes well, you can show additional detail for the first set of tasks in Phase 1. If possible, the team should attend the presentation.

Review for the Process Group

The review for the process group after analysis can begin with the organizations that support multiple processes in the group. Then you can move on to the individual processes, starting with the most critical process. A variety of dependencies exists between processes in the group, so consider the most closely related processes.

Setting the Baseline

After the management presentations have been completed, you are prepared to set the baseline plan. In most project management systems, multiple schedule dates are allowed for each task. There is the planned schedule that corresponds to the baseline, an actual schedule where you will record progress, and the working dates. You will get the working dates each time you load and access the software for scheduled dates. This adds up to three sets of start and finish dates for each task that you can compare and analyze.

Costs

You can associate the earlier estimate of costs with the scheduled costs. This will provide you with an idea of when costs will be incurred throughout the project. An important graph you can create with this information is the estimated requirement for funds in terms of cash flow.

KEY QUESTIONS

Have you thoroughly reviewed your plan? Does it really fit with the strategy?

What can go wrong in terms of infrastructure, process, organization, procedures, and policies? Make a list and review your plan in terms of each of the items on the list. Can you easily change your plan? Is it flexible? Does the plan accommodate change?

If management wanted to speed up the project, change the plan, modify the resources, or slow down the project, how would your plan stand up under these changes?

EXAMPLES

Monarch Bank

Recall that the effort began with the installment loan collection process. The implementation plan was divided into the following subplans: consolidation into semicentralized centers, development of the automated system, implementation of the new process at one site, and replication across all sites.

The following set of processes consisted of additional collection and charge-off processes. For the credit card collections process, a new schedule template was developed using the lessons learned about structure from installment loan collections. Due to the size of the infrastructure and network effort, these were split into separate projects. A cumulative set of lessons learned was developed and presented at the start of each business process improvement project for each process.

TRAN

Recall from an earlier chapter that the old bus driver timekeeping process required every bus driver to complete a timesheet even if he or she had no exceptions to what was scheduled. Timesheets manually flowed to a central operations group for review and to payroll for a second review. The implementation strategy included causing no disruption to the business. The new process implementation was divided into the following phases:

- Phase 1—Establish network to the TRAN bus bases; move to an exception basis for completing timesheets.

- Phase 2—Realign functions so that entry of exceptions occurs at the bus bases; the central operations group will do extensive review; payroll's role will be reduced.

- Phase 3—Bus drivers enter exceptions to timesheets online.

    In the first phase, the exception basis meant that the 75 percent of the drivers who had no problems or delays did not have to complete a timesheet. This may not seem like a large benefit, but this change in procedure eliminated more than 130,000 pieces of paper that once had to be filled out, handled, and stored on an annual basis.

    The first phase was divided into two projects: the exception basis change and the network. The following exception basis factors were examined in planning the implementation:

- **The bus drivers would change procedures.**

  They were unionized and used to standard procedures. This action would impact their pay process. They needed reassurance.

- **For the base staff, there would be fewer timesheets, but each exception must now be evaluated even more carefully.**

- **Central operations would experience little change because they handle exceptions.**

  There was a major impact on payroll: 130,000 forms translates to a stack of paper 45 feet high of input that no longer has to be reviewed. Substantial adjustments would have to be made.

Notice that in all of this there is no automation.
The subphase was divided into the following:

- Pilot project test of the new process for bus drivers
- Development of new procedures for exception reviews at the bus bases
- Organization analysis of the payroll area

  The plan called for implementation in April. In order to meet this deadline, the procedures and pilot project test would have to be completed in March. The tasks for the pilot project test included the following:

- Development of a form to be signed by bus drivers prior to the pilot project
- Development of training materials and questions and answers for the bus drivers' team
- Definition of modified procedures for exceptions at the bus bases
- Training procedures for bus base staff in handling bus driver questions
- Design of a manual report on exceptions by central operations

  The finalization of the bus base procedures would occur after the pilot project. The payroll analysis was complex. Payroll staff were still required to review exceptions. The organization analysis began after the pilot project and expanded to include all of payroll functions.

This demonstrates how a business process improvement project can change as events in the project take hold.

Stirling Manufacturing

The business process improvement project was to implement the new production scheduling process in one business area. This would then be expanded to other business areas. An integrated detailed project plan for implementation was developed for the first business area. The lessons learned here provided information to make substantial changes to later implementations. The network implementation was extracted as a separate project for several business units. Additional tasks were added for training, network testing, and conversion. To ensure that the system meshed with the culture and environment of the organization, a pilot project process was created for each business area. This appeared to slow things down. However, because of the pilot project, training could be reduced. Conversion was also reduced because it was learned that the best approach was to establish production schedules from ground zero.

As the implementation plan was created, it became clear that schedule changes must be traced back to the process and to specific issues. An issues database was created. The issues database record had fields that identified the tasks to which they pertain. The schedules contained the issue identifier for the tasks in comment fields. The issue database had a field for the process. A process definition file referenced both the issues and the tasks. The value of this information cannot be underestimated. In a business process improvement project there is wide interconnection between work. When something slips in the schedule due to dependency, management wants to know what can be done to adjust it. Tracking this manually is usually not feasible.

GUIDELINES

- **In the implementation plan, factor in the learning curve of the team working together.**

Many managers just assume that people will work out any interpersonal problems. In projects with lower visibility and less pressure, this may be true but not here. Allow more time for initial tasks.

- **Include in the scheduling any delays in management review and approval.**

  Don't assume that management will instantly act or react. Anticipate a delay in review and approval. Plan for other tasks so that the project is not delayed.

- **Factor in the learning curve with the new technology.**

  Allow for the necessary effort on the part of the employees to gain limited proficiency. This tends to be overlooked in the presence of schedule pressures.

- **Remember to include system interfaces between current systems and new systems that will support the new process.**

  Here is a technical area that is often poorly estimated and managed.

- **Apply standard project management methods.**

  Employ any standard techniques that your organization employs. Deviations make the project stand out and attract attention.

- **Do not stress the uniqueness of the business process improvement project to the team or to others.**

  Keep a low profile with the plan. Make sure it resemble other plans on the surface. The more that your plan is perceived as different, the more likely that the approval time will be delayed.

ACTION ITEMS

1. Write a task list for implementation, including the highest level 100 tasks. Use indentation to show how detail tasks fall under summary tasks. Label the tasks with task numbers. Add dependencies to the list. You can enter this information into a project management software package or a spreadsheet. Use the following format, as it can be pasted into a table in many project management systems:

Number	Task	Dependency (predecessor)
1	1000 Project management	
2	1100 Develop plan	
3	1200 Review plan	2

2. Create a resource list for the implementation plan. Make sure that your list is complete in terms of involvement by business areas and contractors for infrastructure work. If you do not know a specific contractor or department, indicate the function (e.g., cable installer). Provide an abbreviation for each resource. A suggested simple format is provided below. This information can be pasted into the project management software.

Resource Abbreviation	Resources
Cable	Cable installer
Acct	Accounting department

Assign the resources to the highest level tasks in the list you created in Action Item 1. Assign someone to be responsible and to do the work. Plug in no more than three types of resources for each task in terms of work. Note that you can distinguish between responsibility and work because an internal manager might oversee the work of several contractors. If your project management software does not allow for a separate field for responsibility, use a comment text field for this.

3. For each summary or major task area, identify the milestone. The milestone is what you will have achieved if all of the tasks under the summary task are completed. Examples are the system is in place, the building is ready, or the process is ready for implementation. Write down how you would know if the milestone were achieved.

You can use the following table. This effort will test how concisely you have defined the tasks and whether you understand what has to be done.

Summary task	Milestone	Test of milestone
3000 Data conversion from old process	Conversion complete	Converted data is validated to be complete

4. Identify ten or more tasks in which you perceive risk. Rank each of these tasks in terms of likelihood of task slippage and impact on the schedule if slippage occurs. (This is likelihood of loss and exposure.)

Use a scale of 1 to 5 (1 is low, 5 is high). Note that you can have low likelihood, but high impact. Create another column to show the result of multiplying the likelihood by the impact: This is the risk in simple terms. Also identify the estimated duration of each task.

Keep this table handy and update it often. It tells you where the real risk lies in the project. People often pay too much attention to likelihood and duration and not enough to impact.

Tasks	Likelihood	Impact	Risk	Duration

5. For each of the high-risk tasks you have identified above, chart whether the risk can be reduced by the items listed below. Use a scale of 1 to 5 (1 is not applicable and 5 is very useful). You can add more alternative actions. The ones listed below are common responses. Adding resources can include not only people, but also tools, methods, and facilities. Breaking up the task means that you will divide the work into smaller tasks to micromanage the work, thereby lowering risk. Extending the time would be useful if the extension would reduce exposure. *Improve resource quality* means selecting better people or resources.

Tasks	Add resources	Break up task	Extend time	Improve resource quality

6. Make a list of implementation issues that you think you will face in the project. Now review the task list and find the tasks that are associated with each issue. Next, for each task or issue, determine the underlying issue that leads to the risk. This exercise will help you validate the tasks and risks as well as the issues associated with implementation.

7. Define several alternative approaches for dividing the implementation into subprojects. One is to divide it by areas of risk (highlighting integration). Another is to divide it by functional area (technology, software, business process, etc.). What are the advantages of each of these?

PART V FIVE

IMPLEMENTATION AND MEASURING RESULTS

CHAPTER 21

STEP N: IMPLEMENT
THE NEW PROCESS

CONTENTS

21

STEP N: IMPLEMENT
THE NEW PROCESS

PURPOSE AND SCOPE

You are seeking to build a prototype system and new process and
then test these together with a pilot project. Doing this will achieve
the following goals:

- Validate that the new process and system work together and can
  replace the old process and system
- Demonstrate and improve the prototype so as to improve the
  new process and market and gain support for the new process
- Validate the benefits and costs you identified earlier

The purpose of the work after the pilot project is to complete the
implementation in such a way as to not compromise the results of the
pilot project effort.

The scope of the step includes the process, system, and the organization. This is the first opportunity for the current organization to
interface and work with the new process and system. It will provide
information on what organization changes are possible.

The scope after the pilot includes all systems and data related to
the new process. This involves design, development, integration,
testing, procedures and training materials, conversion of information
to the new process, training, and setup of the systems for the new
processes. The final part of the scope is implementing the new
process and eliminating the old process.

END PRODUCTS

The major end products in the first section are a workable new
process and a prototype system. This is the first time you will have

something more than a piece of paper or report. You will have something that works. The end products of this step will serve as the basis for full-scale development and implementation of the new process and system in the next step.

You should have enthusiastic employees in the business departments after they have seen the prototype and participated in the pilot project. What was vague in the past is now tangible.

The major end product of the second section is obvious—the new process and systems are in place and working, and the old processes have been eliminated. Other supporting end products include procedures, test plans and results, integration results, completed software, training materials, and technical and business staff ready to work with the new processes and systems.

RESOURCES

Your cast has grown. Not only do you have technical people involved in infrastructure change, but you have system developers for the prototype and staff from business departments involved in design and testing. It expands even more with full implementation.

APPROACH

The implementation of the new process can be considered in two sections. The first section ends with the pilot project implementation of the new process and support structure. It includes infrastructure and systems work. The second part includes completing the development, installing the new process into the organization, and cutting off the old processes. The second part also entails conversion, integration, testing, training, cut-over, and organization change. Your objective is to have the new process supported by infrastructure, systems, and organization at the conclusion of implementation. The old process will be eliminated.

Prototype vs. Pilot Project vs. Production

The pilot project takes the prototype, builds the new process over the system, and tests the new process and system together. The production process goes beyond both. Production encompasses integration of all components, testing, conversion, and widespread use.

What would happen if you combined the pilot project and prototype into a single prototype? You would work simultaneously on changes to the system and to the process. This makes it more difficult to finish the system and the process concurrently in terms of getting a stable product. Also, it is difficult for staff members who do not develop systems to attempt to work with both at the same time.

As a side effect of the prototyping and pilot project effort, the current process may be improved. In one case, the improvements in the current process made long-term change unnecessary. The business process improvement project was stopped and called a success.

Prototype Dangers

Prototyping can be very seductive. You get positive feedback. Changes are being made. There is visible progress. But there are dangers:

- Departments can push to use the prototype in production. This can be discouraged at the outset and throughout implementation.

- Requirements can waver back and forth. In such a case, schedule a meeting to discuss different approaches and to have decisions made.

- Prototyping and pilot projecting can bring to the surface a number of issues beyond procedures and systems, such as faulty or incomplete policies or misconceptions about the process and variations in practices.

Full Implementation

After working with the prototype, you will design and develop the production process and system. Integration will occur within the process and with other processes. Integration with management will also occur. You will develop procedures, training materials, and any necessary forms. File conversion includes manual files and/or computer files and databases. Existing data may fall short in terms of the new process, requiring additional data.

You will perform testing and training for the new process. Testing includes both manual and automated steps. Procedures, training materials, and training must be completed. Finally, you will cut over to production and eliminate the old process. You will concentrate on those activities involving process.

Because of the work done on the prototype and pilot project, you can probably reduce the design effort. If you selected client server technology and database management systems wisely, you can reduce your development effort by reusing portions of the system developed during the prototype and pilot.

Action 1: Design and Develop the Prototype

You have a strategy and plan for implementation. One of your first steps is to develop a prototype system to support the new process. You should now be able to develop the initial prototype without a great deal of additional input and data collection. If you are going to reuse the same system or if you are only concerned about process, you could proceed to the actions for the pilot project activities.

At one time the concept of a prototype implied a model of the system. The prototype provided an idea of the user interface and data elements, but it could not process information. Today, prototypes still lack interfaces to other systems, substantial logic, reports, and any batch processing. This sounds like much of the system is eliminated from the prototype. However, the prototype does encompass the user interface and the ability to enter, update, and view transactions.

This section is based on intranet or client-server systems. From a business view, intranet and client-server systems are systems based on network, microcomputer, and database technology. The client refers to the computer workstation software, while the server contains the databases and processes the transactions. Although not less costly than traditional systems, client-server systems do provide flexibility and modularity to support prototyping. Client-server applications and development currently dominate new systems development efforts. Client-server applications have grown out of the increased power of microcomputers, along with availability of network technology. In this concept, functions of a system are divided so that the client side handles the user interface and basic functions while the server side focuses on data and processing. Division of the workload reduces communications traffic and allows customization of the client software. Intranet involves only a web browser as a client. The software resides on the server. In that respect, intranet systems are a subset of client-server systems. For a prototype you might have a skeleton of the server and a fairly complete client. This was the case in the examples.

Begin with the workflow. Associate a status codes with each workflow step. Identify which triggers a status code change. Workflow is extremely important because it provides the guide to navigate through the screens. Note also that a key advantage of the new process will be the workflow support. The existing system, if it is online, will typically have static screens.

Next, define the transaction queuing or waiting lines for transactions. As transactions progress through the workflow, how do they queue up for processing? Three alternatives are simplest first, first come first served, and priority classes. By using status codes and queuing, when an employee enters the system, the highest priority transaction with a specific status code will appear. When this transaction has been completed, the next one will appear, and so on.

Also determine the job functions in the new process. In the Monarch example they are receptionist, junior collector, collector, specialist, and supervisor for installment loan collections. Each job function has a specific role in the process. In a Graphical User Interface (GUI), you would define menus and pull-down menus at the top of the screen. You have security since each job type will have an individual, but similar menu.

Define the databases for the prototype. These consist of core databases and support tables or databases (e.g., zip code lookup). In a recent insurance prototype the core databases included customer, policy, property, and insurance line. Support tables included letter generation, policy amount from a code, flood zone area, and status codes.

Next, define the characteristics of the data elements for the prototype. Decide on the approach to accessing the databases. This is the access or index key(s). The selection of the data elements for the keys will affect performance and design of the system. The key is the basis for the sorting of the records in the database. Picking the wrong key can lead to disaster because the system response time might be excessive; you might not be able to reach the right information.

With the menus, workflow, and data elements defined, define the screens and the GUI. Here are some suggestions for screen design:

- In a GUI, you can elect the degree of control of the system over the employee, or vice versa. In a software-controlled system, areas are shaded and blanked so that you restrict the employee choices. Don't do this if you want to allow staff members to respond to exceptions in workflow. User control should be kept in mind. This also allows flexibility.

- Put only a few choices on the top menu. If you clutter up the main menu, you will confuse people. Hide many of the menu items under the top line.

- Use button symbols that are intuitive. Company logos are good examples.

- Avoid repainting the screen.

- Validate fields across the entire screen and not on a field-to-field basis.

- Use accelerator keys and toolbar buttons to enhance speed.

- Position controls based on ease of use.

- Use text labels rather than too many boxes.

In development, try to avoid standard programming languages unless they are visual and object-oriented. Otherwise, the initial development and successive changes will take too long.

Try to use tools with which you are familiar. It is difficult to learn a new tool and, at the same time, become proficient under severe time pressure. Use available PC software, such as spreadsheets and electronic mail, as much as possible. Database management systems and fourth generation languages are candidates for tools as well.

In selecting the tools and methods, employ the following criteria:

- Completeness of tools to reduce development

- Flexibility to make changes quickly in the prototype

- Reusability of the computer code to move to a production system

Do not depend on a major infrastructure improvement just to do the prototype. This will delay development and will likely reduce the reliability of the prototype.

The first prototype is ready when you complete testing. Do not wait for users to test it. They will lose faith in the system if they see that it does not work. Test the parts that you know work and find areas where you know that failure will occur due to being incomplete.

Here are some steps to include before you announce the first version of the prototype:

- Complete the menus and navigation between menus and screens. This will provide an overall impression.

- Develop several screens for entry and update of information. This will allow users to carry out a transaction.

- To the extent that it is possible, implement the status codes and some of the workflow tracking capabilities. Queuing of records will not be possible in the first prototype.

Action 2: Review the First Prototype

Explain to department managers and staff their role in the development of the prototype, which will be to use and review the prototype. They will simulate part of the process with the prototype. They will also complete a review sheet for each prototype version, indicating issues and improvements.

For the review, consider the following:

- Environment—where and under what conditions testing will be done
- Specific roles of individuals
- What happens after the review

Here is a sample sequence of steps for the review:

- Explain the roles and steps to be followed.
- Give a demonstration of the system, showing clearly where it ends.
- Have the staff use the prototype for several hours.

- Distribute forms on which staff members can provide criticism, suggestions, and recommendations.

On the suggestion form, include a line for the date, space to comment on ways that the prototype is better or worse than the current system, and a place for suggestions and comments. After each person works with the system, have him or her complete the form immediately. Leave the system for people to use after this test period, along with additional forms.

The first review provides an initial reality check. This is the first time that these people have seen something tangible. You may receive very definite opinions. This review typically sets the pattern for future work.

The first prototype should take about one month or less to develop. A review should take two to three hours.

Action 3: Work Between Prototype Versions

Prototyping is a continuous process. Successive prototypes will be developed and delivered for review every few weeks. The prototype will never go into production. This is the basis for system development and process evaluation later during the pilot project.

At any time you have a list of potential changes. It is useful to categorize the list and to track it. By seeing the changing mixture of work you can detect a trend toward stability. Categories might include the following:

- Adding features or capabilities
- Adding non-index data elements and screens
- Fixing what was previously done
- Modifying the basic structure of the system

There is overlap in these categories. One change may fall into several categories. The last two categories are the most important, because correction or implementation may undo much of the work you have done.

What are possible actions for each item on the list?

- Implement the item in the next prototype. If you wait, you risk undoing even more of what you did.
- Set the item aside for later consideration. The item may be vague or there may be indecision about implementation.
- Defer the item if it interfaces to existing systems until the production system has been developed. There is no point in spending time on these items unless the prototype will be the basis for production.
- Renegotiate with managers and staff to drop, change, or replace the item. This is possible in the early stages of prototyping before people become too set in their ways.

Review each item and act upon it as it arises. Leaving important items unresolved will impact the prototype. Pay special attention to workflow management, database indices, and specific functions to ensure early definition.

Group the list of items and changes by versions of the prototype. With each version of the prototype you will find more items to fix. Typically, you should include all changes in one area of the system for release in the same version.

How will you know if you are making progress? If the percentage of items to build in the prototype is diminishing, this is a good sign. The same rule applies to the number of errors that have to be fixed. No critical items should remain on that list. Figure 21-1 gives an example.

Is the Prototype Being Used and Tested?

A lack of reported problems and issues is not a sign that all is well. The absence of issues often reflects a lack of testing. Or people may be doing the same testing again and again, so that nothing new is learned. There is a third possibility—that the same people are doing the testing and they have run out of ideas and become stale.

How do you prevent this problem? Examine the testing yourself. You can also plot several charts. The data from these charts originates from the testing of the prototype itself. Most large software firms conduct similar testing. Figure 21-2 attributes the issues and items uncovered to their source. This is subjective, but it does give some idea of what is being found. Figure 21-3 gives the chart of open,

Figure 21-1:
Sample Graph of Open Items by Severity

This chart allows you to show which problems have yet to be resolved by impact.

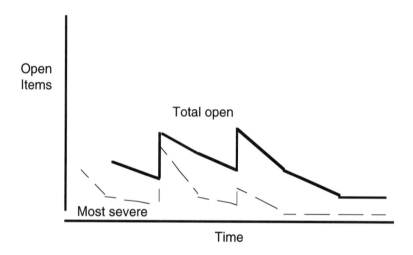

Time

Comments:
- In this figure there are three versions.
- The remaining open items at the end will be addressed in the production version.

Figure 21-2:
Issue Classification Chart

This shows the distribution of issues by type.

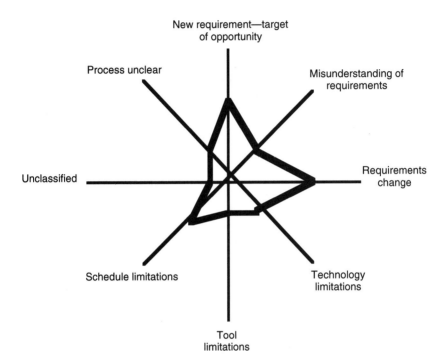

Comments: This is an example of a good prototype. There are few issues relating to misunderstanding. New targets of opportunity have surfaced. The company is not limited by tools or technology but is limited by schedule, as is almost always the case.

Figure 21-3:
Found, Open, and Closed Items

This chart is useful to track progress in resolving issues.

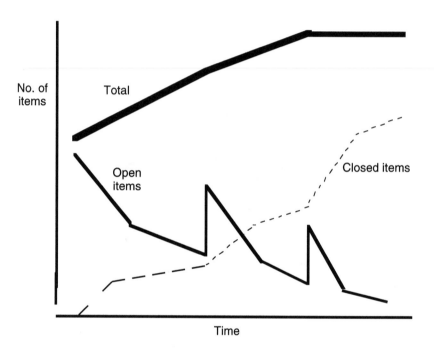

Comments:

- The discovery rate is decreasing, which may or may not be a positive sign. It depends on how the system is being tested.
- The closure rate is fairly even, which is good, indicating even progress. A rate that sharply increases at the end might indicate false closures.

closed, and found items. You hope that the rate of finds diminishes with each new prototype. However, if a new version opens up many options, the find rate will increase. In addition, if different people test, the rate may also increase.

To ensure that there is adequate testing and feedback, rotate staff when you test the prototypes. Try to replace all of the people over time. You might also bring people back after several intervening prototypes. If you replace only a few people, you risk contaminating the testing, because junior people will become biased by what the existing staff indicate.

Direct the testing. That is, indicate what is available in the latest prototype and where the staff should test. Then follow-up in these areas.

How often should you deliver a new version of the prototype? It depends on the situation, but once a week or once every two weeks is often recommended. Some factors to consider are the following:

- The larger the time gap between prototypes, the greater the chance that the staff will become disconnected from the process.
- The fewer the number of prototypes, the less feedback you will have.
- Issuing versions too frequently means that items remain open. Users will become frustrated because they did not get a chance to test the last prototype before another shows up. This can be very frustrating.
- Agree on version frequency in advance so that staff members can plan their testing time.

Action 4: Complete the Prototype

Decide on the final version for the prototype. Not all open items will be resolved until the production phase. However, no critical items or major errors should block access to testing, even though functions may still be missing. The major criterion is that the final prototype be ready for pilot project use. You must be able to test the process sufficiently using the last version of the prototype. The prototype should contain enough major functions so that the scope of testing of the new process will not be limited.

Example: Monarch Bank

For the installment loan collection system, eight prototype versions were developed. The scope of the system expanded and several rounds were needed to get uniformity across the different locations that had earlier devised different processes. Credit card collections took only three versions, due to the stability and experience of the installment loan prototype.

Example: Stirling Manufacturing

Fourteen versions of the prototype were generated over 18 weeks. This high number was due to the number and variety of exception conditions in manufacturing that had to be addressed.

Here, as at Monarch Bank, people became involved and enthusiastic as they saw their ideas and suggestions rapidly implemented.

Action 5: Conduct the First Stage of the Pilot Project—In-depth Assessment

Employ a two-stage approach for the pilot project. The first stage is an in-depth assessment of the new process in the system using a small group of people. The second part is a test of the process and system across a range of people and situations.

The processing of each transaction or type of work is examined. You usually begin with the most common situation, then consider known exceptions. After this, validate that you have completely examined the process. Obtain a sample of work and talk to other departments to find other exceptions. In addition to coverage, you are interested in the following:

- Comparing the current and new process in terms of ease of use and performance
- Detecting ambiguities in the new process (i.e., gaps in procedures and policies)
- Testing new policies to see their effect on the process
- Evaluating controls so as to detect errors
- Assessing the effectiveness of the measurement process

To get this started, assemble a small team. Ask the team members to prepare a list of situations that the process should be able to address. Divide the situations among the members. Each team member describes in detail how the new process should address the detailed situation. The result of this exercise is sometimes referred to as a *model*.

Document and test each model in the pilot project. This is tedious work that requires detailed business knowledge. This is one of the few times that you need dedicated effort by knowledgeable staff. The rewards are substantial. Not only do you test the process, but you use the models as a basis for user procedures, training materials, and training. Thus, you achieve economies of scale and consistency. During this time, track issues that arise, just as you did in your work on the prototype. You can implement changes in either the process or the system, or in both.

Example: Monarch Bank

For Monarch Bank installment loan collections, more than 60 models were defined, including the following:

- Customer does not speak a standard language.
- Customer is carrying out fraud.
- Faulty billing is being processed by the computer.
- Bank branch employees are mishandling payments.
- Customer is avoiding contact with the bank.
- Supervisor is out and substitute handles referrals.
- Workload queue of loans is handled by two collectors—day and evening.

The models were employed to assess the effect of changes in bank policy toward delinquent accounts. Three staff members, along with two systems staff members, developed the models.

Example: Stirling Manufacturing

More than 50 models were defined for Stirling Manufacturing. Only three of these were for normal work; the remaining were for different types of exceptions due to inventory, quality, scheduling, and other conditions. Developing these models was challenging because the team of four did not have direct knowledge of the entire complete manufacturing process. Each member of the team conducted interviews and visits to determine exceptions.

Action 6: Conduct the Second Stage of the Pilot Project—Wide Range Assessment

In this second stage, the process and system will be employed by a wide range of people with different requirements. These testers will have a knowledge of the process and background of the project. They represent a cross-section of the company. Not only will these people help refine the process, but their work on the pilot project will get them interested in what you are doing. The process will gain their support as they improve it.

Many failures in business process improvement projects have occurred because the second stage was neglected. An automated teller machine model failed because it was tested only by those who had designed it. They never realized that it was too complex.

The goals of the second stage are as follows:

- Uncover the learning curve for the process.
- Determine how easy it is to use the process.
- Solicit suggestions for improvement.
- Obtain commitment and support for the new process.

The Continuous Demonstration

At Stirling, a technique was employed that was highly effective. The process was demonstrated on a continuous basis throughout the day—like a continuous running movie. The demonstration consisted of a five-minute introduction followed by a short demonstration of how it worked. Members of the audience were then invited to try the process and system.

The continuous demonstration approach collected a large amount of information quickly. As refinements were made to the process and system, new demonstrations were held. This method also generated enthusiasm for the process.

To carry out a continuous demonstration, you will need a large conference room. The computer should be outfitted with an overhead projector to show the screen. Several computers should be spread out around the room. Develop an evaluation sheet for all attendees. The only mandatory part of the demonstration is that all attendees must complete the evaluation form. The evaluation form should contain the following information:

- Date
- Position of the person
- Number of years employed by the company
- Rating of the following on a scale of 1 to 5 (1 is low, 5 is high):
  —Ease of learning
  —Ease of use
  —Completeness
  —Improvement over the existing process
- What did you like best?
- What did you dislike most?
- What would make the process and system better?
- What do you like best about the old process?

Tabulate the responses over time. Also, modify the questionnaire to include the most common responses in a list. People can then rate these on the scale of 1 to 5 (1 is low, 5 is high). Allow space for written comments.

More than 200 forms were collected during the pilot project at Stirling. Fifty people attended two or more sessions with different pilot project versions. Changes were made to the pilot project system on the same basis as they were made on the prototype. Changes to the process and system were synchronized. To add to the interest, a list of improvements resulting from feedback was posted.

Here are some benefits of the demonstration approach:

- Widespread feedback was obtained.
- Reduced resistance was encountered later.
- Bottom up support for the new process was generated.

- There was a more stable process and system after installation.
- More exceptions were addressed.

Action 7: Deal with Policy Issues

Policy issues come to the forefront during the pilot project. Policies determine what people do and how they will do their work. The pilot project can create momentum for change and for testing policies. Through the new process and system you find a better way to do something. At the start of the prototype, very few policy changes are known in detail. The prototype sheds little light on policy issues because the focus is on the system. Once you reach the stage of the pilot project, each model is mapped against current policies. You have to determine if the current policy can stand as is, should be changed (formal to informal, or vice versa), should be replaced, or should be dropped. If the policies are not changed in the pilot project, it will be difficult to change them later.

Once an issue is discovered, carefully define a new policy and evaluate it in terms of the old policy. Define precise terminology for the policy.

Here are some of the questions to be answered for a new policy:

- What is the impact of the policy on control and audit?
- How easy is it to circumvent the policy?
- How would someone know if the policy were violated?
- What should the scope of the new policy be?
- How should the company transition from the old policy to the new policy?

You can then prepare a written report of the following:

- New policy
- Corresponding old policies
- Differences
- Benefits and impacts
- Effect of the new policy on the new process

- Effect on the new process if the old policy is retained
- Transition approach
- Impact on other processes

Here are some examples of policy issues:

- Monarch Bank
  —When is a loan delinquent?
  —When should they start collecting?
  —When is a customer a chronic delinquent?
  —To which loans should senior staff be assigned?
- Stirling Manufacturing
  —Who is in charge of what schedule?
  —How is priority assigned to scarce testing facilities?
  —How often should schedules for production be updated?
- TRAN
  —What union rules changes are possible?
  —How often should bus schedules be changed?

Action 8: End the Pilot Project

The pilot project is finished after you have validated the process and the system. You may elect to continue it while doing conversion, infrastructure work, integration, and other activities discussed in the next chapter. Ending the pilot project is also a state of mind. Do you wish to freeze the process? Is it truly ready for production work? Have you demonstrated it to the right people?

Action 9: Document the Pilot Project and Prototype

You can now write up the survey results and demographics. Prepare a summary presentation to management highlighting the results of both the prototype and pilot project to capture the essence of the experience.

One subject to cover is the team members. Do they work well together? Can they continue to work together in the next part of implementation?

You can also document the differences between the old and new processes, as these are now in as sharp focus as they will get. Revisit the comparison tables developed in preceding chapters and update them. Costs, benefits, and impacts can be revisited.

Finally, refine and write up the implementation plan for the remainder of the work, incorporating what you have learned about raining requirements by job type and level.

Action 10: Build the New Infrastructure

While the prototype and pilot project effort were progressing, work was being done on the infrastructure. Remember that changes here require the most time and money. Let's divide the discussion into infrastructure based on technology and infrastructure not based on technology. A basic guideline is that you do not want the infrastructure effort to get too far out in front of the pilot project because the pilot project experience may modify details of the infrastructure. On the other hand, you don't want the infrastructure to lag. If it is delayed, the momentum you established in the pilot project may be destroyed.

Technology Infrastructure

Technology infrastructure includes telephones, cabling, communications and networks, hardware, software, and staffing. Some specific concerns here are that much of the activity is sequential, decisions on technology are made too early, and changes are not synchronizing with the infrastructure. Some specific suggestions are as follows:

- Communications and networks are long lead items. Start them as soon as possible. They are often the least impacted by findings from the pilot project.

- Establish communications to handle the maximum you expect over the next three to five years. It is cheap to install additional cabling now, but much more expensive in labor if people have to return later. Labor is often the dominant cost.

- Delay hardware purchases as long as possible. Price performance increases and obsolescence mandate this. There are fewer economies of scale and discounts in purchasing the hardware at the start.

- Purchase hardware based on the experience of the prototype and part of the pilot project. Get more hardware power than you think you require because it may be expensive to upgrade and politically unacceptable to ask for more money later. Upgrades can be expensive in labor if you have to upgrade 100 computers.

- For certain main components, such as central hardware, hold back money so that you can buy more later when you have more experience with the requirements generated by the pilot project.

- Give a great deal of attention to integration and testing. The risk in technology infrastructure is typically not in the components but in integration.

Non-Technology Infrastructure

Non-technology infrastructure includes modifications to the buildings, parking lots, office layout, office improvements, and furniture. This is both broad and specific to the situation. Use critical path analysis on the infrastructure project plan. Also focus on issues. An example of an issue is design alternatives.

Action 11: Integrate the New Process

Integration is a general term that infers successful assembly of the parts. When you work on a business process improvement project, you cross many organizations, policies, infrastructures, etc. Implementing a new process involves much more integration than the systems part alone.

Components of the New Process and System

Integration attempts to mesh each step of the process with the relevant part of the system. Integration also tests the interface between the staff members and the system. During integration, you reapply the scenarios of the previous chapter and generate user and training procedures.

The New System and Other Systems

Integration can be complex due to some of the following factors:

- The new system and the interfacing systems do not have matching data elements.

- The different systems process information at different times so that there are compatibility issues.

- One or more existing systems may be quite old and the data they employ may have questionable validity.

Each of these factors may require additional programming for interfaces.

An individual interface between systems can be one of several types. One is a batch interface in which one system produces a file and passes it to a second system. This is the simplest to test. An online interface is the second approach. Dynamically, one system may pass a transaction to another. The third interface might be a manual one. Here, one person takes data from one system and enters it into another.

The total interface is then a combination of interfaces. For example, Monarch Bank's new system for loan collections accesses the old installment loan system in several ways. The loan system passes the file of delinquent loans along with payments to the collection system. This is a batch interface. Imagine that a collector has a customer on the telephone. The customer asks, "How much will it cost to pay off the loan?" The collection system may not have this information, but it can retrieve it online from the installment loan system. You might take the productivity statistics from the collection system for each collector and enter these into a spreadsheet—a manual interface. Another interface would be required in which the customer makes loan payments through a checking account.

Obviously, you would like to eliminate manual interfaces. They involve additional work and are not as reliable as an automated interface.

Factors considered in building and testing an interface are as follows:

- Verification of proper timing of the interface
- Exact data elements to be passed including their format and order
- Method employed to carry out the interface
- Confirmation that the data was received
- Method for verifying and editing data in the interface
- Approach for correcting any errors that are detected
- Recovery if the interface fails or is not present

The New Process and Other Processes

The process interface includes the following:

- How information is tracked between the two processes
- Method for balancing and checking the interface between the two systems
- Method for handling errors generated by the two processes
- Approach for obtaining combined information from the two processes

Here are some additional concerns:

- **Consistency of procedures by the staff members who perform the processes.**

  If procedures differ, the staff may become confused, and processing will take longer. This will also create more errors. In some cases, this inconsistency has increased the time required by both processes.
- **Policies that impact multiple processes.**

  Conflicting policies are often a major problem. Different processes may be governed by different laws.
- **Infrastructure shared by multiple processes.**

  The concern is that performance of one process will not interfere with that of the other process.

Processes and Policies

The pilot project covered policy impacts. The final new process and system must fit within the policies. In testing you will review the policy and then turn to the process to see how smoothly and completely it follows the policy. If you want to circumvent the policy, will the process allow you to do this?

Processes and the Organization

Analysis of how the process and organization integrate leads naturally to thoughts on reorganization. You have already integrated a staff member with the process and system. At higher levels, you face issues such as the following:

—How will the organization supervise and manage the process?

—How will the organization deal with problems and exceptions that arise?

—How will the organization address policy issues and ensure policy enforcement?

Begin by defining the job requirements for specific functions of the process and system. This will tend to redefine the jobs of people who work with the process directly. Next, move up to the role and activities of the supervisor. Continue moving upward and toward generality.

At Monarch Bank, specific roles in the process were defined: clerical support, handling early delinquent customers, collections, tracking down customers who are difficult to locate, and handling complex situations and difficult customers. These translated into the following respective job titles: clerk, junior collector, collector, skip tracer, and specialist. A person who tries to evade the bank is referred to as a *skip*. The employee tracking the skip is called a *skip tracer*. A supervisor's duties include handling referrals from staff, measuring performance of the staff, conducting follow-up training, and monitoring the system use.

As you define the staff and supervisor roles and job descriptions, you may begin to consider how many staff members a supervisor can direct. With supervisors and staff defined, you can look to the role of a manager. This bottom-up method can reduce the levels of management.

Processes and Management

The integration between the process and general management moves you from the tactical handling of work and transactions addressed above to more general issues:

- How will management be able to control the entire process?
- How will recurring problems be tracked and identified to management?
- What is the impact of management's decisions on organization and process?
- What are routine management reports?
- What exception management reporting will be performed?
- What information does the process provide for errors, productivity, performance, cost, and staffing?

Not surprisingly, with all of your other work, this may be overlooked. People often just take it for granted that definition will follow. Here are some guidelines:

- **Develop a strawman reporting method for the process based on your knowledge of the process and system.**
  A strawman is a model or sample of the reporting method. Put yourself in the position of a manager. If you ask people what they want, you may be disappointed. They do not know the process as you do and they may ask for much more than is possible.
- **With the strawman defined, you have set the scope and format for integration.**
  Once you refine this with examples and discussion, you can document it as a group of procedures to be employed with the process.

Action 12: Convert the Information

Often, when you implement a new process and system, you must convert the information in the old process. Data typically exists across the automated system, manual files, and even local files on microcomputers. Conversion can be the reason that the business process improvement project flounders. If the data is not converted completely and properly, the entire new process is jeopardized. Consider what might be wrong with the existing information:

- Information is faulty because there has been no update or validation.
- Data in the manual and automated parts of the old process is inconsistent.
- Information may originate in other processes and systems. These may have changed, contaminating the data.
- Data in the system is not in the proper format.
- Missing data must be found, captured, and entered.
- History data is in a different format than that of the active master file.

Even with modern technology, data conversion may not be a simple task. It may require extensive manual labor. After all, what would a computer program match against?

In conversion, quality and completeness of information are crucial. Error-free transactions require accurate information at each step. Otherwise, additional manual effort may be required to find and enter the correct data, in which case productivity suffers. Poor data at the start may even deteriorate.

Begin with the new process. Determine the requirements for conversion related to sources of information, quality, and processing characteristics. Now review the results of Step 5 when you considered the old process in detail. What problems surfaced related to data quality?

Next, decide how to get the information into shape for the new process.

Here are some factors to consider in your conversion decisions:

- **Timing**

  If you transfer or reconstruct data too early, you will have to accommodate changes to the data prior to the new process being implemented. This may require an entirely new, temporary updating process. If you are too late, the conversion will delay implementation.

- **The quality of the information**

  Test and sample the information to determine quality.

- **The location of good data**

  Is it in manual files or some other computer system?

Converting Manual Files

In many business process improvement situations, you review manual files, capture data from the files, and then archive the file. Here are some guidelines:

- **Arrange files into batches and put them in a central location.**

  If the information in the files changes, the division into batches helps in locating the files.

- **Carry out a quick survey of the batch.**

  Handle the usable files first. Separate the problem files for work by more experienced staff.

- **Consider scanning and optical character recognition (OCR) for data capture. However, the success in recognition is often too low and will require manual entry.**

  In many cases you cannot get all of the information you seek. You must carry out trade-offs between value on the one hand and effort and schedule on the other. Determine the minimum information needed to bring the process into production. However, you can wait on collecting other customer data from the files.

Example: Monarch Bank

In Monarch's case, there were more than two million loans. Monarch Bank required the customers' telephone numbers. Fewer than 90,000 had valid telephone numbers. No effort was made to clean up the telephone numbers in the installment loan system because most did not require collections.

Action 13: Integrate the Parts of the Process

Integration means putting together separate items, then testing these items together. If A has three possible tests and B has four possible tests, then the number of possible combinations is 12 (3 x 4). Both normal and exception conditions must be tested in combination. You can never completely test everything, so some errors are latent and surface later.

Which items should you integrate?

- **Loosely connected**

  An example is the employee and the computer system.

- **Physically connected**

  The two activities are performed by the same people even though they are part of different processes.

- **Tightly connected**

  The items are totally dependent on each other.

- **Functionally connected**

  The items perform related functions, but are not totally dependent on each other.

The degree of integration and the type of connection affects the extent of testing required. The more integrated the process is, the greater the likelihood that the process is effective. Reduced effectiveness relates to the processes being loosely connected.

In planning the integration testing, take advantage of loose connections between parts of the process and systems to reduce the amount of testing required. Also, systems integrate behind the scenes while process integration tends to be more visible. This generates a wider variety of tests.

Consider different types of testing. Begin by finding the major parts of the interface that have risk in terms of their impact on the process. Then determine the type of testing required. Here are several types:

- **System testing**

  In this type of testing, only the automated part of the process is tested. The overall process is not tested.

- **Process, non-system testing**

  In this case, the process is tested. At the points at which automation occurs, insert a black box to avoid system testing. This is suitable for exceptions.

- **Transaction testing**

  Here a transaction is taken through the entire process, both system and manual.

- **Performance testing**

  In this type of testing, you see how the process and system behave under stress loading. You can determine throughput (volume of work over time) and response time to do the work.

- **Acceptance testing**

  This is testing by the department staff and management to see if they will approve the entire process.

Decisions related to the test approach include the following:

- **How will you obtain the data?**

  Will you use standard production data from the current process? Will you collect data separately?

- **How will you test?**

  Go back to the scenarios and build test scripts. A *test script* is a set of procedures for doing a test. The script identifies the anticipated result. People are reluctant to spend time creating scripts, but they should at least use their scenarios from their pilot project efforts. Scripts are beneficial because they provide formal structure for testing.

Next, carry out the following steps:

- **Set up the process and system.**

  Purge old test data from the process, set up a computer test environment and process test environment, and assemble staff for testing.

- **Carry out testing and monitor the testing.**

  Often, you can gain useful information from observation of the staff carrying out the process. The people doing the work may miss details because they are concentrating on the process. Also, conduct short interviews during the testing. Do not hesitate to stop the testing and restart it.

- **Analyze test results.**

  Tabulate the portion of the results that is quantitative. Look at the subjective opinions and reactions. You will find new information that may contradict lessons learned in the pilot project. Determine not only what to do but also why this happened. Was there a problem in the pilot project? Was it carried out for too narrow a scope? Generate changes in the procedures as well as error reports for correction to the system.

  Client-server systems employ a general communications network across an organization. As such, the software shares the network with other workload from electronic mail, fax machines, and so on. To be realistic you should test when this load is present.

If performance is a problem, look at these areas:

- **Network**

  The network design and communications hardware may not be able to handle the load. Like PCs, communication hubs, routers, and gateways come in variety of models with different performance levels. In addition, the network design typically divides the body of users into segments. Your new system may overload a segment.

- **Database interface between client and server**

  The client software generates database requests (in the form of structured query language [SQL] commands). If you don't write them efficiently, performance suffers.

- **Databases and hardware**

  The bottleneck could be the server hardware, operating system, and database workload.

- **Computer-based monitoring software**

  This software can indicate problem areas and where the system resources are consumed. In terms of countermeasures, you can upgrade or modify networks relatively quickly. It takes more effort to modify and optimize the database requests. Hardware upgrades can be expensive, but they are generally routine. If you have to redesign the database, the project may be in trouble. After you find all of the issues (or as many as you can), fix them in parallel.

Action 14: Archive Data

Ask department managers how long information should be retained, and they will probably answer "Forever." The organization does not have physical or computer space to store all of this information. Experience indicates that the area of archiving and retaining historical data tends to receive little attention during business process improvement implementation. The problem will be solved later through the accumulation of history data.

Some of the issues involving history data are as follows:

- Are the actual originals required, or can microfilm copies be used?
- Is history required for all transactions or only for certain records?
- If you archive computer-based data, subsequently modify the system, and then require the archived data, how can you retrieve the information?
- What retention policies are necessary and how will they be enforced?

To begin, consider the information associated with the old process and system. After some or all of it is converted, what will happen to the original or source information? This is a good place to start considering archival storage. Establish a basic process for archiving and retaining records. Include the following:

- Identification of the minimum data elements for retention
- Specification of the method of storage and indexing of information for later retrieval

- Method of updating old history data with "new" history data
- Determination of what history information will be available online or easily accessible
- Method of accessing remote history data if software changes
- Clean-up procedures for data prior to archiving

How you address these issues impacts the technology. Technology is changing rapidly in terms of image storage, data compression, and price performance. Even so, consider the old reliable approach of microfilm for certain types of records. Microfilm is less flexible, but it may cost only a fraction of other storage media.

Action 15: Choose Backup and Disaster Recovery Methods

Linked to, but separate from, history data are the issues of recovery and restart. If you need to resort to backup, how will you recover the process and system? How will the data that was generated or obtained while the backup was in use be loaded or transferred into the process? Much has been written about system backup and disaster recovery, but what about the process? *Restart* means starting the process and system up again so that no transactions are lost or processed in error.

How can a process fail? Some examples are as follows:

- The system fails, causing the process to fail. For example, in a supermarket when the point-of-sale system fails, the checkout line process fails. The store must close.
- People with extensive process experience may leave, causing the process to deteriorate rapidly and fail.
- Physical disaster strikes, preventing the process from being performed. Hurricanes, earthquakes, riots, and fire are examples of disasters.

The first step in addressing backup is to isolate the few critical processes—those that you cannot allow to fail. Having identified these, add in processes on which the critical processes depend. For other processes, data will be collected, but the information will not be processed.

Proceeding now with the critical processes, determine the risks to the processes, not just to the systems. There are wonderful disaster recovery plans for major systems; however, they often do not include getting critical staff to work to use the recovered system.

Some considerations in developing your backup plan are as follows:

- What is the minimum level of a process in terms of operation? Can only one or two functions be supported? For example, for an insurance company, billing and claims would be considered more important than new application processing.

- How long will it take to establish the minimum level of the process? What happens with the data, customers, and so on during this period?

- After you define the minimum process, what is the recovery sequence to restore the process?

The simpler the process, the easier it is to bring in backup staff to do the work. Also, the more modular the work, the greater the flexibility in placing work for processing.

Example: Monarch Bank

Monarch Bank's initial archive was intended to retain the entire history of a loan online. In actual practice, this was expensive and not performed. The requirement dropped to the past year's transactions. Data older than one year was retained in a separate stripped down system that retained only financial information. Each month the system removed data over a year old and passed it to history, where a general update occurred.

The backup method was initially to generate summary reports for distribution, enabling staff to call customers about delinquent loans. After two years without a failure, this method was dropped. Instead, money was spent on improving hardware and the network to reduce the likelihood of failure. Staff members were cross-trained so that a skeleton staff could make collections. Cut-off levels were set under which loan collection occurred during the period of the backup use.

Action 16: Construct Online Process Procedures

A body of material has now been accumulated to aid in development of the procedures. This includes the concept of the new process, the scenarios and work performed during the prototype and pilot, and comparison tables. Employees can also draw on their own experience and knowledge.

In the past, organizations documented processes with procedures. Procedures for the computer system were then separately documented. This approach can result in the following problems:

- The process and system procedures do not agree and are not tied together.

- Documentation is paper-based and is not retained.

- Updating the procedures is impossible because distribution lists are not maintained and people who did get updates throw them away.

Technology has created an opportunity to construct online procedures for both the system and the process in word processing, then move it into an online help system. The system is graphical and supports key word search and indexing. All three example companies employed this approach, which offers several benefits:

- Online updates occur for the system.

- Updates are controlled because only employees can read the information.

- There is no distribution issue because anyone using the system can access the procedures.

- More frequent updates are possible.

The procedures should be prepared by department staff members who will work with the process and system. By participating, these staff members will gain a sense of ownership. The procedures will be in their language. Also, their participation increases the chances of the procedures being used.

Action 17: Train the Staff

Develop training materials when you develop the process procedures. The materials should draw directly from the scenarios of the
pilot project as well as from test scripts. Include an overview of the
process, as well as detailed training exercises.

The following guidelines have proven useful:

- Always provide an overview of the process and system to
  participants at the start of training. Include parts of the process
  that are not within their job descriptions.

- Link the process to the policies.

- Describe what management expects from the new process so
  that people will know what they are to do in terms of performance.

- Include hands-on work with the new process.

- Ensure that the cut-over to the new process occurs soon after the
  training is completed. Any gaps will cause problems in retention of the process knowledge.

- Use department staff extensively in the training.

- Consider using the train-the-trainer approach so that there is
  wider involvement.

- Share war stories and experiences that support performing the
  process properly.

Action 18: Define Organization Structure and Assign Staff

After the pilot project process, the impact of the process on the
organization becomes clear. Details become clear when you create
the comparison tables. The models allowed you to define the steps in
the work, and defining jobs in terms of the process bottom up has
been covered.

Define the organization structure and assignment of staff into the
various roles after relating the positions to the process. You could
continue bottom up and associate names with positions in an organizational chart that you created with the process fit to the roles. This
method detracts from an opportunity for organizational improve-

ment. A second approach is to now move top down. Define the scope of departments based on the processes as they have been redefined. As you establish the overall organization, you can fit together what you have done from top down and bottom up.

Assignment of staff to roles should not be left solely to the managers. The business process improvement team has acquired experience and knowledge of the staff. This can be useful input. Each level of the organization near the process can be populated by the appropriate managers and staff.

As the cut-over approaches, the lack of fit between the current organization and the new process becomes evident. Organization change is needed. Here are some options on timing of such change:

- **Prior to cut-over**

    This period will be disruptive and may prevent successful implementation.

- **As part of the cut-over**

    At this point, it will be enough to get the new process going.

- **Shortly after the cut-over**

    This is probably the least disruptive period.

- **Long after the cut-over**

    At this point, it will be too late, as the old organization has seized on the new process.

- **Independent of cut-over**

    This period appears feasible, but it negatively affects integrated change, the overall purpose of business process improvement.

Action 19: Cut-Over to the New Process

In the past, a variety of approaches have been proposed for cut-over to the new process. Three of these are as follows:

- **Parallel**

    Operate the new system in parallel to the old system. At an appropriate point in time, terminate the old system.

- **Pilot Project**
  Install the new system with one group in production (not in the pilot project mode discussed in the previous chapter). Then expand it.
- **Cut-off**
  Simply stop the old system. The new system takes over.

The parallel approach is not feasible because of resource and money limitations. Expanding a pilot project process appears attractive but also is usually not feasible. The new process impacts surrounding processes and systems. Isolation is not often feasible, so it is all or none.

This leaves the cut-off method. This approach requires notification of staff. A date for cut-off must be set and it cannot be changed unless a crisis arises. Cut-off can be accomplished by function. That is, you could enter all new work as of a certain date in the new system. You would then have to service both the old processes and new process until you complete all of the transactions from the old process. This only works if the transactions time is very short. Otherwise, there is usually a general cut-off date. You might assign specific staff to handle the last of the old process.

If an organization has multiple processes, you must typically determine the order of implementation and cut-over. You would not always implement the most important process in the group. You might, instead, implement a smaller, less critical process to hone your skills, gain experience, and demonstrate success. This will help to overcome resistance. Also, implementing a less important process will aid in testing the network, hardware, and software. You might even be able to use some of the department staff from the first process to help in later implementation.

How do you force the issue of change to the new process from the old? You know that the old process and system are not efficient. To encourage transition, consider this strategy. Calculate the true total cost of the old process. Allocate the total cost directly to departments using the process. This cost burden will help to terminate the old process.

To eliminate the old process, first eliminate its supports. Terminate the old automated system. Remove the documentation and procedures as well as the files for the old process. Sever interfaces. Block any work that might be started by the old process. Be alert to ensure that the process and system are eliminated. Downsizing will be addressed in more detail in Chapter 33.

Multiple Processes

Recall that you are implementing new approaches and improvements for a group of processes. Much of what has been discussed applies as much to a group as to an individual process. However, consider the complexity the group adds. Extend the prototype effort across the group of processes. This will work if all of the processes in the group use the same system. The infrastructure work to support the processes in the group can be combined.

The difference in working with a group often occurs in the pilot project. It can be time-consuming and lead to delay if you have to undertake pilot projects sequentially. Here are some suggestions:

- **Set up separate groups for the first stage of the pilot project, in which models are developed.**

  Alternatively, you can use the same group of people for multiple processes.

- **Develop specific models that cross the processes in the group.**

- **In the second stage of the pilot project, have some of the demonstrations oriented to staff members who work with one process.**

  Also explain how the other processes in the group are impacted by the change.

MANAGEMENT PRESENTATION AND COST-BENEFIT ANALYSIS

When you show the pilot project to managers, have the business department staff do the entire demonstration. Introduce it and then move to the sidelines. The staff members' passion and conviction will influence management. At the end of the demonstration, return to the stage and go over the plans for the next step and review the costs and benefits.

When discussing the costs and benefits, be direct. If it will cost more or have fewer benefits with what you have learned, admit this. Money and time have been invested in the prototype and pilot project, as well as in the infrastructure. This fact, combined with the enthusiasm of staff members, will likely influence management to continue. The cost from this point on is limited.

Due to the effort and elapsed time, you will have to present to management during the second part of implementation as well as at the end of the project. Prior to production use of new process, you will be focusing your presentations on updates to the project plan and status. You will be measuring your progress against your planned schedule. You will be doing the same with costs.

At the end, you will be showing management how the new process and systems work. Again, let business staff demonstrate everything. This validates management's first concern of function and replacement of the old process. Then you can turn to operational cost and recap development costs.

The staff can point to operational efficiencies. However, you have not yet changed the organization so you cannot emphasize benefits. Hence, you can use this presentation as a political tool to move on to organizational change.

KEY QUESTIONS

Did the first stage of the implementation goes without any problems? If so, it may not be realistic enough. Involve more of the people in the current process in the pilot project to bring together plans and reality.

What surprises have you have encountered in the second stage of implementation? Make a list. If you can't identify any, things are going too smoothly. You will be more likely to run into unpleasant surprises later.

What is your assessment of team and management enthusiasm for the project? The project team members should be pleased because they are approaching the end. Management should be supportive because they are closer to getting the benefits from their investment. Some middle managers and people who are going to be negatively impacted by the new process may be apprehensive or negative about changes.

EXAMPLES

Monarch Bank

Infrastructure issues with Monarch Bank related mainly to preparing physical buildings and office space. Some of the problems encountered were the following:

- Missing and inaccurate building plans
- Elapsed time to get building permits and inspections
- Limited communications capacity in buildings
- Security problems
- Inadequate power and utilities
- Glare from the sun on the work areas

All of these were surmounted, but only through having people dedicated to problem-solving.

Experiences from the full implementation included the following:

- **Conversion**

  Telephone numbers in the bank's old system were not accurate. Someone suggested converting the telephone numbers from other accounting systems. This did not work because the data was no better. More than 85,000 telephone numbers had to be manually tracked down and entered into the system. Additionally, the collection system took advantage of additional loan information on the customer. This information was not in the old installment loan system, so it was necessary to retrieve the loan applications and then enter the additional information into the new system manually.

- **Training**

  Staff members were divided into sections. Each section consisted of 50 people, divided into groups of five. The first part of the training consisted of an overview of the process, which included a demonstration. The first set of five staff members received two hours of intensive online, hands-on training working with the process and system. Two people from the first group were selected to train the next group. The trainers had proper supervision. As training ended for each group, two people become trainers for the next group. After training, the employees returned to their desks and did any remaining conversion and data entry from manual files. Shortly after training was completed, the new process was activated.

After the first group had been trained, training became the responsibility of the staff and managers from departments. The business process improvement team only monitored the training and answered questions. This is a variation of the train-the-trainer approach.

- **Organization change**

  At Monarch, upper management solicited the business process improvement team for advice on how to organize the business departments. A trial run was conducted with one small group to shake down organization details. It worked. As the large rollout of the collection processes occurred, management changed the organization right behind the process. Although the team members were intimidated at first, they recognized the purpose and effect and embraced it. Middle managers who might have resisted were moved to other staff positions.

TRAN

TRAN had major issues in both technology and non-technology infrastructure. A few of the issues were as follows:

- Temporary installation of cabling was necessary due to building work delay.
- The attempt at integration revealed incompatible telephone equipment.
- An opportunity to eliminate a facility surfaced, changing the plans.
- During excavation, hidden utility lines were severed.

Experience from the second section of implementation included the following:

- **Conversion**

  In the case of TRAN, they converted the basic bus schedule information. However, this schedule was linked to a physical map of the region served. Each bus stop had to be pinpointed on a map, and "geo-coded" into the system. Rough latitude and longitude were not sufficient because they had to locate the side of the street for the bus stop. Many hours of tedious manual effort were involved in the process.

- **Training**

  For TRAN the new software system was established in parallel to the old. Staff members spent their time between using the old process and doing data setup and conversion for the new process. Training came through conversion.

- **Organization change**

  Rapid change was not possible at TRAN. Public agencies cannot introduce sudden major changes. The implementation strategy was a phased organization change and restructuring over the period of a year. The same benefits were obtained, although it took a little longer. Public agencies can be downsized and restructured just as private companies can be, but different techniques and timing are required.

Stirling Manufacturing

At Stirling Manufacturing, the process involved the sharing of schedule and issue information for production. The prototype provided the user interface to the information and supported manipulation and analysis of data. It did not contain actual production information, nor did it interface to production systems. This prototype answered the question, "What is the value of providing shared information on production to multiple managers at the same time?"

Examples of issues for Stirling Manufacturing were as follows:

- Cabling and networking of incompatible hardware were mandated as more people wanted to use the system than originally conceived.

- Cabling was difficult in the manufacturing area.

- Old cable was first thought adequate and then had to be replaced.
- The network load was higher than anticipated due to the combination of scheduling, electronic mail, computer aided design (CAD), and other traffic.
- It proved difficult to gain priority for the work among all other projects with limited funds available.

Experience from the second section of implementation included the following:

- **Conversion**

  Existing production schedules were reviewed in Stirling. This revealed problems with the data. The schedules did not match reality. The old data was scrapped. This is not uncommon and is part of business process improvement implementation.

- **Training**

  At Stirling, training was based on an expansion of the pilot's continuous demonstration process discussed in the preceding chapter. Training was combined with input and validation of the schedules.

- **Organization change**

  The implementation of collaborative scheduling allowed managers to build, review, and share information on their project plans. This had several interesting organizational effects. First, the dedicated staff members who were responsible for doing the schedules in the past were reassigned to other work. Second, the lower level managers had more and better information than the higher level managers. Upper management began to empower these managers to make decisions on priorities. In one business area, the scheduling staff survived doing summary schedules in the old system. They extracted information from the new process and system and entered it into the old system. Management in this unit, it seemed, still favored the old system and were willing to pay for it.

  The process and system were implemented successfully at first. The organization remained intact. Time went by. The people who assisted in the new process development found themselves stymied and blocked. There were no changes and benefits. Managers from the old school subtly began to reintroduce practices from the old process. Gradually, the old process re-emerged in the guise of a new process with a new system. The cost was more than three million dollars, but there were no savings. All of the managers continued to pay lip service to the "new process," but upper management had ceded authority to middle management. They didn't get it back.

GUIDELINES

- **Instruct staff members to focus on substance rather than appearance during the prototype and pilot project testing.**

  Make sure that people focus on how a specific transaction is addressed in the system.

- **Look for new opportunities for business process improvement to surface during the pilot project.**

  At this point, write them down. Wait until later to work on them. Avoid promises until you have thought through the opportunities.

- **Alert management as soon as you discover the need to develop a radical new business process improvement approach.**

  The pilot project may lead you to the realization that the new process is not going to meet the issues and underlying problems without organization change. This should be explained to management early.

- **Process implementation must accommodate or address issues of style.**

  Any manual part of a process performed by different people in different locations will generate variations based on style and circumstance. In the bus driver example, some drivers completed their time sheets before their work and adjusted it later. Others completed it later. The new process required time sheets for only exception conditions, so all time sheets were completed at the end of the work period.

- **Use testing for political advantage.**

  Test results are viewed as academic information to be used for technical work. If you believe this, you are mistaken. If department staff have been involved in testing, and results are favorable, ask these staff members for testimonials.

- **Consider using parallel implementation or multiple implementation.**

  If the implementation of a process is successful, consider implementing multiple processes at the same time. Thus, you will reduce the number of separate changes and provide economies of scale of implementation for the team. The dangers are diffusion of resources among multiple processes and confusion among department staff. In many cases, the balance is on the side of multiple processes.

- **Delegate responsibilities to departments as soon as possible.**

  During implementation, a business process improvement team may be tempted to hold control over the process. Instead, hand over control as soon as possible. The business process improvement team should move into the background and monitor the process.

ACTION ITEMS

1. Identify the people who will be involved in the prototype and their roles.

Individual	Role

2. Identify the people who will be involved in the pilot project and their roles.

Individual	Role

3. Write down the requirements of the prototype in the left column. In the right column note the specific results or conditions under which the requirement is met.

Requirement	Condition

4. Track each successive prototype in terms of the following factors. This table can be employed to determine trends toward stability. The time lag in this section refers to the elapsed time between the issuance of the previous prototype and this prototype. The major change is the major improvement that was included in the prototype. In the final column, indicate what remains to be done. If the last two columns do not change, there is a problem and the developers are likely concentrating on minor enhancements.

Prototype number	Time lag	Major change	Left to do

In the second part of implementation you are concerned with conversion, training, policies, and organization change.

5. Prepare a list of process tasks that include online system functions. Use this as the rows in a table. Now take the candidate list of job titles and use this list as the columns. In the table, enter an X if that job performs that task. Otherwise, leave it blank. This table helps you define job descriptions.

New Process   Job Titles

6. Do the same as above except use the old process steps as the rows. By analyzing and comparing the two tables, you will be able to determine how jobs will change.

Old Process Tasks   Job Titles

7. How does the current set of employees fit with the old tasks? Write down the names of the people in the rows. Put the tasks of the old process in the columns. In the table, use the rating system of 1 to 5 (1 means the person does not perform the task at all, 5 indicates that the person is almost totally responsible for the task).

People   Old Process Tasks

8. Determine how the employees would fit with the new process. Enter their names as rows and the tasks of the new process as columns. Use the rating system of 1 to 5 (1 means the person is not suited at all, 5 indicates that he or she is a very good fit) to indicate the degree to which you or others feel they are suited to the task.

People   New Process Tasks

9. You can now use your analysis from Action Items 1 through 4 and create a new table of people vs. job titles. Use the rating system of 1 to 5 (1 means there is no fit, 5 indicates an excellent fit). This table shows you possible candidates for specific jobs in the new process.

People   Job Titles

10. You now can create a new organization from the previous work. Write down the job titles in a standard organizational chart. Create several different charts for the following models:
    - As flat an organization as possible with as few levels of organization as is feasible.
    - Organization by function to cover specialization

11. Use the graphs that you developed in the chapter to track system progress.

12. Track the progress of conversion of databases and files. Use the following table in which the table entries are comments on status.

Database or File	Conversion Attribute			
	Completeness	Accuracy	Format	Quality

CHAPTER 22

STEP O: DEFINE AND MEASURE SUCCESS

CONTENTS

22

STEP 0: DEFINE AND MEASURE SUCCESS

PURPOSE AND SCOPE

The purposes of measurement are to get support for the continuation of the business process improvement, to measure the progress of work on the project, and to determine whether benefits were achieved from the investment in the project. Measurement of the old process and new process gives an understanding of what is happening. Measurement will allow you to control the new process. By measuring an activity or process while it is in operation, you can affect its direction and behavior. You also measure to support the decision-making process.

Measurement can relieve much of the doubt and worry that is common during such projects for the following reasons:

- People fear change.
- People have doubts about the value of the business process improvement.
- People have observed past failures.
- The changes may take place over an extended time.
- Employees rely on certain key processes for their livelihood.

The measurement process is important to disaster recovery, a major area of data processing. All major computer installations have disaster recovery plans for critical systems, whether the disaster is natural or man-made. Business resumption planning was developed to address the recovery of the general processes—staff, files, procedures, and other resources. Measurements are one of the triggers for business resumption and disaster recovery.

The scope of the business process improvement measurement includes all parts of the project, from initial conception and selection of processes to the post-implementation review of results. Measurement also is a regular part of the new process.

END PRODUCTS

The major end products are measurements and a database of supporting measurement data for later analysis to support process improvement. The technology and systems will be measured in a later step.

RESOURCES

In some cases, early in the project, you will do the measurements yourself. As the work progresses, you will start to rely on other people in the project to collect the information. Still later in the project, you will probably rely on automated data collection.

APPROACH

When choosing a measurement method, address the following areas:

- **Data collection**

  Can you collect the data in an automated and consistent manner that will admit standards and comparison over time?

- **Efficiency**

  Is the measurement method cost-efficient so that the cost of gathering, analyzing, and reporting is reasonable?

- **Flexibility**

  Is the measurement method flexible enough to allow detailed, ad hoc questions to be addressed? Can the measurements adjust to handle more work?

- **Verification and validation**

  Are the measurements capable of verification? Are they sufficiently complete and of acceptable quality?

- **Interplay with decisions**

  Can you isolate the measurement method from management decisions? If you cannot, a management decision may affect future measurement.

- **Process effect**

  Is the measurement process unobtrusive, so that measurement has no negative impact on the process?

- **Perceived value**

  Do all of the people involved in collection and analysis receive some value from the measurement? If not, the measurement method may fall into disuse.

  Measurements can be classified in a variety of ways, including the following:

- **Frequency**

  Is the measurement regular, periodic, or ad hoc?

- **Level of detail**

- **Black box model**

  Total results are measured, no examination is made of the detailed performance or the internal workings of the process.

- **White box model**

  Information is collected on the process and the steps in the process with automated tools. White box analysis and testing allow the data from inside the process to be combined with the results. This supports the analysis of more detailed issues.

Measurement is an overhead activity; it does not yield the end product of the process. Detailed measurements can disrupt the process and lower productivity. Thus, there is a trade-off between the value of measurement on one hand and cost, time, and effort on the other. To justify the cost and effort of measurement, consider who will be receiving the information gained from the attempts to measure. What does each derive from the measurement?

- **Department employee**

  Feedback on performance, rewards for good performance, and indication of areas of improvement

- **Supervisor**

  Statistical data on volume and performance by employee and by the group over time, along with a comparative analysis

- **Management**

  Summary performance reports, cost, and performance comparisons with other institutions

- **Outsiders** Assessment of the value of the loan portfolio, the adequacy of lending practices, and an understanding of financial charge-offs

As information ages, its value and use decrease. You can see this problem in military processes in which movement is rapid and change is quick. The same pressure exists in business. If errors occur in a critical process, decisions could be incorrect or timing could be off. Operational impact is possible. For example, if year-end accounting was incorrect and the errors were undetected, it may be impossible to reconstruct the data within a reasonable time. In business process improvement, you focus on critical processes, so measurement and analyses should be performed in a timely manner.

Action 1: Define the Measurement Strategy for a Process and Improvement Project

Such a strategy encompasses the following:

- **Identification, collection, analysis, presentation, and decision processes for normal situations**

  This applies to the current business process as well as the new process after it is implemented.

- **Approach for measurement in the event of ad hoc requests or abnormal conditions**

  While an advanced prediction is not possible, you could hypothesize situations in which you would need more detail or in which a specific issue relating to budget, quality, or resources arose.

At Monarch Bank, the normal measurement process consisted of a series of summary reports and online access to a database of summary information. This information was provided for transactions above the level of an individual loan. For exceptions, the process yielded detailed information that allowed management to "drill down" to individual loan level data. This was successful, because the detailed data was sufficient to handle the issues that arose.

TRAN measured the timekeeping process for bus drivers by considering errors and examining inputs. This is normally sufficient, but in some instances additional ad hoc data collection was necessary.

Stirling used general measurements in terms of production schedules for items being manufactured. For more detailed information, additional manual collection was necessary.

Because you have substantial risk and investment at stake, you should also measure the business process improvement project. This measurement goes beyond schedule and cost. You want to know if you are going to achieve the anticipated results. Otherwise you may risk not detecting a problem until it is too late—after people in the department have labeled the project as a failure. Use the following for measurement information:

- Normal project management methods for summary information about the project
- Detailed data collection and analysis method to probe into the business process improvement project in depth

Action 2: Define the Measurement Criteria

Some common measurements are as follows:

- **Cost**
  - Operational cost of production use
  - Effort to maintain, enhance, and support the systems
  - Capitalized cost of equipment and other components
- **Performance**
  - System response time
  - System throughput—volume of work per unit time
  - Error rates
  - Down time and time to repair/recover
  - Number of simultaneous users on the system

—Availability of systems and technology for work
- **Other**
  —Turnover of computer support staff
  —Assessment of documentation of systems
  —Age and obsolescence of technology and systems
  —Number of original programming staff with application software
  —Size of system in terms of total program size and number of programs
  —Size of the databases and files
  —Response time to implement an enhancement

Infrastructure

Measuring the infrastructure is situation-dependent. Some common examples include the following:

- **Cost**
  —Operation and maintenance cost
  —Installation, upgrade costs
- **Physical attributes**
  —Number of locations
  —Staffing per location
- **Systems and Technology**
  —Stability of operations facilities
  —Availability of facilities
  —Safety record of facilities

Organization and Staff

Go beyond simple costs and head count. Here are some examples:

- **Cost**
  —Direct staff cost
  —Management cost
  —Overhead and burden costs

- **Noneconomic measurements**
  —Stability of organization—frequency of organization change
  —Staff roles, responsibilities, and levels
  —Employee turnover
  —Employee sick-outs
  —Staff seniority
  —Performance evaluations of staff morale
  —Number of employee problems
  —Time and effort consumed in training

Measuring Interfaces

Interfaces between and among processes are an important measurement source. Many errors and problems with processes arise in the interfaces. You can change a process, but if you don't address the interface, you are still likely to have problems. A recurring theme in the literature is that processes with the most potential improvement will cross multiple departments. Therefore, measure an interface as follows:

- Timeliness of interface
- Volume of work in the interface
- Error rate of work in transactions in the interface
- Time and resources required to support the interface
- Error rate of the interface
- Availability of the interface

Following is a summary of a few of the measurements:

- Type of work
- Volume of work by type
- Overall time for processing
- Error rate by type
- Rework and error correction time and effort

For all of the components (infrastructure, systems and technology, etc.) you can also collect information over time. You could collect some information at lower levels of detail, down, perhaps, to the level of an individual staff member.

The criteria discussed above lead to what data will be collected. You may have a choice as to how the data will be collected. Pick the approach that is the most consistent and can be defended in a presentation as being objective.

Given the potential problems arising from insufficient information and analysis, you might tend to err on the side of collecting more data. If you collect more information, people employ more of their time to gather and provide you the information. They will expect you to return with results that use the data they provided. If you don't use the information, you lose credibility. People will become sloppy or less willing to collect the information next time, believing that it will not be used.

Action 3: Determine the Analysis Approach

From this information defined you can construct ratios between and composites among categories. Examples are as follows:

- Cost per transaction
- Throughput per employee
- Response time per transaction
- Cost per employee of infrastructure and systems
- Errors and cost of rework per transaction
- Distribution of time between system, interfaces, and manual part of the process

You can develop trends on the basis of individual cost or performance items as well as for ratios and composites.

Action 4: Do the Measurement

Carry out the measurement as quickly as possible. Organize the information as it is collected to ensure that there is completeness and that it makes common sense. Consider building the presentation as you go.

Measure the Current Process

Standard measurements are probably available. Since you are improving this process, it is likely that these measurements are poor, or that the current measurements are not indicative of the state of the process, or both. Measurement of the current process is limited by the following:

- Limited funds to invest in new measurements for the process on a regular basis because it is going to change with the new process

- Staff who are aware of the project and may resist or slant any additional measurements you take

You can start with the current measurements and consider the complaints people have about the process, such as the process being expensive or prone to errors. More complex comments might be that it is inflexible and incomplete. For most current processes, measure the total process. This typically means measuring the part of the process that deals with exceptions. Often, the exception effort is separate from the measurement of the process and skews the results. Suspect this to be so when you notice that standard measurements do not match up to complaints.

Measure the New Process Concept

If the organization doesn't have a process in place, just a concept and a design, follow up on the comments in Steps 6 and 7 to build a model to simulate or estimate how the process might behave. The key here is not the exact data. The measurement here may indicate that a high probability exists that the new process will produce benefits that justify implementation. Limits exist. Any information and results you derive must be comparable to the measurements of the current process. Demonstrate that the new process will be an improvement.

Also estimate the results of the process for different alternatives. These alternatives may involve centralized or distributed organizations, various types of technology, and others.

Measure the New Process

In Step 10 a new process was developed that incorporated measurement. To implement it, be sure that the measurement process is in place. Begin by collecting measurements. Look for information that helps you compare results of the planned process vs. the old process. You also want to ensure that the measurements reflect reality. For example, in the Vietnam conflict, measuring progress through number of acres held or body counts did not work. The number of defections and interviews, as well as the nature and mix of goods on the Ho Chi Minh trail, were more enlightening. In narcotics interdiction do you measure success by the volume of drugs seized, the street price of the drugs, the number of arrests, or the number of people in treatment programs? These examples point to the need to validate the completeness of the measurements.

Measure the Business Process Improvement Project

Apply the normal measurements of project management, in terms of schedule and cost. To do this, determine the general perception of the project. Is progress noted? Much of the work and milestones have to do with infrastructure and design of the new process. Is the design sound? Is the project retreating into making small process changes? Is the new process beginning to look more like the old process?

Action 5: Present the Measurement Results

As you prepare the presentation, try it out on the people involved in the process or project. The feedback may indicate if you have missed some key message from the data.

Embedding Measurement into the Business Process

The best way to embed measurements into a business process is to collect data automatically by a system. This is a benefit of workflow software. Status tracking of a transaction or piece of work occurs as it flows from step to step. You can record the time, person, and any other pertinent information for each step. Use manual collection only as a fallback because it is subject to interpretation and variance.

Ad Hoc, Reactive Measurement

If an issue arises and the current measurements are inadequate, first state the issue clearly. After collecting additional data, write possible outcomes and actions. Then define further data you want to collect.

The next issue is the data collection method. You don't want to disrupt the process. Some ways to collect additional detail are the following:

- Collect data through the system.

- Conduct an overall review of the process. This may take more time, but you can collect the additional data as part of the review, and this will be less disruptive of the process. Also, issues are really symptoms. A review will reveal the causes.

- Conduct direct, informal observation of the process.

Multiple Processes

With a group of processes, there is a need for a consistent measurement approach across the group. Differences can exist in the level of detail based on the importance of the process, but measuring even smaller processes will allow you to benchmark the processes.

In the case of Monarch Bank, there were eventually five collection processes, which employed a common set of measurements. For the smallest process (charge-off and recovery), the numbers did not make much sense, because there were only a small number of users. However, showing the group in one picture proved to be useful.

The Competitive Edge

You will achieve success not only by the new process, but also by the story revealed by the measurements of it. You are constantly competing with other projects for management support in further business process improvement efforts. This is one reason for being proactive in measurement. Another reason is that, if you constantly measure your project and process, people will trust what you do. There will be fewer ad hoc, disruptive measurement efforts.

Train yourself to look behind the data. Is a rise in crime due to more crime, or to improved reporting? Jumping to simple interpretations leads to the questioning of results. Next question the data. Then hold the process itself up to question.

Search for simple minimum standards of measurement. Measurement is overhead. Automation reduces the burden, but you still have to analyze and then report on the information. It is easier to expand measurement rather than cut it back. Also try to use the measurement information to generate ideas on how to improve the process. As long as you have the data, why not do more with it?

WHY DOES MEASUREMENT FAIL?

Areas of failure include the following:

- **Collection of the wrong information**

  A survey team collects information on a process, including basic volume and work statistics. They fail to collect information on rework and errors.

- **Collection of information that is too general to be of use**

  You collect information on trends on a country but do not pick up information on a specific company in the country.

- **Information gathered at the wrong time**

  You are thinking of investing in a small business. You observe the business on the weekends, notice that it is busy, and assume that it is a real money maker. During the week, however, business is slow. Be sure to gather information at a variety of times.

MANAGEMENT PRESENTATION AND COST-BENEFIT ANALYSIS

Management presentations are based on presenting process measurements as you go. You want to set out what measurements were used, what results were expected, how the measurements were conducted, the results of the measurements, and an explanation of the variance from what was expected.

KEY QUESTIONS

Do the measurements and observations of the process match up with what people think? If not, either your measurements are in error, or you have a perception or political problem.

Can before and after comparisons be made easily in terms of the processes?

Have people's expectations and goals changed? Are the measurements keeping up with these?

Are you being realistic or biased in terms of measurement?

EXAMPLES

Monarch Bank

Monarch Bank implemented measurements as follows:

- **Staff performance in terms of volume of calls, results of calls, and activity per employee**

  This information helped to measure and compare employee performance as well as overall performance. This also allowed for the measurement of process performance on an individual level.

- **Aggregate staff performance in terms of total volume of calls and work, number of busy signals on incoming calls, and total collection activity**

  This data used the individual production results to assess an office and group. It also gave a total production picture, including the cost of operations.

- **Quality and results**

  In collections, this consisted of payments received, the mix and nature of delinquent loans, the monies recovered, the number of charged-off loans, and all customer complaints. It included delinquency and payment statistics, as well as the rate of payment after collection activity.

- **Performance and results ratios**

  These combined process performance data with information on the results of the process. Examples included the percentage of customers who promised to pay and actually did pay, cost per delinquent loan, collection activity per delinquent loan, and the number of delinquent loans and their aging.

- **Systems and technology**

  Given the volume of work in distributed collections, measurement was onerous in the old process. Many telephone calls were needed to determine status of collections for more than 500 offices. This horrific experience drew support from management for automated measurement. The new process tracked all collection activity down to the individual collector and loan.

- **Infrastructure**

  At Monarch the infrastructure issues involved telephones, data communications, physical files, and office layout. The semi-centralized organization that was first improved resulted in substantial infrastructure problems. Multiple locations had to be retrofitted and upgraded to support online systems and the improved process.

- **Organization**

  Measurements of organization were implemented first for the old process. There was a determination to achieve real, tangible savings. Measurements included not only head count by job, but also a duty matrix (duties vs. staff) in which more duties in the new process were performed by lower level staff.

- **Interfaces**

  The interface in the new process and system brought to light many problems papered over in the old installment loan system. The system was more than 20 years old. When the new online system interfaced to the old loan system, many data errors and problems surfaced. In the past, paper reports hid these errors. The new system queued loans for collection based on data in the old loan system. Bad data in the old loan system led to poor collections.

- **New process concept**

  The new process was presented and validated in a manual walk-through. Industrial engineering analysis provided the time to perform individual steps. People were convinced of the benefit of the new process concept by the credibility and logic of the workflow and by the detail of the analysis.

TRAN

- **Systems and technology**

  The old hardware was unreliable and required massive operations support. Maintenance changes to software systems were time-consuming and often generated more errors. People who had originally supported the software had departed. The staff in place had little clue as to how it functioned.

- **Infrastructure**

  The TRAN infrastructure began in old facilities. During the business process improvement project, management obtained new facilities. Supporting both the new and existing infrastructure during the transition to the new buildings with the same staff resulted in several crises. Stability and availability were reduced.

- **Organization**

  TRAN lacked measurement of the organization beyond a head count. To measure the impact of the new process, it was necessary to determine how many people performed specific transactions. The organization information flow revealed flatness and change with the new organization.

- **Interfaces**

  Bus drivers' time sheets served as input into the timekeeping system, which then interfaced to payroll. The payroll system was 15 years old; the timekeeping system was ten years old. The interface required much manual support during each processing run. The effort and errors involved in the interface were then measured, highlighting the problems with both processes.

- **New process concept**

  It was not possible to simulate the new process. The process was to be a complete replacement of the current method. Therefore, this measurement approach relied on external information. Other similar agencies provided data. Adjustments occurred due to size and working conditions. This proved to be credible and later was verified by the new process.

Stirling Manufacturing

- **Systems and technology**

  The old process for production management required a substantial part of a mainframe computer. Errors required the entire system for reprocessing. A weekly production run took more than 28 elapsed hours. This meant that the system and database were not current. The aged information was of limited value.

- **Infrastructure**

  The condition of some of the buildings was a major infrastructure issue. The firm was spread out over a campus of ten buildings. Problems in communications between buildings and the presence of the manufacturing equipment made the situation worse. This became such an issue that the extent of communication outages was a major measurement.

- **Organization**

  The new process involved managers and staff doing their own scheduling, while the old process involved professional schedulers. They were able to measure both processes in a consistent way, even though the approaches were varied, by defining a general role for schedulers and managers and then collecting data on their activities. They allowed for total overlap among the schedulers and managers in order to uncover the impacts.

- **Interfaces**

  The scheduling system did not interface directly with purchasing, assembly modeling, or timekeeping. The reconciliation effort for these systems required substantial manual work. Initial business process improvement work did not fix this problem, but the measurement data led to management pressure to revamp the process. This was accomplished later with automated interfaces.

- **New process concept**

  They embarked on a prototype and pilot process for implementation. The pilot allowed for the collection of detailed information on the process. A simple computer simulation model was used to evaluate the workflow.

GUIDELINES

- **Use self-supporting measurements.**

  In order for measurements to be useful over an extended period, the data collection process should be self-policing. Ensure accuracy by seeing that it is in people's self-interest to collect the information. Have a backup for each individual who is collecting, analyzing, or summarizing information.

- **Match measurement reports and graphs to style.**

  Give management an opportunity to have a say in which graphs and charts they would like. Show them several alternatives.

- **The measurement technique should be flexible.**

  A process and system will age over time and grow in complexity and eccentricities. Be sure that the measurements you have selected adequately address these changes. Measurements cannot do this if it is entirely manual. Also, the measurement method must address exceptions as well as the normal process.

- **Use measurement data to identify process bottlenecks.**

  Measurement data is used not only to improve the process and but also to find the next bottleneck in the process.

- **Use accepted measurement practices.**

  See how other processes are measured. Are any of their measurements adaptable to your process? If they are, use them.

- **Continue to improve your measurement techniques.**

  Keep the data collection and gathering method constant, but continue to improve the analysis and reporting of measurements.

ACTION ITEMS

1. Rate how easy measurements will be for the process group you have chosen. Use a scale of 1 to 5 (1 is difficult or not measurable, 5 is easily measured or strongly yes).

Measurement	Availability	Accuracy	Completeness	Quality

2. For the systems and technology corresponding to the processes you have chosen, make a list of the measurements that you could gather and rate these according to the criteria defined in this chapter. Use a scale of 1 to 5 (1 means very difficult to collect, 5 means that it is easy to obtain).

Systems	Measurements

3. Repeat Action Item 2, but rate the infrastructure. Again, start with the list developed in the chapter.

Infrastructure	Measurements

4. Repeat Action Item 2, but rate the organization. Begin with the list in the chapter.

Organization   Measurements

5. Repeat Action Item 2, but rate the interfaces between processes.

Interfaces   Measurements

6. Recurring data collection is sometimes necessary but difficult. Rate each process on ease of recurring data collection using a scale of 1 through 5 (1 is impossible to collect, 5 is easy to collect).

Process/ criteria	Automated capture	Manual effort to collect	Manual effort to analyze

CHAPTER 23

STEP P: FOLLOW UP AFTER IMPLEMENTATION

CONTENTS

23

STEP P: FOLLOW UP AFTER IMPLEMENTATION

PURPOSE AND SCOPE

Here are the objectives in this step:

- Ensure that benefits of the new process are achieved.
- Defend the integrity of the processes from attacks and degradation.
- Explore and capitalize on investments to make further improvements.
- Proactively enhance and support the integrity and performance of the processes, their infrastructure, and their organization.
- Use success in the implementation to move on to new processes that will be improved.

END PRODUCTS

There are several end products in this stage. First is an assessment of the benefits and costs after implementation, to be presented to management. Second is identification of other possible areas of improvement. Third is the application of lessons learned from the project to other work. Your final end product is the turnover of the ongoing management of the process.

RESOURCES

Although you can assess the new process and gather information yourself, involve your replacements so that all of you can prepare for the turnover of the ongoing support of the process. You want to phase yourself out of the project.

APPROACH

You are finally in production and the new process works. Unfortunately, people are often now so tired that they don't even want to expend the effort to measure the results. However, if you miss this opportunity, it will be difficult to return to gather data later. You will have lost your rapport with the staff. You will probably not have enough time to gather data later. It will be harder to collect information because you will have to reestablish contacts.

Issues during Operation

Here are some issues that can arise after process improvement:

- **The benefits of the new process are not measured, but the old and new are compared.**

  People forget the old process. The benefits of the new process can now be questioned.

- **People question the process itself.**

  With no measurement of the process, people may question the process because the default visible measurement is cost (which has a negative connotation).

- **Surrounding systems change, forcing an unplanned process change.**

  This is why you must plan changes and enhancements to systems and processes on a group, rather than individual, basis.

- **Staff members leave who were with the process when it was implemented.**

  They usually do not transfer their knowledge prior to departure, and the remaining knowledge is limited.

- **New exception situations arise.**

  No one addresses them formally, so staff members begin to develop procedures of their own, which work around the process. The process is now jeopardized as more work moves outside of its framework.

- **The organizational change on which the process depended did not occur.**

   The process now does not fit the organization, so the organization changes the process to fit the organization.

- **Other processes, independent of this one, are changed by other teams.**

   The other new processes are not compatible with the new process, so potential benefits are not realized.

- **Competitive pressure and the business force change.**

   No one changes the process to conform with the new conditions. Management is frustrated and creates a parallel process for the new work.

- **Technology changes, but the staff are stuck with the old technology.**

   Morale sinks as old technology continues to age.

- **A better way emerges.**

   The new process triggered creative thoughts, but no one formalized changes as part of the process. This results in process variations.

Not only should you respond to these situations, but you should also anticipate and monitor the process and its surroundings for signs of pressure and change. In traditional information systems, the technical staff responds to user requests for changes to the system. When you move to processes, you learn that you must be more proactive. One way to do this is to implement subtle manual process changes.

Process Maintenance vs. Enhancement

Maintaining a process means that you take action to ensure that the process continues to meet its goals and requirements. Maintenance refers to being able to accommodate situations with the current process. Examples include taking steps to reduce response time or errors to acceptable levels and continuing to provide the same information.

A process may be forced to respond to new pressures and requirements. Meeting new requirements or attaining new performance levels are referred to as enhancements. These may entail substantial changes. An enhancement may apply to a process, organization, or infrastructure change. Examples of process enhancements are as follows:

- Handling additional volume with the same process
- Processing a new type of exception transaction
- Obtaining additional staff performance statistics from the process

Enhancements tend to be proactive. That is, a requirement surfaces and the process is enhanced to meet the requirement. Maintenance, on the other hand, tends to be reactive. The mixture of maintenance and enhancement work then is an indicator of the state of the process. Some observations on this subject are as follows:

- A lack of maintenance and enhancement may not indicate success; it may indicate that the process is not being used. If you do not drive a car and leave it in a garage, it does not need maintenance or enhancement.
- The greater the percentage of total effort going into enhancements, the more the process is being used. This is because people expect more from the process and have defined additional functions.
- Excessive maintenance may mean that people are attempting to adapt the process to new work without change. A good effort is being made without success.
- Enhancements are easier to measure because they require resources and, hence, management approval. Maintenance can often only be detected through observation.

The actions in this step are in no particular order. Some of them are optional, depending on the state of the process improvement.

Action 1: Appoint a Process Coordinator and Monitor

Critical processes are so important to the business that organizations should create the role of the process coordinator and monitor. You can begin by identifying a staff member for a group of related processes. This position would be part-time so that you might also appoint a primary and secondary coordinator. The duties of the coordinator include the following:

- Collect information on the processes and issue a process report card.
- Review infrastructure and organization issues related to the process. (This includes requests for changes as well as analysis findings.)
- Recommend and design specific changes and improvements to management as well as alerting management to problems.
- Manage the implementation of process change.
- Coordinate the training of new staff in the process and collect the experience and knowledge of departing staff.
- Coordinate the change to computer systems supporting the process.

This is not a job for the department supervisor because the process may cross multiple departments and the supervisor is in only one department. The supervisor may have vested interests in the organization and may not be loyal to the process. Also, the supervisor may have too many other duties.

There are two levels of coordination in business departments. The first level is the tactical day-to-day operational coordination of departmental work. This requires detailed process and systems knowledge. The second entails a wider area across organization and policies. At the second level, the coordinator may have less hands-on knowledge but be more politically savvy.

Choose a middle level or junior staff person with experience in the systems and processes for the role of process coordinator and monitor. Such a person is more interested in change and less tied to the old ways. You may get double duty out of this person by also having him or her act as a system change coordinator. A more senior person could be the alternate, second coordinator. Measure the process coordinators by the performance of the processes and the quality of their measurement and reporting. Encourage process coordinators to get together to share ideas.

The existence of a process coordinator does not reduce departmental accountability. Process measurement includes the extent to which each department is performing its part of the process and its quality.

Action 2: Fill Out a Process Report Card

A process report card (a process evaluation) is completed by collecting all of the measurement information. It is important that there be multiple report cards, one for each process in the group, so as to provide a comparative basis.

Here are some items to include in the process report card:

- Overall grade/evaluation
  A Acceptable; no improvement required
  B Process works, but improvements (enhancements) are possible
  C Process works, but benefits are not being achieved
  D Process does not work all of the time; there is a high error rate
  F Process fails and is not acceptable
- Specific grade components
  —Organization
  —Staff
  —Systems
  —Technology
  —Infrastructure
  —Error rates
  —Resources consumed by process
  —Throughput
  —Response time
  —Subjective opinions
  —Open process items

- Objectives for the process
  —Short-term
  —Long-term

To implement the report card approach, first identify the coordinators. Next, coordinate the assessment of 10 to 15 critical processes. This will give you a sample set of report cards. This is referred to as the *process report card baseline*.

Action 3: Generate a Process Annual Report

Organizations produce annual business reports, organization charts, and other similar documents. Surprisingly, they do not report on the processes. In many organizations an annual process report is encouraged. This report basically contains graphs and findings for critical processes. It also relates the work in the next year in terms of projects to the list of critical processes. In one large energy company, among the annual process report, technology assessment, the competitive assessment, the information systems plan, and business strategies, the annual process report received the most attention.

The annual process report provides information to management and staff on the state of their processes. If the information is faulty, you will hear about it quickly and you can learn from this feedback. You will also see that after the report is issued, more of the systems, organization, and infrastructure documents will tie directly to critical processes.

Action 4: Evaluate Process Costs and Benefits

The typical question posed in a post-implementation review is about costs and benefits. You probably defined a long list of benefits ranging from economic to organizational impacts. The situation can change when you reach an operational state. People are less concerned with benefits, because the effort represents sunk costs; anyway, you will have to live with the process. In addition, the relative weighting of the benefits and what you considered important has changed.

The categories of benefits resemble the three standard levels of management and are as follows.

Operations

The first hurdle is operations. The focus here is on the functioning of the process. If the new process did not successfully replace the old process, there is no point in measuring higher level benefits. Questions to ask are as follows:

- Does the new process handle the workload?
- Is the performance satisfactory in terms of volume, response time, and error rate?
- Is the new process stable? Or is there fluctuation in performance?
- What are the managers' and employees' opinions on the process?
- Does the new process address all exceptions?

Management

Now you move to the more traditional cost-benefit analysis. Consider first only tangible benefits. Intangible benefits should be reflected in operations and strategy. Here is a partial list of the information you want to determine:

- **Cost-related**
  - Operating costs (Direct staff and organization costs for the new and old processes)
  - Support costs (Technology, systems, and infrastructure costs for the new and old processes)
  - Development costs for the new process
- **Performance-related**
  - Error rates and rework for the new and old processes
  - Volume handled for the new and old processes
  - Staffing levels for operation for the new and old processes
  - Staffing levels for support for the new and old processes

After you have gathered the necessary information, you can then perform the standard cost-benefit analysis.

Strategy

Business process improvement should do more than yield a good report on costs and benefits. Go beyond the standard impact analysis. Consider benefits to the organization, policies, and general infrastructure. Return to the comparison tables you created for the new process. Create updated tables and put them side-by-side. Ask the following questions:

- Do the new process and change support the vision?
- Does the process implementation change the organization and infrastructure as desired?
- Does the process support flexibility in the business?
- What is the impact of the new process internally on morale?
- How does the new process help management direct activities better?
- Does the new process have an impact on the external community (e.g., suppliers, customers, investors, and regulators)?

The answers to these questions are subjective. You can survey managers for their opinions. You can assume that the new process was never implemented. Ask yourself what has changed. You can also consider the vision, management, external impact, and other factors and see if you can broaden their impact because of the new process.

Intangible Benefits

You have looked at tangible benefits. However, you will find a number of intangible benefits that people agree are present and consider to be benefits. The problem is how to use these intangible benefits without affecting or detracting from the quantitative benefits. Here are some examples of intangible benefits with suggestions on how to quantify them:

- **The new process is easier to learn and use.**

  There may be fewer errors. Training time and costs should be less. Productivity and morale may increase.

- **Information is easier to find and is accessible.**

  Look at how the time for retrieval has lessened. The number of complaints from customers when you could not find their information may have dropped.

- **More history information is available than before with the old process.**

  Look at how much time was spent in the old process on retrieving and reconstructing history compared with the new process.

Reviewing the Costs and Benefits

Make sure that you are not the only person who can support the costs and benefits. Have a direct source for the information, even opinions. To get opinions and find people to give testimonials, ask people what they would do if they returned to the old process. Problems with the old process (which the new process lacks) will surface.

Work Left Undone

In reviewing benefits, you will probably notice items that have not been completed or closed out. For example, some of the old infrastructure may still be in place. You may clean up and finish data conversion. Documents and files may have to be purged. Furniture may have to be removed. Staff may require reassignment. Take care of this housekeeping prior to completing the benefit analysis.

Action 5: Plan the Next Step

In your plan and strategy, you formulated an approach and direction as to which processes to address next. Implementation and politics could have entered the picture. It is time to revisit this issue and negotiate with management to go to the next process group. A manager could have been favorably impressed with your efforts. The requirements of the business could have changed so that you must alter your focus and address processes you had originally planned to ignore.

Action 6: Detect and Remedy Process Deterioration

As the process ages, negative changes may occur. Software increases in complexity and size as it ages. Infrastructure supporting a process is not maintained. Technology becomes obsolete and must be upgraded. The process itself can degrade in many ways, including the following:

- Infrastructure deterioration affects the process.
- Technology deterioration affects the process.
- Organization change affects the process.
- More of the work is performed outside of the process.
- Procedures within the process are not followed.
- Different people use different procedures.

Process deterioration can be summarized as spending a great deal of time and money and ending up where you started. You are probably worse off because you raised management's expectations and wasted resources. You also destroyed a future opportunity because people will now be reluctant to revisit this.

Some of the recurring examples of process deterioration include the following:

- **Manager replacement**

  A new manager changes the process to reflect his or her style. The manager made his or her mark, but the changes were not thought through and the process decayed rapidly. That was fine with the manager, who then moved on to another disaster.

- **Loss of critical staff**
- **Systems and infrastructure deterioration**

  Sometimes the computer system or building decays to the point where the process performance is affected. When a process begins to decay, the rate of deterioration quickens.

- **Inadequate response to change**

  Management uses a stopgap measure that ends up being in place for years.

- **Organization change**

  The organization changes through downsizing and outsourcing. Qualified people are gone. The remaining staff may not know the process. At one company, employees saw that layoffs would be coming, so they destroyed the procedures. Then they could not be terminated.

- **Old process remnants**

  Individuals continue to use the old process but pay lip service to the new. The result is that people are using a mixture of the two processes.

- **Conscious effort to return to the old process**

  Management and staff in the department work to move the process back to the format of the old process. The process is old; the system is new.

- **Lack of orientation for new staff**

  Once a process has been implemented, the departments may not train new staff. Someone assumed that there would be no turnover, or that people would learn the process through osmosis. Thus, new employees are dumped into the process.

- **Power shift**

  Power positions can change quickly. A manager in another area may attempt to steal staff or take over the functions of a process. In some cases, an entire process can be lost if you lose the critical people.

- **Emergence of shadow systems**

  These may be workarounds to the new process or be created to support new work that no one could put through the new process.

How to Detect Deterioration

Here are some guidelines for detecting deterioration:

- **Review how the process is supposed to function.**

  This gives you a baseline of what is supposed to be done.

- **Review any measurement information on the process.**

  Data might be available on staffing, volume, response time, and error rates. You are looking for variances.

- **Determine if there have been any staffing changes.**

  Can the time of the change be related to the measurement data? Identify the new staff.

- **Contact employees outside the process who use output from the process or feed it.**

  Determine any issues or trends that they detect.

- **Contact employees in the department and observe the process.**

  Consider how exceptions are handled. Go to the key people and get their opinions. Ask new employees how the process works and what they find wrong with it.

The purpose of this effort is to detect opportunities for improvement and problems. There are three types of information: quantitative, observational, and perceptions. Rather than separating these, concentrate on using all of the information to address the following:

- What change has occurred? Why?
- How could the process be improved further?
- What is the sequence of actions that are appropriate?

Alternatives for Action

Some alternatives for action are as follows:

- **Do nothing.**

  Let the process drift and continue to decay. Don't reject this option out of hand. Often, things have to get bad before anyone intervenes. This method has been used in some companies with management's approval. A trigger can be defined as to when a crisis level is reached; management then has justification to act without political risk.

- **Remedy the situation by tweaking only the process.**

  This is the after-the-fact temporary approach. This approach is popular with managers who want to move on to another job and do not want to see a major project through to conclusion.

- **Develop a plan to improve the process again.**

  This would include buying new technology and developing new systems and infrastructure. Don't expect much enthusiasm for this alternative. People have spent money on the process and do not want to continue to do so.

- **Adjust the organization and policies.**

  This is probably the most feasible approach if you want afford-able change.

Doing nothing is not as bad as it seems. If you attempt to tweak and change the process too often, you threaten its stability. You also consume political points. This situation is similar to firing an un-manned probe to a distant planet. If you frequently fire rockets to adjust the trajectory of the rocket, you will consume too much fuel. Instead, let it get sufficiently off course and make major course corrections. Processes can be handled in the same manner.

Action 7: Intervene to Fix Process Problems

Intervening in a process can have several goals. The major goal should be to implement a process of self-correction and self-policing. This means that you will not have to revisit the process again and again. Another goal is the assertion of control over the process. You can actually accomplish both goals. If you cut through middle management and work directly with the employees on the process, they become involved and dedicated. They align with you and your control rises. You can also pave the way for eliminating middle management.

Some of the risks of intervention, along with suggestions for risk minimization, are as follows:

- **Demoralization of staff**

  The morale of the people involved in the process drops. How you intervene and what their roles are will be important factors.

- **Underlying issues**

  If you attempt to intervene, you must address basic organization and infrastructure issues. A fundamental flaw in the new process may require basic change. Unless there is a crisis, there is a lack of will to make the change.

- **Raised expectations**

  People think that you will carry out a major, cheap, effective short-term fix. This appears to happen often, but seldom really does. Often, some new headline issue grabs people's attention.

Intervention Approach

Consider carrying out the implementation in stages. First, you must understand what is going on currently. Collect a limited amount of information and determine the initial action desired from your alternatives. Because you may review multiple processes, you cannot afford to spend a great deal of time on every process. Instead, allocate your time.

Intervention has both a short-term and long-term focus. The short-term focus is to fix symptoms of problems, while the long-term focus is on the problems themselves.

MANAGEMENT PRESENTATION AND COST-BENEFIT ANALYSIS

Assuming that you prepare a process report card every year, you might construct the following graphs:

- Cost, performance, and volume over time
- Ratios
- Cost per transaction in process
- Average time per transaction in process
- Error rate vs. staff turnover
- Division of cost of work over time—staff, infrastructure, technology, etc.

Figures 23-1 through 23-4 are sample process management graphs of Monarch Bank. You can use graphs like these to enhance interest and knowledge in the processes. For one process you can detect trends in deterioration and performance. Perhaps the most important use of such graphs is comparing multiple processes.

Graphs for Multiple Processes

Suppose you identified 10 critical processes for the business. Using the measurement information, you can develop comparative graphs on processes. An example appears in Figure 23-4. You can use such a graph to do the following:

- Compare processes that are not easily compared (accounting vs. inventory)
- Identify common trends for multiple processes, potentially traceable to the same cause
- Determine candidates for process improvement

Use the review to prompt action. The presentation of positive results gives management the opportunity to be proactive without risk. This proactive attitude is desirable in process change.

KEY QUESTIONS

Is anyone is working with the process in terms of measurement and improvement? Lack of activity has both positive and negative sides. On the positive side, it may mean that the new process is fine and that people are using it as intended. However, it can mean that the process has already been changed by the people who operate and use it. These changes could have gone undetected up to now.

Did anyone determine what changes have occurred since the new process was implemented? Has the volume increased? Has the mixture of work changed? Has the scope of work changed? Are there more exceptions? Have policies changed?

Figure 23-1:
Example of Measurements for One Process
at Monarch Bank

This chart allows you to measure the effect of the new process.

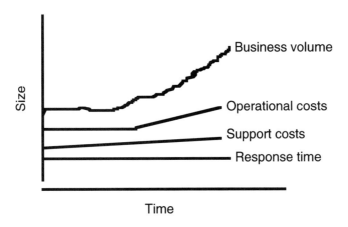

Notes:

- Coordinates for height are different for each graph.
- This is the desirable case: Volume increases and operational costs increase more slowly, while response time and support costs remain relatively fixed.

Figure 23-2:
Example of Impact of Transition from Old to
New Process at Monarch Bank

This chart reveals the impact of transitioning from old to new process.

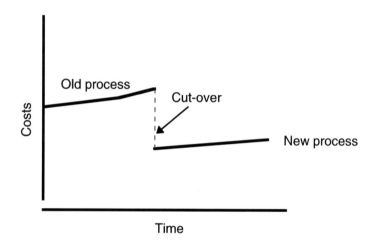

Notes:

- The old process is becoming more expensive to operate and support.
- After the cut-over, the new process is not only less expensive, but also more robust in that it can handle higher volumes without substantial cost increases.

Figure 23-3:
Detailed Comparison of Old and New Processes at Monarch Bank

This is a common chart used to reveal the overall difference between old and new process.

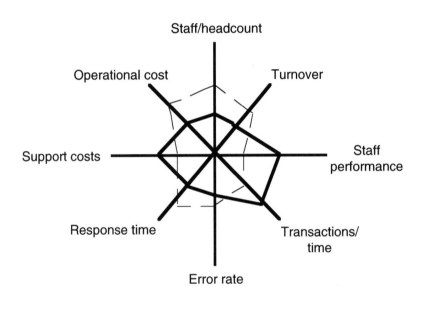

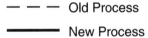 Old Process

—————— New Process

Notes:

- The new process for collections had higher support costs due to new buildings and systems; however, these costs were more than compensated by lower operating costs. Since support costs are relatively fixed in terms of volume of business, the advantage of the new process increased with volume.

- The new process improved throughput, response time, performance, and required less staff. Morale became better, so turnover declined.

Figure 23-4: Comparison of Two Processes over Time

This chart allows comparison of the two processes over time, which is useful for ongoing measurement.

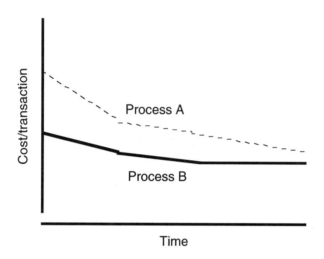

Notes:

- For simplicity, only one criterion was specified—cost per transaction. In general, you would compare two processes on multiple criteria.

- Process A—while having a higher unit cost—has a declining cost, while Process B has stabilized. You would probably want to explore Process B to see if more improvements could be obtained.

EXAMPLES

Monarch Bank

Monarch is, perhaps, the best case of the three in the book. Things went as expected all of the way through the project. The process worked well. Savings were greater than anticipated in the following areas:

- **Staff savings**

  As people observed and participated in the process, more savings opportunities were identified.

- **Productivity of staff members**

  This improved in terms of their ability to detect problem loans. These parameters were fed into the loan approval process and resulted in fewer delinquent loans.

- **Delinquent customers**

  By isolating customers who were repeatedly delinquent, Monarch Bank reduced the number of people in this group.

- **Collection of funds**

  Improved collections resulted in faster collections of funds.

Strategic impacts were as follows:

- Monarch gave high priority to expanding the process improvement effort in related areas.
- Reduced delinquent accounts created a favorable reaction among investment groups.
- Customers who had carried out fraud were detected and fraud incidence dropped.
- The success created pressure on other parts of the business to improve their processes.

The process report card was put in place for each process—installment loan collections, credit card collection, and so on. Statistics were generated monthly. A deputy manager was appointed as coordinator for each process.

The process for installment loan collections underwent few changes until credit card collections was implemented. Credit card managers learned from the installment loan collection process and made improvements. These improvements were deployed retroactively to the installment loan process. This approach continued because each group found new ways to implement the process.

TRAN

The new process for scheduling bus drivers created waves of change. The ability to analyze more routes in the same amount of time permitted many more schedule changes. Union contract terms could be better analyzed in terms of impact. This resulted in lower costs. Other benefits included a reduction of 40 percent in scheduling staff and realigned routes to save six buses.

Strategically, service was improved because the time lag for transfers between buses was reduced. The process was also able to handle special events to generate more revenue. Management felt more in control of the process. Beyond improved service, TRAN evolved from a reactive agency to one that is proactive.

For the bus driver timesheet process, the new process reduced paper form use by more than 70 percent. This translated to more than 150,000 forms that did not have to be filled out and checked. This led to a staffing reduction. A feedback measurement process was instituted for error reporting. Errors dropped by 46 percent as a result.

Stirling Manufacturing

What was successful in manufacturing scheduling and control for six areas was a mixed success in the seventh area. The new process began to revert back to the old one. Meetings and directives were not successful. As a result, the problem business area was left alone and isolated until all surrounding areas were addressed. With a crisis evident, the new process was reinstalled. It took hold only after organization changes had been made.

Example of Failure

An insurance company implemented a process for scanning, imaging, and workflow routing. Benefits cited beforehand were as follows:

- **Strategy**
    - —Faster introduction of new insurance products
    - —Improved customer service
    - —Improved quality
- **Management**
    - —Cost avoidance by handling growth with existing resources
    - —Elimination of the time documents waited for work
    - —Improved workflow
- **Operations**
    - —Documents scanned and stored (then indexed and retrieved as images at workstations with large screen displays)

Claims were made as follows:

- Misplaced files would be reduced.
- Lost documents would be reduced.
- Bills handled per clerk would increase by 20 percent.
- Speed of error check would increase by 60 percent.
- Storage reduction will be reduced by 80 percent.
- Speed of processing will be reduced by four days or by 40 percent.
- Floor space will be reduced by 60 percent.
- Staff will be reduced by 30 percent.

Unfortunately, none of these claims came true. The new imaging system was not compatible with the old hardware. Legal requirements for some documents reduced the savings. Eventually, the staff operated the old and new process in parallel, and the new processes eventually failed. The problem was that the claims arose from partial information rather than from direct observation. Also, the extent of review centered on only a few activities.

GUIDELINES

- **Don't declare victory too early.**

  Wait until you are able to measure the benefits and assess the operational state of the process in terms of stability.

- **Make sure that the process continues to be measured.**

  When benefits have been determined and interest wanes, you still want to measure the process.

- **Adopt the retrofit approach.**

  The retrofit approach is one in which you return to make changes in the process that reflect cumulative knowledge and experience in implementation.

ACTION ITEMS

1. Revisit the original issues that were to be addressed by the new process. Evaluate these and develop a new list of issues based on the new process. Place the old issues as rows and the new as columns. In the table enter one of the following codes: N–no relation, C–changed, U–unchanged, I–improved, E–eliminated.

   Old Issues   New Issues

2. How many people are involved in each process in the process group? List the organizations as rows and the individual processes as columns. Enter the change between the old and new process. Run a total at the side and bottom. This will indicate how resources were redeployed.

Organizations	Processes	Total
Total		

3. Use the data in Action Item 2 to create pie charts for the distributed reduced head count.

4. Create a bar chart in which each organization has two bars (one for old process and the other for the new process). The height of the bar is the number of people.

5. Return to the tables and charts of Steps 5 and 7 to develop new charts and tables for what really happened after implementation.

6. Develop a table that gives side-by-side characteristics of the old and new process.

Process	Volume	No. of Exceptions	Error Rate	Availability	Response Time

7. For each of the categories below of lessons learned, create specific lessons using the data elements:

Type: _____

Title: _____

What happened: _____

_____

What should have been done: _____

_____

What should be done in the future: _____

_____

What would be the benefit: _____

_____

Implementation suggestions: _____

_____

Categories:

P—project management process

M—management review and control

I—infrastructure

T—technology

O—organization

S—Staffing

V—vendors

I—issue handling

SY—systems

A—architecture

CHAPTER 24

STEP Q: MEASURE
STRATEGIC SYSTEMS PLAN RESULTS

CONTENTS

24

STEP Q: MEASURE STRATEGIC SYSTEMS PLAN RESULTS

PURPOSE AND SCOPE

The major objective of measuring is to determine whether you achieved the benefits within the costs that were projected in the plan. To do this requires that you measure before the plan is implemented and that you are able to estimate the benefits and costs as part of the planning.

Another objective is to support presentations and later analysis. Remember that you are implementing new processes, systems, and technology that will last a long time. This extended period actually allows you to define and detect some trends.

Measurement allows you to know if you have achieved any benefits for the technology and whether the technology is consistent and capable of interfacing with the current systems and technology that were not replaced. Establish a regular, ongoing measurement process that will yield information for the planning report on measurement. Routine measurement will reinforce positive plan results in the minds of people involved.

Measurement allows you to deal with political realities. You obtained management support for an extended period of time. Resources were taken from other projects for process improvement. Expectations are high. Managers put themselves somewhat at risk by backing you. They need factual material to assure people that it was all worthwhile. Also, lack of measurement can attract political enemies and leave a plan open to attack. A political opponent might say, "If this planning is so good, why is it that we don't even know if we are better off?"

You want the scope to be broad at the onset so that when you collect interesting data later, you will have something with which to compare. Include qualitative and quantitative measures that go beyond just tangible dollars and cents.

END PRODUCTS

Here are some end products of measurement:

- Measurement before the strategic systems plan
- Measurement of the planning process to produce the plan
- Measurement of the allocation process for resources to support the new technology
- Measurement of implementation of the new systems and technology
- Post-implementation measurements
- Lessons learned from the work

All these categories except "Lessons learned" fit a narrow definition of measurement. Measuring by articulating lessons learned naturally fits with understanding how things work and how they can be made better.

RESOURCES

While you are the primary player here, there is a supporting cast. You will need people to supply you with numbers for the planning and finance area. Another person is needed to work in the area of budgeting. Find people who can review the measurements and put their own interpretations on them.

Establish the tools and databases to make measurement easy for yourself and your assistants. Be in a constant measurement frame of mind. When you observe a process or are in a meeting, ask yourself "What information can I derive from this in terms of measurement?"

APPROACH

Action 1: Measure throughout the Planning Process

You will want to measure certain general items throughout the planning process. You will not be able to collect all of the detail, but you will outline your optimistic expectations.

- **Revenue**
  —Total sales and revenues
  —Breakdown of revenue by source
  —Breakdown of revenue by business unit
- **Costs**
  —Total costs
  —Breakdown of costs by business unit
  —Systems and technology costs and their breakdown
- **Organization**
  —Total number of employees
  —Breakdown of employees by business unit
  —Total number of systems employees
  —Breakdown of employees by job classification
- **Production (if appropriate)**
  —Total number of units by type produced
  —Production effort required per item per type
  —Characteristics of quality
- **Customers**
  —Total number of customers
  —Characteristics of mix of customer base
- **Business processes**
  —Number of people involved
  —Technology supporting the process
  —Number of organizations involved
  —Number of steps in the general transactions
  —Number of exception transactions
  —Volume, error rates, rework statistics

These cover the basic areas addressed by the strategic systems plan. To see improvements or estimate impact from strategies and action items, get down to this level. Going into much more detail can be costly. First, it will take more time and effort. Second, the actual collection of detailed information in some areas, such as business processes, may affect the business process.

When you measure, gather both qualitative and quantitative data. Seek to validate the information as you go. For example, if someone indicates that the current system does not support the business process well and that the time to process a transaction is excessive, you would look for two things. First, you would verify that the time for the transaction is too long. Second, you would request that the staff show you how the system inhibits the process. On the other hand, you cannot afford statistical surveys or sampling.

Also do subjective verification. That is, when you are in a department collecting data, observe what is going on, determine how organized the operation is, and note specific tasks and duties that validate the measurement. Get opinions and examples. These activities make measurement more interesting, as well as providing validation.

At the time you specify the measurements, also define your method for answering the following questions:

- How will information be stored?
- How will data be analyzed?
- What graphs are necessary?

Measurements and measurement graphs address specific purposes. Here are some examples:

- **Monitoring of a business process or some regular set of events**

  An example is tracking the production volume of work or other standard statistics. This category is useful in showing that you are receiving benefits from the new process or system on a recurring basis.

- **Tracking the status of a project or giving a general picture of what is going on**

  These charts relate how the planning process and projects are doing. GANTT charts are one category of measurement. Budget vs. actual charts are another. A third way to draw up a chart is to plot the number of open issues at a given time.

- **Relaying detailed information related to a specific topic or issue**

  Here you zoom in on the characteristics of an issue. Show the impact of the issue if it is unresolved and alternative approaches for resolution.

- **Giving a perspective on trends over longer time periods**

  Produce graphs and tables that span the period of several years. They support the strategies and objectives of the plan.

Develop some sample graphs with realistic data. Create more charts and tables than you would ever use. Sort these into the above areas so that you have models for each area. These will assist you later if you have to produce measurement charts on short notice. Show managers sample charts and ask for their input on which they would like to see. This conveys your organized approach to measurement.

Action 2: Use the Lists and Tables in Measurement

In the remaining sections of this chapter, specific guidelines are given for measuring aspects of the plan, the planning process, and the implementation of the plan. In each case you should refer back to the original tables and lists that you created in the plan. Use the previous tables and update the tables with three additional columnsas follows:

- A column to indicate status
- A column to indicate the impact or change
- A column to contain any comments you might have

There are several benefits to this approach. First, this makes the work incremental from what you have done. Second, when you present the results to management or staff, the presentation is based on material that they have already seen. Third, it provides a degree of continuity across the planning process.

Three assessments were discussed that should be undertaken prior to the development of the strategic systems plan: internal, industry, and technology. Each can provide valuable information for measurement.

Some sample measurements can be developed into tables or charts:

- **Internal technology used by division-age of technology and systems, interfaces, importance of the business divisions, percentage of employees in division whose duties depend on automation and degree of automation in terms of critical business processes**

Figure 24-1 gives the example for TRAN for the financial and operations areas.

- **Potential technology-the range of application of the technology, the benefits, the costs, the impact on key processes, the implementation effort, the ongoing support effort required, the risk involved, and the interfaces with other technologies**

  Figure 24-2 presents a radar chart for several technologies for TRAN.

- **Industry summary statistics-a series of operational and financial factors**

  Collect these and place them on the same graph. Use number of employees, sales, expenses, types of products or services, etc.

- **Issue measurement—range of a number of dimensions of impact**

  Examples of dimensions are number of employees affected, number of critical business processes impacted, estimated direct financial impact of issue, etc. Create a radar or bar chart that gives these and others as dimensions and then plots different issues in terms of impact. This assists in rating which issues are most significant. This figure gives a rating of the current business process in terms of systems and technology. You could then overlay the figure with the status of the new process after the systems and technology have been improved.

Action 3: Measure the Planning Process

You seek measurements that relate how the planning process is proceeding and what results you have discovered so far. Chart the following when you conduct measurements:

- **Characteristics of planning issues**

  The distribution of issues indicates where the problems are in the planning process and the extent of the problems. Look for the following types of distributions:

  —**Distribution of planning issues and opportunities by the number that impact each division (organization spread)**

Figure 24-1: Internal Technology Characteristics

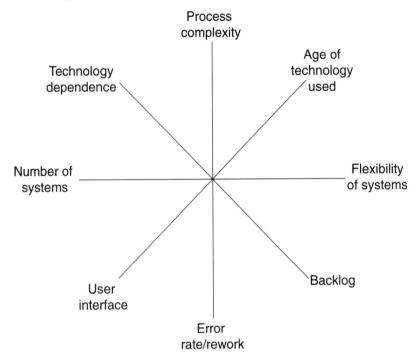

This indicates how many issues cross multiple organizations. An example is shown in Table 24-1.

—**Distribution of planning issues as to when, in the future, they will impact the company in a substantial way**

Table 24-2 contains an example.

—**Distribution of planning issues and opportunities by their dependence on technology**

An example appears in Table 24-3.

• **Objectives, strategies, and planning action items** Look for the following types of distributions:

—**Distribution of planning issues by planning objective**

This shows in a comparative way how objectives address issues.

Figure 24-2: Potential Technology Evaluation

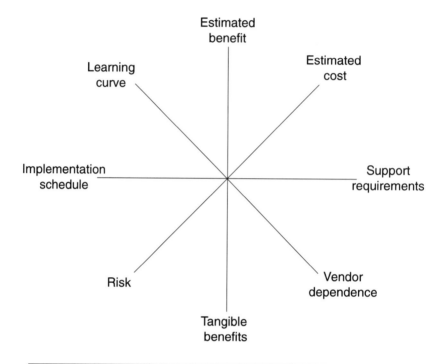

—**Distribution of planning action items by strategies**

This is similar to the above.

—**Distribution of planning action items by type**

This is the distribution of action items by policy, process, procedure, and project (Table 24-4).

—**Distribution of planning action items by required resources**

This shows the number of action items that require funding divided into intervals of funding levels (Table 24-5).

—**Distribution of planning action items by business division impacted**

This reveals the number of action items that pertain to each major business division.

Table 24-1: Distribution of Issues and Opportunities by Division

Issues/ Opportunities	Finance	Operations	Marketing	Planning
Response time	4	5	2	1
Cost of operations	2	4	2	2
Exceptions	4	4	2	2
Inflexibiltiy	3	5	4	4
Manual procedures	3	4	2	2

This chart shows that Operations is suffering most in terms of issues.

Table 24-2: Distribution of Issues and Opportunities in Terms of Impact

Issues/ Opportunities	Year 1	Year 2	Year 3
Response time	3	4	5
Cost of operations	4	4	5
Exceptions	2	3	3
Inflexibiltiy	4	4	5
Manual procedures	2	3	4

Table 24-3: Distribution of Issues and Opportunities by Technology Used

Issues/ Opportunities	Client- server	Network	Host computer	PCs
Response time	4	5	4	1
Cost of operations	3	3	4	2
Exceptions	2	2	5	2
Inflexibiltiy	2	3	5	2
Manual procedures	3	1	5	2

This chart shows that the host computer systems are the major contributors to the issues.

Table 24-4: Distribution of Action Items by Type

Action Items	Policy	Procedure	Project	Process
Intranet	2	3	5	5
Client-server	4	3	5	5
Use of e-form	5	5	1	2
Review of form data	4	5	1	3

Table 24-5: Distribution Action Items by Required Resources

Action Items	I/S staff	Network	Business unit	Vendor
Intranet	5	5	3	2
Client-server	5	5	5	2
Use of e-form	1	2	5	1
Review of form data	1	2	5	1

—**Distribution of planning action items by resource type required**

This chart shows how action items require the same resources.

—**Distribution of planning action items that are interdependent**

This is useful to show dependencies on architecture-related projects.

Action 4: Measure the Allocation Process

The allocation process is the method employed to generate the project slate. Measure the following characteristics of this process and its results:

- **Mixture of systems projects submitted by division**

  This measurement chart or table should show that all divisions have project candidates. It should also indicate that several divisions benefit from one project

- **Mixture of systems projects submitted by type (planning action item, ongoing development, maintenance, enhancement, etc.).**

This measurement helps in the evaluation of candidates for the project slate.

- **Distribution of systems projects by proposed schedule timeline**

  This chart is interesting in that it reveals how much could be completed in one year. If almost all of the projects can be completed in a few months, you have evidence that the plan is probably tactical rather than strategic.

- **Distribution of systems projects by initial priority ranking**

  Assign priorities on a 1 to 3 basis (1 is high). The distribution can be based on the number of projects as well as on a weighted average of costs or elapsed time in the schedule.

- **Mixture of systems projects that require the same resources**

  This chart helps to address resource over allocation and resource conflict. This can assist in focusing on specific resource conflicts. Note that you also have the factor of time. If one project follows another and uses the same resources, there is no conflict.

- **Distribution of systems projects by business process**

  Because business processes are so important, this chart helps to determine which projects touch the most critical business processes. It also supports those projects that cross multiple processes.

- **Distribution of systems projects by technology area**

  Support for the architecture is contained here. The message here is to demonstrate how the technology is essential for the projects. This helps procure a higher priority for the architecture projects.

- **Mixture of existing systems projects and new project slate**

  This chart reinforces the difference between the proactive planning method and that of the past.

Action 5: Measure Systems Implementation

The obvious measurements of a project are budget vs. actual and the schedule of work as shown in a GANTT chart. However, how do you measure multiple projects? First, collapse each project that is interrelated into a set of milestones by itself. Then roll the projects together into a single summary project to obtain an overall picture. Second, create a master project. Each of the individual projects will then become a subproject in the master project. Most project management software packages support these operations.

As a method of measurement of an implementation schedule, use the management critical path, which draws attention to the tasks that have risk. These tasks can then be analyzed and adjusted. Since there are many management critical paths, you usually select those that include several projects or tasks with risk.

Action 6: Measure Systems Post-Implementation

Measurement here aims at determining whether the anticipated benefits were achieved. Here are the measurements for this:

- **Completion of planning action items and systems projects**

  This measurement indicates that the percentage of items that have been completed ahead of schedule, on time, or late. Also indicate items and projects that were never completed.

- **Tangible benefit comparison**

  This is a table in which the rows are the areas of benefits. The first column is the estimated benefits. The actual benefits appear in the second column. Comments and verification appear in the third column.

- **Impact on business processes**

  For each business process (as a row) you can list the benefit areas as columns. The entry in the table is the tangible benefit achieved for that business process.

Planning Lessons Learned

One form of measurement is to look at useful lessons you gathered from the planning process that helped not only within the plan but also across the organization. You can also look at whether the lessons learned have been applied.

What are categories for lessons learned? Here are some suggestions:

- Improvements in the planning process that could be used next time around
- Priorities
- The project slate
- Implementation of policies and procedures
- Architecture-related projects
- Measurement approaches

Each lesson learned should be categorized and then analyzed in terms of impact. Take immediate action on a lesson learned so that it is not forgotten. It should become part of the training and procedures. Conduct informal presentations on lessons learned.

A measurement table would have the lessons learned as rows. The next column would represent the impact in terms of policies and procedures. The third column would address benefits. A fourth would provide lessons learned.

You may decide to change administrative procedures due to lessons learned. To show why you are doing this, add another measurement table. Place the lessons learned as rows and the business processes as columns. The table entry will be the degree of impact of the lesson learned on the business process.

Ongoing Measurement

Trends are among the first things that come to mind with ongoing measurement. Some examples of trends are the following:

- **Total system project costs vs. total benefits**

  By year, establish two graphs-one for costs and one for benefits. Use this data to plot cumulative costs and benefits.

- **Project slate**

  To measure the impact of the planning process, take the project slate from the previous year and estimate costs and benefits. Calculate the costs and benefits with the plan. Now create a measurement chart that shows what did happen with the plan vs. what would likely have occurred without the plan.

- **Planning issues and opportunities**

  Measure and plot the mix of issues and opportunities over time. If the planning process is working, the priority and impact of issues should decline over time. In addition, opportunities should eventually outnumber issues.

- **Planning action items**

  Track the mix of action items and project candidates from the plan. At the start of plan implementation, have a number of architecture projects. Once these projects are completed, there should be a surge of projects that address business requirements that rely on the new architecture. Over multiple years you can trace the changes.

- **Elapsed time of implementation**

  It is valuable to track how long it took between the date that an action item was defined or created and the date it was closed due to completion.

MANAGEMENT PRESENTATION AND COST-BENEFIT ANALYSIS

The costs of collection and analysis appear substantial in contrast to the end products. However, much of this information will be gathered and assessed for other parts of the plan along the way. Data collection and sensitivity to measurement should become a habit.

The benefits extend beyond demonstrating success. Your efforts reinforce managers who supported you and the planning effort politically. You also support the ongoing planning process. People also obtain a better sense of their worth through measurement. The external data provides management with ongoing benchmarks.

KEY QUESTIONS

What is success in a project or systems work? What is failure? Are there any guidelines?

Is there an effort to measure the business processes and compare the results with measuring the systems work and efficiency?

Does anyone reconcile the system and the business process?

EXAMPLES

Monarch Bank

At Monarch, there was no thinking about measurement. However, management raised questions about the architecture. The questions were unanswered and the pressure grew. If the situation had continued, there would have been questions raised about process improvement. The project leader then embarked on measurement. Looking back it would have been better and saved a great deal of time to address measurement earlier as part of the process of improvement.

TRAN

While measurements were taken beforehand, they had to be modified and recalibrated to accommodate the relocation of the organization and its reorganization. The organization changed during the planning process. The key measurements during the planning process were the distribution of issues and action items by division and the action items implemented. Statistics on implementation increased grassroots support.

Some of the most interesting measurements related to the allocation process. The pre-project slate measurements pointed to the fact that 40 percent of programming went for projects in a specific division for which there were no tangible benefits. Why had this occurred? It had become a habit and had been the rule for more than five years. After the allocation process, the measurement results were totally different. In place of projects that lasted one or two months, there were eight- to twelve-month projects. Benefits were enforced by measurements and audits during the projects themselves.

Stirling Manufacturing

For Stirling, the major measurement was elapsed time in manufacturing (i.e., cycle time). All proposed action items and projects were evaluated by their impact on cycle time first. Then other factors such as cost and quality were considered. Measurements here included statistics of systems use, numbers of users, response time, and volume of work.

In terms of post-implementation measurement, cycle time of manufacture was accompanied by personal endorsements of the systems that were implemented. Management regarded the personal side as important. Individual managers and staff were encouraged to voice their opinions, both good and bad. Concrete examples served as tangible benefits.

GUIDELINES

- **Be creative in generating interest in measurement.**

  In terms of marketing measurements, you might label it tracking or management control. The term measurement can be viewed as too technical or passive. To interest people in measurement, show sample graphs and charts with data that is representative of realistic data.

- **Define measurements by working forward and backward.**

  You can delineate the measurement, analysis, and presentation process by moving forward from data collection. Determine the process by working backward from the charts and tables of a presentation.

- **Always take more measurements and collect more information than you require.**

  Management may ask questions. You may have to plunge into more detailed information. If you have already collected this, you can respond quickly with little additional effort.

- **Test your measurement charts on a friendly employee to receive valuable feedback.**

  Measurements and charts are subject to different interpretations. For example, if you demonstrate that sales are up by five percent, some people will view this as favorable and others will ask why the percentage is so low. Be critical of your own charts. Show them to people without any explanation to get their reactions. Ask them what they think the charts indicate. Rework the charts if necessary to clarify your data.

- **One reason for performing measurements is that, if you fail to do measurements, others may develop measurements of their own.**

  These measurements, unsupervised by you, may not tell the same story as what you would say. Doing the measurements is part of control of the planning process.

ACTION ITEMS

1. For an area of measurement that was covered, define the measurements you would employ in your company.

2. Now define what data would have to be collected to provide the measurement. Also, identify what analysis is required for the graphs.

3. What graphs, charts, and tables can you generate from your measurements?

4. How would you validate that the graphs and data are correct and relate the proper message?

5. Let's suppose that you are going to present measurement graphs to two different audiences-senior management and the people in your department. Which graphs would you use for each audience? What differences are there and why?

PART VI SIX

MANAGING THE PROJECT

CHAPTER 25

PROJECT COMMUNICATIONS

CONTENTS

𝟤𝟧

PROJECT COMMUNICATIONS

PURPOSE AND SCOPE

The purpose of this chapter is to help you take a balanced approach to communications. Many people take communications and presentations to extremes. They spend too much time worrying and preparing. Others just walk into a room and ad lib. Take each contact, presentation, or telephone call seriously. Be ready to address almost any aspect of the project at a moment's notice. On the other hand, have some enjoyment with the project experiences and lessons learned.

Conveying the message is very important in project communications. This goes beyond getting a single message across one time. Project communications involve building and maintaining communications paths with many different people, since projects involve team activities and decisions. You can perform good work, direct people well, and show good results, but poor communication within and outside the project team can negate all the things you are doing right. Communications are also useful in gathering information and resolving problems more effectively.

To reach the goal of a balanced approach to communications, you will define each step in the communications process, considering almost all forms of communications, formal and informal.

The scope of this chapter includes communications in various types of reports and presentations.

END PRODUCTS

The general end product is successful communications as revealed by support and limited effort in dealing with communications problems. More specifically, the end products are the presentations in the process improvement projects. Smaller end products are the various points of communications during the project. It is important to pay attention to these informal communications in a process improvement project. Mistakes can be costly in terms of the time it takes to reverse and repair damage.

RESOURCES

The people involved in this step go beyond the project management. Work for good communications among the project team members. Miscommunications by one member of the team can affect the rest of the team, the project leader, and the project.

WAYS TO COMMUNICATE

Always be ready to communicate effectively. Beyond the ability to address issues and crises, this is one of the most important attributes of a good project leader. If your demeanor is sour or down, the audience may interpret this as indicating a problem in the project. It is all right to show anger, concern, or worry if that helps in getting an issue resolved or in advancing the project.

Communications have become more complex because you communicate with more people than the typical employee did in the past. Also, you have more choices of the medium of communications. Here is a short list of the possibilities, with specific guidelines on using each one:

- **In-person informal communications**

  This is the best for discussing something or gathering information. It is the best in process improvement projects because the direct contact reinforces the personal contacts. You can get a better overall impression of what is going on if you go to a person's office rather than running into someone in the hallway. Many different topics can be explored in this casual atmosphere. You get more of the person's attention without interruptions. When you stop by, indicate why you are there, what information you need, and how much of the person's time you need.

  If someone contacts you, be ready with a smile and look the person in the eye. Always be ready for any informal visit. You might even enter your own office as if you are a visitor and see what impression you are conveying.

Whether you are the sender or the receiver, check facial expressions. Does the person you are talking with appear closed up by having legs or arms crossed? Do either of you appear nervous? Scan what is on a person's desk. It will tell you what the person's priorities are.

- **Formal meetings**

  This is a chance to cover topics with a larger audience in a structured format. More ground can be covered. There is an opportunity to gain consensus. Formal meetings require more preparation and thought.

- **Telephone**

  This is a good medium for following up on specific nonpolitical points if the person is remote from you.

  If you are on the receiving end of a call, answer with a greeting and your name. Let the caller do the talking. Just listen. Try to detect from the caller's tone whether he is nervous, upset, or angry.

  Maintain a telephone log of all calls. This will help jog your memory later. If a caller makes a specific request that impacts the project, ask for the request in writing so that it can become part of the project file, since it could affect the work or the schedule.

- **Telephone contact with an intermediary**

  Careful here—any message you convey is subject to misinterpretation. Stick to a straightforward message that is clear and unambiguous. Organize your thoughts before you call.

  After identifying yourself on the phone, establish rapport with the person answering. Then move to the message. Imagine that you are writing down the message along with the intermediary and speak at a pace that allows this.

  If a secretary or assistant calls you on behalf of someone else, get the details, then repeat the message back to ensure that you have received it correctly. If you are asked to come to a meeting, do some research. How big is the room? Which department controls the scheduling of the room? The answers to these questions can reveal who the other audience members are and tip you off as to what may be covered.

- **Voice mail**

  Keep the message brief. Make notes before you call, writing down the subject and key points. If the call is for information only and needs no response, indicate this. For your own voice mail line, keep the greeting short and avoid being cute, which may distract the caller.

- **Pagers**

  Adopt a code system for each person you will be paging frequently. For example, if the need for contact is urgent, enter 911. If the need is informational, enter 411. Returning pages promptly indicates to the sender that you treat the business seriously.

- **Facsimile**

  Try to get as much on the cover sheet as you can. Try to use electronic mail instead of faxes since it is more private. If the person being faxed is not located near the machine, call and alert the person that you are sending a fax.

  Fax the message yourself to ensure that it was sent. Someone else who doesn't really care might insert it into the machine and walk off. The fax may fail. Someone else walks up and removes your pages and leaves. Finding the pages neatly stacked, you mistakenly assume that the fax went through successfully. Also, watch the time of day. If you fax at lunchtime, it's possible no one will be there to pick it up. If you fax at busy times and are able to get through, then your fax may end up on the back of someone else's. If you are going to send copies to several people, address each person on a separate sheet. Always hand-sign the cover sheet.

- **Electronic mail**

  If you are going to send a lengthy e-mail message, write it first in a word processor, since this is a much better editor than the e-mail text editor. Also, many e-mail systems do not have a spell-checker.

  Make sure the subject line is short and clear. Include any issue or topic that is the focus of the message.

  Establish group mailing lists in the e-mail system for the inner project team and outer project team. This will save you from having to type in all of the e-mail addresses each time.

- **The Web and Internet**

  The intranets, the Internet, and the World Wide Web have so much useful information for projects that being selective is the best skill to acquire. Don't flood the receivers with too much information.

  If you are going to post documents or information on web pages, then concentrate on content. Don't spend a lot of time on making it cute by customizing HTML code. Cute stuff can backfire since the audience may assume that you have nothing better to do. If you are going to establish a web site, maintain the site with up-to-date information or go back to e-mail. Remember that a key duty will be maintaining any and all Web information you establish.

- **Groupware**

  Some people employ groupware like electronic mail. However, groupware has the advantage of allowing several people to comment or to build documents together. In using groupware, stick to the basic features. If you use exotic features, other people may not be able to participate fully.

- **Videoconferencing**

  This is one of the more abused media forms, even while in limited use. To cope with limited communications capacity, only a limited number of frames are transmitted per second. This means that the image is jagged. Use the videoconference to show charts, tables, photos, or drawings. You can then communicate by voice or text in discussing the figures.

  This is a communications form that has a great deal of potential for some applications. For example, in engineering and manufacturing, the technician on the floor can ask questions of a design engineer regarding a drawing. For construction companies, videoconferencing is one of the best electronic tools available, since it puts multiple construction sites in touch with each other and with headquarters.

- **Memoranda and letters**

  Keep written memoranda and letters short and to the point. Adopt a simple writing style. Avoid long sentences and complex terms. Make sure the subject is short and to the point.

Think about what follow-up measures you will take to ensure that the message got through.

- **Reports**

  When writing the report, keep in mind who the audience is and keep the focus narrowed to this. Print on one side of a piece of paper. Although this consumes more paper, the document will be easier to follow. Number and date each page with the title so that it can be reassembled if separated. Always assume that any written communication will be copied and distributed.

Message Failure and Success

What constitutes success in project communications? The message not only gets through to the receiver, but you also receive action or a response.

What constitutes failure in project communications? The message was misinterpreted or ignored. The failure is always the fault of the sender, who is responsible for all steps in preparing, sending, and following up on the communication.

APPROACH

Action 1: Define the Purpose and Audience

Whom do you wish to reach? Think about the person or people you are trying to reach. What do the people think of you and the project? What is their attitude? What is their knowledge of the project? What can you assume they know so that the communication can be shorter? What are they likely to do after they receive the message? To whom will they pass the communication? Answering these questions will help you to determine the degree of detail and background required, set the tone of the communication, and determine what medium is most appropriate.

Why do you wish to communicate? What would happen if you did not communicate now? With the overload of information in many organizations, treat any of your communications as if it costs great money and effort. If you are in doubt and the reasons for the communication are unclear, then wait. Is the reason for communicating complex? That is, do you need to address a number of issues? Consider breaking down the communication into addressing one person at a time or addressing smaller groups.

Action 2: Form the Message

The message is not the communication. The message is contained in the communication. Based on your skill, the receiver may or may not be able to decipher the message from the communication. To avoid confusion, first construct an outline of what you want to say. In general, your outline should include the following:

1. An introduction that identifies the problem or situation
2. The detailed steps of the message (who, what, when, where, how)
3. The desired action of the recipient
4. Expected feedback from the message

Example: Stirling Manufacturing

As part of process improvement, the project manager at Stirling had to request a detailed blueprint of the offices in a remote location in order to lay out the network and estimate costs. However, a blueprint can mean different things to different people. What if some vague diagram were provided? It would be worthless and the information request would have to be repeated. The communications outline first listed the request and reasons behind it. This was followed by the date required and what was to be done with the information. The last item was a sample blueprint of the headquarters building as an example. This was appropriate and provided the necessary example along with the information on the request.

Action 3: Determine the Medium and Timing

Confine all discussion of issues to in-person contact or direct telephone contact. You want to have direct interaction with the person so that any questions can be answered. Use electronic mail or groupware for routine messages. Avoid facsimile because of the many possibilities for missed communications. Keep communications informal. Use formal meetings and settings as a backup for escalation and for general impressions.

After you select the medium for the message, think about how the receiver will respond and what media will be used. Assume that the messages will fly back and forth.

Timing is important if you want to get someone's attention. When should you send the message? The answer, as you saw in the discussion of various media forms, depends on the medium, the objective, the audience, and the message.

Action 4: Formulate the Communication

In this step you now package the message inside the communication. Whether you are dealing with verbal or written media, if it is important, expand your outline and build the communications. If the communication is verbal, create a series of bullet items. If the communication is written, prepare the document. Write with words of ten letters or less whenever possible. Write in simple sentences, usually no longer than 10 words, and form short, succinct paragraphs. Avoid jargon—especially project management jargon, such as *critical path*, *PERT*, *GANTT*, and *critical resources*.

Action 5: Deliver the Communication

If the delivery of your communication brings many questions from the recipient, suggest that you go over the message with the person in a face-to-face situation. If complex questions arise during direct contact, set another meeting to resolve all the issues raised.

Action 6: Follow Up on the Communication

If you send messages and you fail to follow up, people may think that the message was not important.

First, make a note in a log as to what you sent and when. Track whether you receive any feedback or response. Plan ahead for follow-up on whether the message was received and what actions are flowing from it. In most cases involving politically sensitive topics, the only evident response may be acknowledgment of receipt of the message, since they will need time to think about a response.

Obviously, to do this for many messages is absurd and impossible. This is another reason for not sending out many messages. If you have to send more messages in total than you can pursue, identify the critical messages and follow up on them. Place messages on issues, budget, schedule, and important resource topics in this category.

Figure 25-1 gives elements to use to track and improve communications skills.

Effective Reports and Presentations

When you think about project presentations and reports, your mind will often turn to technical details and in-depth discussions of issues. Most people want to plunge in and make a list of details and then formulate a report or presentation. This is unwise. Here are six topics which must be considered in creating an effective report or presentation.

- **Medium or format**

  What is the medium of the message?

- **Length**

  How long will the communication be?

- **Organization**

  Where will you start your presentation? Where will it end? How will you get from the start to the end (order of presentation)?

- **Method of argument**

  Will you use project data, your authority or experience, or project history? What will be the basis for your support?

- **Attitude toward audience**

  What is the attitude you wish to convey toward your audience (friendly, hostile, polite, informal, etc.)?

- **Impression**

  After your message is heard or read, what do you want the audience to think of you?

Figure 25-1: Sample Form for Communications

No.: _____ Date: _____

Title: _____

Audience: _____

Purpose: _____

Message: _____

_____

_____

_____

_____

_____

Media Selected: _____

Expected Action: _____

Expected Time of Action: _____

Actual Time of Action: _____

Real Action that Occurred: _____

Lessons Learned: _____

_____

Notes:

   Assign a number to each form so that you can track it later.

   File these by subject or by date.

With this as your strategy, you can begin to assemble information, tables, graphs, plans, etc. This is the evidence for your presentation.

Presentation Style

Next, choose one of three presentation styles:

- **Descriptive Report and Presentation**

  An issue, situation, or opportunity can be described to an audience. You begin with an introduction to the subject. Next, establish your credibility. Why are you qualified to talk about this? Here you might cite project experience. Third, give an overview of the topic. This is followed by the details on the subject. Now bring the audience back to the initial topic so that they can relate the overview and detail to the topic.

  This style works for a travel show or for some academic presentations but has limited effectiveness in project management. In projects you are often trying to gain support or approval. Description often is too general, leaving too many loose ends.

- **Analytical Report and Presentation**

  Here you might be reporting on an issue in a project. You start with identifying what you are analyzing. First provide your credentials. The question addressed next is "What is the current state of affairs with the issue?" You can move from general to specific and back to general, as in the descriptive presentation. Now identify the methods and tools employed in the analysis. You end the presentation with conclusions and recommendations.

  This style is good for milestone assessment and other evaluation type work, but is not well suited to the major presentations of the project.

- **Persuasive Report and Presentation**

  Concentrate your effort and practice in this presentation style. As with the other two styles, you begin with an introduction and qualifications. Next, what is the need? What are you trying to address? Avoid the solution or benefits. After answering these questions, answer the question, "What will happen if the need is not addressed?" Point out grim and unwelcome consequences. Then change the tone to one of optimism and talk about what will happen if the need is addressed. What benefits will accrue? You have warmed up your audience and prepared them well. Now move to the solution.

Meetings

Some general suggestions regarding meetings are as follows:

- Do a great deal of preparation for meetings. Collect agenda items for meetings in advance.
- Actively run the meeting. Keep meetings focused on an agenda.
- Minimize meetings due to the effort and the impact of lost time on the project.
- Meet to discuss lessons learned rather than to discuss status.

Here are some specific comments on types of project meetings:

- **Project Kickoff Meeting**

  You are starting the project. The meeting will introduce members of the project team to each other and set the stage for the project. Have people introduce themselves and explain what experience and expertise they bring to the table. This is especially important since you are establishing the tone for the project in this first meeting.

  Prepare for the meeting by developing the project plan from the template, but leave out the lowest level of detail. Delegate that task to the team members. Set down the ground rules for communications, reporting, work, and issues. Make this as structured as possible. If you start out vague, then you have damaged the project at the onset. To build the group into a team, develop the initial list of issues and detailed tasks as a team.

- **Milestone Meeting**

  This is a meeting where a milestone or end product is presented and reviewed. As the meeting begins, provide the audience with checklists of questions and guidelines for evaluation. Let the people know what you expect to get out of the meeting. What actions are possible? As you go through the review of the end product, make notes on an easel or board as to what issues and questions are raised. At the end of the review, start going through the list on the board and either get closure or assign topics out for analysis.

- **Issues Meeting**

  Identify the two or three issues to be addressed and who should attend for each issue. Set strict time parameters for each issue and invite only those needed to each issue discussion. Identify action items for each issue and decide how to follow up on these.

- **Lessons Learned Meeting**

  These meetings can be based on achieving a specific milestone. You would ask what people learned in doing the tasks that led to the milestone. Another option for this kind of meeting is to take a time period and ask for lessons learned for that period. In either case, start with a general discussion. Then identify the following elements and record them so that others can benefit:

  —How the lesson learned can be generalized

  —How someone would use the lesson learned in practice

  —The benefits of the lesson learned

  —Who to contact if a person has questions about the lesson learned

  —How to add further detail later to the lesson learned

  —How to measure the results of the lesson learned

MANAGEMENT PRESENTATION AND COST-BENEFIT ANALYSIS

These steps are involved and you may be tempted to skip some of them. However, if you casually handle communications, then with all of the issues that have to be handled for process improvement you run the risk of miscommunications. Different incidents of miscommunication can be cumulative in impact. Experience shows that the workload lessens as you follow the steps.

KEY QUESTIONS

What is the level of your awareness of being able to differentiate between the message and the overall communication?

Think through the communication process you use today. How often do you have to clarify messages that were not properly received?

How much project time is spent on determining status? How much is spent on issues?

Do you have any standard guidelines for presentations to management? Do these fit all of the types of projects in your organization?

EXAMPLES

Monarch Bank

For Monarch Bank, the problem was that people were used to a variety of different communications media. No standardized pattern existed. This created communications problems because people employed their own style between written, voice, and electronic media.

The project manager was able to standardize the distribution of project plans and issue management. Extending standardization any further would have consumed too much effort and engendered too much hostility.

TRAN

TRAN is a political organization. From the start it was realized that communications would be a key factor if the process improvement project were to succeed. Periodic reviews were conducted for all communications in the project. Before any major meeting, political factors in communications were discussed.

Stirling Manufacturing

Communications on the project at the Stirling Manufacturing started with electronic mail and faxes. Problems arose because the faxes would get out of sync. While preparing a response to the first fax, a second fax would come in. These faxes were mixed in with standard daily work. Faxes were lost. Electronic mail growth was slow and uneven.

The project manager stepped in to help by supporting electronic mail use. Once e-mail was established, usage soared.

The lesson learned here was that these events could have been foreseen and planned for in advance. The project manager had to react to each situation. Some of the problems could have been prevented with better planning and organization.

GUIDELINES

- **Think of the self-interest of the audience when you supply project information.**

  Remember that the importance of a project lies in the eyes of the beholder.

- **Avoid secondhand communications.**

  Secondhand communications means going through intermediaries. You know from the elementary school game of "telephone" how messages get changed as they pass from person to person. Also, it is highly unlikely that the intermediary will convey the passion, interest, or other emotion that accompanied the message. This lowers the likelihood of the message leading to success.

- **Democracy in a project has its place, but so does autocracy.**

  In a collaborative environment for a project you seek to encourage greater communications about issues, lessons learned, and project status. However, also maintain order in the project and stomp out any rumor mills. This is a challenge between democracy and authority for the project leader.

- **Detect indirect resistance by observation.**

  When people communicate with or respond to you, they convey their feelings and attitudes. You should be able to detect resistance on specific topics. Maintain frequent one-on-one contact to detect changes or nuances in demeanor.

- **Manage small leaks of information while they are small.**

  Most project leaders can cope with leaks of information about the project to people outside of the project. The basic problem is that what might be an annoyance in the project becomes a major crisis through the retelling of the information again and again by different people. Coping with substantial disinformation is time-consuming. If possible, determine the source of the leaks and discuss the issue with that person.

- **Be consistent in what you relate to each of the members of the project team.**

  Assume that everything you tell someone on the team is known to the entire team in less than one hour.

- **Operate on the assumption that you might create an enemy in each meeting.**

  Enemies (or friends) are made during the process of communication. Once you have made an enemy, it will be difficult, if not impossible, to undo. Be considerate and avoid unnecessary criticism of others throughout the communication process.

- **Keep the volume of written memos among project members as low as possible.**

  The volume of memos is usually inversely related to progress. Experience indicates that memoranda volume increases when the project is under stress. People naturally want to cover themselves and appear busy. If people are working productively on the tasks, they have little time for memos.

- **Confine your meeting time to issues.**

  Project issues are often more interesting than project status. People tend to want to get involved and put their fingerprint on issues. People are bored by status.

- **Use simple language and avoid arcane jargon.**

  Using unfamiliar or arcane words was encouraged at one time as a demonstration of intelligence. Now it is viewed negatively because people miss the meaning of what you are saying. The communications path to a person consists of first understanding the language, then understanding the words, and then deciphering the meaning of what is said. If people can't understand you, your communications are not going to be effective.

- **Vary the project report formats.**

  If you continually use the same format and structure for reports, you will not have an impact on your audience. Your goal is to obtain a decision and an understanding, but the message may be blocked by the format of the project reports. Design a series of formats—one for use with routine reporting, another series for analysis, and a third series for decision-making.

- **Share project information.**

  Sharing project information builds trust. People often hold project information close to the vest. They think that if it gets disclosed, their position will weaken. This occurs more often when professional schedulers are tracking progress for management. It is always better to share information on the project. You don't have to share the political perspective or details about issues in progress, but be open about status and activities.

- **In order to raise morale, look at the worst that can happen.**

  In communications, when you encounter a difficult issue or crisis, take the time to examine the worse case scenario. Often, this is not as bad as people may have thought.

- **Have people leave their present agendas and schemes outside before a meeting.**

  As a project leader, you will have to address these agendas directly at the beginning of the meeting. It is better to tell people to leave their "guns" outside and see you privately at a later time.

- **Try to sit in on meetings for different projects and teams.**

  Learn something about style and what works and does not work, no matter what the content might be. Focus on the flow of the meeting, the interaction of the people, and the structure of the meeting.

- **Keep project meetings to no more than an hour.**

  Meetings that last more than an hour tend to generate more heat than light. Extended project meetings tend to disrupt other work. People may get too worked up about an issue during the meeting and productivity will then drop for some time after the meeting.

- **Provide a forum to encourage the sharing of lessons learned.**

  If you do not, you will suffer the penalty of repeating the lessons. Having the team members share their experiences provides reinforcement and support. Otherwise, a team member will have to go through the same processes as other team members without the benefit of the experiences and lessons learned by the others.

- **Vary project meeting dates and times to increase the level of awareness.**

  Periodic meetings are often preferred by people who like routine. But holding periodic project meetings will lull a project team into complacency. Also, issues do not conveniently mature and become ready for resolution on the same schedule. Drop the periodic meetings. Make the next meeting "to be announced" and notify people several days in advance.

- **Stick to simple visual aids and have handouts in case these fail.**

  The more you depend on extensive audio-visual aids, the more likely they will break. Exotic visual aids include electronic CRT screen projectors, nonstandard slide projectors, and overhead projectors without substantial fans. Do not trade content for slickness. Do not rely on equipment that has no spares or on-site support.

- **Evaluate yourself after a presentation.**

  After a presentation there is a tendency to want to forget everything and go on to something you like to do. But first, sit down and be your own worst critic. Did you achieve the results you were after? What did the audience do in the meeting? How did they react to you? How did they react to other speakers?

- **Consider chart appearance.**

  Charts can be confusing, even if the information is valuable and correct. The choice of colors, shadings, format, lettering, fonts for letters, and wording are all important. Create your presentation and set it aside for some time. Then go back and shuffle the presentation order. Pick up a chart at random and see if you can understand it. In a project presentation, discuss the impact of the chart—not the detailed meaning of the chart.

- **Hand out all materials at the start of the presentation to make life easier for the audience.**

  The old argument was that people would read ahead of your presentation and would lose interest. However, people get more from the information if they have the materials in front of them. Also, handing out materials at the beginning of the presentation minimizes surprises.

- **Hold informal meetings more often than formal.**

  The more formal meetings you have, the more people will become involved in the issue. With more heat and attention, many people are likely to defer action. It is best if possible to resolve issues and get decisions informally and with a low profile. The decision can later be announced formally. Also, informal meetings often convey more information than formal meetings. Formal meetings tend to have a rigid agenda with less time for questions. The presentation tends to be more rigid in terms of overheads, slides, and handouts. In informal meetings you can get questions and issues out more easily since there is less structure to the meeting. One good strategy is to have an informal pre-meeting to solicit issues and questions to be covered later at a formal meeting.

ACTION ITEMS

1. Go into your project file and grab several memos or copies of electronic mail that you generated. Review these by asking the following questions:

   Does the communication fit the audience?

   Can you discern the message through the communication?

   What was the result of the communication? When did it happen?

2. Start keeping a log of your communications. Note the date and time of contact, the person contacted, the nature of contact, the response, the date and time of response, and the action that resulted.

3. Develop an approach for modifying your method of communicating. Start with one media form at a time. Work on electronic mail and faxes, since these are relatively short and focused.

CHAPTER 26

MANAGEMENT COMMUNICATIONS AND SUPPORT

CONTENTS

26

MANAGEMENT COMMUNICATIONS AND SUPPORT

PURPOSE AND SCOPE

This chapter focuses on key events in your management contacts during the life cycle of a typical process improvement project. The previous chapter gave general guidelines on communications; in this chapter more specific, pointed suggestions are given. The purpose is to help you win support. This chapter provides practical advice as well as tips on how to avoid failure.

While you can recover multiple times from problems and failure within the project team, you get very few chances with management on a process improvement project. If you are successful in your first major presentation to management, the favorable impression you create will last a long time. However, the margin for error is small. If you don't pay attention to management communications and their nuances, you could undo all of your other good work.

The scope of this chapter begins with getting the project idea approved and moves through the completion or termination of the project. Both formal and informal communications with management are included.

END PRODUCTS

The end products are the various presentations and meetings that you hold with management. End products can also be extended to include the results of the communications with management.

RESOURCES

While the project leader is the obvious resource, in process improvement you want to involve people from the user and IT departments as well as those on the team. During presentations you do not want to take credit for the work. Give credit to the team and the departments.

APPROACH

The traditional method in project management is that as you approach a major event or milestone in a project, you put together a formal presentation to management. The presentation then may or may not occur. If it does, some follow-up may be required, but the attention returns to the work. The contact with management is a temporary event, perhaps viewed as an interruption in the process.

This concept of communications with management is fundamentally wrong. Instead, consider management communications as an integral part of overall communications. It is important to manage your management communications in terms of weekly tracking of contacts and scheduling of contacts for the next week. Informing and working with management on a continuous basis are major roles for the project manager which are just as important as obtaining status and addressing issues. Communication is especially important when there is continuous contact with management.

The discussion of this approach to management communications is divided into informal and formal communications. The most effective strategy is to use informal methods as a basis for communications and smoothly and continuously build up to formal presentations. The formal presentations will then be followed up on by information communications.

About the Audience

The old school of thought was to keep your manager informed and that would be sufficient. However, managers come and go. Also, the elapsed time of the project may be such that the manager may move to another position. A suggested alternative is to identify and keep informed a set of three to four managers in different parts of the organization. These people will be your direct audience for both informal and formal communications. For process improvement this spreads the risk if one manager leaves. It also provides you with additional input.

With which managers should you develop a rapport? Choose a combination of general, high level managers and line managers who are interested in the outcome of the project, or who are supplying people to the project. Make a list of several managers of each type to call on if you need backup.

This method has several benefits. First, you have a plan in place for backup if one manager leaves. You also have continuity, since the existing managers can assist in updating the new manager as well. A third benefit is that you have a wider audience to give you feedback before formal presentations.

Informal Communications

Here are some benefits of informal communications:

- The managers can give you their reactions to a presentation informally prior to formal presentation. People tend to be more open in a one-on-one situation.

- You provide others with information on issues. They can then take the information and work the issue for you behind the scenes. It is often best to solve politically sensitive issues "off-line."

- Status information can arm others to answer any questions or concerns about the project. This prevents both defensiveness when someone questions the project and the need to call you to clarify a point.

What do these benefits add up to? You become more proactive. You are getting information out to people. When formal presentations occur, they are almost anticlimactic, since several members of the audience already know what you are going to say. This also means less chance of a surprise.

How to Make Contact Informally

Here are some pointers on informal contacts with management.

- **How to contact managers** Plan on casually running into several managers each week. Planning and "casual" contact appear contradictory, but they are not. Plan how you can informally contact managers in the hallway, copier room, or their offices. Study their work patterns. Usually, the best time to run into people or stop by their office is early in the morning.

- **Extent of contact** Plan on no more than five minutes of total contact, unless the manager indicates that he wants to spend more time with you.

- **What to cover in the contact** Always start with status. Let the manager know some good news first. This is a positive way to start the day. If you want to discuss or present an issue, gradually lead into it. Starting with the issue is too negative.

  If you desire feedback on the major points of a formal presentation, reveal some of the key parts of the presentation for reaction. You get not only the manager's reaction but also the manager's understanding. This typically means that the manager can provide assistance during the presentation.

- **A manager's concerns and comments** The previous point stressed the transfer of information from you to the manager. It works both ways. The manager may hear something that impacts your project. The informal contact allows the manager a chance to inform you without a record in writing.

- **A manager's ideas** Incorporate the ideas suggested by the managers and then provide them with feedback by showing how the presentation or report changed after their input.

With this amount of contact, you and the project are quite visible to certain managers. However, to others you are unknown until there is a formal presentation. This is desirable. If you receive a great deal of management attention openly, people will become jealous and may take shots at the project. To keep a low profile, favor a structure with extensive informal contacts and little obvious visibility.

Formal Presentations

Before the Presentation

Whether it be a report or an oral presentation, try these guidelines:

- Keep all materials in a draft form. Label them as a draft.

  This will give people the impression that they can have input prior to the final form, as well as providing you with the ability to improve and make changes. The more people are involved, the more feedback you will get and the more buy-in you will receive.

- For verbal presentations, ask line managers of the project team members to be present along with team members. Plan to spread the credit around.

- Use successive dry runs to keep improving the material.

During the Presentation

Here are some tips to consider in making the presentation:

- Minimize the number of charts. Too many can be confusing.
- Hand out all charts at the beginning. This allows the audience to see the entire presentation and surprises are avoided.
- All charts should express complete thoughts and sentences. If you use lists without additional information, people can misunderstand what is going on.
- Encourage feedback and questions. Follow up on each item either in the meeting or shortly afterward.
- Make sure you have dangling items so that you have the opportunity to follow up afterwards for more marketing.
- Walk around as you give the presentation and be animated.

After the Presentation

Follow up after the presentation with managers who were in the audience and further explain any points that were unclear. Asking what they thought is too direct and shows a lack of confidence. If a manager has an opinion, he will express it.

Immediately after the presentation, grade yourself by using the following checklist:

Presentation Evaluation

- **Material**

  How well was it organized?

  Was the material relevant to the theme of the presentation?

  Were people able to understand it easily? Did they ask what terms meant?

  Was there too much material?

  Did you find that you lacked material to respond to specific issues?

- **Presentation style**

  Were you too formal?

  Did you receive many questions or comments?

  How did you respond to comments?

  Did you read from the charts?

- **Audience**

  Who attended the presentation?

  Were the key players there?

  Was the audience attentive? Were there any interruptions?

After a presentation, take the time to write down the answers to the above questions and file this evaluation for reference. If needed, refine the presentation to the way it should have been.

Critical Marketing Milestones

Almost all projects, even the smallest, have key milestones and end products. Here are the milestones to consider in detail.

Marketing the Idea for Process Improvement

- **Background**

  Project ideas don't just surface on their own. Someone has the idea and either that person or somebody else follows up by becoming the champion for the plan concept. The fate of the idea is closely linked with the person who is pushing for approval of the idea.

- **Purpose**

  The aim is to gain approval from a manager to develop a project plan and determine the initial feasibility. This is positive, since it gives management an inexpensive way to assess the will of the person who is pushing for the project.

- **Approach**

  The favored approach is to build support for the project gradually. Sell individual managers one-on-one. Show how the project concept fits in with their own interests. Avoid a pitch based on vague terms and concepts.

  To generate enthusiasm as well as gain approval, show the benefits of your plan. For example, a project leader in one of the examples did this for her network by pointing to how issues could be resolved through a network. This was much more effective than trying to sell dry network concepts.

- **Suggestions and hints**

  Try to have managers adopt the project idea as their own and then act as apostles in marketing it to other managers you cannot reach yourself. Your plan is to build a set of cadres to support and sponsor the idea. Keep the idea verbal so that it is flexible. Once you put it in writing, you will tend to become locked in.

- **Measuring your performance**

  The obvious measure is approval of the concept for planning. In addition, assess the degree of enthusiasm and excitement for the project.

  Another test is to ask managers what their impression is of the project.

Marketing the Process Improvement Project Plan

- **Background**

  It is not enough to gain approval of the project plan; you must obtain resources as well, garnering political support to get the necessary funding.

- **Purpose**

  You should obtain the following after initial approval of the project plan: support for providing resources to the project for the first stage of work, interest in the project for continued contact, and management input on the plan.

- **Approach**

  One technique is to reveal the overall, high-level plan to managers. Show the major task areas, general dates, and dependencies. Then refine the plan and come back with more detail, as well as resources needed. It is too much to expect people to grasp all of the detail the first time. Presell the project top down and bottom up at the same time. Focus on the people who will benefit from the successful completion of the project.

- **Suggestions and hints**

  Incremental marketing is the key. This gives you a further opportunity for management contact and contact with the future beneficiaries of the project. Make it appear in form if not in reality that the development of the plan is a team effort. Make sure that you give people credit for their input.

- Measuring your performance

  Did you obtain approval?

  Do people have a clear idea of the project and are they supportive?

  Did you obtain resources to get started?

Communicating Project Status to Management

- **Background**

  Conveying status information is not just walking up and saying the project is going along well or writing a memo to that effect. Strive to continue to build rapport and strengthen support. Treat the supplying of status information as a continuous process rather than a periodic activity you do once a week or once a month.

- **Purpose**

  The basic purpose is to enlist and build support for the project. A more immediate purpose is to convey an understanding of the project status. Another purpose is to pave the way for the resolution of issues.

- **Approach**

  Provide status in informal one-on-one meetings. Start with the overall state of the project and then zoom in on a detailed issue or specific milestone. Then relate an interesting war story or experience. Alert managers to a looming issue so that they can prepare for it.

- **Suggestions and hints**

  Develop a version of the status of the project and what you want to say each morning. Rehearse this informally with a member of the project team. Then set out on your mission to relate the status to one or two managers. Do this several times a week. Managers you contact will become involved and more interested. They will look forward to your contacts.

- **Measuring your performance**

  How many people have you contacted this week?

  How has your relationship grown with them since you started?

  Are they more interested in the project now?

Presenting an Issue

- **Background**

  Present the issue or opportunity along with alternative actions, and get a decision. This way, you are presenting solutions as well as bringing up problems.

- **Purpose**

  The purpose of the presentation of an issue is for management to understand the impact of the issue, why action is necessary now, and the suggested decision, actions, and anticipated results. Avoid getting bogged down in the details of the issue.

- **Approach**

  The first stage is to alert managers through informal communications that an issue is coming. This will mitigate any feelings of surprise. Next, follow the steps for issues suggested later in the book in Chapter 18. When you have the materials ready, present a complete picture.

- **Suggestions and hints**

  Don't cry wolf over an issue. You can alert management and indicate that you are tracking it. Let it mature. Carefully plan the sequence of issues and opportunities that will be presented to management. Insert positive opportunities in between issues to avoid leaving a lingering negative impression.

- **Measuring your performance**

  The bottom line is whether you receive approval for the decision and actions you proposed.

  More than that, however, did you establish a positive pattern of managing issues?

Obtaining Management Decisions

- **Background**

  Many immediate management decisions after a presentation will be negative. To deal with this, during the presentation indicate what you will do while the managers ponder the presentation. In that way, you can continue the project. The managers will know that work is still going on and will feel less pressure to make a decision.

- **Purpose**

  The purpose is to obtain a decision, but as important as a decision is, your ultimate goal is support.

- **Approach**

  Presell the decision through the informal contacts. Informal approval is easier to obtain than formal. Avoid a formal memo of the decision if you can. The formal presentation can stress the actions that flow from the decision, rather than the decision itself.

- **Suggestions and hints**

  A basic suggestion is to indicate that a decision will be needed way in advance. Then show that this decision does not bear any significant risk for management. Instead, focus on the benefits that will flow from the actions. This turns the spotlight away from the decision. As you approach the decision, move the attention to actions—again moving the focus from the decision. This will make the decision more natural.

- **Measuring your performance**

  Did you get the decision you wanted when you required it? How much good will did the decision cost? How hard did you have to sell the decision?

Coping with Poor Management Decisions

- **Background**

  You wanted a management decision and you got the wrong one. They did not approve the requested resources or the budget. What do you do?

- **Purpose**

  The purpose is not to go back in and reverse the decision. What you seek to do, rather, is to mitigate the effects of the decision on the project. It is most important to keep up progress and momentum in the project. Do not let a cloud of doom hang over the project.

- **Approach**

  First, analyze why the undesirable decision was made. What is the difference between your perception of the situation and management's? Next, look at the impact of the management decision—immediate and long-term. How can you counter the effects of the decision to protect the project and keep up the work?

- **Suggestions and hints**

  Expect that poor decisions will be made. This often happens through a misunderstanding. Once key managers have taken public stances that cannot be reversed, figure out how to work informally behind the scenes to counteract the negative effects of the decision.

- **Measuring your performance**

  Were you able to control the damage from the decision?

Have you determined how to go back to management with pieces of information to get some change in the decision?

Taking Action After the Decision

- **Background**

  Actions flow from a decision. If no actions follow a decision, the decision is likely to have little meaning. If the gap between the decision and the subsequent actions is too big, people will not be able to understand and relate to the actions.

- **Purpose**

  The goal is to implement actions immediately after decisions are made.

- **Approach**

  Include the actions in your presentation. Link the actions to the situation by explaining what benefits will likely follow. Then you can back into the decision.

- **Suggestions and hints**

  Make sure that you have a complete list of actions ready to go. Actions can be policies and procedures, as well as resource actions.

- **Measuring your performance**

  Were the actions implemented?

  Do people clearly see the connection between the decisions and the actions?

Changing an Improvement Project

- **Background**

  On many projects lasting six months or more, you will be faced with selling project change to management. This occurs naturally for several reasons. For example, change external to the project may affect the project. Also, knowledge gained from the project team can be employed to change the project.

- **Purpose**

  The goal is to accomplish the change in the project while maintaining the confidence of management in the project.

- **Approach**

  Bundle all possible changes into the marketing of the change. If you change the project many times, management will lose confidence in you and the project. Managers might think that things are out of control.

  Indicate why the change is needed by explaining what will happen if things continue as they are. Then move to the benefits of the change.

- **Suggestions and hints**

  Point out at the start of the project that the project could change due to events. Keep alerting people to this possibility. Then, as you approach the change, give attention to some of the different problems that could be solved by change. Indicate that you are packaging the solutions into a major change and that after this the project will move into a period of stability.

- **Measuring your performance**

  More important than getting the change approved, do you still have management's support and confidence?

Terminating a Process Improvement Project

- **Background**

  This is unpleasant but necessary. The project leader should be the champion of termination. Don't protect a project that should be killed off.

- **Purpose**

  The purpose is to reach a decision on terminating a project, or at least initiating a major overhaul.

- **Approach**

  Start by building up the project from an overall perspective. Emphasize what has changed since the original purpose of the project was approved. This will help to ensure that no one places the blame for the termination. Then point to the effects of termination. Don't focus on the sunk costs. They are gone. Press for approval of the termination actions.

- **Suggestions and hints**

  Always consider termination as an option for any project. If nothing else, it forces you to validate the need for and benefit of the project.

- **Measuring your performance**

  Did you achieve the right outcome? Was termination successful without any placing of blame?

Potential Problems of a Presentation

Here are some problems that you may run into and what you might do in response.

- **You are not given a chance to present.**

  This is often due to scheduling or to other logistics problems. Don't personalize it. Try to get temporary approval so that the project can continue. Then present it next time. It is often better not to present than to be forced to present with insufficient time remaining.

- **The key managers did not attend the meeting.**

  If you know in advance of the meeting that this will happen, consider removing yourself from the agenda. If the audience is not right, then you may waste the impact of the presentation. On the other hand, if an enemy of the project is going to be out of town, you might want to move up the presentation.

  If you show up and the key managers do not, make the presentation. After the presentation, go to each manager's office and offer to provide an informal, short presentation. This is your chance for follow-up.

- **You failed to respond adequately to questions and comments.**

  When people ask questions, listen carefully. Let them fully explain their ideas. Don't interrupt. Break up the points they raise in a sequence of numbers. Then address each directly.

KEY QUESTIONS

How do you prepare for presentations now? How do you prepare documents? What preliminary reviews do you receive?

Do you make the same mistakes repeatedly in presentations?

Do you take the time to evaluate yourself after a presentation?

Do you combine marketing and sales with providing information for understanding of the project?

EXAMPLES

Monarch Bank

At Monarch Bank, the project leader was able to encourage one upper level manager to be a champion of the project. This worked for more than a year. Then that manager was transferred so that there was now a black hole in sponsorship. Through many hours of work, the project leader was able to get several other managers to act as sponsors. It would have been much easier had this been done at the start. When the next process improvement project was started, at least three managers were involved at all times.

TRAN

In this government agency, management communications was a continuing concern. Many different managers had to be kept in the communications loop. Within the business units it was necessary to also keep the various line managers of the departments informed on the project.

Stirling Manufacturing

In Stirling Manufacturing, the project managers had to cope with authority while the project was centralized and driven from the top. Academically, this might appear to pose no problems due to the existence of top management support. However, the projects were hampered by the lack of support from the divisions and groups.

In each case, the project managers succeeded with management only by showing the benefits of the projects to their own organizations. The lesson learned is that you must appeal to self-interest of management to gain their understanding, involvement, and support.

GUIDELINES

- **Positive management exposure leads to success in getting resources.**

   Only in theory do projects compete only for resources. In the real world they also compete for management attention. Work on getting management attention in order to get resources.

- **Telling management too early that a project is a success can lead to its failure.**

   Treat success as expected. Always caution that more milestones remain to be achieved. Exude a feeling and impression of cautious optimism. If people think that the project is a success, they let down their guard. When a problem later arises, it is a surprise and you find reduced support.

- **Align a project to management's self interest.**

   Always show how the project supports the self-interest of the organization and the managers. To do this, indicate the benefits that will accrue. Prepare tables of benefits and show how the project is aligned with the needs of management and of the organization.

- **Look at the worst that can happen in a project and then minimize its likelihood.**

   What is the worse that can happen in the project? Make a list of the top five items. These can range from lost resources to the disappearance of management support. Think about how you would respond if any of these occurred. This is not just contingency planning; it is also a way for you to practice problem-solving before you are in the heat of battle.

- **Keep the managers of team members informed of the status of the project.**

   Try a dry run of all of your presentations on the project team. This will solicit the input of team members, inform them of the "party line" on the project, and allow them to help in marketing the project.

- **Keep project information you present to a minimum.**

  Be very careful about the level of detail and amount of information you present. Do not present detail unless it addresses a specific issue. Avoid cumulative project statistics except for budget vs. actual and plan vs. schedule in general. Concentrate on short-term issues and project status in routine meetings.

- **Always plan to present in a period of five to ten minutes.**

  In a project presentation if you are told you have 20 minutes, assume that you will actually have 5-10 minutes to present the project. This will force you in planning to give attention to issues and decisions you need to have the audience consider. If you plan for 20 minutes, you may find yourself filling time with status information.

- **Summarize project status in one page.**

  Lengthy summaries will not be read. The purpose of giving project status is to inform and allow for understanding or decisions, or both. A single page containing schedule (summary GANTT chart), project spending and budget (a graph of budget vs. actual), issues, and key events will often suffice.

- **Include alternatives and implementation in a discussion of issues.**

  At the end of many advertisements is often some action for the consumer to perform, such as a making a telephone call. It is the same in project management. If you discuss an issue in a meeting without getting into alternatives or actions, it seems theoretical. People are not pressed to take action.

- **Be self-assured in presenting issues.**

  A project's external appearance reveals a great deal about the past and present issues within a project.

- **Maintain a low profile.**

  Lack of project visibility does not equate to project insignificance. A low profile has advantages, as discussed earlier in the chapter.

- **Read between the lines and determine what is going on through impressions, appearances, and symptoms.**

  Do not wait for a neon sign with a message from management. Figure out what is needed and initiate action.

- **Give team members due credit.**

  A person who takes all of the credit is eventually a one-person project team. If you take too much credit, managers will become doubtful of other things you say or write. The team effectiveness will diminish.

- **If you want to use humor, make jokes about yourself or your own project.**

  This shows that you have the ability to laugh at yourself. Making too many jokes at the expense of other projects can make your project a laughing stock.

- **Portray yourself as confident and knowledgeable about the project.**

  A leader's demeanor tells the management team far more than many project charts and graphs. If a leader appears beaten down or nervous, this will have a negative impact on managers. Also avoid saying "I don't know; I will follow up on that."

- **Keep content as a priority over presentation.**

  Concentrating on the format and style of the presentation while neglecting the content will lead to trouble. People who see the presentation may immediately become suspicious about the project. If problems exist, keep them out in the open. Note also that if you make a slick presentation with no problems, the same level of presentation will be expected in the future. Don't present and do work that you would not do on a regular basis.

- **Be ready to answer questions during a presentation—don't wait until the end.**

  Encourage questions at the start. When asked a question, repeat it in your own words to the audience. Then answer it. If you do not have an answer, write it down in front of the audience and get back to the audience and questioner.

- **Try to be placed in the middle of the agenda.**

  Being first on an agenda is not always an advantage. Yes, you get the audience when they are fresh. You also know you will have your assigned time. However, being in the middle or last has more significant advantages. You can compress your presentation. The audience will be more likely to remember your presentation, since it came later. However, if you are at the end, you do risk being bumped.

- **Remember your goal—to get approval.**

  People try to make a management presentation at a very high level. They want to make it appear strategic. But in fact, management sees many presentations, most of them probably poor. Many managers would rather be doing something else. So get to the point. Take a marketing-oriented approach. Your goal is to obtain approval, not applause.

- **Always be prepared to present the status of the project or discuss an issue with management.**

  Some people attempt to isolate project management from other duties, but this is impossible. At any time you may run into an upper level manager who asks about the status of the project or a specific issue. If you say that you will look into it, you convey the impression that you are not on top of the issue or project.

- **Always end with the default actions that will be taken.**

  You make a presentation and the managers say they will think about it. This is basically your fault because you did not end the meeting with closure. You left too many loose ends. Waiting for management approval is a common excuse for inaction. Instead, offer actions to be taken as you wrap up your presentation.

- **Debrief the project team after a presentation—or someone else will.**

  After a project presentation, hold an informal meeting with the project team. If you do not, word will filter back from other participants. Then you may spend much more time correcting false impressions. Schedule a project team meeting within 15 minutes after you get back from the first meeting.

ACTION ITEMS

1. Identify three or four key managers who are critical to the project in terms of their approval of major milestones. Develop a plan for how you could contact them informally at the start of the day.

2. Prepare yourself for the informal management contacts by making sure that you are aware of status and issues. Begin to update one of the managers. After doing this once a week for several weeks, expand your contacts to another manager. Every few weeks, add another manager.

3. Review your last formal presentation. What preparation in terms of contacts did you make? What efforts did you make to practice the presentation? What surprises arose during the presentation? How did the audience participate in the presentation?

CHAPTER 27

TRACKING AND ANALYZING PROJECT RESULTS AND STATUS

CONTENTS

27

TRACKING AND ANALYZING
PROJECT RESULTS AND STATUS

PURPOSE AND SCOPE

The purpose of this chapter is to help you be more effective and efficient as a project manager in the day-to-day work of directing the project. Good daily habits and an efficient work pattern are not intuitive; most managers have to learn them. The goal here is to teach you how to set up work patterns that will help you stay on top of the project. You should be able to administrate the project and still have sufficient time to address issues and opportunities and to communicate with management and staff. You will learn ways to be proactive, rather than merely reacting to events.

The scope of this chapter covers the day-to-day project management activities that you face. Specifically excluded are addressing issues, dealing with crises, and measuring the progress of the project. These topics are so significant that separate chapters are devoted to each one.

END PRODUCTS

The end products include the reporting and analysis of the process improvement effort. This encompasses normal reporting of status and progress as well as budgets. It also takes into account the presentation of issues and reporting on issues.

RESOURCES

The central resources are the project leaders of the improvement projects. However, in collaborative scheduling the team members will be updating tasks and addressing issues at the direction of the project managers.

APPROACH

Here is a list of tasks on which you will spend your time as a project manager.

Group I—Administrative Tasks

- Determining the status of the work
- Tracking the progress of the work
- Updating and maintaining the project plan and budget
- Carrying out administrative tasks (e.g., performance reviews, hiring, terminating)

Group II—Project Work Tasks

- Doing actual work in the project
- Motivating the staff
- Analyzing the project
- Meeting with and reporting to management
- Evaluating the quality of the work and milestones

The tasks in Group I concern overhead and administrative work. The activities in Group II tend to be proactive—you plunge in and do the specific tasks or take on the issue. Spend most of your time on the tasks in Group II, as these move the project ahead. In contrast, reactive tasks in managing a project occur when you fail to track the project adequately. Then a problem occurs and you must react. By the time you have addressed that problem, another surfaces. You are always behind.

The more proactive work you do, the more you tend to be aware of what is going on in the project. The more reactive work you do, the less you are in control of the project and the more events control you. Assume some manager greeted you in the hallway and asked, "How is the project going?" Could you respond with detailed information? If not, concentrate more on the tasks in Group II to work towards better control of the project.

Note that project control, as people commonly define it, includes some items from both groups.

To track where you are spending your time, at the end of each day write down the rough percentage of time you spent in both groups. After you have done this for several weeks, determine whether any patterns exist based on the day of the week or the time of the month. Work toward increasing your time in Group II activities.

DETERMINING THE STATUS OF THE WORK

The basic objectives are to know what is going on in the project and to know where the project is going. Tracking projects allows you to resolve issues early and to take advantage of opportunities. A project can be tracked from different perspectives:

- **Project team**   The levels of morale and work satisfaction color the perspectives of team members.
- **End user of the project**   This perspective looks at the products that result from the project.
- **General management**   The priorities are costs and schedules.
- **Line management**   Line management is concerned with the use of their resources in your project.

In collaborative project management, the project team members track progress and alert the project manager of any problems or issues arising in their tasks. This is much more effective than the traditional approach, in which the project manager was left to ferret out the problems and status alone. To ascertain status, go to each team member and ask how the work is going. This will yield status information. If you ask directly for a status report, you may get a rosy, unrealistic view as the team member tells you what he or she thinks you want to hear.

TRACKING THE PROGRESS OF THE WORK

The first goal in tracking is to understand what is going on. Once you understand a situation, you can think about decisions and actions. When you are trying to understand what is going on, you often stumble upon targets of opportunity. This occurs when a team member mentions an idea for a small change or improvement. This often costs nothing and does not involve any high-level management action. When this occurs, take action and implement it right away.

Here are several approaches to tracking work:

- **Track all work and tasks in the project with the same level of detail and effort.**

  This appears fair and makes some sense when you first consider it. However, it is not a very intelligent use of your time given that it does not take into account the stages of various issues or the timing and duration of tasks.

- **Track work based on the mathematical critical path.**

  This is a traditional approach focusing mainly on the critical path tasks. These are tasks that happen mathematically to fall on the longest path. The problem with this approach is that it is not sensitive to risk and uncertainty. Also, it is not sensitive to time. Logically, you should spend more time on tasks that are in the near future.

- **Track work based on the managerial critical path.**

  The managerial critical path is a set of paths in the project plan that contains tasks that have substantial risk. How do you know which tasks these are? Look at the existence of issues and problems associated with tasks, as well as the uncertainty inherent in the tasks. Using this approach, start with the tasks that are happening now that have risk and expand to those that have risk in the next two months. Then extend your examination to all of the tasks on the mathematical critical path that carry risk.

The third approach is favored since it is most reasonable in terms of the resources available and it is centered on minimizing risk.

How should you track routine tasks? In collaborative scheduling, you want the team members to participate and let you know what is going on one-on-one. Also, randomly check on some routine tasks.

Collecting Information

The first step in tracking work is to collect the following information:

- **Information from team members**

  You want to track what is going on with each team member, individually. Drop by each team member's office. Why not have them come to your office? You don't interfere with their work as much by visiting them. Also, when you visit others, you can see what they are working on. This is useful in tracking people who are part of the project's core team.

  During the visit, encourage team members to talk about their tasks in their own words. Take notes yourself and don't use forms. Don't use checklists or task lists and go down each list. These approaches are all too formal and may lead to answers of "okay" or "so-so" that aren't helpful. Prepare for these meetings by reviewing the tasks and issues each team member is working on. After the meeting, return to your office and prepare the team member's part of the status report.

- **Information from observation**

  Observe what is going on in the project firsthand. This is very important, since you can use this to update the tasks that are active in the project. Observation does not help in updating the estimates for future tasks, but it can tell you what is going on now.

- **Information from meetings**

  You attend many meetings on the project and with management. At the end of each meeting, ask if there was anything discussed in the meeting that has bearing on your schedule. Did you learn anything that will have an impact on resources? Do you foresee changes in methods and tools?

Work should be tracked continuously. In the past, if status or progress reports were due monthly, people would collect data on status and do tracking just before the end of the month. After the presentation of status, tracking would become a low priority until the end of the next month. A better approach is to be aware of what is going on all of the time because situations in projects can change rapidly. Continuous tracking will allow you to understand what is going on at all times.

Along with continuous tracking, update your schedule and plan as you get the information, at least twice a week. A daily update is not necessary, as this requires too much effort for what it gives you.

Problems in Tracking

Management Wants Frequent and Detailed Reports

This may occur because of problems within the project. It can also be due to a faulty project reporting and control process. Project control should be sensitive to the size, type, risk, and importance of a project. It is also dependent on the stage or phase of the project. For example, management would want more information during critical stages of construction.

How do you cope with this? Start with increasing informal contacts to let management know what is going on. This will provide management with more information. Next, propose a summary reporting process that can replace the existing detailed reports. Prepare the information yourself. Don't shift the burden to others on the team, since this can lower productivity and morale.

You Inherit a Poorly Run Improvement Project

It has been assumed until now that you have been the project leader from the beginning. What if you are taking over a project in trouble? Your initial actions upon takeover should pertain to tracking. Here is a sequence of actions in project takeover:

1. Determine the status of the project and assess the team. Don't ask for more resources or money yet. Find out what is going on in the project. In finding out the status, you can assess the project team members in terms of their productivity.

2. Conduct analysis of the project to determine what could be done to improve project performance and results. Follow the steps for analysis given in this chapter.

3. Assess the current open issues and see if you can make some quick progress on some of these.

4. Develop a new project plan and approach and present it informally to management. Indicate what can be done with limited incremental resources.

5. Implement changes as soon as approval is given. Implement a more formal project reporting process. Management is giving

you more resources. Reciprocate by giving management additional information on their investment.

You Have to Deal with False Information

False information on the project can originate inside or outside the project. The damage it causes can be extensive. Your time may be consumed dealing with problems that are perceived but not real. This reduces both productivity and morale. Management may get the wrong impression about the project and institute countermeasures without asking you. This can be a major issue in that a new layer of management may be created.

To prevent this problem from occurring, first, keep your ear to the ground and determine what is being said about the project. Second, draw in the project team to do the same and to support you. Third, stay in informal contact with managers you can trust to get early warning signs of problems.

You Lack Technical Knowledge

You are managing a project in which you lack technical knowledge. What do you do? You will obviously make an attempt at trying to learn the technical words and concepts. However, you will still lack detailed hands-on experience. Identify several informal technical advisors who can help you in reviewing plans, assessing milestones, and determining how methods and tools are being employed.

UPDATING AND MAINTAINING THE PROJECT PLAN AND BUDGET

If you are using a standard project management software package, here are the actions for updating the project plan and budget:

1. Update the current schedule bottom up.

That is, go to the most detailed level of tasks and update these. Mark the relevant tasks that are complete; change the duration, resources, dependencies, and dates where necessary. If you are doing collaborative scheduling in which the team accesses the schedule, then set a deadline for the update. Review the update.

2. **Move into the future and enter new task detail in the schedule.**

You may actually change the structure of the schedule based on your knowledge now.

3. **After making changes to the detail, set the actual schedule.**

This will recompute the critical path and overall schedule.

4. **Go to the databases that you have established for issues and action items.**

Update these as well, based on status.

At this point you are prepared to analyze the schedule. Note that the approach we have suggested focuses on doing routine work and no analysis. Give attention to the detailed tasks in updating. Keep analysis separate from updating.

CARRYING OUT ADMINISTRATIVE TASKS

A project manager performs many mundane but significant tasks. These include performance evaluations for team members, recruiting and interviewing potential new team members, dealing with personnel problems on the team, checking up on the timekeeping and human resources of the team, and monitoring vacation time and sick time. Administrative duties also include maintaining project files, determining training needs, and reviewing what other projects are doing. These are important duties. However, control the amount of time spent on them. Plan when you will do administrative work and group these duties into one portion of the workday. For example, try devoting the early morning hours several days a week and see if this is enough time to handle the work involved.

MOTIVATING THE STAFF

Some project leaders either downplay this or pay it lip service. They assume that getting a paycheck is sufficient motivation. Or, they may get people together and give a motivational talk.

Here are some better ideas on motivation:

- When gathering status on the project from team members, show not only a sincere interest in their work, but also try to see what you can do to help them.

- Group motivation should be done through addressing issues and paying the team overall compliments. Group motivation has its drawbacks. First, if you do it often, it loses impact. Second, diligent workers may feel slighted when you compliment a group of people in which some members slacked off.

- Follow up on suggestions by the team members concerning improvements or problems. Give them credit for their suggestions.

- Compliment people who raise many problems—the more the better. Hiding problems or not taking action is a recipe for disaster.

ANALYZING THE PROJECT

Divide the analysis into specific actions. A guideline here is to divide the update and the analysis. Do the update and the analysis at different times, because they require different skills.

Action 1: Validate the schedule.

Review the milestones, dates, and summary tasks of the schedule to see if they make sense. If events suddenly shift, check to see if you left out a dependency or missed some tasks. Use the project management software to determine completeness of the tasks and the impact of change.

Action 2: Assess the mathematical and managerial critical paths.

You want to determine how these paths have changed. If a task has become critical, why did this happen? If the path is longer due to greater detailed task durations, this indicates slippage in the work. Is the path length due to more information on the work that increased the number of detailed tasks? This is a common occurrence and not unexpected.

You might lower or raise the risk when you update the task, depending on the issues. Lower the risk for the task if the issue has abated or been addressed. Raise the risk if the task has grown in importance, if there are new issues and if the assumptions made about the task are no longer valid.

Action 3: Compare the planned and actual schedules.

Use tables and GANTT charts that compare the actual and planned schedules. To analyze them, go back to the start of the project and work forward in time. Consider where the schedule first began to slip. Then move ahead to note areas where slippage increases. Start with a high level outline form of the project and then step down into more detail. Figure 27-1 gives an actual vs. planned GANTT chart.

Action 4: Do actual vs. planned cost analysis.

Create a spreadsheet using project management software. You can produce a table in most project management software packages that gives the planned or actual work performed by resource (rows) over time (columns). This table can be exported to the spreadsheet. With both the planned and actual work exported, you can compare the results in terms of hours.

To do cost analysis, use the spreadsheet to convert work into money considering regular pay, overtime, and other cost factors. Figure 27-2 gives a cumulative actual vs. budget analysis. Note that in this example the actual cumulative expense lagged behind the planned expense for some time. At the current time this project is now over budget in terms of cumulative costs.

Action 5: Analyze variations.

If you have found variations, why did they occur? The obvious reason is that the task dates and durations slipped. A second reason is that more information is reflected in changes in schedules and dependencies. Third, you may have added more tasks and detail that can impact the overall schedule through a rollup to summary tasks. Fourth, you may have restructured the tasks in the schedule.

Figure 27-1
Actual vs. Planned GANTT Chart

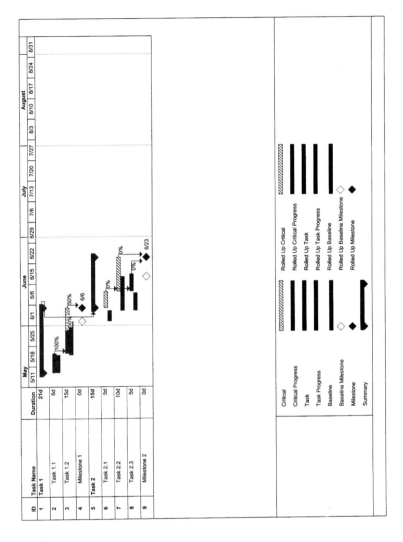

Figure 27-2: Cumulative Budget vs. Actual Expenses

In this diagram the actual cumulative expenses are shown in the dotted line. As you can see the project started more slowly than was budgeted. This is not unusual. Then it exceeded the budget amount, probably in an effort to acceleterate the project. Finally, spending tapered off.

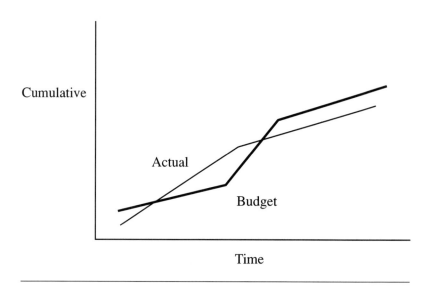

Cumulative

Actual

Budget

Time

Action 6: Perform a "What if . . .?" analysis.

At the end of the actual analysis, analyze the impact of shifting resources, adding resources, changing project structure, or deleting resources. See what happens if you shake things up. This can lead to some interesting ideas for project change.

Perform Financial Analysis

You will want to review the actual expenditures by area. Set aside time to do this analysis on a regular basis. Take the reports you are provided by accounting and review these in light of the plan. Here are questions you should ask:

- Have part-time people working on the project been charging too many hours to the project? Relate the part-time people to the tasks that they are performing to formulate your answer.

- Are the facilities use and equipment charges valid? Go back to purchase orders and the plan for your information.

- Is the overhead and burden assigned to the project excessive?

If possible, maintain your own spreadsheet for budget items. If you hold yourself accountable to maintain numbers, you are more likely to have the discipline for the analysis of the data as well.

Common Analysis Problems

The above questions are inductive in that they proceed from validation to consideration of variations. Analysis can also be inductive when your analysis is based on an issue. Here are three examples:

- **Problem 1: The schedule is standing still, but you know that the work and progress are going well.**

  Probably tasks are missing from the schedule. When these are added to the schedule, the schedule will likely show slippage. Yet, when you post actual results, this should be fixed.

- **Problem 2: The work is showing limited progress, but the schedule shows even less progress.**

  The schedule probably does not reflect dependencies or work correctly.

- **Problem 3: The number of issues is growing. Not all the issues are getting addressed. However, the schedule is remaining unchanged.**

  You have not reflected the issues in the dates of future tasks. Allow for these additional issues and recognize that, when these are factored in, the future tasks will slip, causing the overall schedule to slip.

EVALUATING THE QUALITY OF THE WORK AND MILESTONES

What is quality? What is acceptable quality? To answer these questions will require effort and definition for each milestone. Checking out the quality of dozens of milestones is not practical, requiring time and resources. Here are some alternatives for evaluating milestones.

- Level 0. Do no review.
- Level 1. Determine if there is evidence of a milestone. This is verification of presence, not content.
- Level 2: Perform a quick check by evaluating only a few items related to the milestone or work.
- Level 3: Conduct a full milestone or work review.

When work is routine and you trust the people involved, impose level 0. Many key milestones will deserve at least a level 2. Few will justify a level 3 review. You can escalate a review from one level to a higher level if you sense problems.

What is involved in a full-scale review? Three setup tasks begin the process:

1. Determine who has knowledge of the project, technology, and situation to be involved in the review. Involving people in a review means time lost from working on your project or other projects, so enter into the review process judiciously.

2. Set the time for the review and try to manage it in such a way that it causes a minimum of disruption to the project.

3. Define the scope of the review. What will be included and excluded? For example, will only quality be reviewed or will the review include the way that the methods and tools are employed?

With the setup tasks accomplished, move to the review itself. Make a checklist of items:

- Materials that will be supplied before the review
- Materials and documents during the review
- People, equipment, and facilities access required for the review

Divide the review into two parts. The first part consists of an overall assessment by the review team with feedback as to the level of detail for the review and the areas of the project milestone or work for review. The second part consists of the actual review.

After the review of a milestone or work, implement the results as soon as possible. This may mean changing the project plan. It may mean resource shifting or change. It can also be a time of getting charged up again in the project. If the results of the review are favorable, the team's efforts are reinforced. If the results are recommended changes, you can tout success based on the changes and lessons learned.

MANAGEMENT PRESENTATION AND COST-BENEFIT ANALYSIS

A major guideline is to meet often informally with management to keep them up-to-date and to garner support. These meetings should be short so that the overall percentage of time spent with management is actually small. Most of the contact should be in informal meetings, rather than in formal presentations. More formal presentations indicate either that the project is becoming more exciting or the project is in more trouble.

Effective Status Reports

Here are three ways to provide status to management:

- Status report based on work and progress. This tends to be a reporting method that focuses on accomplishments. The detailed work and milestones accomplished are enumerated.
- Status report based on issues. This report identifies the various issues still open and their priorities. It also highlights the issues that were resolved.
- Combined status report based on both work and issues.

To ensure consistency across many projects, adopt a standard reporting method, preferably the combined approach.

You will want to provide both quantitative and qualitative information to management at the same time. The form in Figure 27-3 provides a reasonable summary sheet for a general project.

The sections of the report are as follows:

- Title, identification, and purpose. This provides some basic information to identify the project.

- Summary GANTT chart. This is a summary high level GANTT chart that provides status.

- Cumulative budget vs. actual chart. See Figure 27-2.

- Summary of issues. This area provides highlights of active issues.

- Milestones and accomplishments. This section addresses achievements.

- Anticipated activity in the next period. This section describes what is likely to occur in the next period.

KEY QUESTIONS

To what extent are you on top of the project? Are you aware of what is going on in the project today? If you had to walk over to the project team and go to the most critical area of the project, where would you go?

Where do you spend your time? How much time is spent in the interactive, more productive work in the project? Have you attempted to spend more time here? What is preventing you from spending more time in these tasks?

Have you adequately delegated the tracking of the project and work to people on the team? Have you adopted a more collaborative tracking approach?

What milestones and work have you recently reviewed? Was the right information available? Were the correct people involved in the review? What results and actions flowed from the results of the review?

Do you find it easy to relate the issues and action items in the project with the project schedule? Have you identified the areas of risk in the schedule?

Figure 27-3: Example of Summary Sheet for a Project

Project Summary Sheet

Project Name: _____ Date: _____

Project Manager: _____

Purpose of Project: _____

_____

Summary GANTT Chart	Cumulative Budget vs. Actual

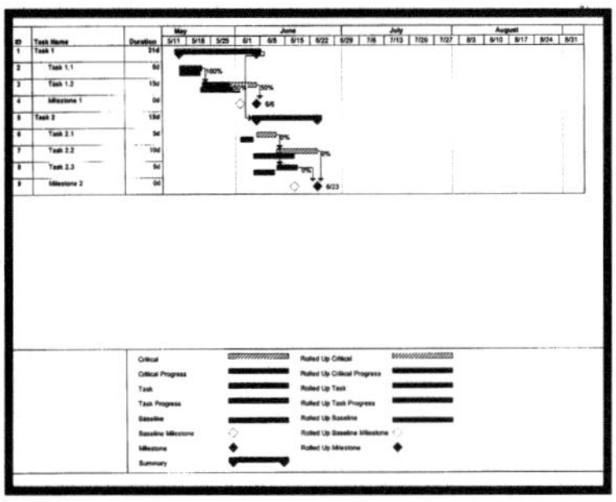

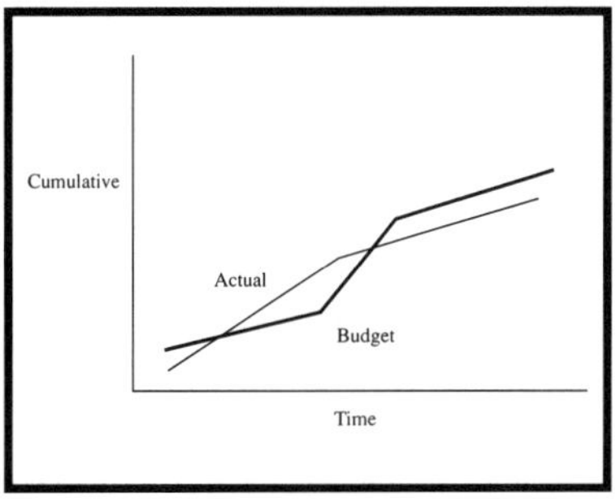

Results/Milestones Achieved in Last Period: _____

_____

Critical Issues: _____

_____

Anticipated Results/Milestones: _____

_____

EXAMPLES

Stirling Manufacturing

The project leader at Stirling Manufacturing quickly saw that the project could not be tracked by one person. It was spread out over too large an area. Moreover, the project leader lacked a detailed network technology background. Managers for regions of several countries were identified as subproject leaders. Even with this change, it was necessary to spend time interpreting the information provided.

GUIDELINES

- **Consider what omens mean and what pattern they imply.**

  As in real life, omens can appear for projects. These can be problems or successes with methods and tools, people, or other resources, for example. Rather than just tactically responding to these, look for a pattern so that you can be proactive in dealing with problems.

- **Take stock of the project when you are too tired to do other kinds of work.**

  When you are tired, you may not want to deal with the project anymore. This is a good time to sit back and review the project overall.

- **Allow ample time to do project analysis before a meeting.**

  Last-minute work on a project before a meeting can result in more chaos than benefit. Use the time right before a meeting to review what you have done before and get focused on issues. Project analysis time should be open-ended and not subject to pressure.

- **Distribute project knowledge throughout the project team.**

  People sometimes associate control of a project with knowledge about the project. For this reason, some project managers attempt to keep knowledge to themselves, believing this will allow them more control. In a modern collaborative environment, this is clearly out of place. Control and knowledge are related, but project knowledge should be distributed throughout the project team.

- **To gain wisdom, sit back and look at a project.**

  A project manager who is constantly working on detailed administrative or issue work loses the benefits of considering the overall picture. Gaining perspective and an understanding of what is going on in the big picture are two valuable aspects of taking time to take a step back.

- **Do project analysis yourself.**

  Do not depend on others to do your work in analysis. First, when this person is not available, you are helpless. Second, in meetings you will be unable to respond to questions related to the analysis. Unless you do it yourself, you are remote.

- **Suspect trouble and check up on the situation if people do not inform you of the progress of particular project tasks.**

  People who are achieving results are usually happy with what they are doing. They are likely to relate their success to you. On the other hand, if you hear nothing, you have a right to suspect trouble.

- **Retain project history so that you are not doomed to repeat mistakes.**

  If a project goes on for a year or more, similar issues and questions will crop up numerous times. Knowing how previous problems were addressed will help you now. Also, note that some issues will recur in different clothes. This may occur with someone who lost out on an issue, for example.

- **Make use of statistical analysis of project data.**

  Project statistics usually abound and are there for the taking. These statistics are often boring to work with and overlooked, but they are most useful. If you do not analyze the data, you will wake up to unpleasant trends too late. With the availability of more statistical tools in spreadsheets and other software, statistics are getting easier to work with.

- **Track and compare multiple schedules for a set of tasks.**

  In many settings, several projects compete for the same people, supplies, facilities, or equipment. You also may want to learn from previous, similar projects. Yet if the schedules and resources are not compatible, it will be impossible to make any meaningful comparison. What a term or task means to one person may mean something different to someone else. Work out a system which allows for comparison.

- **Look for the real project bottlenecks.**

You have been taught that the project bottlenecks can be found on the critical path. It seems logical that if you can shorten or rearrange the work, the bottleneck will disappear. The reality isn't this simple. You are watching the critical path, but problems arise from a task off the critical path. This occurs because the critical path does not include risk and uncertainty; it includes only length and duration. Real project bottlenecks cannot be detected easily by looking for the red line on the GANTT chart. How can you prevent bottlenecks? Go through the schedule and label tasks according to risk. Then filter or flag these tasks. Consider how close these are to the critical path. Continue to keep a close watch on those with the least slack.

- **Allow for a difference between resource allocation and resource usage.**

Resource allocation is the assignment of resources. Resource usage is the consumption of resources according to specific schedules and calendars. These may not match, for several reasons. The resources are allocated at the level of higher level tasks but are consumed at the level of more detailed tasks. Also, the overhead associated with a resource is often not factored into resource allocation. For example, you may allocate someone for six months to a project. However, the team member is on vacation for two weeks and in training for another two weeks. Allocation and consumption would be different.

- **Add tasks related to error fixing and rework at a detailed level.**

The inability to cope with the need to rework in a project affects likelihood of eventual success. Many people just extend a task duration to reflect fixing errors or rework. This does not convey what is happening and creates communications problems. Instead, add in the actual tasks that have extended the duration of the task. If you allow the task to be slipped, you lose history and accountability later.

- **Examine project boundaries periodically.**

  During the duration of a project, the nature and boundaries of a project can change. As a project leader, you should examine the project boundaries as part of your "What if . . .?" analysis.

- **Manage a project for long-term payoff.**

  Patterns of work behavior, relationships between people, and experience with methods and tools often long outlive the original project. Side effects of a project may long outlive the project impact. Keep the long-term view in mind throughout the life of the project.

- **When you see a problem coming, give warning.**

  Do missed deadlines have penalties? For example, you deliver a milestone a month late. In many cases, the project grinds on. Maybe no one will say anything. But you lose credibility when you don't see a problem coming and take some ameliorative action.

- **Determine deadlines by need rather than playing games with deadlines.**

  A middle level manager wants to look good. This manager imposes unrealistic deadlines on the project. If the project team can make it, this will reflect favorably on the manager. This sounds fine, but this will only work once or twice, if at all. People become wise to this strategy and start to give dates more conservatively to compensate.

- **Manage tasks that have risk as well as those that are easier to handle.**

  Balance your time between different project management tasks. If you devote too much of your time to tasks that are comfortable, you will not be coping with the tasks that have risk in the project.

- **Assign as many cheap solutions and resources as possible.**

  Depend as much as possible on simple, cheap resources. You will be pleasantly surprised to see the benefits from the expenditure of a small sum.

ACTION ITEMS

1. Using the list of Group I and Group II activities in this chapter, list how much of an average week is spent in each activity. Make a list for several project managers around you, also.

2. Evaluate your technique for assessing milestones in your project or the process in a project with which you are familiar. Should you adopt a more formal process in evaluating milestones and work?

3. Review your update and analysis process for your project. How well is it organized? Have you divided updating activities from analysis? Does the analysis that you do get translated into actions and schedule changes?

CHAPTER 28

COLLABORATIVE
SCHEDULING AND WORK

CONTENTS

28

COLLABORATIVE
SCHEDULING AND WORK

PURPOSE AND SCOPE

The obvious goal is to achieve the objectives of the improvement project within budget and schedule constraints using a collaborative project management approach. This definition of purpose should be expanded to include the interests of the organizations and individuals participating in the project.

The scope of the project is defined. However, the roles and responsibilities of the project team are more broad than that of the traditional project manager, as seen in the previous list of the duties of the project team members.

END PRODUCTS

While there are no specific end products in terms of reports and presentations, the end product you seek is an information sharing environment in the process improvement project. This is the true sign of information sharing and collaboration.

RESOURCES

Collaboration in a process improvement project means that everyone on the team is involved. Each member of the team participates in scheduling and communications. You must motivate the team to participate in this. Give them opportunities within the team for participation.

APPROACH

Process improvement projects represent a challenge because of factors such as the following:

- The culture and interests differ among team members and companies.
- Many individuals assigned to the project have normal, non-project duties that they cannot give up for the project; dividing their time among project and non-project work is a major challenge.
- Different companies may employ a variety of IT methods and tools which do not easily support integration and lead to incompatibilities.
- Projects have hidden dependencies that are revealed only later in the project at critical times.
- The goals of the project may not be relevant to many of the team members.

At the heart of these issues is the problem that the project leader does not have total authority over members of the project team.

Collaborative Management

Here are some key ingredients of a collaborative management approach:

- Each person on the team is responsible for identifying detailed tasks, updating tasks, addressing issues associated with their tasks, and participating in joint project work.
- A substantial percentage of the project work is assigned to more than one person. In some cases, 30 to 40 percent of the tasks are joint among two or three people.
- The project manager shares all project information except the really political elements with the team.
- Project leaders share information amongst themselves. This includes schedules, issues, and lessons learned.

- Project leaders work together and with line managers in assigning people and other resources to tasks on a routine basis (typically weekly).

What are some of the benefits of a collaborative approach?

- People working together and sharing information tend to trust each other more. They grow closer together.
- Working on issues together helps to build skills of the people in the project.
- The project is more likely to end successfully on time and within budget.
- A ready forum is available in which to gather lessons learned.

Action 1: Define the Project Concept and Identify Other Work

The activities are intended to build a common vision of the objectives and scope of the project, identify all of the things that team members are doing, and explore issues in the project identified in the project concept. In addition, you will be defining together how the project will help each person on the team.

Review the Project Objectives and Scope

Go over the objectives and scope of the project with each team member individually. Show how the team member's self-interest is aligned to the objectives of the project. Also show each team member how he or she fits into the project.

After you have met with each person, assemble the project team. To avoid a rehash of what you did with each person, go into the alternative purposes and scope that were considered in the project concept definition. Also, look at the project from several alternative perspectives. These include the following:

- **Business perspective**

  Show how the project is contributing to the organization. This will help reinforce the feeling that each team member is making a contribution.

- **Technology perspective**

  Look at the project from the view of the methods and tools that will be employed in the project. Show that the project is employing modern techniques and that these techniques are well established.

- **Management perspective**

  Explore the management controls and reporting that will be done in the project.

As you are doing this, you can indicate why each person was chosen for the team and each person's role in the project.

In this first action you are also defining the benefits of the project for the team members. In the past, little attention was paid to individual team members and what team members would get out of the project. Yet, this is extremely important when working with team members because your project is competing for their attention with their other work. A prime strategy is to appeal to self-interest. Here are some things to do:

- Have each team member give you a resume when he or she joins the project.
- Have each team member identify career goals and objectives for the next five years.
- Have each team member create a new resume that they would like to have after five years.
- Based on previous collaborative actions, work with each team member to identify tangible things that they will learn and do as well as the knowledge they will obtain from the project.
- Now have each team member create a resume that would represent work at the end of the project.
- Identify issues and barriers to achieving these personal goals.
- Make these issues generic and add them to the list of issues in the project.

Build a Limited Project Plan for Each Team Member

At the team meeting, indicate that you are sensitive to the fact that most, if not all, of the team members also have line responsibilities as well as work on other projects. Visit each person to determine what he or she is working on and what the schedule is. Try to obtain a copy of the project plans for other project work. Give as the reason for this the fact that you must build an overall project plan that reflects the realities of the availability of the project team members.

It is useful to build a small plan for each person with his or her other work. Each task the person performs in a line organization would be one task in this plan. You would also have the person's tasks in other projects in a summary level.

With this done you have a project plan for each team member. When you construct the schedule for the project, you can combine it with these other plans and then filter on each resource to see the total commitment for each person on the team. You will be able to see points in time when people are overcommitted. Then you can plan and negotiate for people's time more effectively.

Negotiate with Line Managers and Other Project Leaders

Work with each manager to define a set of near-term priorities for each key team member. Next, focus on the short term of two to three months. If you negotiate for work beyond that, conditions and situations may change.

Besides accomplishing the setting of priorities with these other managers, this step provides two other major benefits. The first is that you are establishing a collaborative environment for sharing resources with them prior to any crisis or major issue. This helps to build a pattern of successful relationships. Second, you are sharing information with them. You want to build upon this relationship to share schedules and future need information far enough in the future to support planning.

Define Issues Together

The issues are particularly important here because you want to use discussions of these as tools to build a common approach for working on problems and opportunities. Here are some guidelines:

- Do homework on several issues and introduce these to the group.

- Consider as issues the following:

  —People on the team have other duties and responsibilities. How can they be effective on the project?

  —The project may be of importance to the organization overall, but it is of marginal interest to some in the team. How will this be addressed?

- As you discuss each issue, summarize how people are to work together.
- Identify how people should report on their project work.
- Identify how people will define their own work.

You can design a template to identify what the upcoming step is in terms of defining the project. Include detailed tasks for each team member and schedule when the team members are to report on these tasks.

Action 2: Develop an Improvement Project Plan Using a Collaborative Approach

Build or Evaluate a Project Template

Do you have an available project template for this project? If not, define a strawman, candidate template for the team members to review. Recall that the template contains high level milestones and tasks. For each task in the template, identify the team member who will responsible. Also, identify which tasks are going to have joint responsibility. It is useful to have 30 to 40 percent of the tasks jointly assigned to foster teamwork. You should also validate the template by evaluating the issues in the project that surfaced in the previous step. Find the summary task in the template to which each issue corresponds. You can also scan down the tasks to see if you and the team have missed any issues.

Once you have a template, meet with each person on the team and indicate that person's areas of the project. Get each person to think about detailed tasks and relate the issues from the previous step to the tasks that they are responsible for.

Go Through a Simulation of Building the Detailed Plan and Updating the Plan

This is an important part of the project since it basically links the work on issues with the initial meeting on purpose and scope. At this meeting, take one area of the plan and act as a team member in defining the tasks in the template. Progress from defining tasks to completing the baseline schedule for the work. Next, explain how the tasks will be updated by the team member responsible for them.

Construct the Detailed Tasks for the Project for the Next Three Months

Each team member can now define the tasks needed to accomplish work that is to be done in the next three months. It is very important that you have identified tasks that are to be jointly performed by team members. Encourage team members to work together to define these tasks in more detail.

Each template task should be broken down into tasks that are not more than two weeks in duration. If you go over two weeks, the task is too fuzzy. If the task is too short, the effort requiring updating will be too great.

Here are some additional guidelines in defining tasks:

- Each task should be able to be defined as a simple sentence starting with an action verb. An example is "Prepare ground for planting trees." If you find that a task has complex wording such as "Dig up ground, fertilize, and water for trees," then split up this task into three separate tasks: dig up, fertilize, and water.

- Have each team member associate issues with the detailed tasks under the relevant template task for the issue. This further helps to validate the tasks and issues.

- Each team member should identify tasks that have risk or seem risky. This will give rise to additional issues or validate the existing issues.

- Schedule meetings with team members to discuss their joint tasks together with you.

Making task definition a distinct step, apart from schedules, dependencies, and resources, will give a more complete task list and prevents team members from getting distracted by other facets of the project.

Establish Dependencies and Assign Resources

After reviewing the tasks, have the team members put in the minimum number of simple tail to head dependencies. If they are in doubt about a particular dependency, leave it out. They can discuss it later. This may indicate that you are missing a task.

In this action each team member will identify critical resources of any type that are a cost to the project or that the project will have to compete for with other projects and normal work.

In reviewing the work in this action, start with the dependencies. Ask team members why the dependency was created. This will lead to a discussion about the surrounding tasks. The net effect of this is to not only validate the tasks and dependencies, but also to get a better understanding of how the work is to be done. The same is true with assigning resources to tasks.

Define the Duration and Dates Based on Previous Actions and the Previous Step

With the tasks, dependencies, and resources defined, each team member can now estimate the dates and duration's for each task. Give some examples to team members so that they have a better awareness of the approach. Here are some guidelines to help the team members:

- Do not pad the dates for contingencies. Put in realistic estimates.

- If you cannot estimate for a specific task, break up the task until you have isolated the part that you cannot estimate. There is probably an issue here that is the reason an estimate cannot be given.

Review each person's work with him or her when you have received all input from team members. By waiting until you have all inputs, you can see the schedule overall.

It is likely that the schedule will not be realistic. It will stretch too long. Don't attack the group by saying that the schedule is not acceptable. Rather, identify where the specific parts of the schedule are in trouble. Go to the person involved on an individual basis and get at the assumptions behind the estimates. If you are lucky, you will find that assumptions have been made that caused the schedule to be longer but that were not necessary.

After reviewing the schedule, you can set the baseline plan and hold a project team meeting to review it. At this meeting, hand out the schedule along with a list of issues and a mapping between issues and tasks. The purpose of this meeting is for the team members to gain a better understanding of the work as well as to focus on near-term risky tasks as a team.

Action 3: Build Collaborative Teamwork through the Initial Tasks

Work now begins on the project. Circulate a printout of the schedule for the next three months. Have the team members mark tasks that have been completed. Add new tasks that were unanticipated or that apply to the future time horizon. If a task has slipped, have the team members create a new task and link it to the current task, also giving a reason for doing so. By repeating this several times, a person gets used to the process of schedule updating. You can then have a team member do the updating online in the network.

There may be a lack of knowledge of project management software on the part of the team members. Don't wait until the people are trained on the software to begin the collaborative approach. Implement manually with paper to get the process of collaboration going.

This will take more time initially but rushing this learning phase of collaboration will be counterproductive.

Address Initial Issues

Early on, establish a pattern for addressing issues. Identify some sample issues that are relatively minor and non-political. Get people in a group and start analyzing the issues. After some discussion, show the team how decisions are made and actions are taken. You can also indicate how the plan is updated as a result of deciding the issue.

As the improvement project gets underway, ask for the reaction of the team to the process. Have team members share their views and suggestions on making the process better. This is a bottom up approach to implement collaboration and one that has often worked. This approach establishes a pattern for dealing with issues in a friendly and non-hostile setting. You can scale up the issues to address those that are more significant.

When you do this with a team, you are accomplishing several goals. First, you are showing the team members that they can solve problems on their own without management. Second, they gain confidence their ability to get things done as a group. Third, you are paving the way for more serious issues to be handled, based upon the pattern of success.

Conduct a Review of Initial Milestones

Review the work of the team members and milestones reached. Also, give attention early in the project to tasks that slipped. You are trying to determine a pattern for the slippage. This is done not to punish a team member but to determine now whether estimates for later tasks need to be revised. Try to get team members to the point of feeling comfortable in dealing with milestone reviews of each other's work. Another goal is to position team members to review each other's work, both positively and negatively. Team members will be able to see that people make errors without incurring punishment.

Action 4: Monitor and Manage the Project from a Collaborative View

This step considers some of the most common situations you will face in managing projects collaboratively.

Exit of a Team Member

Prepare the team to address this situation before it arises. At the project kick-off, point out that team members will come and go. Turnover is inevitable. Have the team members identify and discuss issues associated with someone leaving. Some of these are as follows:

- The departing person takes knowledge with them.
- It is difficult to capture all of the knowledge before a person leaves the team.
- The work of the departing team member falls on the shoulders of the people remaining.

The exit of a team member brings not only problems but also benefits and opportunities. First, by the time someone leaves, progress has been made in the project. Work has been started and the person may not be critical to the project anymore. When someone leaves, it gives the team a chance to find a replacement with different skills that are needed for future tasks.

Transitioning between Project Phases

Longer and larger projects are typically divided into phases. Each phase often has a formal ending prior to the start of the next phase. How can a project leader take advantage of this for the project? First, the project leader can gather the team members together and gather lessons learned about what went on in the project. It is better to do this at the ends of phases than to wait until the end of the project. The knowledge will probably be lost then due to the elapsed time. Also, identifying the knowledge and getting agreement from the team builds teamwork and consensus.

Dealing with a Major Issue in a Collaborative Way

It is likely that the team will face a major crisis or issue in the project. For many of the most difficult situations, you have to rely on upper management for resolution and support. For other problems, have the team work together to address the crisis. The collaborative effort on the part of the team can help the project leader focus on potential actions and decisions.

Changing Project Direction

A project can change direction due to management action, external factors, or events in other related projects. The project leader should prepare the team for eventual changes in direction early in the project to avoid problems later. For example, the leader might propose several changes in direction based on detailed knowledge of the project. This allows the team to work with a reasonable hypothesis of change.

Action 5: Bring New Team Members into a Collaborative Environment

To bring a new team member into the project, include the following actions in a one-on-one session:

- Walk through the purpose, scope, issues, benefits, and other elements of the project concept.
- Indicate the history of the project and what changes occurred during the project and why.
- With this broad overview, review each team member and what their expertise is and what they do.
- Indicate how the new member will work with the existing team members.
- Review the issues with the new team member.

Next, introduce the team member to the project team. First state the new member's expertise and then explain how this person fits within the project. Indicate areas of joint work involving this new member and others. Have the new team member give some experience and lessons learned from previous projects.

Finally, set up and monitor the new team member's initial work. Each new team member should be assigned both individual and teamwork tasks. This will allow the new team member to experience a team approach.

MANAGEMENT PRESENTATION AND COST-BENEFIT ANALYSIS

While there are no management presentations, there are opportunities for presentations within the improvement team. These presentations by team members to each other on aspects of the project. The result is feedback and collaboration. You gain more interest and enthusiasm.

If you don't adopt a collaborative approach in process improvement projects, then you incur the high cost of putting the load on the project leaders. The energy of the project leaders is diverted away from productive tasks. The team is not motivated to participate. Team members feel detached. Remember that team members are doing other work, too. If the process improvement project is managed the same way as every other project, the benefit of differentiation is lost and team members will lose their motivation to work on the improvement project.

KEY QUESTIONS

Do you have an approach for doing work in a collaborative environment? Notice that the word *work* was used and not *projects*. It is helpful to have a pattern of joint work habits.

How are projects managed that involve several divisions of your company? How are division-specific issues and problems addressed?

How are projects managed that involve outside consultants and contractors? Do the consultants have any role in defining the tasks and work? Who evaluates the milestones?

EXAMPLES

Monarch Bank

The project manager fostered a collaborative atmosphere for the team from the start. This continued for years of process improvement. Morale remained high despite setbacks and crises.

TRAN

TRAN was not used to a collaborative environment. Rather, the project started as a standard project with the project leader setting and tracking the tasks. This did not work. People on the team set higher priorities on their normal work. With some coaching and trying out collaboration, a pattern of collaborative behavior was set.

Stirling Manufacturing

Due to the size of the project, it was impossible for collaboration to extend across all players in the project cast. The approach was to have extensive collaboration among members of the core team.

International Bank Credit Card

An international bank wanted to implement new processes for credit card products across Southeast Asia and Australia. They decided to base the project in Singapore. A core team was appointed. All of the team members were based in Singapore. The banking organizations in each country were separately and individually accountable for their financial results. Bonuses and other rewards were based upon performance.

The project groups in all of the countries were told to participate by management. The management in each country assigned to the project junior staff members who had little bank knowledge. At the kickoff meeting in Singapore, attendees were told about the project and given the project plan. The plan for each country was basically the same. There was no recognition of the different cultures in the region. The team members were given no opportunity to provide input to the plan or to identify the issues of their individual markets.

What should have been a successful project turned into a nightmare. Staff members returned to their countries and went back to their own work. They generally felt isolated from the project. The project team tried to direct and dictate the project effort. The project failed after three months for the following reasons:

- Management of the bank operations in other countries fought the project and pushed for other projects that were more closely aligned to their profit goals.
- The core project team became demoralized because of the lack of cooperation.

The bank had no choice. It had to roll out credit cards to be competitive. Having learned the lesson of failure, the bank decided to try again. The approach employed was a collaborative one with a steering committee composed of business managers in each country.

The project plan was created in a collaborative manner. The team members jointly developed the tasks as well as issues. Special attention was directed to cultural differences and the individual competitive situations in each country. This project was completed three months ahead of schedule.

GUIDELINES

- **As the complexity of the project grows, the benefits of collaboration grow.**

  The projects most unsuitable for collaboration are those that are small and short and performed in one location. For very large projects there must be a practical partitioning of the work among organizations and collaboration occurs at upper levels between groups.

- **Surround people who resist with people who participate and endorse collaborative scheduling.**

- **Work with the other managers to set priorities.**

  People are sometimes pulled off the team to do other work not related to the project. If you and other managers have jointly set goals, this problem will be less likely to occur.

ACTION ITEMS

1. Identify potential opportunities for collaborative work outside of projects. On projects, try to have about 30 percent of the project tasks assigned to several people. Select a small project with several organizations involved and build a collaborative team. As the project goes on, attempt to gather lessons learned to improve your techniques for the next project.

2. Examine your organization in terms of past collaborative efforts. This helps to see how ready an organization is for information openness and sharing.

CHAPTER 29

MANAGING PROJECT ISSUES

CONTENTS

29

MANAGING PROJECT ISSUES

PURPOSE AND SCOPE

The purpose of this chapter is to help you manage and direct the outcome of single and multiple process improvement issues. An issue is something that must be addressed; otherwise, progress may slow and the improvement project may deteriorate. An issue can be a problem or an opportunity (positive or negative). It can relate to something within the team or to technical, managerial, and political situations. How and when issues are handled impacts the project schedule and the plan. If not addressed, an issue can blossom into a full-fledged crisis. In process improvement at any given time there are often many unresolved issues. Issues can remain unresolved for political reasons, because that part of the improvement project is further down the road, or for many other reasons.

You will be provided with guidance on identification, analysis, decision-making, and implementation of solutions.

The scope includes all of these activities, across the entire project.

END PRODUCTS

Keep the following list of end products in mind.

- Identification of process improvement issues
- Tracking of the issues during process improvement
- Process improvement issue resolution through decisions and actions
- Follow up after actions have been taken on issues

Each of these end products is interrelated to the others. In process improvement, you do not necessarily want to solve issues the minute they arise. Many process improvement issues have various nuances and facets. If you address the issue too soon, you may be attacking a symptom and not the underlying problem.

RESOURCES

The first thought that occurs to many people is that the only resource involved in issues management is the project manager. However, for process improvement to be successful, you must gain consensus and agreement from management and employees regarding changes, problems, and opportunities. The cast of characters in dealing with process improvement issues tends to be much broader than in standard projects.

APPROACH

A systematic approach is efficient in addressing issues. Through analysis of multiple issues, you will be able to address families or sets of issues. You also will be more effective in dealing with management.

At any time in a project, active issues may or may not be interdependent. Most process improvement project problems and slippage can be traced to specific issues. Issue management tests the range of a project manager's capabilities far more than project control or project administration. Required skills include identifying an issue, collecting data, performing analysis, developing alternatives for resolution, obtaining concurrence on the solution, selling the solution, and implementing the solution.

Table 29-1 contains a list of issues that you might encounter in a substantial project. The list has been drawn from projects tackled over the years. The potential impact of each issue is indicated.

How to Spot Potential Problems

These questions apply to opportunities as well as to problems. For each question, rate an issue on a positive or negative scale from -3 to $+4$, where positive numbers indicate benefits and negative numbers are disadvantages. The rating 0 means no impact. When finished, you can generate a bar chart such as that in Figure 29-1. Two examples for the manufacturing company are given in Figures 29-2 and 29-3.

Table 29-1: List of Sample Issues

ISSUES	POTENTIAL PROBLEMS
Project restructuring	Parallel effort and reduced project time
Loss of key a person from the project	Slowing of the schedule
Team morale drop	Reduced productivity
Line manager opposition	Road blocks to decisions
Falling behind schedule	Milestones slippage
Expanding scope	Milestones slippage
Competition for money and resources	Slowing of the schedule
New regulatory changes	Changes in nature of the project work
Conflict over work assignments	Lost productivity and low morale

- What is the urgency of the issue to the project?

- Are other organizations affected by the issue?

- Which business processes are impacted by the issue? To what extent? Include here procedures and policies for the process.

- How does the issue relate to the systems and technology in place?

- Does the issue have any impact on the company overall? For example, are many side effects generated by a decision on the issue?

- Is there any fallout from the issue on the customers and suppliers?

- What is the impact of the issue on the infrastructure (buildings, office layout, parking, telephones, etc.)?

- What is the effect of the issue on other projects?

Determine to leave the low priority issues alone unless they are grouped with a high priority issue. At the construction firm, it was decided that work would be performed only on issues with ratings of −2, −3, and +3. These are the most severe issues in terms of either benefits or costs. The other issues were put on hold until they grew more beneficial or were grouped with an important issue.

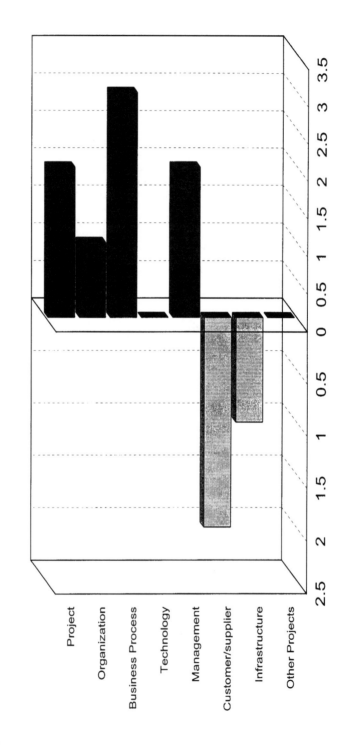

Figure 29-1: Sample Rating of Issue

Figure 29-2: Radon
Control of Vendor Work

In this example, the issue has a negative effect. The project, infrastructure, and technology are affected the least.

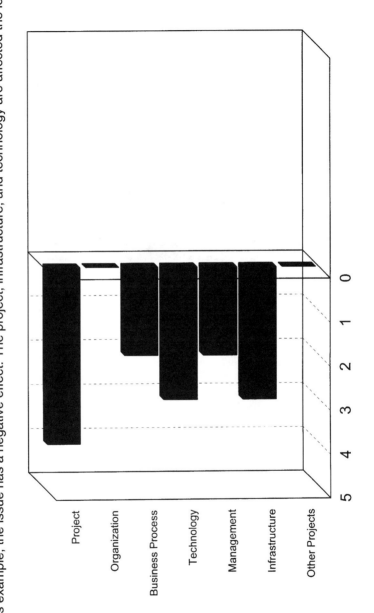

Figure 29-3: Radon
Potential Faster Network Devices

In this example, there are clear benefits to faster local area network links.
However, acquisition of the technology could impact the project schedule.

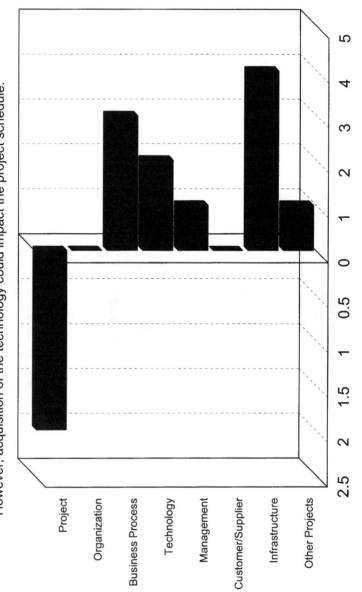

How an Issue Becomes a Crisis

When an issue surfaces, you are faced with several choices. If you adopt the wrong approach, you could make the issue worse. Just calling attention to the issue can be harmful. For example, suppose that you notice that the project is falling behind schedule. You could react by telling everyone that "We must all do more work to catch up." This may instill panic. People on the team may react by slowing down. Another reaction is to recruit a number of new team members. They have to be brought up to speed. This takes people away from productive work. Coordination and decision-making are slowed down. The issue grows into a crisis.

The Issues Database

Seek an organized approach when tracking process improvement issues. A data base is useful and requires minimal effort. Both data base management systems and groupware can support an issues database. Another alternative is to use paper. However, generating the reports and doing analysis will require more intensive manual work. Since process improvement projects tend to generate many issues, it is no surprise that the companies in the established a standardized available system on a network.

Having each project manager spend time developing databases that are not compatible with other project managers' work is not the best use of time and effort. You want standardization across all projects.

Here is a list of data elements to employ:

- **Identifier of the issue**

  Use a separate code for each issue.

- **Status of the issue**

  Based on where the issue is in the life cycle, sample codes might include the following:

  I—identified

  A—assigned and being analyzed

  AD—awaiting decision and resolution after analysis

  R—resolved

F—followed up on

RE—replaced by another issue

T— terminated or eliminated

- **Priority level of the issue**

  Define several levels of priority:

  A—extremely important in that the project is impacted within days if not resolved

  B—the project will be impacted in weeks if not resolved

  C—impact is marginal on the organization and project

- **Organization impacted**

  This is the major organization affected by the issue.

- **Date the issue was created**

  This is the date the issue formally begins to be tracked.

- **Description**

  This is a summary description of the issue.

- **Impact of the issue if not resolved**

  This field identifies the effects of not addressing the issue.

- **Related tasks**

  These are the tasks (by number) in the schedule that are impacted by the issue.

- **Related issues**

  This includes how the listed issues are related.

- **Person assigned to the issue**

- **Date of expected resolution**

- **Resolution code**

  Examples:

  R—replaced by another issue

  D—decided

  S—shelved indefinitely

  T—terminated

- **Decision on the issue**

  This is a statement of the decision made.

- **Actions**

  These are the actions that flowed from the decisions made.

- **Comments**

  This field is for free-form comments on the issue.

  Typically, each issue is associated with a series of events or actions. An event log would have the following elements:

  - Identifier of the issue
  - Event number—A unique number assigned to the event
  - Event date
  - Person recording the event—May be different from the person responsible
  - Type of event—Meeting, telephone call, fax, and e-mail
  - Result of the event
  - Comments

The event log links to the issues data base using the identifier of the issue. The index to ensure uniqueness is a combination of the identifier and the event number. How would you use these files? Set these up as data bases on a file server. The information can be accessed by the project team members. Access to update the log could be controlled.

Use the data base to summarize issues for a project. A sample rating is in Figure 29-4.

Across multiple projects you can integrate information by the following criteria:

- **Priority of the issue**

  This can isolate all high-priority issues so that management can address the entire set of issues on an organized basis.

- **Organization**

  This can indicate the extent to which issues are impacting specific organizations.

- **Families of issues**

  By clustering by families of related issues, you can attempt to deal with groups of issues as opposed to single issues.

Figure 29-4: Example of Issues Report for One Project

Priority: High

Type of Issue	Date Opened	Issue ID	Issue	Status Closed	Date	Resolution
Work	3/1/97	005	Ability to track work performed remotely.	Open		
Technology	4/1/97	008	Decide on network card	Closed	5/15/97	100 Mbps Ether net card

This table is from the Radon example. It assumes that the person who receives the report is familiar with the issue so that a description is not necessary. The report is first sorted by priority. The other sorts are by type of issue and date opened.

You can also analyze the issues by aging analysis. That is, you can develop a histogram of open issues over time. Consider Figure 29-5. There are lines for the total number of issues for all projects and for the number of high-priority issues.

Common Mistakes in Addressing Issues

Over time, we have identified eight recurring problems or failures in addressing issues. Let's discuss each of these in terms of how it can happen and the impact:

Figure 29-5: Open Issue Graphs

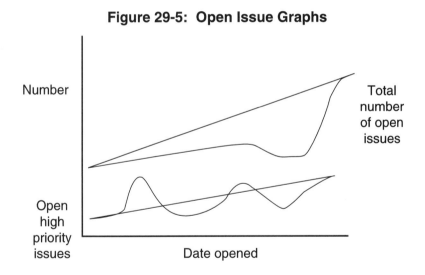

The purpose of these graphs is to draw attention to open issues that were opened long ago. These are the aged, high priority issues. The total number of open issues graph is typical in that overall it is the most recent issues that are unresolved. The other graph of open, high priority issues is troubling. It shows two humps of issues that are aged. This means that there are substantial old and high priority issues remaining.

- **Being unaware of the issue**

  If you keep too narrow a focus, you will find that you are missing details. You will be missing signs and symptoms of problems. Instead, be constantly on the lookout for more issues.

- **Misdiagnosing the issue**

  Once you have identified the issue, a common error is to plunge in and attempt to address the issue without analysis. Misdiagnosis of the issue is likely. Then you either make the issue worse or lose credibility as a manager.

- **Not selling the decision to management**

  After the issue is identified and the analysis performed, a decision is made and seems logical. If the project manager jumps in to act on the decision without selling it to management, problems may occur. Actions taken as a result of the decision can affect resources, costs, and the schedule. If management wasn't consulted, the bill for these extra costs may be a shock. Failure to market the decision to management opens the door to attacks on the decision as well.

- **Making decisions without planned action**

  A decision is announced. Everyone who hears it asks, "What does it mean?" The answer is "nothing," unless the decision is followed by action. Some people seem to think that they can announce a decision and then wait for weeks to take action. As time passes, the credibility of the decision is questioned. When the action finally comes, the situation may have changed, making the decision inappropriate.

- **Acting without the framework of a decision**

  Another problem occurs with project leaders who are action-oriented. They move from their assessment of the problem to immediate action. This is fine in a true emergency. However, this can be deadly. First, the actions will appear as chaotic without the framework of a decision. Second, the actions will probably be incomplete, requiring additional actions. These may contradict or overlap the previous actions.

- **Failing to act when you should**

  Some people cannot decide when to act. While many favor a conservative approach, action must be taken immediately after the decision is announced.

- **Acting when you should wait**

  This is a common mistake with new project managers. They make decisions and take action on the spot.

- **Taking actions that are inconsistent with decisions made**

  This occurs because people do not think through whether the actions support the decisions.

Seven steps to address process improvement issues are given to ensure that these problems will not happen to you.

Action 1: Recognize the Process Improvement Issue

It often starts with a question or offhand comment. "What's happening with Harry?" is a question leading to a personnel issue. "I heard you won't need that piece of equipment by the first of the month after all." This can imply that the project is behind schedule. A verbal message may be the first symptom of an issue.

Respond by answering the following questions:

- **Does the symptom relate to a current active issue?**

  Is it just another symptom of a known problem? If so, employ this information to gain a better understanding of the current issue with which it is associated.

- **Can the symptom be grouped with anything else going on?**

  You can group by organization, technology, management, customer, and supplier. If you see no such connection, wait to raise the issue.

- **What are the characteristics of the issue?**

  At this point, define the issue. Use the database of issues and fill in the elements. A form is included in Figure 29-6.

- **What priority should be assigned to the issue?**

  Set priorities by urgency of the project. Do not use other criteria, such as benefits to the organization or management, since mixing criteria complicates decisions on priority.

- **What should be done with the issue initially?**

  Discuss it with the project team to collect ideas and to see who has the most interest in the issue. Assign the issue to someone

Figure 29-6: Sample Issue Form

Issue Management Form

ID: _____ Name: _____ Priority: _____

Title: _____

Description: _____

_____

_____

Impacts if not addressed: _____

_____

Assigned to: _____ Date assigned: _____

Issue Activity

Status	Date	Who Entered	Action/Result

Date Resolved: _____ How Resolved: _____

Comments: _____

_____

who cares about it. Giving an issue to someone who dislikes the subject will result in it getting little attention.

Action 2: Analyze the Improvement Issue

Use a combination of direct observation, interviews, review of documents, and meetings to collect the information for the analysis. In collecting the information, don't draw attention to the issue. Instead, talk about symptoms and impact. If you zero in on the issue, people may expect too much in terms of resolution. Also, by tagging the issue too early, everyone accepts the preliminary definition, which may be in error.

Start with the person who proposed the improvement and collect as much information as you can. Find out how the project team and the work can be affected, as well as the end products of the project.

Categorize the issue for the data base, using the topics and information earlier in this chapter. Next, draw up the following table. This table allows for different interpretations of the issue (from conservative or minimal to radical). Obtain different views from the various members of the project team and others. For each interpretation, list the symptoms of the issue in one column, the impact of the issue in another column, and the principal dimensions of the issue, based on the interpretation, in the last column. An example is shown in Figure 29-7.

Interpretation	Symptoms	Impact	Dimensions

Now focus on the effects and benefits of the issue on the project itself. Construct another bar chart, using the following categories. An example is given in Figure 29-8.

Figure 29-7: Example of Categorization of Issue for Radon Control of Vendor Work

Interpretation	Symptoms	Impact	Dimensions
Lack of control over vendor	Excessive invoices; invoices for unapproved work	Cost overruns; schedule slippage	Accounting and financial controls
Weak project management	Lack of direction to vendor	Lose control of project	Project management
Weak central management	This is only one example of weak controls	Decentralized organization undermines any central initiatives	General management

Figure 29-8: Radon Example
Distribute Project Authority to Regions

In this chart, there are potential negative effects for the work, commonality of tools, and more complex project management. On the other hand, the schedule might improve. Quality with local oversight will improve. Other projects are not impacted. The cost and resources might be less using local resources

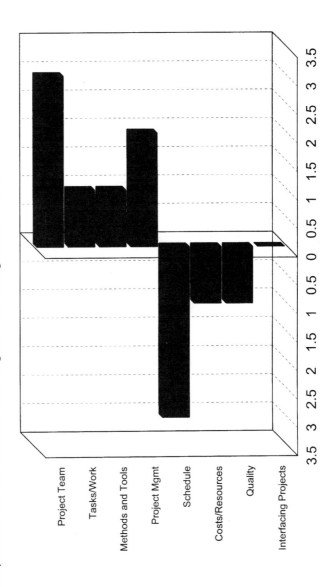

You can also use the following perspectives to analyze the project:

- Project team
- Tasks and work performed
- Methods and tools employed in the project
- Project management and control
- Schedule of the project
- Costs and resources required
- Quality and nature of end products and milestones
- Interfacing projects

Action 3: Define Alternative Decisions for the Improvement Issues

As you perform an analysis, also define alternatives for decisions. Consider the following suggestions or actions and estimate the effects that will accrue to the project, organization, or team.

Alternative 1: Do nothing.

This is the alternative to adopt most often. Wait and let the issue mature. As it does, the impact of the issue will become more evident. Note that even if you do not take action, you continue to track the issue; you still treat the issue as valid.

Alternative 2: Restructure the improvement project with no new resources.

This alternative helps you see what you can do with the resources you have. It forces creative thinking in organizing the work.

Alternative 3: Apply resources to the issue without regard to cost.

If you consider applying resources to the issue in virtually unlimited amounts, you can see the limits of what can be bought. This is an important alternative because it reveals the true limitations of resources. When you apply additional resources, you actually slow the project, since there is more coordination involved in the handling of the resources (bringing people on board and setting up equipment, for example). Always be ready to answer the question, "What could you do with additional resources?"

Alternative 4: Reassign resources within the process improvement project team.

This alternative is often useful for personnel problems and conflicts within the project team. Consider setting up subproject teams of different people to see if that works. This alternative tests your knowledge of the project team and also defines the limits of their flexibility.

Alternative 5: Remove resources from the improvement project.

This could be applied to personnel issues. It could also be considered after a major phase of work in the project is finished, when you are trying to downsize.

Alternative 6: Expand the scope and/or purpose of the improvement project.

The issue may be very important to the project. However, taking the issue on in the project will lead to the scope or objectives of the project being expanded. If this is a possibility, consider an overall strategic change in the project to address more than the one issue. If you let the scope expand naturally to handle the issue, you are likely to run into schedule problems and resource shortages as you scramble to address the expanded scope or purpose.

Alternative 7: Reduce the scope and/or purpose of the improvement project.

This is the flip side of the previous alternative. If you encounter a major obstacle, you may wish to avoid direct confrontation with the cause. Instead, you might consider downsizing the project and avoiding the problem. This is not cowardly, since with success you can often later return and expand the scope.

Alternative 8: Treat the issue outside of the improvement project.

Under this alternative, you are attempting to insulate the project from the issue. You will attempt to address it away from the project.

Alternative 9: Change the mix of methods and tools in the improvement project.

Look for a better way to do the work, using better or different methods and tools. The trade-off against the potential benefit is that there is a learning curve for the new approaches.

Action 4: Make Decisions

After considering alternatives, think through each in terms of defining the potential actions that will flow in support of the decision. Employ the following table to analyze the situation further before making a decision.

1. Issues Addressed	2. Alternative Decisions	3. Actions	4. Effects	5. Risks

Select different issues to address (column 1). For each, identify several alternative decisions (column 2). For each decision, identify actions that will implement the decisions (column 3). What would be the likely effects of the actions on the issues? This is column 4. These effects are not guaranteed, which leads to column 5, in which risk is identified. This approach will allow you to resolve incidents of conflict in resources.

The actions typically involve politics, changes in the plan, and resource actions. After you select the decision and identify the actions, inform management of the issue and the recommended approach.

Action 5: Announce the Decision and Actions

Announce the decisions and the actions at the same time. Complete paperwork on the actions prior to the announcement. This strategy will let people know that you are serious. Also, benefits will begin earlier and people will be more likely to be supportive.

Action 6: Take Action

Take all actions at the same time. Change the project team, resources, plan, and scope all at once. If you attempt to do it sequentially, you will end up having a mixture of old and new for some period of time. You want to establish an entirely new mindset. This is another reason for considering bundles or groups of issues at one time.

Action 7: Follow Up on the Actions

The results of the actions and decisions should be seen quickly after implementation for most issues. In follow up, ask several questions:

- Did the issue get addressed or were only symptoms treated?
- Are side effects of the actions and decisions creating new issues?
- Do additional areas exist in which one can apply the same actions and decisions to handle even more issues with little more effort?

Managing Groups of Issues

Typically, you have to address many improvement issues. They are in different stages of being identified and addressed. How can you more effectively manage groups of issues?

Here are some guidelines for considering multiple issues.

- View all of the open issues at one time and compare the mix of issues now with that of months ago. Do you see some lingering issues? Has the number of important issues increased? Has the average time to resolve an issue increased?

- If you devoted a solid day to working on issues, what could you accomplish? What things get in the way of resolving the issues?

- Do you know the status of the issues? How effective is your tracking?

MANAGEMENT PRESENTATION AND COST-BENEFIT ANALYSIS

Presenting issues to management in process improvement projects must be done carefully. Most of the communications should be carried out informally and not in formal meetings. Formal meetings inhibit the discussion of sensitive political issues. During a series of informal contacts, you can raise the symptoms of an issue to alert the manager first. Then in successive contacts you can elevate the urgency and need for action in a measured and organized way. Managers often will appreciate this approach because you are protecting them from being blindsided by another manager who asks about a specific issue.

Leaving an issue unresolved over an extended period can be costly to the process improvement project. It can weigh down morale and halt progress on the project. So while there is a cost in implementing a more formal approach to issues management, it is more than offset by the management benefits of an organized, structured approach.

KEY QUESTIONS

How good are your abilities in each of the following areas?

- Identifying issues
- Determining the ramifications and impact of issues
- Deciding on the issues and timing of announcements
- Defining the action items to be taken

Does the organization have a standardized issue management approach?

Does the organization have standardized software for issue management?

What escalation process is employed for issue resolution?

Are decisions clearly separated from actions? Are actions linked to decisions?

Do you know how many issues are open and closed in a specific project?

Do you know which issues have the highest priority

What is the age of the oldest outstanding issue?

EXAMPLES

Monarch Bank

Due to the lack of experience of the project manager, no standardized approach for dealing with process improvement issues was initially employed. This had very negative results on the project. Without a formal method, the same issues kept surfacing. Just when an issue was apparently resolved, the person who lost on the issue would resurface the issue in a different way. Another problem was that actions and decisions were not followed up on. This led to some crucial actions not being taken or being done incorrectly.

After several months, the problem was corrected with the implementation of the formal issues approach in this chapter. There was also a side benefit to the process improvement project. The overall management of the improvement project became more formal and structured at higher levels—benefiting the overall project.

TRAN

A modification of the approach presented in this chapter was used at TRAN. Because there were so many issues that were active at most times, it was felt that tracking all of the issues was not possible while still doing the work in the project. The approach that was taken was to have regular meetings to decide on the top ten issues and opportunities. These then were tracked and managed. At each of these meetings, the status of the existing issues was reviewed and updated.

Stirling Manufacturing

The leader at Stirling Manufacturing thought that issues could be handled as they arose. This worked for the first ten or so issues. Then things became more complex. The elapsed time to resolve an issue dragged out and more issues were active at the same time. People would call with status reports on issues. The names and titles of the issues were very similar since they all involved the network. This created more confusion and return calls. To compound the situation, management wanted to have information on specific topics. Reviews of these requests indicated that they were tied to the issues.

After the issues database and formal approach to issues management were implemented, the situation improved somewhat. However, the project leader was the only one doing the entry and tracking. The problem was that the issues management function was not made into a collaborative effort with the field project leaders.

GUIDELINES

- **Deal with political problems in a project to avoid project collapse.**

  Political issues in a project can undermine morale. If several are allowed to fester and multiply, the situations will feed off of each other and get worse.

- **Consider large and small issues together.**

  Patience in a project includes not jumping on easy issues. It is a real temptation to resolve simpler issues quickly. Everyone feels good that something is getting accomplished. This is a false sense of security. If the bigger issues require resolution that undoes what you just announced, your credibility is lost and you have to start over. This is another reason to consider issues in groups.

- **Determine the relationship between issues.**

  A few underlying causes can generate many seemingly independent issues and many more symptoms. What can happen is that several issues or causes of issues join hands and begin to cause impact across the project. Group issues by the areas of the project such as the resources used, the organization involved, or the method being used. Take action on a group of issues, if possible.

- **Reward people (including yourself) for identifying issues.**

  This motivates you and others to be on the watch for new issues. It can be overdone if people just complain. However, if the focus is on finding issues or suggesting improvements, the complaints have a positive effect.

- **Know which issues are constraints.**

  A constraint is something that you cannot change. What issues do you accept as constraints and which do you address? This is a key decision, since it determines how the issue is interpreted.

  Look at a stand-alone issue as a constraint. A stand-alone issue is rare and exists in a vacuum. No other issues are involved. Whatever action is taken will impact only that issue.

- **Decide whether an issue is secondary or artificial.**

  For every real issue, a project may have 5 to 10 artificial issues. When symptoms of problems appear, you may fix a symptom only to see another appear if you failed to pinpoint the real issue. Before you treat symptoms, decide if the issue represented is artificial or secondary.

- **Analyze the underlying source and concern behind the issue.**

  What is behind the issue is almost more important than the issue itself. The issue may be just one manifestation of an underlying problem. Understanding the cause of the issue can lead you to discover whether additional issues stem from the same cause.

- **Know when something is out of scope to keep a project on schedule.**

  Many issues relate to parts of the project that are not within the original scope of the project. When one of these comes up, the team and leader cannot deal with it quickly since it is beyond what was originally in the project. Test the scope with each issue.

- **Delegate the task of researching issues and follow up in tracking.**

  It is impossible for you to follow up on every issue. You must delegate. To be successful, track how the follow-up is going and how the issue has changed or has been transformed through further analysis.

- **With issues involving outside vendors, prevent one vendor from criticizing another.**

  This is not an unusual practice. Be aware that it can happen and point this out to each vendor prior to a meeting. During the meeting, if a vendor is not present, try to mitigate any criticism of the vendor and turn the conversation into action steps regarding the issue.

- **Address basic project issues to prevent the project team from working on less important, though visible, work.**

  During a project, management issues can emerge. Usually no emergency exists for most issues. However, if the elapsed time without resolution continues to grow, the team may get the impression that management does not care or is not interested in the project. The team may think that the issue is not important. This can lead to a lack of confidence among team members. The team members may work on tasks that are not impacted by the issue. If the issue is important, the tasks related to the issue are usually important.

- **Test the degree of flexibility in a plan gradually rather than precipitously.**

  Changes in a project occur over time. Change tests flexibility. Change is often generated by the solution and resolution of issues, so change depends on how issues are sorted out. Each time you resolve an issue, you may change the plan, testing the flexibility.

- **Accompany changes in project leaders with a change in project scope.**

  When you make the major change of replacing a leader, consider other changes, including project scope.

- **Take time to gain an overall perspective after setbacks on issues.**

  You cannot expect to win on every issue. What do you do when you lose? Take an overall perspective on what just happened. You will gain a more general view of the situation and gather lessons learned for the future.

- **Resolve political issues to prevent polarization of a project team.**

  Political issues that remain unresolved can begin to split the project team. Work to resolve these issues and prevent the team from working against itself.

ACTION ITEMS

1. For a project that you are working on, identify several issues (both open and closed). Determine the step that each is currently in. Next, assess how effectively each issue was addressed in previous steps.

2. Try applying the alternative decisions that were identified in the issues in Question 1. What did you learn about the issues after doing this that you did not know before?

3. Look back at several attempts to address issues. Were the benefits and effects as anticipated?

CHAPTER 30

OVERCOMING PROJECT CRISES

CONTENTS

30

OVERCOMING PROJECT CRISES

INTRODUCTION

The word "crisis" may sound ominous. However, a crisis can be viewed as an opportunity. It is a chance to gain management attention, to get decisions made and implemented, and to redirect the project. In process improvement projects, a crisis can be employed as a trigger to change the organization. In other words, use the crisis to address a number of political, organizational, policy/procedural, and technical issues at one time.

PURPOSE AND SCOPE

The purpose of this chapter is to provide techniques to address crisis situations so that not only is the crisis resolved, but also the crisis is resolved to the advantage of the team, the organization, and the project.

More specifically, the goals are as follows:

- To help you sort through the perception of a crisis vs. a real crisis
- To provide tips on how to analyze and assess a situation
- To support you in using a crisis to the advantage of the project

The scope of this chapter includes situations such as technical problems, organizational upheaval, project leader change, and major team changes, as well as more classical budget and schedule crises.

END PRODUCTS

The obvious end product is the favorable resolution of the issues that provoked the crisis. However, from a management perspective you want more than this. You want to set a pattern and process for resolving crises in the future. It should, hopefully, become easier to deal with issues and crises.

RESOURCES

Beyond yourself, you will end up involving upper level managers as you work the issues that led to the crisis. In process improvement, you might have a crisis in that some of the senior old time staff may resist changes in workflow. Even with your best efforts, you are not getting through. With the clock ticking you must escalate it to the level of a crisis to get management attention. Here you will involve upper management, senior department management in the department that is changing, and managers from related departments.

APPROACH

A crisis is a culmination of events that forces the project management, and organization to deal with issues. Thus, when issues become critical, you have a crisis.

Crisis is a matter of perspective. Issues typically become critical to the project team first, then they escalate and progress through the organization. When does an issue become a crisis? This is subject to interpretation. Some of the major factors affecting whether an issue has become critical are the following:

- Current state of the issue
- Rate of decay of the situation
- Increase in impact in the project or organization
- Age of the issue—how long it has been active

A crisis in a project is a situation that requires rapid decisions and actions. If action is not taken and the crisis is real, the situation worsens, impacting the cost, the schedule, the quality, or some key attribute of the project.

What can you do about a crisis? You can understand and solve it. You can also guide and orchestrate it. You can play a role in defining the timing and presentation of a crisis, affecting the media surrounding the issue. That is, a crisis is open to interpretation.

The basic strategy in dealing with a crisis is as follows:

- You can affect and impact how a crisis is handled and resolved. Therefore, be proactive.
- A crisis can be employed as a tool to carry out fundamental change.

A significant point to keep in mind is the difference between perceived and actual crisis. In a project it is important to act upon perceived crises as well as actual crises. Otherwise, if people perceive a major problem and you do nothing as a project manager, you and the project lose. You can use the perception of a crisis to achieve a breakthrough in the project in terms of resources or other factors.

If you announce that some situation or issue is a crisis, you have to back up your statement. If, on the other hand, you begin to point out that the impact of an issue is getting bigger, and risk and danger are growing, people get the impression of urgency without the word crisis. That is the preferred strategy. Save the term *crisis* for true emergencies.

When people see a project crisis, it is usually because they perceive an impact on their organization, the project, the project team, or some project resource. This perception can stem from internal as well as external factors. Thus, you must consider how these perceptions arise, how to determine if the crisis is real, what to do about it, and how to implement decisions.

Over the years, it has been found that certain projects are prone to crises. Here are some examples:

- The project is large or involves many people. This makes the project more visible and subject to misinterpretations and rumors.
- The project is political. Reengineering projects are typical here. Enemies of the project create crises based on some event.
- The project involves outside entities or external factors that can affect the project. An example is a project to remodel retail stores. The success of the project is subject to trends in industry and technology, as well as to what competitors are doing.

- The project extends over long periods of time and is exposed to many different factors.

Crisis Assessment

Symptoms are visible signs of the crisis. They may or may not be related to the actual causes. When you are sick and go to a doctor, the doctor is trained to observe the symptoms as a means of diagnosing the cause. Treatment is applied once the cause has been found. In the last few decades, doctors have been taught to listen more carefully to patients and to spend more time analyzing the symptoms, as opposed to rushing to diagnosis and treatment. This technique also applies to projects. Spend a generous amount of time assessing the symptoms. If the manager is remote from the project, symptoms typically surface as part of a review.

Here are some common symptoms of crisis:

- A lack of decision-making or only partial decisions are made
- Attempts to leave the project team
- Overrunning the project budget
- A lack of enthusiasm for the project
- Unresolved important issues
- Excessive calm as people try to ignore the crisis
- Excessive excitement as people address the crisis

These and other symptoms are usually visible if you are on the project team. However, the team members may be so accustomed to the symptoms that they do not even notice them after awhile, especially if the symptoms are not visible outside of the project. Other major sources that may alert you to a crisis are management and someone outside the project.

Predicting a Crisis

Many times you can predict a crisis. Although a crisis can appear suddenly it is more likely due to the impact of an unresolved issue that grew. You may be aware of the situation and issue. You may have pointed it out to management but nothing was done._For example, the schedule may reach a critical point and the project begins to fall behind. However, critical resources are not approved for the project. Eventually, a schedule crisis results. Because you predicted the crisis, you would have been able to prepare for it early.

Here are some guidelines in making a valid prediction:

- Take a broad perspective over time. This allows you to see what has been accomplished in the project, the rate of progress, and trends in the project.
- Look at how long important issues have remained unresolved.
- Observe how the project manager and the team have dealt with previous situations.
- Think of other projects in the past that are similar to this project.

An exercise at the end of the chapter asks you to take a project and define potential crises. It is important for you to sit down at least once a month and assess potential crises in your project. Then attempt to figure out what countermeasures you would take.

Causes of Crisis

Once you understand the symptoms of the situation, you can begin to sort out causes. Usually some combination of factors contributes to most crises.

Here are categories of causes of a crisis:

- **Political**

  Someone or a group is out to sabotage the project. The group may not even care about your project; people may just want your project's resources and money for their own project.
- **Technical**

  An inherent technical problem or flaw in the systems and technology in the project should be addressed.
- **Managerial**

  This could be management indecision or a management vacuum. Whatever the cause, the symptom is managerial in nature.

- **Organizational**

  The organization structure and roles inhibit the employees from coping with the project issues.

Here are some more specific causes of crisis:

- **Policy**

  Is the crisis due to a new or existing business policy? An example might be a crisis resulting from a new approach to accounting or budgeting. A crisis may also arise related to how people are allocated to projects.

- **Internal project structure**

  The basic project is based on goals and scope that are now less relevant. The project did not change relative to the evolving goals and scope.

- **Resources**

  The resources in the project are not performing as expected and cannot address the problems.

- **Management**

  Management attitudes or positions toward this project or other projects have changed. There is less support.

- **Project leader**

  The project leader may be the problem. The crisis is occurring because the project leader is not doing the job. Perhaps the project leader has let issues slip or did not validate the quality of the work.

- **The work**

  The quality of the work is not adequate. The work may not be complete. There may be a requirement for extensive rework or additional work that causes the schedule to fall apart.

Use a process of elimination when working with the above causes, since more than one cause can exist. Start by assuming that something in all of these is contributing to the problem.

Coping with a Crisis

The First Steps

Suppose that a crisis or important issue is before you. What steps should you take to address it?

Action 1: Determine whether the crisis is real or perceived.

Ask yourself, "What has changed to make this situation a crisis?" Another test is to ask, "If nothing is done, what will happen? How will things worsen?" If your answers to these questions are that nothing has changed and the situation will not likely deteriorate, you have a perceived crisis.

Action 2: If the crisis is real, determine the scope of the situation and how much time you have left to make a decision and to implement it.

If the crisis is perceived, not real, decide what is behind the perception. Why do people feel that a crisis exists? Don't take action until you can answer this. Also ask who benefits if there is a perceived crisis. The perceived crisis may be a result of a misunderstanding. The analysis should reveal some interesting communications paths of the project. Take this opportunity to learn more about informal communications in the project. Determine the action that is appropriate. If you attempt to deny that a crisis exists, you will not be credible. Instead, think about what you want to say and the scope of your response. This is especially pertinent if you wish to use this opportunity to advance the project politically or to gain resources.

For example, go to management and indicate that the situation is bad but not hopeless. Identify what should be done before a crisis does erupt. This approach has several advantages. First, you are not crying wolf. Second, you are warning management before the crisis arises that the possibility exists.

Action 3: Implement the decision.

Here are some questions to answer for a real crisis:

- What other issues should be addressed as part of the actions involving the crisis-related issues? Handle as many open items as you can. It is important to determine the scope.

- What are the long-term approach and solution? Knowing these will ensure that short-term actions do not negate the long-term solution.

- What are alternatives for short-term actions? How do these alternatives group together?

The Strategy of Doing Nothing

Doing nothing is a reasonable alternative to action. Most of the time you should wait and organize a response to the crisis. Taking action without thinking through the consequences can make the situation worse. Time allows a situation to mature. Time allows you to work behind the scenes to get the situation resolved. Time also increases anxiety so that people will welcome a resolution and decisions that they would have resisted several weeks before.

Example: Software Development Project

In this classic case, the project slipped. Management overreacted by throwing more people into the project. The people already in the project suddenly had to stop working and bring the new members of the team up to speed. The project slipped further behind. The lesson learned here is that a more intelligent approach would have been to reduce the size of the team and increase accountability.

Here are some events that can occur if you leave the crisis alone:

- If a crisis is emerging, the existing symptoms may become more acute. Additional symptoms may appear. The problem will worsen.

- The issue may be noticed by someone else who may address it before it becomes critical.

- The situation may not change at all. This does not indicate that the issue is solved. It typically means that nothing is visibly new about the situation.

- The problem symptoms may abate or disappear with time.

Our basic recommendation is to let an issue mature and emerge on its own. This allows you time to plan on what to do. This strategy also will help convince people of the urgency later.

How do you protect the project if you decide not to do anything? Alert management to the issue and indicate that you are watching the situation and planning for action. Point out that taking action may not be needed and you don't want to overkill the issue.

Inaction may appear to be a weak way to handle a possible crisis. However, you do accomplish something, even by waiting to act. First, people are on the alert. Second, you will be able to judge the scope of the issue more precisely. Third, you will have more time to rally management behind a course of action.

Traditional Project Management

In traditional project management, the project data and schedule are often tightly held by a scheduler and the project leader. Few people are aware of what is going on, since the projects are managed separately and are only loosely coordinated. This can set the stage for disaster, as a project can slip or an issue can remain hanging for weeks. When management is finally aware of the problem, too much time has passed and the action that must be taken is too drastic. The decision is rushed.

Without open sharing of project information, little chance exists of getting help from other projects. This also tends to make the situation worse. It is more difficult to approach other managers for ideas, given the closed nature of the process.

In employing the traditional approach, you are often forced into using the written word, be it electronic mail or memorandum, to indicate the problem. Going on record in writing can lead to trouble, as the problem is now out in the open.

Collaborative Management

In a shared information environment, all of the project team members, as well as other project leaders and members, have access to the issues and the project plan. This is an environment that encourages people to offer suggestions and help. People feel that they are working together even though they are on separate projects.

Here are several advantages of using the collaborative management mode in handling a crisis:

- The team members work together to head off the crisis, thereby building and reinforcing the strength of the team, as well as solving the problem.

- A crisis tends to be identified earlier and addressed earlier. Therefore, it is less likely to turn into a serious crisis.

- The factors in one project that are creating havoc are often present in other projects. With the shared information the issue can be addressed systematically and not ad hoc on each individual project.

- Team members who have worked on other projects may have experienced similar problems and can give good advice.

Dealing With a Crisis Using Modern Tools

The modern tools discussed in earlier chapters include collaborative project management in a network, electronic mail, groupware, and shared databases. Several basic features and effects of the new software contribute to its usefulness during a period of crisis, including the following:

- Information is shared and available to more people.

- People get the information faster than with other means.

- You can respond faster so that the volume of mail, messages, or transactions per unit time is increased.

With all of the benefits these tools bring, they also have a potential drawback. First, misinformation or incomplete information can be spread faster. Second, if this occurs, more people find out about it. It is difficult and in some cases almost impossible to correct false impressions. Third, team members must have access to the tools, be trained, and be active users of these tools so that they can receive the messages.

What is a good strategy for using technology to deal with a crisis? During the period leading up to a decision and action, minimize electronic mail and other media. Leave the project plan alone until decisions are made. After a decision has been made, take the initial actions without the electronic tools. Once these have a beneficial impact, start using the electronic tools again. Update the issues database and project plan. By then, the crisis will have passed. In summary, use the tools when you have more control of the situation and its outcome.

The Consequences of a Crisis

In a true crisis, management and the project work will be impacted while people deal with a crisis. Let's consider potential impact.

- **Paralysis of the project**
  People are waiting until the situation is resolved.
- **Deferred decisions**
  Decision-making is slowed.
- **Withdrawal of support**
  People outside of the project who supported it suddenly are quiet and almost hidden.
- **Departure of some team members**
  As a crisis continues, people start to jump ship.
- **Sudden increase in management involvement**
  Due to the situation, management is now heavily involved in the project.

The positive impact a crisis has on a project is that it gives the manager a chance to redirect and reenergize the project.

Improve your Crisis Management Skills

Hone your skills prior to an actual crisis. One of the hardest but most important skills to develop is the ability to have perspective and patience when confronted with a set of symptoms.

Here are some suggestions to help you accomplish this:

- Examine your list of outstanding issues. Ask if these are complete. Add to the list any politically sensitive issues.

- With the complete list, note the age and importance of the issues. Sort the issues in order of importance. Within a group of issues of the same importance, sort by age.

- Take the top five issues in importance and age and assess what the trend has been for each. Has the issue deteriorated, remained the same, or improved?

- For each issue, develop a scenario for the reasonable worst case. That is, how could each issue turn into a crisis? What would be the symptoms of a crisis? What would cause the issue to worsen to this extent?

- Now determine how you would detect deterioration in each issue.

- With an assumed crisis, attempt to develop countermeasures you could take.

Following these suggestions will help to prepare you for a crisis. Get in the habit of evaluating issues each month to raise your level of awareness of the possibility of a real crisis.

Action 1: Determine the Crisis Issues to Be Included in the Decisions

Include as many issues as possible. You want to fix as much as you can so that you can stabilize the project. Typically, one or two issues that must be addressed are obvious. What is not as obvious are additional political and organizational issues.

Here are two examples from projects.

- The project crisis is that the schedule and cost are getting rapidly out of control. The cause was not the work itself, but the fact that the scope of the project had been expanded slowly to include additional work. What decisions are possible? First, you can create a larger project plan and team. You can request additional funding. The drawback of these plans is that they may slow the project while they are being put in place.

  A second course is to curtail the scope of the project immediately. This might help the core of the project, but it will create enemies of people who were expecting the additional items that were promised.

A third approach is to create a new super project and divide the project into subprojects. The core activities of the original project might be divided among several subprojects.

Which is the best approach? We are in favor of the third approach, even though it involves the greatest change. It requires changes in the plan, budgets, and staffing. You may encounter political resistance. You may be faced with management turning you down. Then you will have to revert to one of the other two alternatives.

- The project crisis is that an outside factor you cannot control is impacting the project. This could be another project or an outside event that is changing the nature of the work and purpose. The symptoms of this are typically doubt and tension within the project. What should you do in terms of defining issues? First, include the immediate impact on the project. Next, sit down and estimate what long-term impact there is on the organization and on the project. Attempt to widen the scope of issues so that they can be dealt with on a higher organization level than the project. If something is beyond your control, escalate it so that management will handle it.

These two common examples will be employed in each step. Note that within each are underlying political issues and also factors beyond your control.

Action 2: Define Possible Decisions and Their Interrelationships

In the first example of the budget and schedule overrun due to expanded scope, three possible options for handling the crisis were offered. With the third option, further decisions are required. First, decide how to divide up the project. Then decide if you are going to expand the scope even further to reach some natural boundary. This example shows that after you define a series of alternative major decisions, you next need to identify smaller decisions within each major decision.

When making lower level decisions, consider including at least one decision in each of the following areas:

- Project purpose and scope
- Project organization
- Interfaces outside of the project
- Project team and staffing
- Project methods and tools
- Approach to communications with management and outside of the project

Are some of the lower level decisions the same for several alternatives? If so, this may cause you to rethink the alternatives.

Here are examples of possible decisions.

Choose to do nothing.
You will not make any decisions now. Instead, you will monitor the situation for changes.

Use no new resources.
A second possible decision is to take no action that would require additional resources. You will live within your existing means.

Change purpose and scope.
You will either expand or contract the purpose and scope of the project.

Work the political circuit.
You won't change the project. Instead, you will go out and position the project and work politically. This method is useful when you have a crisis in interpretation of the project.

Add resources to the project.
Determine if the project could benefit from additional resources to address the crisis. Consider this only as a last resort. Substitution of resources is included in this decision.

Modify the methods and tools in the project.
This is also dangerous. If you change the methods and tools during the project, you will slow the project and cause the need for more time spent in training.

When considering subsidiary decisions, assess timing and dependencies. What would be the trigger for a later decision? If decisions are dependent, you may need to announce the decisions at the same time, but implement them sequentially. That is, you might change the project scope and the structure of the plan. Changes in resources would also follow.

Action 3: Determine Potential Actions

You have now identified the range of possible actions required to implement a decision. Take each decision and fit it into one or more of the categories in the following list:

- Changes In the Budget
- Changes In Staffing
- Changes In the Project Team
- Changes In Objectives and Scope
- Changes In Methods and Tools
- Changes In Organization
- Changes In Technology
- Changes In the Schedule and Deadlines

The action itself may involve a combination of activities, such as announcements, analysis, reorganization, procedure, policies, staffing, training, facilities, and equipment. It is important that you think an action through. If you neglect some parts of an action and people become aware of it, your credibility will be questioned. Once this occurs, the lack of confidence in you will expand to the entire action, as well as to the decision itself.

Action 4: Make and Present the Decisions

Three sequential events are involved in this step:

- Making the decision

- Announcing the decision
- Taking action based on the decision

To be most effective, the time between each of these events should be very short to prevent any buildup of resistance or short-circuiting by a manager. Rapid progression of events also reinforces the impression of you being action-oriented. If team members receive an announcement of a decision and this is followed by silence and inactivity, doubt and anxiety are created. Progress on tasks may slow.

Making the Decision

To prepare for making a decision, compare and analyze alternatives. Use Table 30-1 for analysis and for presentation to management.

Table 30:1 Decision Chart

Major Decision	Supporting Decision	Impact	Benefit	Risk	Comments

In the columns for impact, benefit, risk, and comments, you can enter information in a bulleted format. Use impact to enter what the expected result is. Benefit is the effect on the project and organization. Risk is the potential exposure and likelihood of problems.

Each decision or supporting decision has actions that must be taken to support the implementation of the decision. An additional factor that can be added for each supporting decision is the trigger or event that led to the decision being made and the action being taken. Use Table 30-2 to record this information:

Table 30-2: Decision Information

Major Decision	Supporting Decision	Actions	Trigger

If you want to pursue this further, create detail for the action items. This detail might include the following:

- How the action will be taken
- Who will take the action
- What anticipated fallout might occur due to the action
- Verification that the action was taken

In some cases, you will recommend a decision to management. In others, you will be empowered to make the decision yourself. In previous chapters on communications we discussed dealing with marketing and selling decisions to management, the team, and the organization. If you seek management approval, you have the above analysis in hand. The more thoughtful the presentation, the more support management will provide.

Who should make a decision? Many would say "Pass it up the ladder to management. They can make the decision and people will follow." If you do this, follow these guidelines:

- Base the level of management required for the decision on importance and scope to the organization. Have the decision made or endorsed at as low a level in the organization as possible.
- Inform managers at higher levels in advance of the decisions and actions. This has several benefits. The informed managers can impact the decisions or actions, if they feel that it is necessary. Also, the managers put distance between themselves and the decisions so that they feel less at risk. With advance notice, managers are better prepared for any issues that may arise. Give some examples of negative reaction that may occur due to resistance to change.

Announcing the Decision

Begin by making your announcement to the project team and work your way to the line organizations. In terms of timing, attempt to make the announcements as close together as possible.

With the announcement, suggest some actions to put into effect right afterwards. These might include project changes, team assignment changes, method adoption or change, or tool acquisition. You want to shift the attention of the people from the decision to the actions. This gets people working again.

An announcement should be preceded by a verbal announcement indicating what is coming. This reduces anxiety and stress and also preserves the surprise of part of the announcement. Never call off an expected announcement. This can raise more issues and doubts.

Taking Actions Based on the Decision

If a decision is not going the way that you think it should, don't continue to press for action. Try to put the decision on the shelf. What if immediate action is needed? Shift gears and work on selling the actions as a stopgap measure in order remove the pressure to make a decision.

Action 5: Implement the First Actions

The first actions are often the easiest to undertake. These don't involve purchasing or hiring and are probably within your span of control. You have considerable discretion as to how to implement these actions.

Here are some suggestions:

- Implement actions in groups, with periods of calm between groups of actions. This allows you to assess the effects of the actions.
- Determine what results should flow from the actions.
- Follow up on the actions to ensure that they are being carried out and that the results are what you anticipated.
- Be ready to step in and modify the action in terms of implementation, if necessary.
- Evaluate the actions individually and as a group.

When implementing an action, play an active role. If new procedures or announcements are necessary, review the material prior to release. Show that these actions mean something to you. If others get the impression that you don't really care and that this is not serious, they may not participate.

Be flexible with respect to actions. While changing a decision may result in actions changed and an unraveling situation, the consequences of changing an action are less far-reaching and may be advantageous.

Action 6: Measure the Results of the Actions and Determine What Further Actions Are Necessary

When you measure the results of an action, pose the following questions:

- Is the work on the project continuing?
- Has the nature of the work changed to reflect the decision and actions?
- What new factors have emerged that should be addressed?
- Do areas of ambiguity or fuzziness need to be addressed?
- Are the results of the actions supportive of the decisions?
- Is the pace of the results consistent with expectations?

People often forget management at this time. Once management gives approval, people go off and implement the decisions and actions. Seldom is there feedback to management on what happened. However, the project will progress more smoothly if you provide feedback to management after the actions have been taken. Keep management informed to retain support for the project.

Decisions, actions, and change can bring harmful side effects. Progress may slow. Other projects may be impacted. Sometimes the actions have not been thoroughly considered. Gaps exist, unanticipated problems arise, and issues are left unanswered. These situations can create enemies. Enemies can then go to management and indicate that all is not well with the project.

Keeping management abreast of what is happening will prevent management from relying on a project enemy for information, misinterpreting the situation, or feeling betrayed and turning against the project, all of which could result in management stopping your planned actions.

This discussion provides further support for taking actions immediately after the decisions. Measurement and marketing of the results must begin soon afterward. Adopt a conservative approach to measuring and marketing the results of an action. Figure out the worst case scenario and be prepared with solutions. Head off misinformation and disinformation on a positive note.

Examples of Decisions

Replacing the Project Manager

Suppose that the decision has been made to replace the project manager. Short of terminating the project or a major redirection, this is one of most significant decisions you can make.

Once the decision has been made, the project manager should be informed. What happens next? We recommend a gap in management. Take time to consider what qualities you want in the project manager. An upper level manager can function as the acting manager of the project.

This approach has the following benefits:

- The interim manager can determine the true status of the project.
- The team gets a breather and an opportunity to tell an outsider what is really going on.
- Project changes can be made with the blame falling on the interim manager, thereby shielding the next official project manager from tough decisions.
- This gives a chance to test team members in assuming aspects of management of the project.

Recruiting from within a project may be easier than recruiting from outside. An insider already knows what is going on the project. No learning curve slows the project. The downside of recruiting an insider is that the person has existing relationships that are now changed. This creates new dynamics. If someone from outside the project is selected, the team members may resent the newcomer and feel that one of the current team members should have been considered. In light of the pros and cons, we recommend that you consider several team members for the position before turning to those outside the project.

If you decide that you must recruit a new manager outside the project, it is essential to find someone who will be able to take over an existing project and not change it to fit his or her preconceived ideas. Key qualifiers are that the new person is an "adapter" and is "results oriented." Also, choose someone who is a fast learner and doesn't require weeks to get up to speed on the project.

Terminating a Project

Beyond the analysis of the project itself, here are some factors to consider when making the decision whether to terminate a project.

- What is the impact on the organization of terminating the project? The project was to deliver benefits to the organization. These will not be received if the project is terminated. What is the impact of the loss of those benefits?

- What can substitute for the project? If the benefits from your project are needed, does another project exist that will result in the same benefits?

- Where can the resources best be redeployed?

- How should the project be terminated?

- What is the impact of keeping the project going for awhile longer?

Note that the following question was not asked: "What is the impact on management credibility or morale?" Do not keep a failing project going only to preserve management credibility.

To terminate a project, you can gradually reassign resources and pare down the project. However, this gradual death is often unproductive. If you need something in particular from the project, create a new task plan and have people moved to work on the necessary tasks. Terminate what is left.

Overcoming Resistance

You may encounter resistance to ending the project. Head this off by stressing the positive results that will occur with reassignment and work on other projects. Recognize the loss that people feel when they have worked diligently on a project that is scheduled for termination.

If team members still resist ending the project, try to convince them that this is the best course of action. Indicate the type of resources, changes, and other support that would be needed to continue. Also, stress what could be achieved in other areas by stopping this particular project now. If you are overruled and the project continues, don't say "I told you so" if the project eventually fails. Conversely, if the project does turn around and is successful, trace this success back to changes made during the time of crisis.

How Should a Project Be Terminated?

Expediency is recommended. The faster resources can be moved, the less time the negative impact will be felt. Take the opportunity to build up the projects that will now receive additional resources.

Have a plan prepared to shut down a project before you announce your intentions.

Here are the actions to take to shut down a project:

Action 1: Freeze all documents and computer files. This will prevent people from destroying project information or end products because they are upset.

Action 2: Get people together from the project team and discuss lessons learned from the project. This allows people to focus on something positive.

Action 3: Let people know one-on-one where they will be going. Let them know what they will be doing.

People on the project team may blame themselves for the project failure. Even if they are to blame, tread lightly. Your goal is not to exact retribution but to achieve a smooth shutdown.

Your goal is to complete the process in a week or less. If lingering tasks have to be done, try to reorganize them so that they become part of a separate small project.

MANAGEMENT PRESENTATION AND COST-BENEFIT ANALYSIS

For a crisis you will have both informal and formal presentations. You will begin with informal presentations. Hopefully, this will get the issues resolved. If it does not, then you should resist moving to a formal presentation. Instead, you should have an informal meeting on the issues around the crisis. Use formal presentations as a last resort.

In terms of costs and benefits, not having an approach for dealing with crises can be very costly in time and on the process improvement project. Not only can the project be delayed, but also the morale of the process improvement team can be damaged. The benefits to having a method for dealing with issues and crises go beyond just issue resolution. You set the stage for working with management in the future because you were able to work through issues with them. Relationships among team members should also be improved.

KEY QUESTIONS

How does your organization identify a crisis? Do you have an organized approach for escalation of a situation? Or do you handle crises on a case-by-case basis?

Who determines if there is a crisis? What is the role of management? What is the role of the project leader?

Does each crisis have a learning curve? Do you make an effort to analyze crises after the fact and extract lessons learned?

Are the decisions that result from a crisis consistent with actions taken? Do actions taken flow logically from decisions?

Is a method for tracking decisions and actions in place?

Is a conscious decision process used to relate actions, follow up, and decisions concerning a crisis?

EXAMPLES

Monarch Bank

While there were no true crises in terms of issues, at several points crises had to be provoked to obtain management decisions and direction. This required in-depth analysis of the individual issues and how the issues combined. The effects of not resolving the issues had to be plausible so that this limited the number of times and situations that it could be employed.

TRAN

At TRAN there were a number of crisis points in process improvement. These included: initial resistance to changes in general, specific resistance to changing forms and procedures, and then resistance to working on new tasks. This is a fairly common situation in process improvement and one that you should be ready to address.

Stirling Manufacturing

The project at Stirling Manufacturing was progressing well when the crisis struck. A manager picked up a rumor that a competitor was putting in more advanced automation than they were. The competitor was implementing a larger network with more functions. Within hours, a crisis atmosphere pervaded the company. When management held a meeting, the agenda should have included an assessment of the competitor's status and what steps to take to deal with the competitor. Instead, several managers who were enemies of the project immediately began to press for a review of the project and determination as to whether it should be killed off. The challenge was to turn this around. The project leader handed out a short project plan he had developed for the specific crisis. The plan contained material that applied generally to a major crisis. The first set of tasks dealt with verifying what the competitor was doing and the facts. Several tasks to be carried on at the same time concerned determining the potential impact of the competitor's move. The next set of tasks identified what could be done to accelerate their own project.

Lessons learned here are that the project leader should take the lead in analyzing a crisis, and that it is useful to assume the worst in a crisis.

Management at the manufacturing firm perceived a crisis when they felt that a competitor would have a network and software available first. Management directed that the project be accelerated without obtaining market intelligence. Later, management found that the competitor was not far ahead and was building a smaller network. Management slowed the project and pulled resources. The net effect was harmful to the project. The decisions made resulted in reduced morale and delay in the project schedule, due to failure to plan. The management had failed in a time of crisis.

GUIDELINES

- **Don't jump to conclusions on either symptoms or causes.**

  Unless a true emergency exists, do not take any precipitate action. Instead, show that you are working on the issue.

- **Ask yourself if there is benefit in forcing a crisis.**

  When faced with a crisis, you have a trump card to play—the timing and posturing of the crisis. You can position the crisis and select the timing of unveiling the crisis and potential solution. If you have been unable to get attention, but you retain management support, consider the cost and benefits of forcing the crisis.

- **Work out a strategy for change in a crisis situation.**

  In project evolution you introduce changes to projects gradually. This can be very smooth at first. However, as time goes on and the number of changes increases, team members experience increasing anxiety and uncertainty.

  In a revolutionary change to a project, a major change is made. This is followed by relative calm as the changes settle in.

  Decide in a crisis whether to take an evolutionary or revolutionary approach.

- **Ask yourself who benefits from how an important issue is resolved.**

  Issues can be addressed, shelved, or made to disappear. They can disappear if one changes the assumptions, purpose, or scope underlying a project. Once an issue is resolved, winners and losers emerge. This is especially true for political issues. Analysis of this outcome can assist you in seeing what is behind the issue and what positions people are taking with respect to the issue.

- **Be cautious when confronted with a critical issue.**

  With a critical issue, the tendency is to plunge in and address the issue. However, first review how the issue surfaced and evolved into being critical. What were the main events along the way? This is important because it helps to frame the issue and give perspective.

- **Draw analogies in project situations to calm a temporary project crisis.**

  One value of having experienced people in a project is that they can provide perspective and experience when dealing with an issue or a crisis. They can recall a similar event in a previous project. Use these stories to calm people during a crisis.

- **Look for different interpretations of a crisis.**

  When people present you with an issue, they sometimes disguise it by emphasizing the action they desire. Alternatively, they may offer only one view of the crisis. As you have seen, many interpretations are possible. Dig deeper when someone hands you a situation.

- **Learn to enjoy dealing with the unexpected.**

  One reason that people enjoy projects is that projects offer the unexpected. Projects tend to involve change. Change typically involves issues. Issues lead to the unexpected. If you don't enjoy projects, it may be because of having to deal with the unexpected. Learn to enjoy this aspect of project management, rather than dreading it.

- **Play out or simulate what would happen if the immediate crisis were resolved. Ask what new crisis might take its place.**

  Do you have the right interpretation of the crisis? Would the solutions you are considering fit? To help answer these questions, jump ahead mentally and assume that the crisis has been handled. What do you think is the next issue that will become critical and, perhaps, a crisis? Does a link exist between the two issues?

- **Follow up on decisions with actions to maintain management credibility.**

Managers should consider both decisions and actions together. Through understanding and seeing the actions, you can better evaluate the decisions.

- **Correlate actions with decisions.**

  To evaluate this, make a table with the rows being the decisions and the columns being the actions. In the table write a paragraph on how the action supports the decision. An action may support many decisions, and many actions may apply to a given decision.

- **Compromise to bring later rewards.**

  When considering decisions, maintain an attitude of conciliation and compromise. When you move to actions, you have less flexibility. Decisions have many shades of gray; actions tend to be more black and white. When considering decisions, you can also trade off with opponents on the decisions vs. the actions. If you have to concede points on the actions, you can eventually recover if the actions prove to be inadequate.

- **If you fail to obtain a decision or you disagree with a decision, pause and let the situation alone.**

  Let things cool off. Take time to gain new perspective. Later, you can resurrect parts of issues.

- **Focus on achieving success.**

  This chapter dealt with the termination of a project. If a project is not terminated but is close to failure, you may overcome failure. However, overcoming failure is not the same as achieving success. When you overcome failure, you naturally feel that you have accomplished something. In fact, you have depleted your energy dealing with a problem project.

- **When you stop a project, give a viable explanation for your actions.**

  Stopping a project without explanation fuels rumors. While you don't have to go into detail, cover the major reasons for the decision. Stress the changes that have occurred since the project was started that necessitated your decision.

  Early project decisions are sometimes made in haste and based on external pressures—only to be reversed later.

- **Be cautious in pushing for a decision to terminate a project while you are still in the early stages of the project.**

  This is a period in which the project was recently approved with a specific purpose and scope. A crisis, or at least a major issue, occurs. A manager may start to question the project itself. The logic might be that the project must be poorly conceived if it cannot get a proper start. However, with time, the project may take off and become successful.

- **Avoid placing blame for a failed project.**

  If a project is failing and about to be terminated, no one needs to go down with the ship. Placing blame is not appropriate. If you do blame specific managers, move to have them leave the company. By placing the blame, you may have doomed them while they are at the firm.

- **Frequently ask, "If the project were stopped today, what would happen?"**

  Ask this even if the project is doing fine. Pausing to ask this helps put the project in perspective in terms of its importance to the organization and business processes. It also helps to indicate what is not important in the big picture.

- **Delay a decision in a project to provide time for perspective.**

  This strategy is beneficial for several reasons. The first is that, if the time is not right for a management decision, you will spend energy on the decision but get nowhere. Also, while the decision may be clear, the follow-up actions may still be undefined.

- **Put a project on hold to provide time for perspective.**

  When you place a project on hold, you can still continue work at a low level. You are no longer caught up with the events, so you have time for perspective. Also, a pause gives project team members time to assess how they are doing in their work and what small changes they might make.

KEY QUESTIONS

How does your organization identify a crisis? Do you have an organized approach for escalation of a situation? Or do you handle crises on a case-by-case basis?

ACTION ITEMS

1. Look back at a crisis in a project (in the past or present, or one about which you have information). Ask yourself the following questions:
    - When was the issue first identified?
    - When did the issue become critical?
    - What were the symptoms that were visible at the time?
    - Looking back, what symptoms should have been visible?
    - What were the causes behind the symptoms?
    - How well trained was the project manager to deal with the crisis?
    - Was management prepared to address the crisis?
    - Could better preparation have been made for the crisis?
2. In a current project, try to identify at least three potential major issues that are either present now or are possible in the future. For each of those, answer the following questions:
    - When was the issue first identified?
    - How much importance do management and the project team associate with the issue?
    - What has been the rate of decay of the situation?
    - What symptoms are currently evident?
    - What are potential causes for the issue?
    - What will cause the issue to become a crisis?
3. Select any three projects that are or were in a state of crisis. For each one, try to determine when the crisis began, what actions were taken, and what results occurred.
4. For these same examples, try to estimate if people had thought through the decisions and actions. What was the elapsed time between the time of the decision and the visibility of the actions? What additional unannounced and unplanned actions occurred?
5. Assess the side effects of the decisions made by the organization with respect to the project. What was the impact on other projects?
6. Consider any project that was terminated. What has changed with respect to the management of current projects? Do you see any evidence of lessons learned?

EXAMPLES, OUTSOURCING, AND DOWNSIZING

CHAPTER 31

EXAMPLE: PROCESS IMPROVEMENT

CONTENTS

31

EXAMPLE: PROCESS IMPROVEMENT

INTRODUCTION

This chapter provides an example of process improvement based on an insurance company, Force Insurance (Force). Force offers insurance to customers of banks, credit unions, and automobile manufacturers. When these institutions offer loans or leases, they require proof of insurance to protect the assets (e.g., home, automobile). If the customer does not provide proof of insurance in a timely manner, Force "force places" an insurance policy on the customer. Because the rates may be high, many customers go out and obtain insurance elsewhere. They then inform Force of their cancellation of insurance. Loan and lease portfolios range from tens of thousands to hundreds of thousands of customers.

Several current processes are presented. The chapter shows how Force progressed through the steps outlined in earlier chapters. The false starts that Force went through are also examined.

Previous Process and Systems Efforts

Over a period of years, Force developed standard batch processing systems for supporting policy placement and servicing. Each type of insurance product had its own system. For example, Force had several homeowner systems and an automobile system. Each system was surrounded and supported by dedicated resources within business departments and systems. Each product had its own variant processes, even though the product and processes were similar. Each product also had dedicated computer programmers and customer service staff.

Force later added online terminal systems; however, the core of the system remained unchanged. Enhancements and new features were added to some systems on an individual basis. The time it took the staff members to perform an enhancement increased due to several factors. First, the original programmers had left a long time ago. Second, there was little documentation for the system. A third factor was that the size and complexity of the system had increased with the number of changes. When an enhancement could not be made in time, the business department would often institute new exception processes and steps as workarounds for the system limitations.

Management grew more frustrated. Every time the business grew, more people had to be hired to support the workaround manual processes. However, when business fell off, Force did not have a corresponding staff decline. Rather than opt for business process improvement, management pursued a new system. Based on the functions of the current system, Force developed a new system for a homeowner's product. It was called Trakker and was built using a Computer Aided Software Engineering (CASE) tool. This tool had had little use in the industry and was not compatible with the company's hardware. The homeowner's product was Trakker's first customer and there were many problems. The system took three years to develop, and the company still had production problems.

Attempts to extend Trakker to other products were rebuffed by management. Some of the managers believed that a homeowner's system could not serve an automobile product. This was compounded by the business staff and programmers uniting to support the automobile product and protect their jobs.

Because the new system did not address the workaround processes, there were no benefits. The underlying processes were labor intensive.

Management eventually decided to embark on a process improvement project. They hired a large consulting firm that had its own process improvement method. The consulting firm brought in 10 people. Many of these were junior consultants; some had never worked on a process improvement project; others lacked insurance experience. The ones who knew the insurance industry did not have experience with business process improvement and vice versa. The consultants trained many employees on the method and its jargon. The method had more than 50 acronyms that the employees had to learn. This consumed the first three weeks of the project, and no work was performed on process improvement during this time. The training was followed by the installation of diagramming software.

The consulting team then fanned out in the organization to analyze every process. Months passed. A book of more than 200 flowcharts was prepared for various insurance transactions.

The consultants conducted an interim management presentation. Several managers asked why the project was taking so long and why it was so expensive. The team's response was, "Business process improvement projects are always large. You have to start clean and understand all processes. Also, it takes time to learn the method."

After several more months, the team developed a concept for a new process. The process for the homeowner's area was designed around the Trakker system. More flowcharts appeared. Out of frustration, management asked the employees who performed the current process if they liked the new process. The employees replied that they had not been involved and did not really know. The consultants held a walkthrough of the new process. People immediately began to raise issues about the surrounding informal processes that the consultants created as workarounds. Additional questions were raised regarding business rules and exception transactions. It was clear that the new process was incomplete.

The project was terminated after more than six months had been invested in it. Force was left with four three-ring binders and no new process. The consulting firm walked away with more than $450,000. The firm's credibility was badly damaged.

In retrospect, failure could be attributed to the fact that Force did not consider industry trends, new technology, the flaws in the Trakker system, and the methods employed in the process improvement effort. Force was not competitive in price, and management had been diverted into the process improvement project from its core business activities. Force was sold to new management.

Force's new management realized that the problems lay in both processes and systems. It pursued a process improvement approach similar to the one described in this book. It took more than three years to complete the work. The results were improved processes and a standard system across all insurance products. Force became competitive again and could offer new insurance products on a timely basis. Eventually, with the new processes and systems in place, Force was able to outsource some of the insurance servicing for additional savings. The remaining organization had three layers of management fewer than before, operating costs were cut by more than 40 percent, and staff was reduced by 45 percent due to improvements, downsizing, outsourcing, and moving some staff to part-time.

PROCESS GROUP SELECTION

The process groups were based around single core processes, or in this case products. Forms, electronic mail, and personal computer tools augmented the group. The alternative groups were Trakker, AutoTrak, LoanTrak, Leasing Track, and MobileTrak. The factors that were considered in the selection of the process group included the following:

- Size of the staff and support required by the group
- Difficulty in supporting new business customers
- Existing known problems with the processes and systems associated with the group
- Major benefits after improving the first process group
- Paving the way for the later process groups if the process is somewhat representative

All but AutoTrak were eliminated based on the following reasons:

- Trakker had substantial problems and the business department was discouraged with it after the first failed process improvement effort.
- Leasing Track did not have the volume to justify its selection.
- MobileTrak was not representative.

AutoTrak met the criteria and was selected to be first. Runner-up was LoanTrak.

ASSESSMENTS AND PROCESS ANALYSIS

Existing Process: Automobile Insurance

Here is the list the company made of part of the process prior to the improvement for input and data capture. This is only one part of the overall process, but it is representative of the analysis and will be the focus of the example. The other parts of the process were treated in a similar manner.

1. Documents arrive via courier delivery and mail.

2. Documents are prepared for microfilm. Documents are sorted by size.

3. A document control sheet is completed manually.

4. The document is microfilmed. A document number from the microfilm is assigned.

5. The microfilm document number is entered from the document into AutoTrak.

6. AutoTrak issues a second control number.

7. The filmer and preparer are logged onto the control sheet log.

8. Total statistics are entered and calculated on a weekly basis.

9. The control sheet is copied to travel with the documents.

10. The original documents are filed by date and AutoTrak number.

11. The physical documents are carried from the mailroom to the data entry area.

12. The data entry clerk enters an average of 15 fields. Each field averages ten characters.

13. The AutoTrak system batch processes the input and attempts to match the input with the existing data in the system. A number of reports are generated.

14. Exception handlers view exceptions and find the original documents to make corrections.

15. Business letters are generated by AutoTrak and letters are microfilmed.

The problems with the process were as follows:

- Microfilm was the central technology because it assigns an identifying number. Microfilm is inexpensive but not flexible and is time-consuming, as it must be printed and staff members must leave their desks to view it.

- Each document was assigned two numbers: one for microfilm and one for AutoTrak.

- Document numbers were only on the first page of the document set when filmed. The second and later pages had no identifier, making retrieval more complex.

- Manual calculations were required, making it difficult to analyze the workflow on a day-to-day basis.

- The workflow allowed paper to cross several departments. Documents can be misfiled or lost.

- Data entry was performed without the benefit of the previous work steps. There was a substantial time gap between the receipt of the letter or form and its entry. There was no trail leading to the document until it had been entered.

- A key field for an automobile was the Vehicle Identification Number (VIN). It is commonly found on the driver's side of the car under the windshield. In AutoTrak, only the last four characters of the VIN were entered. At least seven characters are needed to ensure a unique identifier.

- The matching process was a batch process based on the VIN. If there was no match on VIN, the system attempted to match on address.

- The rejection rate of non-matches and multiple VIN matches was 25 percent. Analysis revealed that expanding the VIN could cut this to 10 percent.

Industry Assessment

After talking to current and potential customers (banks, credit unions, etc.), Force employees found that these customers wanted the flexibility to be able to do some of the insurance servicing themselves with Force's system (insourcing) as well as using Force's staff and system (outsourcing). The old process could do only outsourcing. The online system was so complex that it was too difficult to train the customer's staff. A Graphic User Interface (GUI) with online help was necessary.

Competitive insurance firms were offering scanning, image processing, and Electronic Data Interchange (EDI). Force did not offer these, which placed Force at a disadvantage. Also, the online screens of the competitors were simpler to use.

Infrastructure and Technology Assessment

The following technologies were identified as candidates for supporting process improvement:

- Scanning
- Image processing and storage
- Optical Character Recognition (OCR)
- EDI
- Workflow software for routing work in the process
- Integration with microcomputer tools to reduce reports
- GUI with online help
- Archival capability
- Internet access for issues and non-confidential messages
- Software that automatically indexes an image
- Client-server technology

With these technologies two alternatives were formulated. In both cases, a key ingredient to supporting process improvement was the degree to which the technologies integrated.

PROCESS ALTERNATIVES AND COST-BENEFIT ANALYSIS

New Process—Alternative 1

The first alternative was to use four of the technologies identified earlier: image processing, scanning, automatic indexing, and workflow software. The steps in the new process are as follows:

1. Documents arrive via courier delivery and mail.

2. Documents are sorted by document size and prepared for scanning.

3. Documents are scanned. The system assigns a document number. The system tracks who the scanning employee is along with productivity. Logs and control sheets are generated by the system.

4. Documents are electronically routed to data entry.

5. Data entry is performed from the image.

6. The AutoTrak system batch processes the input and attempts to match the input with the existing data in the system. A number of reports are generated.

7. Documents are automatically indexed. Exceptions are electronically routed to exception/rejection staff.

8. Exception handlers view exceptions and find the original documents to make corrections.

9. Business letters are generated by AutoTrak.

Force employees compared this list with the list of current process steps. Here are some observations:

- The new process eliminates the following steps in the current workflow: 3, 4, 5, 7, 8, 9, 10, and 11.

- The batch matching program is still used, slowing the process down.

- Workflow software tracks where each transaction is after being captured and indexed.

- Savings lie in keying data from the image instead of paper (the image appears side-by-side on the screen with the entry fields), reduced paper handling, and reduced handling of rejected items.

- Microfilm viewing, which requires people to leave their desks, was eliminated.

Benefit Analysis—Alternative 1

The benefit analysis revealed the following:

Improved efficiency of data entry—20 percent	
(2.2 people @ $30,000/year)	$ 66,000
Reduction in rejections due to 7-digit VIN	
(1 person @ $30,000/year)	30,000
Reduction in microfilm viewing	30,000
Total savings	$126,000/year

The person who did the microfilming would not be eliminated until all insurance products were considered. The microfilm viewing savings would occur gradually as the old insurance policies already on microfilm expired. Fractional savings would be realized by moving people to part-time work from full-time work.

New Process—Alternative 2

The second alternative uses all of the technologies mentioned earlier. The workflow steps are as follows:

1. Documents arrive via courier delivery and mail.
2. Documents are sorted by document size and prepared for scanning.
3. Documents are scanned. The system assigns a document number. The system tracks who the scanning employee is along with productivity. Logs and control sheets are generated by the system.
4. EDI transactions enter here. The new system matches the transactions to the database in an online mode. If there is a total match, the system updates the database in AutoTrak and updates the audit trail.
5. Exceptions are routed to exception/rejection staff who review these and either enter the data with online update or place them in a separate stack for return.

This alternative automatically posts the transaction to the database after it has been matched online and identified. For example, in the case of an insurance cancellation, the employees would scan and index the policy number, the cancellation transaction, and the date. The system would search the database and find a match. The cancellation would be automatically performed. An audit trail would keep track of all transactions.

Some key advantages of this alternative are as follows:

- All of the benefits in alternative 1 are received.

- EDI and scanned documents progress through the same steps, where applicable. Thus, Force receives the benefits of automated posting for EDI transactions as well.

- Much of the data entry is eliminated (more than 70 percent).

The drawback of this alternative is that there is additional systems work to design and program the online matching and updating of the database.

Benefit Analysis of Alternative 2

The areas of savings are as follows:

Elimination of 60 percent of the labor in data entry $198,000

(70 percent of work is eliminated, leaving a buffer;
60 percent of labor is 6.6 people)

Reduction in rejection handling (same)	30,000
Total	$228,000/year

These are substantial and recurring savings. However, these must be traded off against the costs. First the unit costs of the technology and systems were considered. Then the company built the costs for each alternative.

Technology and Implementation Costs

The cost categories are listed below. Which ones the company buys and how many depend on the alternative selected.

Hardware

1 Microcomputer workstation with large screen, cabling, and network attachment	$ 4,500
1 Database server and software with network attachment	15,000
1 Image cartridge storage device (holds 332GB)	77,000
1 Scanner server	2,800
1 Scanner equipment (55 ppm with 500 page capacity)	29,000
1 Laser printer	1,500

Software

1 Scanning software (server)	4,000
1 Scanning software (workstation)	100/each
1 Automated indexing software	15,000
1 Network operating system and utilities	2,000
Software development tools	6,000

Development

Alternative 1	10,000
Alternative 2	35,000
Training	3,000

Storage Estimation

In order to size the number of image storage devices, the company began by deciding on the need for two devices for backup because this was a single point of potential failure. Next, the number of documents and pages that the device could support were estimated. This allowed the company to determine how long the device could be used before it filled up with images.

Calculations were performed across all of the processes for all insurance products. Storage for images and for printed reports that were microfilmed were calculated. Using a document as a page, the calculations were as follows:

Number of documents/week	60,000
Number of documents/year	3,120,000
Storage requirements/page	50,000 bytes/page
Number of pages/gigabyte (GB)	25,000
Total storage required for one year	124 GB
Number of printed pages/month	1,000,000/month
Number of printed pages/year	12,000,000/year
Storage requirements/page with data compression	about 2,200 bytes
Number of pages/gigabyte	450,000
Total storage required for one year	26.67 GB
Total of image and printing per year	150 GB/year

Thus, the storage capacity will last more than 2.2 years.

Configuration and Cost for Alternative 1

The configuration and costs for automobile insurance are as follows:

	Quantity	Item	Extended Cost
Hardware			
	20	Workstations	$ 90,000
	1	Database server	15,000
	2	Laser printers	3,000
	1	Image hardware subsystem	108,000
Software			
	20	Image software licenses	2,000
	1	Scanning server software license	4,000
	1	Automated indexing software	15,000
	1	Network operating system	2,000
		Software development tools	6,000
Development and training			
		Development	10,000
		Training	3,000
		Total cost	$258,000

The payback period is slightly over two years. Note that the one process is absorbing the cost of an image storage system that can handle all processes so that if only the one process were considered, a smaller image system could be obtained, reducing the payback period.

The payback period is slightly over two years. Note that the one process is absorbing the cost of an image storage system that can handle all processes so that if only the one process were considered, a smaller image system could be obtained, reducing the payback period.

Configuration and Cost for Alternative 2

This configuration was approached on the basis of adjusting from alternative 1. This is a useful approach in marketing an alternative because it highlights the differences. The adjustments and their impact are as follows:

Reduce the number of workstations by 5 (less employees)	$ -22,500
Reduce the number of software licenses by 5	- 500
Additional development	+25,000
Net change	$ 2,000

Notice that process improvement and downsizing allow for the offset of the development effort. The total cost of Alternative 2 is $260,500. The total benefits are $228,000. The payback is less than one and a half years.

General Benefits and Costs for All Insurance Products

The analysis for Alternative 2 was replicated to all insurance products using the same analysis performed earlier. The total savings was $590,000 per year. However, the microfilm-related savings was added because the microfilm position and maintenance on the equipment was eliminated, except the viewers for the old documents. This is an additional $68,000 per year in savings. The total annual savings was $658,000.

The total cost was $925,000. Some savings resulted from reusing some workstations and better pricing on software development due to the volume of work. The payback period is less than two years. But there are more savings. First, the savings only count people involved in the process. Head count reductions at this level translate to fewer supervisors. In fact, two supervisors were eliminated, raising the annual savings to $758,000, with a payback of less than 18 months.

MARKETING AND STRATEGY

Marketing the New Process

The audiences for the new process included upper management, financial staff and managers, employees, and middle management. For upper management, the emphasis was on the vision of how streamlined the new process would be. The comparison tables helped here. The financial analysts reviewed the numbers and verified that they were correct.

Some employees did not care for the current processes. They viewed them as being antiquated. However, the scanning system was demonstrated in another firm and won them over.

The major resistance was from middle management, which attempted to obstruct the project in several ways. Managers maintained that the staff had unique skills so that all or almost all of the processes had to be retained. Given the nature of the work, this was rejected. In fact, because Alternative 2 performed interpretation of data and matching automatically, a lower level of staff person would be needed in the future. Nevertheless, to be conservative, the same type of staff person was assumed in the analysis.

The second barrier was the difficulty in transition to the new process and the danger this posed to the level of service. A phased implementation strategy addressed the transition point by point.

Implementation Strategy

It takes time to create the design and do the programming for the matching and updating. However, Force did not want to let the benefits of the alternatives slip by. The strategy was to implement

Alternative 1 at the same time as the Alternative 2 system development was being performed.

This strategy offered the benefits of Alternative 1 earlier and moved the company toward the eventual process with less disruption. It also gave us a fallback position if the programming were delayed.

IMPLEMENTATION

The actual implementation proceeded following the strategy. After the automobile process was addressed, pressure from management grew intense to speed up the implementation for the other processes. Additional contract staff were hired to work on some of the processes. The added cost of this was more than $125,000. However, the costs were recouped through the faster attainment of benefits.

Organization Change

Organization change followed the process implementation. The number of supervisors was reduced after Alternative 2 and the other parts of the process were completed. While the other processes were improved, the organization plan was developed. Essentially, the plan called for the merger of the work along functional lines. That is, all data entry and clerical support were centralized, as was customer service. This led to even greater savings, partially offset by cross-training expenses for staff to learn multiple products. With the organization divided along functional lines, it became possible to outsource the clerical and support functions, thereby achieving even more benefits.

CONCLUSION

At Force the focus was on a combination of technologies as opposed to a single technology. Major changes were carried out in workflow and organization as a result of this combination of technologies.

The example of Force reveals some of the political complexities as well as technical challenges of business process improvement. It also illustrates the way that "new methods" can destroy attempts at process improvement.

CHAPTER 32

OUTSOURCING

CONTENTS

32

OUTSOURCING

PURPOSE AND SCOPE

The first purpose is to determine whether outsourcing will bring sufficient benefits to outweigh the costs, issues, and management of the outsourcing. Beyond that, you want to ensure that the transition to an outsourcing firm is accomplished with minimal disruption. You also want to ensure that the relationship is controlled.

The scope begins broadly, including many potential areas for outsourcing. Then it narrows to a specific set of activities (similar to the selection of a process group in Step B).

END PRODUCTS

The major end products include the following:

- Identification of potential opportunities for outsourcing
- Evaluation and prioritization of outsourcing candidates
- Evaluation of specific activities and recommendations
- Generation of a project plan for outsourcing implementation
- Completion of implementation
- Measurement of the results of outsourcing

RESOURCES

Although you can perform some of the analysis yourself, you will need to involve more people at each step when implementing outsourcing. How these people are introduced into the project is a major concern because you want to ensure that the business processes continue with effectiveness and efficiency.

APPROACH

Outsourcing is the transfer of specific functions and activities from one organization to another organization and the first organization retains proper control and oversight. Outsourcing can be a partial or total solution to changing a process, organization, or infrastructure. Examples of tasks that can be outsourced are as follows:

- Information systems functions—data entry, computer operations, PC support, hardware maintenance, software development, etc.

- Accounting functions relating to suppliers and customers using electronic commerce, also known as Electronic Data Interchange (EDI)—accounts payable, accounts receivable, receiving, shipping

- Courier services and mailing services

- Transportation and shipping

- Warehousing

- Customer service

- Order fulfillment

Outsourcing is viewed in some companies as a strategic partnership. Both sides bring strengths to the table. They share chemistry and similar cultural values. Recent outsourcing contracts, in which both companies work to develop new products, exemplify this. One example is a software firm that develops systems for a company. The company shares the costs and time, then enjoys future potential revenues from outsourcing system development.

Prime candidates for outsourcing are companies experiencing growth or decline. Growing companies use outsourcing to accommodate increased volume. Declining firms use outsourcing to control costs and try to regain control of core areas.

Outsourcing makes a company the hub of a network in which vendors are the spokes of the wheel. Firms are increasingly viewing themselves this way. If the network prospers, the company will prosper—if outsourcing is done well.

The economical appeal of outsourcing, especially in a global economy, is great and is increasing with reductions in trade walls.

Consider outsourcing on a periodic basis. This approach will make the underlying business processes more efficient.

Outsourcing has four dimensions:

- Relationship of the business to the outsourcing issue (why)
- Extent of outsourcing of the activity (what)
- Type of outsourcing vendor (who and how)
- Duration of outsourcing agreement (how long)

A simple graph of these dimensions appears in Figure 32-1. This graph gives two examples. The first example shows a limited activity that has been outsourced for a moderate duration to a contractor with a very restricted charter. Examples of such tasks are mail services and PC installation. The second example is that of a large-scale outsourcing agreement, such as warehousing.

Outsourcing cannot be taken lightly. Some outsourcing agreements typically extend for five or more years. In order to achieve economies and to recover initial start-up outsourcing activities, a vendor will often require multiple-year contracts. Also, the company does not want to change vendors frequently. This is especially the case if the company hires temporary employees who must be trained to perform the work correctly.

Over time, the outsourcing vendor and the company develop a relationship and mutual trust. With a new vendor, the relationship must be established all over again. Replacing the supplier or vendor results in a difficult interim period until a new supplier is found or the organization can perform the function internally.

REASONS TO OUTSOURCE

Following is a list of reasons a company would want to outsource. Note that the reasons overlap. In almost all cases, when asked why they chose to outsource, companies responded with multiple reasons. However, there is usually one dominant reason. Here are some common reasons given for outsourcing:

- **Cost savings with less staff**

  Staff salaries and benefits are the largest expense component of most companies. If the outsourcing activity is one that has

Figure 32-1: Outsourcing Dimensions

Relationship to business

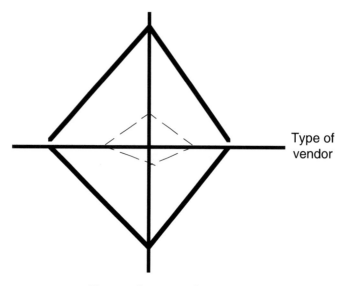

Type of vendor

Extent of outsourcing

— — — — Example 1

Example 2

peaks and troughs and does not involve critical expertise, the savings are real and no expertise is lost.

- **Cost stability**

  If the cost of an operation is growing out of control, outsourcing can provide cost stability because a vendor has a legal agreement to provide a specific service at a certain cost.

- **Lack of expertise**

  If the company has to take on a set of duties for business reasons but lacks expertise, the new operation may not work well. Once management realizes that they lack the necessary skills, they outsource to a vendor with many more years of experience. The outsourcing vendor may be able to address nagging technical problems. The reason for hiring consultants in implementing Enterprise Resource Planning (ERP) software is due to a lack of expertise internally.

- **Cash flow savings**

  An outsourcing vendor may promise immediate savings. Alternatively, the outsourcer may purchase the capital equipment from the company. Examples include computer equipment, facilities, and other types of equipment. These generate positive cash flow for the company.

- **Business process efficiency**

  The company may outsource part of a strategic business process, such as manufacturing, to achieve greater efficiency. An example is the assembly of a component structure.

- **Tax advantages**

  This depends on the situation. A company may possibly realize immediate tax advantages through outsourcing. What were capitalized expenses may be expensed. Hiring a certain type of vendor in a disadvantaged area may provide additional benefits.

- **Resources shortage**

  A subsidiary of a large firm was given a head count ceiling for staff. The subsidiary was growing, but management refused to raise the ceiling. The subsidiary outsourced several functions.

- **Need to focus on core capabilities**

  If management and staff do not have to be involved with the outsourced activity, they can turn their attention to more important functions.

- **Personnel problems**

  A specific business function may have a high concentration of staff problems. This could range from drugs and alcohol to poor performance. By outsourcing the activity, the problems migrate to someone else.

- **Target of opportunity**

  An outsourcing vendor makes an irresistible proposal to a firm. Even though the company has not formally considered outsourcing, the terms may be too attractive to pass up.

- **Peaks and troughs**

  Normally, a company has difficulty rapidly hiring or downsizing to meet demands. If business fluctuations are significant, outsourcing is a way to address the variation. The outsourcer may be providing the same service to many companies, so peaks and troughs in one firm are offset by troughs and peaks in others.

- **Desire to become more competitive**

  This is a combination of some of the above factors. Moving an operation to a separate company overseas is an example of using outsourcing to become more competitive.

- **A new business activity**

  If you begin a new venture or move into a new area, you must acquire expertise quickly. One way to do this is to outsource initial support and performance. As business grows, you can bring these functions back.

- **Improved customer service**

  If a department has not been able to achieve adequate customer service, an outsourcing vendor that is service-oriented and measured on service performance may be a good alternative.

- **Improved management control**

  An outsourcing relationship may offer greater control over operations.

- **Support activity distraction**

  Employee time may be diverted into a support activity. An example is non-computer people attempting to fix computer problems. As a result, major work is being neglected.

ISSUES WITH OUTSOURCING

There is a positive side of outsourcing, but there are negative issues as well. Some of the most common are as follows:

- **Lack of vendor expertise**

  The vendor is no better at the work that the company's employees. The vendor may have claimed specific expertise. However, the work that is provided indicates otherwise.

- **Increased costs**

  The original cost of the contract often increases because the vendor negotiates add-on work. Costs can balloon out of control.

- **Overdependence**

  Management and staff feel comfortable with the vendor. They rely on vendor staff for critical processes and decision making. When this trend is recognized, management and staff are too far along the road to change quickly. The business is impacted.

- **Inflexible contract terms**

  The outsourcing work is going badly, and the organization would like to renegotiate the contract. However, this cannot be done because no one read the fine print.

- **Loss of control**

  The vendor begins to take control of the work and indirectly begins to manage some of the organization's departments.

- **Loss of in-house expertise**

  After the agreement is signed, the organization's in-house expertise starts to disappear. It becomes difficult to manage and change the process.

- **Conflict of interest**

  The vendor gains expertise and experience by working with the organization. To make more money, the vendor markets this expertise to the organization's competitors. If the contract does not prevent this, the organization has little recourse. The organization may be able to get out of the agreement, but the vendor will still have the arrangement with the competitor.

- **Vendor turnover**

  If there is a change in vendors that perform a specific function for your firm, the transition from one to the other may be difficult. Each firm may have a different style as well as method in doing the work.

- **Loss of interest**

  The vendor may have wished to expand into the outsourcing business that it performs for you. However, after some effort, the vendor is unsuccessful. Your business is no longer in their mainstream of work. They may not devote as much attention to it, even it is profitable.

There are some tricks of the trade that some vendors practice. Be on the lookout for these.

- **Rotating staff**

  Some vendors start a project with their best managers and staff. These employees make rapid progress. After the start-up period, the vendor substitutes a "second string" staff. If the work is routine, this may not be a problem, but productivity may fall and the quality of work may not be as high.

- **Using bait and switch**

  The vendor staff is extremely helpful. The employees do work beyond that for which the customer is paying. The vendor starts charging for additional services. Soon, the customer is paying the vendor more money than initially budgeted.

- **Charging for additional tasks**

  Every time the customer brings up issues, the customer finds that handling these is not within the scope of work.

- **Using proprietary tools and methods to lock the customer into a long-term relationship**

  The vendor comes in and does the work. The tools used are proprietary. The customer now faces increased obstacles to learning what is going on and taking over the work. This occurs in some data processing centers where the vendor has specific tools to maintain and operate computer programs.

Figure 32-2 provides an example of the financial picture for some large contracts. The flat line is the contract price to the customer. The curved line is the vendor cost. In the initial period of transition, the vendor will incur more costs. After this period, the vendor will likely attempt to drive costs down through efficiency.

Figure 32-2: Example of Financial Aspects
of Outsourcing Agreement

This chart can be useful in explaining the financial impact of outsourcing.

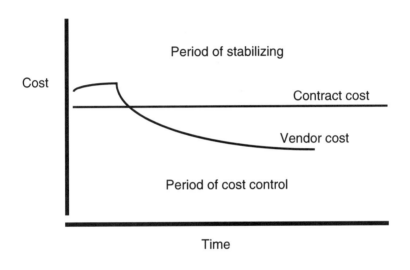

Action 1: Evaluate the Feasibility of Outsourcing and Identify
Candidates

A company must be willing to deal with greater complexity if it
wants to outsource. Outsourcing increases complexity because the
company loses total control. The company changes from being integrated to becoming distributed, and distributed things are more complex. The trade-off is that by assuming this complexity, the company
can grow in terms of service and revenue. Outsourcing encourages a
company to develop a more strategic focus. Doing the detailed work
inhouse directs your attention to tactical function rather than the
overall picture.

To show where in the business outsourcing would benefit the company, define the vision of the company and identify key business processes. Some factors to consider are as follows:

- **Business volatility**

  How much has the business changed? Are the organization and infrastructure stable? If they are not, outsourcing could lock in obsolete technology.

- **Competitive position**

  Would outsourcing help or hurt the organization's competitive position? Would it remove key advantages and knowledge?

- **Environment in the industry**

  What are other firms in the industry and similar industries doing? What experience do they have?

- **Current state of the process**

  Is the process ready for outsourcing? Is it efficient?

- **Retention of intellectual property**

  Does the outsourcing involve the transfer of intellectual property to the outsourcing firm?

- **Alliance benefits**

  Are there true benefits to the future of the company from an outsourcing agreement that appears to be a joint venture?

Which part of business processes should be considered for outsourcing? There are extreme ranges—from a specific function (for example, mowing the grass at your home) to assigning the entire function (doing all the gardening). The point at which you initiate outsourcing might not be permanent. If the outsourcing relationship works, you may outsource more. If it doesn't, you might bring back these functions inside or hire someone else.

Factors that affect the decision of the area to outsource include the following:

- **Relationship to critical business processes**

  This has to do with competitive advantage and maintaining control.

- **The feasibility of splitting the activity out from everything else and managing it**

  If you outsource a specific activity that is in the middle of a process, problems here could shut down the entire process.

- **The availability of someone to manage the transition and operation of the outsource vendor**

  Take the broadest possible view at the beginning of the outsourcing. You can always eliminate some areas from outsourcing.

Action 2: Develop an Outsourcing Plan

As with general business process improvement, you must develop an outsourcing plan. First, establish a competent and relevant outsourcing team. Select team members who know the processes and who work in departments that will manage the outsourcing vendor. Also include an accountant and a lawyer. The team members will identify alternatives and determine an initial set of risks and benefits. They will gain management commitment to do the investigation.

The project will start with the investigation and go through to the transition of work to the outsourcer. For large outsourcing projects, the duration can be a year or more.

The outsourcing plan should include the following:

- **The specific area to be outsourced**
- **Interfaces**

  Address how this area interfaces with other areas of the business. These interfaces may cause problems later if not evaluated during this early stage.

- **The benefits of outsourcing**

  Identify these, along with the potential drawbacks of outsourcing.

- **A backup approach**

  Assuming that the outsourcing is consummated, there must be an approach for a backup if the outsourcing should fail.

- **Measurement and control**

  Identify how the outsourcing will be managed and the resources required for management of the vendor. The cost of these resources can be substantial (5 to 10 percent of the total outsourcing cost), diluting financial savings. Spell out how the vendor performance will be measured. Use a vendor scorecard, which may include the following:

  —Number of vendor staff involved

  —Turnover of vendor staff

  —Problems and outstanding issues—the quantity, severity, and age of the problems

  —Volume of work performed

  —Range of work being addressed

  —Response time in doing the work

  —Work quality

  —Cost of the outsourcing, as well as cost of management of the outsourcing effort

  —Benefits of outsourcing to this vendor

- **Expanded work policy**
- **Changes in business activity needed prior to outsourcing**
- **Transition steps**

Action 3: Measure and Evaluate the Activity

Evaluate and analyze in detail the activity being considered for outsourcing. The analysis will provide a list of changes that might be implemented in the short term to prepare the process for outsourcing. If the activity requires non-deferrable major work, remove it from consideration.

Analysis should also identify the key people involved. Who stays? Who can move to the vendor? What internal company knowledge do these people have?

Analyze the economics of the activity, including the capital and operating costs and the tax implications of outsourcing. Treat this work as preparation for disposing of an asset.

Action 4: Identify Potential Vendors

The scope of the outsource function will determine the number of vendor firms you should consider. Literature, industry contacts, and referrals may indicate leads for potential vendors.

If you must hire several vendors, the complexity level will rise. You must manage each vendor, as well as conflicts and problems between vendors.

Include vendors who have relevant experience in outsourcing work. Also consider the size of the vendor and its expertise.

Your goal is to come up with a vendor list of three to five firms.

The range of outsourcing alternatives is broad, which is in part due to the definition being wide in scope. Here are some alternatives:

- **Another division of a company**

  One example is a division that provides parts or services to other divisions or a subsidiary company.

- **Former employees or independent contractors**

  If a core of people perform a function well, but that function is not a core function, you may be able to encourage those employees to form a company of their own. You can then outsource the work to them. This can save money in employee benefits and achieve some of the benefits cited earlier.

- **Contract labor**

  You can hire someone on a contract or part-time basis to perform specific tasks. This alternative applies to a wide range of professional services, such as designing architecture for computer programming.

- **Professional outsourcing vendors**

  You can contract with a vendor that specializes in the specific outsourcing activity, such as accounting, system integration, and customer service.

- **A company that performs the entire process**

  An example of this would be a firm that specializes in shipping.

- **Subcontractors**

  Subcontractors have been used for centuries. A subcontractor performs a specific set of functions year after year. The aerospace industry uses subcontractors. When a company wins a contract, it hires a subcontractor. If the company does not win a contract, the subcontractors don't have work, This eliminates the expense of keeping employees on staff to handle new work.

- **Third-party utilities**

  When a company uses Electronic Data Interchange (EDI) or electronic commerce, it often uses a third-party network. This network acts as an intermediary to control the information transfer between suppliers and customers.

Action 5: Get the Activity Ready for Outsourcing

Make the changes to the process that you identified in Action 3. People sometimes elect to stop the outsourcing plan here if they find that they have improved the activity to the extent that outsourcing benefits are no longer sizable. By improving the process at this point, you also measure it. This establishes the measurement process for outsourcing later.

Action 6: Obtain Outsourcing Bids

The request for proposal for vendors should contain the following:

- Statement of what the vendor must provide
- Additional work that may be requested
- The management process for proposal evaluation and award
- The pricing of services and goods to be provided
- The contract terms of the outsourcing agreement
- The measurement, management, and dispute resolution processes
- A standard outline for vendor proposals

To retain control, develop your own contract. If you accept and slightly modify the vendor contract, you may be at a disadvantage. Show the potential firms the current process, ideally without disrupting current work. Hold a bidder's conference at which you answer questions. Make clear to firms the key parts of the outsourcing plan from the previous Actions, especially the benefits expected, how the firm will be managed, and the process for controlling changes and additions.

Action 7: Conduct Outsourcing Negotiations and Seal the Contract

The project team will conduct the evaluation, which typically includes vendor presentations, site visits or contacts with vendor customers, and in-depth questioning of vendor staff.

The contract negotiations focus on these issues:

- Scope of responsibility and services
- Project management
- Skills and abilities to be provided
- Availability of staff
- Warranties
- Rights to proprietary information and indemnification
- Change process and control
- Dispute resolution
- Measurement process
- Penalties for failure of performance
- Agreement cancellation and termination
- Protection of secrets
- What other customers they can serve and what services they can provide
- Review process
- Technology upgrades over the life of the contract

Specific business and systems activities may require additional terms.

Action 8: Implement Outsourcing

Once you have selected a vendor, you will begin the transition process. Both the vendor and the company appoint transition teams. Human resources is involved in working with the staff. Appoint a key technical person because technical process and infrastructure issues will occur during the transition. A senior technical person is useful in resolving issues and ensuring a smooth transition.

There are several transition alternatives. You might simply transition at a specific date. You can establish a learning period during which the vendor acquires detailed knowledge and the relationship with the vendor is finalized. A third alternative is to divide the activity into units and then transition each unit.

Action 9: Manage the Outsourcing Relationship

Identify a company manager as the chief interface with the vendor. Let the vendor know that no additional work or tasks can be performed without this person's approval. No one else in the company has jurisdiction. The manager will develop measurements for the outsourcing vendor's performance using the vendor scorecard. He or she should have regular vendor meetings to review issues, problems, opportunities, costs, and performance. The manager will track any open items and issues and will give upper management a scorecard of the vendor's performance.

Action 10: End the Relationship, if Necessary

As with the transition to outsourcing plan, the vendor and company need to assemble teams to carry out a transition back to the company. It is helpful if both sides identify people who have not been involved in problems and issues.

The transition addresses turning over not only the process, but also the infrastructure. Transition involves knowledge and training. Vendor staff may have to be hired as consultants to deal with technical issues.

MANAGEMENT PRESENTATION AND COST-BENEFIT ANALYSIS

Provide management with feedback during each of the outsourcing actions discussed earlier. The focus of management at all times is likely to be on answers to the following questions:

- Is outsourcing still proving to be economically attractive?
- Did you select the right outsourcing vendor?
- What are the impacts on the business processes?
- What changes have occurred in the process since outsourcing began?
- Has outsourcing had any impact on employee morale and job satisfaction?
- Are you planning the transition and conducting management of the outsourcing efficiently?

KEY QUESTIONS

Are you making headway on defining outsourcing opportunities?
Have you successfully transitioned a business function outside?
What are outstanding issues with the current outsourcing vendor?
Have you identified a complete set of activities for outsourcing?
What lessons can be learned from existing outsourcing agreements? Have you applied these?
Did you receive bids and proposals from multiple vendors? Or has the requirement been so narrowly defined that only one firm will bid?
What has been the growth in the business volume with the outsourcing firm since you started? Has the scope of activities expanded?

EXAMPLES

Monarch Bank

The review of the overall credit card and installment loan collections and charge-off area revealed several outsourcing candidates:

- Skip tracing
- Repossessions of automobiles and other assets secured by loans
- Legal action to recover delinquent balances and fees

After proceeding through the outsourcing actions outlined earlier, employees found that repossessions and legal action were suited to outsourcing. As a method for maintaining customer relationships and for improved later collections, skip tracing was made more efficient and retained.

Several outsourcing firms were retained for repossessions and legal action. This allowed work to shift from one firm to another in the event of poor performance. It also provided incentives for vendors to do good work.

TRAN

Outsourcing was examined for customer information on bus routes, information systems, and facilities maintenance. The process for customer information was in poor condition. It had to be modernized and automated with a software package. It was then outsourced, saving more than 30 percent of the original estimated cost. Facilities maintenance was also outsourced.

Some areas of TRAN's information systems, such as programming specific TRAN systems, could not be outsourced. Generic functions, such as repairing and installing microcomputers, were outsourced. They identified a backup vendor for continuation and support.

The benefits went beyond cost savings. Outsourcing precipitated a reorganization that allowed for downsizing and a focus on basic business processes.

Stirling Manufacturing

Stirling was already employing subcontractors. Because of the political nature of the process improvement effort, this was outsourced. They also realized that availability of funds for new initiatives would vary over time. Hiring full-time employees for major new projects would have led to higher costs during a downturn. Therefore, Stirling resorted to contracting out major new projects that internal staff later took over.

Computer Manufacturer

A computer manufacturer outsourced all of its shipping functions to a logistics company. For a mail order computer firm, shipping is a critical business process. The manufacturer's intent was to improve product distribution, control shipping costs, and handle growth. They expected multimillion dollar savings and accommodation of growth without increased staff. Previously, the company had projected hiring more than 500 employees to handle growth.

The scope of the outsourcing agreement included all inbound and outbound shipping and domestic and foreign service and repair transportation. The outsourcing vendor was to use its own trucking operation, software, management expertise, and formal processes. The manufacturer expected to make money by imposing the workload on top of its existing structure and by hiring only a few workers.

GUIDELINES

- **Have alternate and backup vendors available.**

  This may sound expensive, but for some activities it is possible. The backup vendor might also be called in to evaluate the work of the primary vendor.

- **Consider dividing the work between several outsourcing vendors.**

  The work, of course, must be divisible. How you design and divide the work to be outsourced determines whether you can use more than one vendor.

- **Reevaluate the outsourcing vendor about halfway through the contract.**

  Don't wait until the end of the contract to evaluate the vendor. If the vendor is not performing as expected, put pressure on the vendor. You can also begin the action steps needed to bring in another vendor.

- **Have a redeployment plan for key people and announce the change prior to the outsourcing vendor selection.**

  Key people should be kept informed to some extent. More importantly, provide information that will make them feel more secure with regard to their jobs after the transition.

ACTION ITEMS

1. Make a list of functions that link or group together for outsourcing. Include some that are not being considered for outsourcing. Use the list for both rows and columns. Rate the closeness of fit of the functions using a scale of 1 to 5 (1 is no relation, 5 is tight relationship and would outsource together). Note that a function can include multiple processes.

Function   Function

2. What interfaces do the functions have with other activities in the business? Develop a table which identifies the nature of the interface as well as issues and potential problems.

Function   Interface   Potential Issues

3. Rank the functions in terms of outsourcing. Use the list of functions developed in item 1 as columns in a table. For rows, use various criteria for assessing outsourcing. This will help you see which are the most appropriate functions for outsourcing. By combining the analysis of items 1 and 2, you can combine functions of different suitability for outsourcing. Use a scale of 1 to 5 to rate the functions (1 indicates a major problem with the function for that criteria, 5 indicates that there is a natural solution).

Criteria   Function

Vendor availability				
Function ready				
Measurement of function completed				
Dependence on co. knowledge				
Involves key bus. process				
Degree of risk				
Potential savings				

4. Develop a list of 10 to 20 vendors and list them as rows in a table. List the functions as columns in a table. Rate the vendors using a scale of 1 to 5 (1 indicates that the vendor is not suitable, 5 indicates that the vendor is suitable). This table will help you to narrow the number of vendors.

Vendor   Function

5. What detailed work is necessary to clean up specific functions? Using a table, set the rows as specific actions needed and the columns as functions. Rate the items on a scale of 1 to 5 (1 indicates little or no effort needed, 5 indicates a great deal of effort needed) to determine the relative degree of effort or problem involved. This table will indicate where the cleanup effort should focus.

Organization	Group
Cleanup steps vs. function	
Training of staff	
Prepare formal proced.	
Develop meas. process	
Streamline current process	
Cleanup information	
Construct new interfaces	
Establish control process	
Downsize	

6. Each function that might be outsourced has its own interfaces between the vendor and the customer organization. The more complete the interface, the more potential problems there are in outsourcing. Use the following table to help you assess complexity. The rows contain elements of the interface; the columns are the functions. Rate the entry using a scale of 1 to 5 (1 is no problem or issue, 5 signifies a major problem). If many rows are rated 4 or 5, the function will be very complex.

Interface	Function			
Process split with outsourcer				
Internal processes depend on outsourced process				
Quality control is major concern				
Outsourced function has exceptions				
Sharing of information and extent of information varies over time				
Interface occurs at different frequencies				
Outsourcer must interface systems				
Error correcting process is extensive				

CHAPTER 33

SUCCESSFUL DOWNSIZING

CONTENTS

33

SUCCESSFUL DOWNSIZING

PURPOSE AND SCOPE

The goal is to provide a step-by-step method for designing and implementing downsizing. Begin to think about downsizing right after you have implemented the new process. Once an organization has invested in process improvement, downsizing will allow it to achieve the benefits that will pay for the investment and make the process even more effective.

The scope of downsizing goes beyond the people doing the work in the process. Include all departments involved in the process as well as supervisors and managers. Another aspect of scope is time. Successful downsizing takes more elapsed time than many people figure on, due to politics, roadblocks, etc. In terms of start and finish, the beginning occurs right after the process has been improved. The end comes only after downsizing has been completed and the organization has been measured.

END PRODUCTS

The end product is a functional organization that improves the performance of the new business processes. Success is achieved if the process performs better at lower cost, is supported by a stable organization, and has not been impacted in a negative way during the downsizing.

There are intermediate end products as well. These include the following:

- The measurement of the organization prior to downsizing
- A strategy for downsizing
- Job responsibilities for staff involved in the process, supporting the process, and interfacing with the process

- Actual organizational assignments
- Implementation of the downsizing
- The measurement of the organization after downsizing

RESOURCES

To design and implement a downsizing strategy requires almost everyone involved in the process, as well as human resources. People are needed not only to do the analysis, but also to eliminate resistance, gain management and staff support, and ensure continuity.

APPROACH

Downsizing will be defined as actions taken to make the organization fit better with the business process so as to reduce organization size and cost. Key questions about downsizing are the following:

- How can a business downsize without disrupting the business process?
- When should downsizing be initiated?
- How should the benefits and success of downsizing be measured?

There is a downside to downsizing. Here are some examples of drawbacks:

- **The best people leave with their knowledge and experience.**

  Companies often have to hire them back at higher cost later as contractors or suffer the consequences. In one manufacturing firm, 85 percent of the people laid off came back as contractors. Downsizing did not reduce costs—it raised costs by 15 percent.
- **Knowledge is lost so that productivity and creativity suffer.**

  In one insurance company management urged senior programmers to retire early. Then they had no one left to work on the Year 2000 problem. So they had to buy new software. This touch of genius cost more than two million dollars.

- **Morale drops.**

    People wonder "Who's next?" The workload increases for the remaining staff.

Many firms implement downsizing before process improvement, which is the wrong order. When firms downsize first and then attempt to reengineer with what is left, the most likely outcome of this order is either disruption or disaster. Yet, this order continues to be employed by short-sighted managers who conveniently move on, leaving behind the chaos that they created.

Here are some reasons to pay attention to process improvement before downsizing:

- If downsizing takes place without process improvement, the people left are junior staff and middle managers. These people do not understand process improvement.
- Downsizing likely will disrupt the performance of the process—resulting in more problems.
- Product knowledge, lessons learned, and customer relations all suffer if downsizing takes place without adequate attention to these areas.
- Downsizing can cause paralysis because of fear, hampering process improvement.

Downsizing is an opportunity to redeploy people to better and more productive work. Do not use it as an opportunity to dump people onto unemployment rolls. When firms do this, they are not only affecting people's lives, they are also saying that experience and expertise in their company is not valued. This sends the message to the remaining employees that the management doesn't care about the people or the processes. It appears that management just want to make money in the short term. It is no surprise that many managers who lay people off to get short-term savings then quickly move on. These managers don't want to be around to pick up the pieces when things fall apart.

The following actions apply not only to new processes that replace or improve current processes but also to entirely new processes. For new processes, start with Action 2 to define a staffing strategy. Then proceed to the other actions.

Action 1: Measure the Current Organization Prior to Downsizing

Recall that you have already measured the new business process. You have a process score- card. Now you will develop an organization scorecard. This will show you the situation with the process changed but the organization unchanged, which will allow you to measure the benefits later. This is similar to process measurement.

Here is a set of criteria to be measured:

- **The relative power of the individual department over the process**

  When there are multiple departments, identify which has more power. This political assessment will be critical for implementation of downsizing.

- **The number of people in the organizations supporting the processes, including part-time and contract people**

- **Issues and problems that have surfaced from the mismatch of the process and the organization**

- **Turnover and longevity of staff and managers**

- **Stability of organization**

  Look at organization charts over time.

- **Cost of the organization**

  Include facilities, space, and utilities.

- **Requirements from other processes**

  Factor out the organization resources that support other processes performed by the department.

- **Distribution of head count and budget by level of the organization**

- **Assessment of policies and rules of the organization in terms of their impact and fit with the organization**

  Note that you will include all departments that are involved in the process. You may wish to create a scorecard for each department.

Your purpose is to show the extent to which the organization does not fit with the process. While individuals can adapt to new processes, it is much more difficult for organizations. Examples of areas of possible change are job descriptions, policies, and rules of the organization. Look at whether these fit the new processes or need to be changed.

This information serves two basic purposes. One is to document that organization change is necessary. The second is to be able to compare the "before" and "after" of downsizing.

Action 2: Develop Your Downsizing Strategy

The downsizing strategy provides the direction for downsizing. The particular strategy you use depends on the specific situation. However, here are some candidate strategies to consider:

- **Focus on the middle of the organization.**

  Under this strategy you basically assume that the people involved in the process remain intact. The reductions will come from the ranks of middle management, starting with the supervisors.

  This strategy is fairly conservative. It has the benefit of reducing layers of management. However, it does not take into account that there may be a need to restructure the bottom of the organization. It also leaves people in place who are not suited for the process.

- **Reduce the staffing involved in the process and then let the management and supervision ranks sort themselves out.**

  This approach is followed in many companies. The bottom is cut out to get short-term savings. If the savings are sufficient, management ranks may remain basically unchanged. This leaves a top-heavy organization.

- **Reduce the staffing involved in the process and then move up to reduce management ranks.**

  This approach takes the most time but will yield the greatest long-term results. It consumes the most time because you must analyze both staff and management positions.

The last strategy is the preferred one of the three. It provides for the most stable long-term solution. Also consider two extreme alternatives—do nothing or radically downsize to minimize costs.

This part of the strategy is the "What." Another part of the downsizing strategy involves "How." Here you consider whether you want to outsource some or all of the work to an external firm. This is not an all-or-nothing decision. You can elect to outsource simpler work in the business process.

This action could end here but you would be missing a golden opportunity. People will be left over from the downsizing. Should you dump them out on the street, as many firms do? First, look around the organization. Find areas where new processes are needed and where current processes are understaffed. Reallocate these people. This approach makes economic sense. These employees have a great deal of experience and expertise. They can support future growth. The firm can still realize economic savings through attrition and through people finding other work on their own.

Thus, looking at your other processes and opportunities for new processes are part of your overall downsizing strategy.

Action 3: Define Interface and Support Responsibilities

Interfaces and support are areas that are frequently ignored. Managers concentrate instead on the business process itself. This is often a big mistake. As stated in earlier chapters, a process does not usually exist alone. Other subsidiary processes relate to the process or other processes performed by the same staff. Part of this can be addressed by considering a group of processes. However, this still leaves you with interfaces and support provided by other groups.

In the analysis you identified how groups were involved in the process. For each group that interfaces you must analyze the staffing provided. These employees cannot be included in the downsizing because they are from other departments. What can you do? Define the staffing demands of the new process on the interfacing groups. Identify responsibilities and requirements. This includes listing the specific responsibilities of the groups. Then negotiate with the departments how the support is to be provided. Note that you have already carried out measurements of the support in the first action.

If you ignore the interfaces and support, problems may arise. First, the departments may cut staffing on their own. This could damage the new process. Second, departments could leave staffing in place, which could also mean trouble for the new process, since an area may be overstaffed.

Action 4: Collect Information and Lessons Learned on the Operation of the Process and Define Job Descriptions Associated with the Process

This is a major action. At the end of this action you will specify exact job descriptions and criteria for each position. Human resources may lack resources, time, and knowledge of the business process, so it is more effective if you do this job and then give the results to human resources to review. When you observe the new process being performed, you can see whether or not there is a good fit between individuals and the actions that they are performing.

The end product of this action is real-world job descriptions that fit the business process. You can't just take the current descriptions and use them because the process changed how the work will be done and who performs it. Also, different skills may be needed due to automation and technology. The job descriptions will be used as a basis for interviewing current staff to find those that are most suited to the new process. There is also another benefit. These job descriptions for those involved in the process can serve as the basis for defining responsibilities for supervisors and middle management.

What should be in a job description? Start with a list of duties, but make them specific to the business process. The duties should include a description of how the technology is to be employed in the process. Performance criteria based on process measurements should be included.

This action step gives you overt reasons for going out into the department and collecting information. A covert reason for this action step is to determine who are the best people for which jobs and tasks. You are also trying to determine levels of job satisfaction. A third purpose is to discover how their duties have changed from the perspective of the people performing the work. This is a good time to consider lower level job restructuring in terms of what specific tasks people perform.

Collect data in interfacing and supporting processes as well. Identify what these people are doing and how their activities fit in with the new process. Determine whether they are doing redundant or unnecessary work because of the new processes.

Action 5: Define Supervisory Levels and Middle Management Positions

Supervisory positions are the easiest to define. They are based on the job descriptions you created for the people involved in the business process. Include the performance criteria mentioned earlier, as well as supervisory tasks associated with the review of work using the measurement methods in earlier chapters. Middle management positions are more difficult to define in that they depend on specific situations and company policies.

Action 6: Identify Key Employees at the Working and Supervisory/Managerial Levels

Based on the data you collected in Action 4, along with data from human resources and past measurement, identify the key people in the new processes. Include supervisors and managers, as well as the people at the lowest level. Also include staff from interfacing and supporting processes. Staffing can play a major role and impact the future of the process performance. In one company, a key person here decided to leave because he did not know what would happen with his job. This had a negative effect on both production and morale.

Action 7: Implement the Downsizing

Some downsizing activities are general. Post job openings and descriptions. Arrange and conduct interviews with managers and staff. Fill the positions as soon as possible to avoid any disruption to the business processes.

Implementation details will depend on your organization's policies and procedures, but some general guidelines are as follows:

- Present the change from this perspective: "We have spent a great deal of energy and effort in establishing the best processes we can; now it is time to find the best people for the processes."
- Consider filling positions bottom up and top down concurrently. That is, ensure that the people who are critical to the process are retained with the process. Identify individuals who are not going to be involved in the as soon as possible. Identify supervisors and upper level managers early as well. This approach will tend to reduce middle-level management head count.
- Seriously consider attracting new people from other departments into the process.
- Begin an orderly transition of staff on a continuous basis. Try to avoid one large, major change, as that would likely be more disruptive.

Action 8: Measure the Process and Organization After the Downsizing

Reassess the business processes, using the approach given in the earlier chapter on measurement. Prepare an overall scorecard. Create a table with columns for the processes before the change in process, the process after change but before staffing changes, and the new process downsized.

MANAGEMENT PRESENTATION AND COST-BENEFIT ANALYSIS

To present the set of measurements from Action 1, you might follow this outline:

- Summarize the process. Give the process scorecard. Identify any outstanding issues. This calms people in that there is a common, stable starting point.
- Present the issues involved in the interface between process and organization. Include the impact of the issues on the process. This highlights how important it is to address the organizational aspects of the processes.

Table 33-1: Business Process Scorecard

Criteria	Old Process	New Process	New Downsized Process
Head count of staff			
Head count of supervisors/mgrs.			
Volume of work			
Staff turnover			
Responsiveness			
Error rate			
Number of exceptions			
IT/IS costs			
Total manpower costs			
Total process costs			
Ratio of IT to total process costs			
Cost per piece of work			

Action 2 is your next presentation because it allows you to provide management with information so that they can determine what downsizing strategy to pursue. Make a list of the ways the downsizing impacts the business. With this list create a "spider" chart like the ones presented earlier in the book. Figure 33-1 is an example from TRAN of aspects of business to consider when they developed a downsizing strategy:

At the conclusion of Action 6, you are ready to present the detailed transition plan to management. Here are guidelines:

- Develop a detailed project plan showing each phase of implementation.

- Determine a list of issues related to morale, impact on process, etc.

Figure 33-1: Sample Downsizing Strategy
Evaluation Chart for TRAN

Here are the two alternatives of doing nothing and of downsizing to reduce staff to a minimum. The strategy of doing nothing is shown in a solid line and the total downsizing is shown in a dashed line.

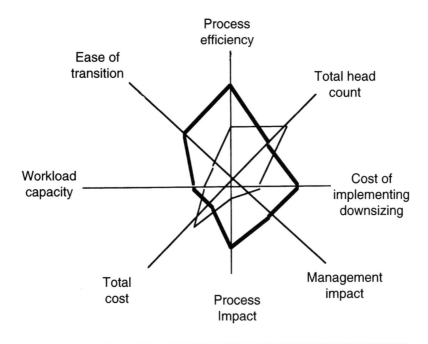

- Relate the issues to the tasks in the plan. Find the tasks that apply to the issues. Indicate that these tasks have high risk. Write down the task numbers that apply to each issue with the issue.
- Define a method for handling issues during the transition with human resources.

During implementation, keep management informed of the issues as well as providing progress reports. Combine the cost-benefit analysis with the measurement of Action 8.

KEY QUESTIONS

What progress has been made due to the new processes? Measure the efficiency, cost, volume of work, and other characteristics of the processes.

How would you rate job satisfaction in the new processes? Back in the early actions you collected data on the old processes. You found out how people felt about their work then. Later you had the opportunity to observe what happened when the processes were improved or replaced. Next, you measured the new or improved processes when you collected data on downsizing. What is the job satisfaction level now?

EXAMPLES

An Overseas Manufacturing Firm

There was an Asian manufacturing firm that made electrical motors and components. They proceeded in the actions of process improvement that have been described in earlier chapters. After the definition of the new processes, it was found that almost 40 percent of the staff was not essential to the performance of the processes. The human resources manager panicked and said, "What can we do with all of these people? If we lay them off while we are implementing the new process, it will cause chaos." He was absolutely right.

Employees were told that jobs would be reassigned and new jobs would be created. They were told to support the new processes and to fit in as best they could. Many were apprehensive and feared that they would soon be out of work.

Things immediately calmed down when several new business processes were announced. New processes were set up to improve the design of the motors. The firm had not had a good history of handling complaints and suggestions for improvements to the motors from the field locations. To remedy this situation, staff was to be assigned to go into the field and collect the information and act as intermediaries between the field offices and the headquarters design and manufacturing units. In addition, completed manufactured motors were only selectively tested. There was a need to expand testing for many more motors. Because of this new direction for the company, additional personnel were needed immediately.

After the new processes were put into place, two parallel efforts began. One was to determine who was best suited to work with the new process. The other was to define the new processes and to write job descriptions for the new processes. These Actions were followed up by interviewing all employees in the existing processes to determine the best fit. No layoffs were necessary. Morale was high and people were assigned to meaningful work.

TRAN

At TRAN, the implementation of the new processes created redundancy. TRAN could not easily downsize except through attrition. If people were left in place, morale would sink and the processes would be inefficient. Figure 33-1 is an evaluation chart used by TRAN.

Management decided to assess their overall organization to determine areas which were understaffed. This turned out to be successful. More than 25 people were reassigned to various areas of operations. Another positive outcome of this approach was that the agency grew and added more services—requiring more employees.

GUIDELINES

- **Before you start, go back through the files and records and collect measurement information from early steps in process improvement.**

  This information provides a benchmark for determining who best fits the process and what people's general attitudes were. You will make more effective decisions if you have this perspective.

- **When collecting data in the department, do not read the old job descriptions ahead of time.**

  Reading the job descriptions will tend to bias your data collection and analysis. Do the work with an open mind.

- **Inform management early about different strategies for downsizing.**

  Managers may not have given the topic much thought because they are occupied with other duties.

- **Seek to involve the people in the process in the analysis.**

  Indicate that a number of options are being considered and that you are trying to find the best approach that will least disturb the process. Take suggestions from those involved.

- **Overcome fears of staff members.**

  To handle the fear factor, talk about the large amount of money, time, and effort spent on the process improvement. Make the logical point that this would be wasted if a haphazard approach to downsizing were taken.

ACTION ITEMS

1. Review the personnel files of the staff involved in the process.

2. Before you begin, contact managers to find opportunities for placing staff members who might be displaced from the processes.

3. Keep detailed notes on each person you contact and interview.

GLOSSARY

Acceptance testing   Testing performed by business staff of the new process and system

Benchmarking   The development of comparisons of your firm to others

Black box   Testing in which you assume inputs into and outputs from a step or process

Business process improvement   A major change or improvement to a process or process group along with its technology, organization, and infrastructure support

Client-server   This is a popular type of system today. Processing is split between the PC at the user's desk (client) and the central computer (server)

Comparison tables   Tables constructed in all steps to assist in analysis and marketing of the work performed

Deterioration   The decay of a business process over time

Downsize   The reduction in head count of the organization

Enhancement   Improvements to a process to meet new requirements

Exception   A variation of the business process to address a specific transaction

Facilities management   This refers to the management of a firm's computer systems by another

Infrastructure   The facilities, equipment, and other support for a business process

Integration   The interfacing and combining of the process and system components

Intranet   A type of client-server system in which the client software consists of the web browser

Maintenance   Changes to a process to meet the original requirements

Method   A set of procedures for performing some function

Organization   The business's structure and its employees

Pilot   The testing and review of both the prototype system and the new business process

Process   A set of procedures and work-flow steps that carries out a specific business function

Process improvement   Steps taken to improve a business process

Performance testing   Testing of the system to ensure that response time and workload are within acceptable limits

Process group   Processes that are related through one facet of a business, such as organization, technology, suppliers, or customers

Prototype   The initial version of the system that will support the new process

Rightsize   To downsize

Scenario   One possible version of the new business process

Scorecard   The criteria for evaluation of a business process

Shadow systems   A manual or automated system created to handle work outside of the business process

Strawman   A model or sample of the reporting method

System testing   The overall testing of the computer system that supports the process

Technology All categories of technology involving computers and communications

Tool A tool supports the performance of a method

Transaction testing Detailed testing of transactions in the new process and system

White box Testing of a component of a process or system internally

INDEX

HARCOURT PROFESSIONAL PUBLISHING SOFTWARE LICENSE AGREEMENT
FOR ELECTRONIC FILES TO ACCOMPANY
PROFESSIONAL'S GUIDE TO PROCESS IMPROVEMENT (THE "BOOK")